Playing the Field

Playing the Field

Video Games and American Studies

Edited by
Sascha Pöhlmann

ISBN 978-3-11-075462-9
e-ISBN (PDF) 978-3-11-065940-5
e-ISBN (EPUB) 978-3-11-065572-8

Library of Congress Control Number: 2019944316

Bibliographic Information published by the Deutsche Nationalbibliothek
The Deutsche Nationalbibliothek lists this publication in the Deutsche Nationalbibliografie;
detailed bibliographic data are available on the Internet at http://dnb.dnb.de.

© 2021 Walter de Gruyter GmbH, Berlin/Boston
This volume is text- and page-identical with the hardback published in 2019.
Cover image: Detail of a Gameboy from 1990 © Sascha Pöhlmann
Printing and binding: CPI books GmbH, Leck

www.degruyter.com

Table of Contents

Sascha Pöhlmann
Introduction: Video Games and American Studies —— 1

Mark J. P. Wolf
Video Games and the American Cultural Context —— 21

Michael Fuchs, Michael Phillips, and Stefan Rabitsch
The end is nigh! Bring forth the Shepard!
   Mass Effect, the Apocalypse, and the Puritan Imagination —— 35

David Callahan
The Last of the US: The Game as Cultural Geography —— 49

Patricia Maier
Mobility and Choices in Role-Playing Games —— 65

Dietmar Meinel
Playing the Urban Future: The Scripting of Movement and Space in *Mirror's Edge* (2008) —— 79

Martin Lüthe
Playing on Fields: Seasonal Seriality, Tele-Realism, and the Bio-Politics of Digital Sports Games —— 97

Stefan Schubert
Narrative and Play in American Studies: Ludic Textuality in the Video Game *Alan Wake* and the TV Series *Westworld* —— 113

Andrei Nae and Alexandra Ileana Bacalu
Toward a Reconsideration of Hypermediacy: Immersion in Survival Horror Games and Eighteenth-Century Novels —— 131

Doug Stark
Ludic Literature: *Ready Player One* as Didactic Fiction for the Neoliberal Subject —— 151

Sebastian Domsch
Strategies against Structure: Video Game Terrorism as the Ultimate American Agency Narrative —— 173

Jon Adams
Why We Play Role-Playing Games —— 185

Damien B. Schlarb
Narrative Glitches: Action Adventure Games and Metaleptic Convergence —— 195

Sabrina Mittermeier
Time Travelling to the American Revolution — Why Immersive Media Need American Studies —— 211

Manuel Franz and Henning Jansen
A Shining City and the Sodom Below: Historical Guilt and Personal Agency in *BioShock Infinite* —— 221

Jacqueline Blank
The Art of *BioShock Infinite*: Identity, Race, and Manifest Destiny —— 235

Veronika Keller
Sounds of Tears: Mozart's *Lacrimosa* in Different Media —— 249

Nathalie Aghoro
Unspoken Adventures: On Sound, Story, and Nonverbal Gameplay in *Journey* and *Inside* —— 259

Contributors —— 275

Index of Names —— 281

Index of Subjects —— 285

Sascha Pöhlmann
Introduction: Video Games and American Studies

The present collection of essays poses two seemingly simple questions: first, what does American Studies have to say about video games? Or, put differently, how can American Studies as interdisciplinary Cultural Studies attend to what has emerged as arguably *the* most prominent medium and cultural force of the twenty-first century, in the US and globally? Second, and just as importantly, how does attending to video games change the way we do American Studies? The essays assembled in this volume postulate a dialectic relationship between disciplinary framework and objects of inquiry, i.e. between American Studies and games, but also between American Studies and Video Game Studies, a field that over the past decades has emerged as its own interdisciplinary platform. The many different explorations undertaken here link these important disciplinary questions to the structural ways in which they might be answered. This relates to the observation that gave rise to the project as much as the need for a theoretical and methodological inquiry into the mutual influence between American Studies and video games as its object of research: that this need is acknowledged quite broadly but still addressed only quite narrowly.

American Studies and Video Games: a Disciplinary Approach

Given the immense proliferation and cultural impact video games have had globally since the 1980s, and given that the USA has been the major site of the culture industry that continues to drive this development both economically and symbolically, few would deny that video games are relevant and even important objects of study with regard to American culture, and that American Studies is the proper context in which to study them. American Studies has a history of embracing new theories, methods, and objects of research as it expanded from mainly text-based philology and historiography to interdisciplinary Cultural

---

I would like to thank Michael Fuchs, Stefan Rabitsch, and Damien B. Schlarb for their valuable critiques of this introductory essay, as well as Jon Adams, David Callahan, Doug Stark, and Laura Symnick for their help with the manuscript in general.

https://doi.org/10.1515/9783110659405-001

Studies that now includes literature as much as any other cultural artifact, and which now also routinely transcends the national limits implied by the name of the field itself. Transnational approaches and a turn to visual culture are only two of several other paradigm shifts that continue to make American Studies a productively fuzzy discipline, and they are perhaps the two that provide the most fertile ground for a systematic integration of video games into the larger theoretical and methodological framework of the field. If it is actually happening at the moment, then this process is not simply taking place by itself but only because some scholars are actively cultivating it, and it is by no means certain that their efforts will be successful in the long run (as for example the integration of film into American Studies was).

Within the institutional framework of American Studies, this work is carried out largely by individuals in efforts that are mainly either local or even personal, with no substantial wider network for scholars to participate and collaborate in. Almost two decades after Espen Aarseth proclaimed "the Year One of *Computer Game Studies* as an emerging, viable, international, academic field," and well over four decades after video games began making a global cultural impact (from the US), researchers in American Studies will find the institutional structures that mark even a budding field only elsewhere, if not in dedicated Game Studies programs then mainly in Media Studies programs, but not, as I contend, within their own field. This state of affairs would feel less like a missed opportunity if American Studies, with its disciplinary multiplicity, was not so ideally equipped for analyzing video games. For example, when American Studies responded to Henry Nash Smith's challenge in 1957 to develop methods that would take it beyond the high-cultural fantasies of literary autonomy espoused by New Criticism, it opened up to Cultural Studies, to the popular, to visuality, or to mediality, and in effect created an ongoing intellectual obligation to engage emerging cultural phenomena and objects of inquiry. Americanists who work on video games feel that this is something they *can* and *should* do, that their theoretical frameworks are particularly well-suited for the exploration of video games as cultural artifacts, and that, in a nutshell, the study of contemporary American culture(s) must also be the study of video games—and yet their field has yet to tap that potential in a significant way.

This situation is not only frustrating to the individual researchers but also has adverse effects on the research as a whole, as it is in danger of lacking the contextualization and historicity that should mark scholarly discourse. Simply put, if you keep being told that you do something nobody else is doing in your field, you might actually believe it, and then fail to acknowledge over two decades of academic video game criticism and many more of games theory. Yet even if the individual researchers avoid the traps of presentist bias and discursive decontextualization, they may find themselves unable to contextualize their work institutionally, try as they might, within the intellectual and material resources available to others. This may mean not being accepted into a graduate program in American Studies, or being accepted and then told that nobody can actually supervise their dissertation; it may mean never actually getting to present one's project in a research colloquium because any such presentation needs to dwell too much on fundamentals; or it may mean routinely paying for any book you need because the library at your institution does not carry them. These are not merely personal inconveniences but symptoms of a larger problem: American Studies has barely begun to explore the massive potential of taking its tools to work on something that is so far left largely untouched but actually sits right in the center of its Cultural Studies workshop.

Again, this assessment should in no way imply that American Studies has not yet turned its attention to video games at all, and it is not meant to disparage the scholarly efforts that started this process of integration decades ago,[1] or those that have worked to consolidate it more recently.[2] There is no need for any avant-gardist rhetoric, and neither this text nor the collaborative project it introduces are offered in a spirit of breaking new ground. Instead of perpetuating the myth that scholars working on video games in American Studies do what no-one else is doing (all of them!), the goal is rather to find the communal in what now still seems individual, and seek ways in which what feels like loose ends may be woven together to form a more coherent tapestry of approaches that might have theoretical and methodological implications for the analysis of video games but also for the field at large.

---

1 Randi Gunzenhäuser described video games as a 'challenge to the sciences' in 2003, and her essay is exemplary of these early, turn-of-the millennium explorations from a number of fields that inquired into the structural and institutional conditions of analyzing video games in order to find out how to ask questions in the first place before trying to answer them.

2 Let me highlight just three recent publications that show how productive work at the intersection of American Studies and Video Game Studies can be. Michael Z. Newman's *Atari Age: The Emergence of Video Games in America*, published in 2017, is a historical work that considers "the cultural significance of the emerging medium" (5) as well as "how people understood and thought about video games as a whole" (6) in its US-American context. Phillip Penix-Tadsen's 2016 monograph *Cultural Code: Video Games and Latin America* exemplifies the hemispheric notion of American Studies as it analyzes how culture uses games and how games use culture in Latin American contexts. This approach is explored further in a special issue of the journal *forum for inter-american research* devoted to "Encounters in the 'Game-Over Era': The Americas in/and Video Games" (vol. 11, no. 2, 2018), edited by Mahshid Mayar. Last but not least, John Wills's *Gamer Nation: Video Games and American Culture* is forthcoming from Johns Hopkins UP in 2019.

By the same token, the issue is thankfully no longer one of introducing video games to American Studies but rather of connecting and consolidating individual and insular efforts, not to create a monolithic 'method'—quite the opposite—but to systematically discuss ways in which video games may present a challenge to the current methods of American Studies, how they might demand new methods, or how they might reinvigorate methods that have become unfashionable but are still part of the field's historical repertoire.

This project, then, avoids the rhetoric of paradigm shifts and newness and instead sets out to explore the ways in which American Studies may systematically integrate video games into its analyses as a dialectic. This is based on the assumption that one never merely takes a certain methodology to a research object in a one-directional way of application, but that the object as much applies itself to the method as the method is applied to the object. In other words, the question is not only how, say, video games may be analyzed ecocritically by adapting the methods Lawrence Buell and others have developed for literary analysis (for example by wondering if and how the four main properties of the environmental text Buell lays out in the introduction to *The Environmental Imagination* (cf. 7–8) might be adapted to theorize the environmental game).[3] The question is also what lasting effects such an engagement might have on ecocriticism itself. For example, what happens to the concept of place that is so central to ecocriticism when it is applied to simulated environments with different rules of perception, embodiment, movement, attachment or symbolic inscription, or how do the unique possibilities of remediating and constructing nature in video games affect our cultural imagination of the natural?

One might describe the unfortunate ludology-narratology debate that preoccupied the early days of Video Game Studies as a consequence of a misguided attempt to impose established methods onto an object of study that resists them, and for good reason. 'Reading' video games as narratives was a perhaps understandable yet fallacious effort to make the object fit the method instead of the other way round; with the benefit of plenty of hindsight, I would describe it as a case of 'when all you have is narratology, all you see is stories.'[4] This de-

---

[3] See Alenda Y. Chang's "Games as Environmental Texts" and Colin Milburn's "Green Gaming: Video Games and Environmental Risk" as prominent examples of a growing body of ecocritical perspectives on video games. Cf. also the special issue of the online journal *Ecozon@* (vol. 8, no. 2, 2017) on "Green Computer and Video Games."

[4] Marie-Laure Ryan's *Narrative as Virtual Reality: Immersion and Interactivity in Literature and Electronic Media*, published in 2001, is an example of how narratology learns from video games rather than simply treating them as yet another story-telling medium, and with this shift perhaps already indicated at the time that the debate would fortuitously not end with entrenched sides.

bate is mainly of historical interest now, especially as it "has turned into discussion whether it really happened in the first place" (Mäyrä 10). Yet it is instructive as a warning on how to integrate new objects of research into an existing methodological canon, especially when other fields are already dealing with said objects of research in their own way.

Disciplinary Fuzziness and Foundational Gestures

Asking what American Studies can bring to the table today in a more general, interdisciplinary discussion and critical analysis of video games should not imply that American Studies has not already been sitting at that metaphorical table and is but a newcomer to a scholarly discourse that has already been well-established by others elsewhere. In fact, a number of significant early contributions to the emergent field of Video Game Studies were made in the context of American Studies (in the guise of "English" in the USA) and have grown from the Literary and Cultural Studies environment of that field. For example, the now canonical essay collection *First-Person: New Media as Story, Performance, and Game*, edited by Noah Wardrip-Fruin and Pat Harrigan, first appeared online at *electronic book review*. Its take on video games is heavily inflected by the publication's core interest in technology and literature, so that one might trace one critical lineage of Video Game Studies back to a particular trend in literary studies. American Studies is one of the fields that Video Game Studies had to emancipate itself from in order to become a field in itself, as the latter needed to establish itself especially beyond the grasp of literary studies or film studies to ensure that these would not "force outdated paradigms onto a new cultural object" (Aarseth) and would co-opt its object of research into existing scholarly practices that would disregard its unique properties. (And for good reason: literary studies clearly exhibited such imperialist tendencies when, high on a misconstrued deconstructionist claim that "*il n'y a pas de hors-texte*" (Derrida 158), it eagerly claimed images, film, and any other medium as part of its proper domain by declaring them all texts.)

Yet I am not interested here in historically sorting out the many paths that led to the formation of the discipline of Video Game Studies, which has firmly established itself on the academic scene in the last two decades as a truly interdisciplinary conglomerate that involves the discourses of Media Studies, design, programming, Literary and Cultural Studies, anthropology, philosophy, sociology, psychology, and numerous other disciplines without fusing them into a singular streamlined approach. The question of what American Studies may uniquely contribute to and draw from this network cannot be answered by identifying influences, especially as this would imply a derivative linearity that would not do justice to the complexity of either discipline. Instead, it seems to me that this question must be future-oriented, and the two fields may now engage in a productive dialogue in which they influence and speak to each other rather than struggle for hegemony of interpretation over a particular cultural field or medium. Espen Aarseth wrote in 2001 that the "colonising attempts" from literary and film studies would continue to happen time and again until "computer game studies emerges as a clearly self-sustained academic field." I believe that this is now the case, and that these fields may now—along with others such as historiography that make up the multiplicity of American Studies—return to the conversation without either an intended or suspected colonial intention.

This conversation seems particularly promising because Video Game Studies and American Studies share a crucial characteristic: they are both deeply interdisciplinary and multidisciplinary fields that are so diverse in their methods, theories, and scholarly practices that these can only be described in terms of family resemblances rather than a few paradigms that would clearly define what these fields are doing and how they are doing it. Any such summary is reduced to tautology (although it hides complexities of definition that are far from easily resolved): American Studies is the study of American culture, and Video Game Studies is the study of video games, but each field would readily admit that its boundaries are fuzzy, fictional, and rather due to pragmatic institutional necessity than an actual epistemological certainty about what exactly it is they are up to. This uncertainty is perhaps even bigger in American Studies than in Video Game Studies: while one of the founding acts of the latter was to debate how a game might be defined,[5] it never doubted that they exist, whereas the former came to wonder more fundamentally whether such a thing as 'American culture' exists at all, and if so, what its modes and conditions of existence are.

Famously, Janice Radway, as president of the American Studies Association in 1998, speculated on ways of changing the name of the association: "Does the perpetuation of the particular name, 'American,' in the title of the field and in the name of the association continue surreptitiously to support the notion that such a whole exists even in the face of powerful work that tends to question its presumed coherence?" (2) Turning against the assumption of an *a priori* cultural unity that is then being studied, "past and present, as a whole" (Smith 197),

---

[5] Even though this debate naturally took place across a variety of publications, I would still recommend Jesper Juul's useful summarizing take on the subject in *Half-Real: Video Games between Rules and Fictional Worlds* (2005), a monograph that remains one of the most lucid and persuasive in the field.

postnationalist American Studies rather inquires into how this "imaginary unity" (Radway 3) comes about if it is not always already there. It seeks "to complicate and fracture the very idea of an 'American' nation, culture, and subject" (17) rather than perpetuate it. Notably, this is not the same as trying to reveal "America as non-existent" (30), as Alan Wolfe claimed in his notorious response to Radway and the postnationalists, but it is rather an inquiry into the reality of the imaginary. It probes how imagined communities are imagined and how they attain reality through symbolic and material practices, and how these shape identities, politics, societies, and individual lives. (Needless to say, video games play a significant role in this imagination of community, and they are unique in how they connect the imaginary and the real.)

This positive uncertainty about disciplinary core concerns and methodologies is nothing new. If there is any tradition in American Studies that really characterizes the field from its inception through its myriad contemporary manifestations, then it is a tradition of persistent self-questioning and a stubborn refusal to let any answer to these questions crystallize into a single and stable unity that would define American Studies beyond the tautology mentioned above. This is why Henry Nash Smith's seminal essay "Can 'American Studies' Develop a Method?" retains its contemporary relevance even though it is clearly rooted in a particular historical and intellectual context. Critically adapting the text to American Studies today, one would certainly want to read "the desire to study American culture as a whole" (206) not as a nationalist fantasy of a pre-existing wholeness but rather as an inclusive desire to consider *any* form of cultural expression, and not merely "the full range of meanings available to us in the arts of complex modern societies" (207). Yet the most relevant aspect of Smith's essay today is the methodological openness he highlights. Perhaps born of necessity as an interdisciplinary attempt to recontextualize the literature that has been decontextualized by New Criticism, it has outgrown this particular desire and has developed into a theoretical and methodological pluralism that cannot be grasped in terms of linear paradigm shifts but rather in terms of an ever-changing interdisciplinary network that holds even though its central node, American culture, no longer stabilizes it. One could say that the pragmatic, improvisational, processual *bricolage* proposed by Smith—"a kind of principled opportunism" (207)—did not prepare the way to a method for American Studies but has *become* its method; there is nothing as permanent as a provisional solution. According to Smith, "[t]he best thing we can do [...] is to conceive of American Studies as a collaboration among men working from within existing academic disciplines but attempting to widen the boundaries imposed by conventional methods of inquiry"; he adds that "inquiries which have their starting-points in various academic departments can converge as they are brought to bear upon a single topic, namely, American culture past and present" (207). The singularity of this topic is as questionable as Smith's assumption that it is only men who work on it, but he is right in pointing out that "Method in scholarship grows out of practice" (207). Something as complex as American culture must be addressed in a combined inter- and multidisciplinary scholarly effort that will never have *a* method but only ever methods in the plural, just like it will always deal with cultures rather than a single unified culture.

This characteristic methodological fuzziness and openness of American Studies corresponds to that of Video Game Studies, where Espen Aarseth's "Computer Game Studies, Year One" in 2001 inaugurated the e-journal *Game Studies* as a central publication platform for the field. Despite its different context, Aarseth's editorial shares notable family resemblances with Smith's programmatic essay. Reading these two texts alongside each other is instructive in that both engage with the challenges and advantages of interdisciplinarity, and how they may productively reconnect on those terms. Aarseth identifies his historical moment as one in which "it might be the first time scholars and academics take computer games seriously, as a cultural field whose value is hard to overestimate," and therefore also a "very early stage" in which "the struggle of controlling and shaping the theoretical paradigms has just started." Aarseth might as well have asked "Can 'Video Game Studies' develop a method?":

> Computer games are perhaps the richest cultural genre we have yet seen, and this challenges our search for a suitable methodological approach. We all enter this field from somewhere else, from anthropology, sociology, narratology, semiotics, film studies, etc, and the political and ideological baggage we bring from our old field inevitably determines and motivates our approaches.

While Smith's methodological musings oppose the dominance of an existing method that he found lacking for its limiting focus on a decontextualized high literature, Aarseth has no such identifiable opponent. He proceeds from the methodological multiplicity that Smith envisions at least as a pragmatic interim goal. Aarseth envisions "uniting aesthetic, cultural and technical design aspects in a single discipline," but this unity is functional and structural rather than methodological, and it is certainly not intended as homogeneity:

> Of course, games should also be studied within existing fields and departments, such as Media Studies, Sociology, and English, to name a few. But games are too important to be left to these fields. (And they did have thirty years in which they did nothing!) Like architecture, which contains but cannot be reduced to art history, game studies should contain media studies, aesthetics, sociology etc. But it should exist as an independent academic structure, because it cannot be reduced to any of the above.

Despite their differences, Smith's and Aarseth's texts share a paradigmatic vector: they both understand that the complexity of their objects of research is such that it may only be addressed in equally complex ways, and that doing so means finding common ground between as large a variety of scholarly approaches as possible. The objective then is to find ways to cultivate this multiplicity without either leveling the differences between these perspectives or establishing a rigid hierarchy between them.

Video Games as Objects of Inquiry: A Methodological Approach

The unique mediality of video games will continue to present one of the biggest challenges to the methodologies of American Studies. For example, it will both enhance and question the so-called visual turn the field has undergone in recent years. Video games lend themselves to be analyzed in visual terms but also cannot be reduced to the visual (just like they cannot be reduced to sound, music, gameplay, narrative, symbolism, or any other single factor that would dominate the irreducible complexity of the medium). Its turn to visuality indicates that American Studies is well past its exclusive philological focus, even though it retains a strong text-based concern. It is worth emphasizing here that this philological tradition is not to be dismissed wholesale as a methodological toolbox when it comes to analyzing video games just because a certain part of that tradition has played such a problematic role in theorizing them. What has come to be identified as a narratological position in video game studies—the notion that games tell stories—has its roots in the long tradition of narrative analysis that dominates the study of American literature today, as narrative forms of literature dominate the literary market and the academic scene. Notably, this kind of narratology is not the same as the narratology that literary scholars speak of when they refer to a particular kind of analysis. Even though the latter has strongly influenced the narratological position on video games, it must not be conflated with it. A terminologically precise understanding of narrative analysis will avoid the double fallacy of either treating games as stories or of interpreting their narrative elements only in narratological terms, thus missing the many other ways in which literary studies may deal with narrative (since narratological analyses of texts are at best a limited, if not marginal subset of literary interpretation today). Philipp Schweighauser draws attention to this distinction in his essay "Doubly Real: Game Studies and Literary Anthropology; or, Why We Play Games," in which he argues that narratology is only a part of literary theory, and a contested one at that. He convincingly outlines useful perspectives on the study of video games beyond that particular approach (focusing in particular on Wolfgang Iser's theory of fiction). Yet I would argue that literary studies has a particular area of expertise that has not yet been even remotely tapped in relation to video games, even though it shares a fundamental property with them that would make its obvious differences all the more fascinating to explore. In fact, this form of cultural expression—once central to the field of American Studies—has been obscured by the intense contemporary focus on narrative with regard to literature: poetry. Like video games, poetry is fundamentally non-narrative in the sense that it *may* be narrative, even strongly so, but that this remains an optional quality. Of course, poetry is mainly textual, visual, and/or acoustic, while video games combine audiovisual, tactile, and textual elements. Yet the tools of poetic analysis may still be more appropriate to the interpretation of video games and their cultural relevance than those of narratology. For one, they will draw attention to the minute details of form and style, to devices such as synecdoche or juxtaposition, to the intricacies of symbolism, and to the play of meaning and its possibilities beyond the constraints of plot, character, and setting.[6] For example, Ezra Pound's theory of Imagism or William Carlos Williams's notion of the poem as a "machine made out of words" (256) may provide literary perspectives on the aesthetics and the symbolic qualities of video games that narrative approaches are missing. One may also add the explorations of the visual beyond the textual by concrete poetry as well as the poetic insistence on the auditory, the sensual, and the performative as much as the textual. This is not to say that narrative approaches to video games are inherently flawed, especially not when considering the sheer diversity of such approaches that barely share anything but that label; it only serves to indicate what else may be found in digging deeper beyond the top layer of narrative analysis in the toolbox of American Studies.

At the same time, the methods of literary analysis—narrative or otherwise—will undoubtedly have to increasingly incorporate the aesthetics of video games into their discursive repertoire as the texts they scrutinize do the same. Just a few brief examples: Thomas Pynchon's novel *Vineland*, published in 1990 and set in 1984, uses scarce references to fictional and real video games (such as "'Nukey,' which included elements of sex and detonation" (160)) mostly in order to situate the narrative in its appropriate contemporary pop-cultural setting; yet his 2013

---

[6] I explore these parallels further in my essay "Whitman and Everything: Playing with the Poetics of Scale," which analyzes Walt Whitman's "Song of Myself" (1855) alongside David OReilly's *Everything* (2017).

novel *Bleeding Edge*, set in 2001, fundamentally draws on games and gaming culture also on a symbolic level, most notably with regard to the digital utopia/dystopia of "DeepArcher," which has "'forerunners in the gaming area, [...] like the MUD clones that started to come online back in the eighties, which were mostly text'" (69). Mark Z. Danielewski's series *The Familiar* goes even further as it explores the potential of the novel beyond the textual: for example, it reveals its own fundamental narrative constructs (or "Narcons") as digital, "nothing but numbers. Zeros and ones" (TFv1 565), and they may "take on multiple shapes whether textual, musical, figurative, abstract, even performative" (TFv1 575). This transmedial take on narration is influenced by video game aesthetics and mediality, which requires a move beyond the literary categories of narratology.[7] The novels use the fictional game of *Paradise Open* as an example of how reading and playing may intersect while remaining distinct. The novels even find a kind of guiding metaphor in software code for their use of visual elements that are always more than mere illustrations: they do include textual code in C++ (e.g. TFv2 111–13), but they also comment on how in the execution of a program "'image subitizes language'" (TFv1 380). This duality is at the heart of its textual, visual, and material aesthetics, and it must be grasped not only in digital terms, but also in the multimedial aesthetics of video games that combine different symbolic forms with an embodied process of interaction.

Interaction might be the right term of understanding how the theories and methods prevalent in American Studies relate to video games as its object of research, as both will mutually affect each other. This includes the more formal approaches I have just mentioned as well as those methods that inquire into the relation between the imagination and identity—in the widest sense of the term —asking the critical questions about race, class, gender, sexuality, (dis)ability, nationality, ethnicity, and so many other categories that American Studies has rightfully focused on in recent decades in its search for appropriate methods of understanding 'American culture.' The theoretical and methodological repertoire that is associated with each of these categories and their intersections are undoubtedly vast and promising, and the notable work that has been done in this regard only indicates how much more there is to be done.

Feminist criticism of video games, for instance, has come a long way since *From Barbie® to Mortal Kombat* (edited by Justine Cassell and Henry Jenkins in 1998). Perspectives rooted in Cultural Studies rather than psychology or game

---

[7] For a multifaceted exploration of the implications of such a move, cf. *Storyworlds across Media: Toward a Media-Conscious Narratology*, edited by Marie-Laure Ryan and Jan-Noël Thon (2014).

design seem desirable now more than ever to spur on this movement; and even though notable work has been done since Mia Consalvo's 2003 essay "Hot Dates and Fairy-Tale Romances: Studying Sexuality in Video Games," both the first anthology on *Queer Game Studies* (edited by Bonnie Ruberg and Adrienne Shaw) and the collection *Gaming Representation: Race, Gender, and Sexuality in Video Games* (edited by Jennifer Malkowski and TreaAndrea M. Russworm) were only published in 2017. The issue of race in video games has been addressed powerfully and repeatedly by scholars such as Anna Everett;[8] she adapted Eric Lott's work on minstrelsy to the new task at hand. Yet these groundbreaking efforts[9] are clearly the beginnings rather than the conclusions to a critical body of work on the subject. And finally, most of the work on video games and social class seems to be done in the social sciences rather than in Cultural Studies, even though a Marxist critique of the largest culture industry today would surely be as merited as a reading of individual games (Nick Dyer-Witheford and Greig de Peuter's 2009 study *Games of Empire: Global Capitalism and Video Games* still remains the most substantial scholarly contribution to that effect.)

All these examples only go to show that video games must be fully integrated into the established and emerging methodological repertoire of Cultural Studies at large, and that American Studies with its strong theoretical diversity must find a way of incorporating video games not just as yet another object of study but as one that may fundamentally challenge the field to reevaluate its methods. Of course, there is also a basic, urgent necessity to address the role of video games in the analysis of American culture from a scholarly perspective, and both the relevance of the medium and the need for a critical perspective on the discourses that surround and constitute it are best exemplified by two separate but connected news items that were published within two days in 2018. On April 9, *Grand Theft Auto V* was described as "the most financially successful media title of all time" (Cherney), earning about six billion dollars in revenue since its initial release in 2013. On April 8, the official White House YouTube channel released a highly controversial, entirely decontextualized supercut video entitled "Violence in Video Games"; this is the video President Trump showed at a meeting with representatives of the video game industry which he called after having speculated on violent video games being the cause of

---

[8] See especially her co-authored essay "The Power of Play: The Portrayal and Performance of Race in Video Games" (with S. Craig Watkins) on this topic.
[9] To these efforts one should add Adrienne Shaw's *Gaming at the Edge: Sexuality and Gender at the Margins of Gamer Culture* (2015), Soraya Murray's *On Video Games: The Visual Politics of Race, Gender and Space* (2017), as well as the edited collections *Queerness in Play, Feminism in Play*, and *Masculinities in Play* (all 2018).

the shooting at Marjory Stoneman Douglas High School in Parkland, Florida on February 14, 2018 (Sirani). These two media events mark the immediate historical context of the project at hand and frame the scholarly challenges ahead: on the one hand, video games are the biggest culture industry out there, not only in economic terms but also in terms of cultural pervasiveness; on the other hand, the discourse on video games is still very much contested, not only because of the revival of a debate most people were already tired of in the 1990s by a president who would prefer not to talk about the second amendment instead, but also because evidently their *cultural* and *political* force remains largely unexplored while their *psychological* and *social* impact is highlighted.[10]

Perhaps it will be American Studies that may provide a self-reflexive element of scholarly critique in adding (or even opposing) more cultural approaches to psychological ones, especially when the latter's premises and methods seem dubious and their results, therefore, questionable. In any case, American Studies can and must be more than simply a counterpoint to other perspectives. Most importantly, the question of what American Studies has to say about video games must be the question of what it has to say that might not as well be said in and by other fields, and what its genuine and unique contribution to the interdisciplinary field of Video Game Studies might be. My own answer to this question is that the most important thing it can offer are critical perspectives on the construction of American culture in and through a global medium, not understanding American culture as a given or Americanness as a unified set of properties, but rather drawing attention to the contested space of Americanness, its symbolic constructions and political implications, its ideologies, stories, histories and myths, its homogenizations and exclusions, and most generally its imagination of community with very real effects. If American Studies no longer assumes there is a singular American culture to begin with (without giving up on the concept of culture itself), then its interest has shifted toward how American culture is constructed, invented, negotiated, and challenged, to what end this imagination occurs, and who gets to do the imagining under which material conditions—and video games are a prominent realm of cultural production in which

---

10 President Trump established the Federal Commission on School Safety in the aftermath of the Parkland shooting. It presented its report to the President on December 18, 2018. In this report, there is only a remarkably brief section on "Violent Entertainment and Rating Systems," which concludes that "scholars and researchers disagree about the effect of exposure to violent entertainment" (63) and highlights the importance of existing rating systems for parental guidance. The Commission thus refuses to identify video games as a singular cause of school shootings, and its conclusion suggesting ways of preventing school violence in the future does not even mention them again.

all these processes are taking place and merit scholarly contextualization, scrutiny, and critique. Transnational approaches have only highlighted further the necessity to understand such cultural processes beyond the epistemological limits of the national. Perhaps no other object of research demands a transnational framework as video games do, as they epitomize the glocal in their distribution on a global market with significant regional specificities. In short, I see the biggest conceptual contribution by American Studies to Video Game Studies in its pronounced skepticism toward its own object of research. The best way to study the role of video games in American culture and the role of American culture in and for video games, it seems to me at least, is to take none of the two as a unitary given. Rather, it serves to understand them as truly mutually constitutive without assuming the priority of one over the other. This is a tall order, to be sure, so it is really time to play now.

Essay Summaries

The contributions in this collection all accept this invitation to play with this dialectic in one way or another, and despite their multiplicity they are far from exhaustive in their approaches to the task at hand. This volume certainly wants to start a conversation rather than end one. It is designed to offer a variety of perspectives rather than a streamlined approach that would make a normative case for a particular position that should become paradigmatic for American Studies. In the spirit of Smith and Aarseth—I hope—this collection highlights the pragmatic over the paradigmatic, either by exemplary analyses or by more theoretical reflections on interdisciplinary methodology. Since American Studies is so many things to many different people, its approaches to video games cannot be reduced to a single or even just a few perspectives, and even though there is a need for discussing what works and what does not, this discussion cannot occur in terms of agreeing on the single right way of doing things but rather of agreeing to disagree productively. This is what lies ahead, then:

The collection opens with Mark J. P. Wolf's "Video Games and the American Cultural Context," which provides a broad historical overview of the combined cultural, technological, and commercial conditions that have allowed the video game industry in the USA to develop and prosper as a central node in what has now become a global video game economy of production and reception.

Michael Fuchs, Michael Phillips, and Stefan Rabitsch expand on the cultural aspect by focusing on a particularly relevant trope in the repertoire of how Americanness is constructed. In "The end is nigh! Bring forth the Shepard!

Mass Effect, the Apocalypse, and the Puritan Imagination," they discuss the game trilogy as an updated Jeremiad with an uneasy relation to the national discourse this mode of discourse has come to define.

In a related manner, David Callahan in "The Last of the US: The Game as Cultural Geography" focuses on the representation of spaces and places in *The Last of Us*, arguing that the game invokes and subverts a variety of cultural and historical subtexts as it traces the westward movement of the protagonists through an American landscape.

Patricia Maier is concerned with a particular form of movement in "Mobility and Choices in Role-Playing Games," in which she analyzes *Skyrim* in terms of the tropes associated with American road narratives, arguing that the game associates different types of mobility with different ethics in its own in-game system of 'racial' segregation, and that it uses the resulting tension to evoke moral decisions in the player without flagging them as such or pre-judging them.

Dietmar Meinel concludes this cluster on movement and spatial representation with "Playing the Urban Future: The Scripting of Movement and Space in *Mirror's Edge* (2008)," in which he adapts the theories of Henri Lefebvre and Michel de Certeau to analyze how the game mediates an urban environment and scripts a particular form of its potentially transgressive traversal, Parkour.

Martin Lüthe turns to a different form of bodily movement in "Playing on Fields: Seasonal Seriality, Tele-Realism, and the Bio-Politics of Digital Sports Games," as he analyses the *Pro Evolution Soccer* and *Madden* digital sports franchises for their relation to the serial and televisual aesthetics of their analog counterparts, and also shows how these games reproduce anxieties of the digital era regarding the fragility and volatility of the human body in general, and the (white) male sporting/slouching body specifically.

Stefan Schubert considers a different area of contemporary US-American popular culture in "Narrative and Play in American Studies: Ludic Textuality in the Video Game *Alan Wake* and the TV Series *Westworld*," and his comparative analysis of these two artifacts (along with other examples such as Mark Z. Danielewski's *House of Leaves*) establishes an abstract theory of the interrelations between play and narrative from an intermedial perspective that attests to an increasing fusion of these forms in the twenty-first century.

Andrei Nae and Alexandra Ileana Bacalu step back three centuries from there for a different kind of comparative analysis in "Toward a Reconsideration of Hypermediacy: Immersion in Survival Horror Games and Eighteenth-Century Novels," which discusses the *Silent Hill* series and Daniel Defoe's *Robinson Crusoe* (among other examples) in terms of their related hypermedial form that seeks to heighten immersion not by erasing but by emphasizing mediation.

Doug Stark then addresses this relation as a fusion in the genre of the video game novel in "Ludic Literature: *Ready Player One* as Didactic Fiction for the Neoliberal Subject." He sets the playfulness of Ernest Cline's fiction and its expansive intertexts in relation to a larger neoliberal practice of gamified self-fashioning within a framework of ludic cultural capital, reading its allegedly sub- or even countercultural gamer ethic as an updated version of Max Weber's protestant work ethic for the digital age.

Sebastian Domsch engages in a different kind of literary analysis in "Strategies against Structure: Video Game Terrorism as the Ultimate American Agency Narrative" in order to describe how video games establish narrative archetypes through their gameplay mechanics rather than the modes of semanticization that are usually considered as integral to their storytelling; listing navigation, survival, accumulation / attrition, and destruction, he focuses particularly on the latter as a 'terrorist narrative' that highlights the tension between individual agency and structure.

This is precisely the abstract concern of Jon Adams in "Why We Play Role-Playing Games," although coming from a different angle that purposefully blurs the line between game and non-game further. Adams argues that RPGs offer a playful way of acquiring algorithmic literacy in a world that has become increasingly algorithmic, and as they teach players how to position themselves critically toward the algorithmic systems that run their lives to a significant extent, and how they might even "game the system" in the process.

Damien B. Schlarb writes about more concrete structural (self-)subversion in "Narrative Glitches: Action Adventure Games and Metaleptic Convergence," as he discusses how *X-Men* (1993), *Batman: Arkham Asylum* (2009), and *Pony Island* (2016) stage moments of metalepsis in which simulated machinic failure becomes part of narrative, showing how video games uniquely use these interstices between the material and the cultural in their meaning-making.

Sabrina Mittermeier explores this connection further from a very different perspective in "Time Travelling to the American Revolution—Why Immersive Media Need American Studies," as she addresses the combination of material, historical, and cultural aspects in American theme parks and video games alike. She discusses how *Assassins Creed 3* and Disney's Magic Kingdom and Epcot represent the American revolution, and how these participatory media fare when confronted with the (often political) demands of historical 'accuracy.'

In another twist that takes us back to video games and constructions of Americanness, Manuel Franz and Henning Jansen discuss historical representation in *BioShock Infinite*. In their essay "A Shining City and the Sodom Below: Historical Guilt and Personal Agency in *BioShock Infinite*," they analyze the game for its history-related content as they argue that its depiction of history addresses individual responsibility and guilt as a driving force of commemorative culture. They show that the game seeks and largely fails to evoke such responsibility and guilt in the player.

Jacqueline Blank continues the discussion of this game in "The Art of *BioShock Infinite:* Identity, Race, and Manifest Destiny" by focusing on a particular visual aspect that is central to how its own variety of Americanness is conveyed to players. Comparing major in-game paintings with historical ones, she shows how the ideological context and purpose of the latter informs that of the former by way of a shared visual aesthetics that critically embeds the gameworld in US-American cultural history.

Veronika Keller concludes the discussion of *BioShock Infinite* with a musical analysis in "Sounds of Tears: Mozart's *Lacrimosa* in Different Media." Using Miloš Forman's *Amadeus* as a starting point, she traces how this particular piece of classical music accumulates layers of meaning through different iterations in various cultural artifacts across media, and how it goes beyond this process in *BioShock Infinite* in assuming not only a symbolic but an interactive role.

Nathalie Aghoro concludes the collection with a focus on sound rather than music in "Unspoken Adventures: On Sound, Story, and Nonverbal Gameplay in *Journey* and *Inside.*" She argues that these games, despite their differences, both use nonverbal sounds to generate individual storytelling experiences that invite players to evaluate social dynamics and world-subject relations as they are fundamental to the exploration of their own agency within the game and at its limits.

With this variety of individual approaches, this collection serves as a basis for an extended debate within American Studies on how the field may deal with video games and how it may change in order to do so. Even though this is what some readers might expect from a more abstract introduction such as this one, it would be unduly limiting to identify more precise potential fields of interest or methodological implications for American Studies here. The beauty and challenge of how American Studies may integrate video games more and be changed by them, however, is that not even a well-meaning speculation would do justice to the potential that is actually out there. I would only caution that we avoid the pitfall of misrepresenting our objects to make them fit a particular method. I see the biggest potential for American Studies in exploring this dialectic between what is studied and how it is studied, and I have no doubt that any analysis mindful of this will prove to be productive in more than one way.

Works Cited

Aarseth, Espen. "Computer Game Studies, Year One." July 2001, www.gamestudies.org/0101/editorial.html. Accessed 15 Jan. 2019.
Buell, Lawrence. *The Environmental Imagination: Thoreau, Nature Writing, and the Formation of American Culture*. Harvard UP, 1995.
Cassell, Justine, and Henry Jenkins, editors. *From Barbie® to Mortal Kombat: Gender and Computer Games*. The MIT Press, 1998.
Chang, Alenda Y. "*Games as Environmental Texts*." Qui Parle: Critical Humanities and Social Sciences, vol. 19, no. 2, 2011, pp. 57–84.
Cherney, Max A. "This Violent Videogame has Made more Money than any Movie Ever." *Marketwatch.com*, Dow Jones & Co., 9 Apr 2018, www.marketwatch.com/story/this-violent-videogame-has-made-more-money-than-any-movie-ever-2018-04-06. Accessed 15 Jan. 2019.
Consalvo, Mia. "Hot Dates and Fairy-Tale Romances: Studying Sexuality in Video Games." *The Video Game Theory Reader*, edited by Mark J.P. Wolf and Bernard Perron, Routledge, 2003, pp. 171–94.
Danielewski, Mark Z. *The Familiar*. Pantheon, 2015–2017. 5 vols.
Derrida, Jacques. *Of Grammatology*. Translated by Gayatri Chakravorty Spivak, Johns Hopkins UP, 1997.
Dyer-Witheford, Nick, and Greig de Peuter. *Games of Empire. Global Capitalism and Video Games*. U of Minnesota P, 2009.
Everett, Anna, and Craig Watkins. "The Power of Play: The Portrayal and Performance of Race in Video Games." *The Ecology of Games: Connecting Youth, Games, and Learning*, edited by Katie Salen, The MIT Press, 2008, pp. 141–66. doi:10.1162/dmal.9780262693646.141. Accessed 15 Jan. 2019.
"Final Report of the Federal Commission on School Safety." U.S. Department of Education, 18 Dec. 2018, www2.ed.gov/documents/school-safety/school-safety-report.pdf. Accessed 15 Jan. 2019.
Gray, Kishonna L., Gerald Voorhees, and Emma Vossen, editors. *Feminism in Play*. Palgrave MacMillan, 2018.
Gunzenhäuser, Randi. "Computerspiele als Herausforderung an die Wissenschaften." *Computerspiele—Eine Provokation für die Kulturwissenschaften?*, edited by Evelyne Keitel et al., Pabst Science Publishers, 2003, pp. 107–114.
Harper, Todd, Meghan Blythe Adams, and Nicholas Taylor, editors. *Queerness in Play*. Palgrave MacMillan, 2018.
Mäyrä, Frans. *An Introduction to Game Studies: Games in Culture*. Sage, 2008.
Mayar, Mahshid, editor. *Encounters in the 'Game-Over Era': The Americas in/and Video Games*, special issue of *forum for inter-american research*, vol. 11, no. 2, 2018, interamerica.de/wp-content/uploads/2018/09/Vol-11.2-ready.pdf. Accessed 15 Jan. 2019.
Juul, Jesper. *Half-Real: Video Games between Real Rules and Fictional Worlds*. The MIT Press, 2005.
Malkowski, Jennifer, and TreaAndrea M. Russworm, editors. *Gaming Representation: Race, Gender, and Sexuality in Video Games*. Indiana UP, 2017.

Milburn, Colin. "*Green Gaming: Video Games and Environmental Risk.*" *The Anticipation of Catastrophe. Environmental Risk in North American Literature and Culture*, edited by Sylvia Mayer and Alexa Weik von Mossner, Winter, 2014, pp. 201–18.

Murray, Soraya. *On Video Games: The Visual Politics of Race, Gender and Space*. I.B. Tauris, 2017.

Newman, Michael Z. *Atari Age: The Emergence of Video Games in America*. MIT Press, 2017.

Penix-Tadsen, Phillip. *Cultural Code: Video Games and Latin America*. MIT Press, 2016.

Pöhlmann, Sascha. "Whitman and Everything: Playing with the Poetics of Scale." *Revisiting Walt Whitman: On the Occasion of his 200th Birthday*, edited by Winfried Herget, Peter Lang, 2019, pp. 55–80.

Pynchon, Thomas. *Bleeding Edge*. Penguin, 2013.

Pynchon, Thomas. *Vineland*. Little, Brown & Co., 1990.

Radway, Janice. "What's in a Name? Presidential Address to the American Studies Association, 20 November, 1998." *American Quarterly*, vol. 51, no. 1, March 1999, pp. 1–32.

Ruberg, Bonnie, and Adrienne Shaw, editors. *Queer Game Studies*. U of Minnesota P, 2017.

Ryan, Marie-Laure. *Narrative as Virtual Reality: Immersion and Interactivity in Literature and Electronic Media*. Johns Hopkins UP, 2001.

Ryan, Marie-Laure and Jan-Noël Thon, editors. *Storyworlds across Media: Toward a Media-Conscious Narratology*. U of Nebraska P, 2014.

Schweighauser, Philipp. "Doubly Real: Game Studies and Literary Anthropology; or, Why We Play Games." *Eludamos. Journal for Computer Game Culture*, vol. 3, no. 2, 2009, pp. 115–32.

Shaw, Adrienne. *Gaming at the Edge: Sexuality and Gender at the Margins of Gamer Culture*. U of Minnesota P, 2015.

Sirani, Jordan. "'Trump: Video Game, Movie Violence Is 'Shaping Young People's Thoughts.'" *IGN.com*, 22 Feb 2018, www.ign.com/articles/2018/02/22/trump-video-game-movie-violence-is-shaping-young-peoples-thoughts. Accessed 15 Jan. 2019.

Smith, Henry Nash. "Can 'American Studies' Develop a Method?" *American Quarterly*, vol. 9, no. 2, part 2, 1957, pp. 197–208.

Taylor, Nicholas, and Gerald Voorhees, editors. *Masculinities in Play*. Palgrave MacMillan, 2018.

"Violence in Video Games." *YouTube*, uploaded by The White House, 8 March 2018, www.youtube.com/watch?v=0C_IBSuXIoo.

Wardrip-Fruin, Noah, and Pat Harrigan, editors. *First-Person: New Media as Story, Performance, and Game*. MIT Press, 2004.

Williams, William Carlos. "Author's Introduction to *The Wedge*." *Selected Essays of William Carlos Williams*, Random House, 1954, pp. 255–57.

Wolfe, Alan. "Anti-American Studies: The Difference between Criticism and Hatred." *The New Republic*, 10 Feb. 2003, pp. 25–32.

Mark J. P. Wolf
Video Games and the American Cultural Context

As the birthplace of video games and a major producer of them, the United States of America is the location of much of video game history, which is usually covered in detail when the history of video games is recounted. Although video games spread to other countries in the early 1970s, particularly to Japan and Europe, the American video game industry remains intimately bound to American popular culture. Popular American themes such as cross-cultural conflict, cultural assimilation, and the importance of personal identity are explored in many games, such as the games of the *Grand Theft Auto* series, the cities of which are very American in their depiction and action. Some games, like *Red Dead Redemption* (2010) and *BioShock Infinite* (2012), even have designs which refer to, and are highly influenced by, American history, even though their settings are entirely fictional.

It makes sense, then, to explore video games within the American cultural context, and how it may have shaped their nature from their very beginning, if even in just a general way. While a large domestic audience may explain how video games quickly became a viable industry in America, other initial conditions must be examined to explain how, why, and in what form video games came about in America.

A Convergence of Conditions

The 1880s through the early 1900s saw the rise of arcades as places of entertainment due to the introduction of coin-operated amusement devices, including the coin-operated mutoscopes and kinetoscopes that paved the way for cinema. Like these machines, early arcade games were simple, visual, action-based, and inexpensive to play, making them similar to much early film, which appealed to a wide mass audience of limited means and education that made up a significant percentage of the American public around the turn of the century. As a nation of immigrants and many languages, visual media—including film, comics, television, and video games—have usually found widespread popularity that crosses language barriers, making them good candidates for export as well. Electromechanical games, housed in upright cabinets, provided the format that would be adopted by arcade video games, and frequently they were shooting games or racing games, genres that would become mainstays for video game makers. So the arcade provided a ready venue for video games to enter, once they could fit the arcade cabinets and be cheap enough to operate.

From the late 1800s onward, the do-it-yourself mentality, an outlook that began with immigrant homesteading pioneers, was increasingly applied to the rapidly-spreading electrical technology. Inspired by entrepreneurs and inventors like Thomas Edison, many boys and young men experimented with telegraph and radio technologies, resulting in the formation of technological elites and the culture of hacking. The boom in technological expansion that came with the Second World War, particular in the area of computer technology, along with other resources like the G. I. Bill that increased college enrollments, encouraged the development of university laboratories, like those at MIT and the University of Utah, which became homes to mainframe computers and the hacker subculture. It was in such places that hacking led to the first mainframe games, like *Spacewar!* (1962), inspired as much by the technology as the American-Soviet Space Race and a renewed cultural interest in science fiction. While concurrent movements in the American art world, such as interactive installation art, abstract art, electronic music, and experiments which combined art and technology, may not have had a direct influence on the rise of video games, they at least helped contribute to an environment that helped validate the minimalistic appearance of early video games.

During the post-war period, television was making inroads into American homes, which were now moving away from the city into the suburbs, where residents had greater leisure time to enjoy family life and activities in the home, including watching TV. Television quickly became a ubiquitous technology, leading German-born inventor Ralph Baer to consider new uses for it. Baer's work eventually led to the first home video game console system in 1972, the Magnavox Odyssey, which was made by Magnavox, a maker of television sets. The close association of video games with television not only helped them quickly become a commercial product, as opposed to an artistic novelty or underground subculture, but also helped determine, along with electromechanical games and popular arcade video games, the kinds of genres that would come to dominate the young medium, namely shooting games, racing and driving games, and other fast-action games.

Throughout the 1960s, projects of the US Government Space Program and Department of Defense provided the motivation, and funding, for the integrated circuit industry, which in the 1970s resulted in the miniaturization and lower prices that allowed integrated circuits to start appearing in consumer products, such as pocket calculators, digital watches, and of course video games. The 1970s were another period of great technological enthusiasm, as home video, home computers, and home video games became popular. Entrepreneurs and investors funneled millions of dollars into electronics ventures and start-ups to meet the demand. The unbridled experimentation and numerous offerings led to a glutting of the market in several electronics industries, including the video game industry as well, which experienced crashes in 1977 and later in 1983–84. Pessimism followed, and it took the success of a foreign system, the Nintendo Famicon (renamed the Nintendo Entertainment System for its North American release), for the industry to rebound in 1985.

Influences after the Crash

The year 1985 marked a turning point in the US video game industry, which would no longer be the dominant producer of video game consoles, with Nintendo and SEGA becoming the two main contenders for industry dominance. The rise of Japanese video games in the US was foreshadowed in 1978 when Taito's *Space Invaders* (1978) became a hit game in the US; it was the first foreign import to find a mass audience there. It is rather ironic, then, that Atari, America's powerhouse video game company of the pre-Crash era, and the first company devoted solely to the production of video games, was given a Japanese name. Taken from the game of Go, "atari" means a situation in which pieces are in danger of being captured on the next turn—a forewarning of the taking over of the market when Nintendo eclipsed Atari in the mid-1980s.

But the US market for video games was growing new sectors, such as handheld games and game systems, home computer games, and new types of technology, like that used in vector games and laserdisc games. Americans have always loved gadgets, and they bought into the new technologies that were appearing, with video games providing a reason to buy a home computer in many households; some of those, like the Texas Instruments TI99/4a home computer, even had a cartridge slot built into it. Home computers also allowed users to write their own games or type in the code for games from hobbyist magazines, carrying on the do-it-yourself tradition. Atari joined in, producing its own line of home computers, including the Atari 400, Atari 800, and the Atari ST series. Home computers also helped video games gain respectability, since they could help teach programming and the procedural, logical thinking that it required; even the Atari VCS 2600 had a cartridge named *Basic Programming* (1979).

America had one of most advanced telephony infrastructures in the world, so with the addition of modems, home computers could use telephone lines and network with each other, resulting in new possibilities for gameplay. In 1978, the first publically-available bulletin board system (BBS) came on-line in

Chicago, around the same time that the first multi-user domain, or MUD, came on-line in Essex, England. The first on-line console gaming came shortly after, with the release of Mattel's PlayCable service in 1981 and the CVC Gameline service in 1983. Mattel's PlayCable delivered games for its Intellivision system, while the CVC Gameline allowed Atari 2600 users to receive games on-line. The CVC Gameline Master Module plugged into the Atari 2600's cartridge port and had an internal 1200 baud modem through which games could be loaded into the unit's 8 KB of RAM, allowing games to be downloaded and played but not saved.

Elsewhere in American popular culture of the late 1970s and 1980s, merchandising and franchising were becoming popular business strategies, with the marketing of movies like *Star Wars* (1977) and its extensive toy lines and tie-in merchandise. With more movie sequels being made than ever before, intellectual property was coming to be seen as the seeds of franchises which could extend over multiple media, with each release supporting the others, giving rise to the early forms of transmedia marketing and authorship which are so popular today. Deregulation of the American media industries during the 1980s also made it easier for corporations to buy up holdings in multiple media and then distribute their content across multiple media.

Early on, then, video games became one more venue into which transmedia franchises could adapt their material. Even the relatively low-resolution Atari 2600 had dozen of cartridges for it adapted from movies, television shows, comics, literature, music, and other intellectual properties. Some cartridges were even adaptations of television commercials, including *Chase the Chuck Wagon* (1983) and *Kool-Aid Man* (1983), both of which are now sought after by collectors. The 1980s also saw video games themselves becoming the source of character-based franchises, such as those surrounding Pac-Man, Mario, and Zelda, which would also spread to other media. Thus, video games had many outside influences helping to bring them into the American public's attention, and by the mid-1980s, they were well-established and well-integrated into the American cultural scene.

But the American video game industry, competitive as it was, had lost its dominance. The Crash destroyed confidence in the market, and Nintendo and SEGA remained the two giants battling it out in the late 1980s. Two other foreign companies, Sony and Philips, had developed the CD-ROM, an optical disc that could store 650 megabytes of data, and by the end of the decade it would begin to replace the cartridge as the main storage medium for games. Although an American game, Cyan's *The Manhole* of 1987, is generally credited with being the first video game to become available on CD-ROM, American video game companies were slow to incorporate CD-ROM drives into their game systems. Japanese companies did so much sooner. A CD-ROM add-on peripheral was released for the NEC PC-Engine/Turbogrfx-16 in 1989, and for the SEGA Mega Drive/SEGA Genesis in 1992; and in 1991, Fujitsu's FM Towns Marty (released in Japan), became the first 32-bit system and the first console system with a built-in CD-ROM drive. Finally, in 1993, an American system, Trip Hawkins's 3DO Interactive Multiplayer, came with a CD-ROM drive, but the console was a commercial failure and ceased production only three years later. But subsequent systems would use CD-ROMs as they became the industry standard, and by 1996, only the Nintendo 64 was still cartridge-based.

The American video industry remained in crisis into the 1990s. Arcades were disappearing as home games improved and were able to compete against them, and even Atari, the flagship company of the American video game industry and the only company to produce arcade games, home game systems, and home computers, had lost some of its relevance and was finally merged with JTS Inc. in 1996, forming JTS Corp., which sold the Atari name and assets only two years later to Hasbro Interactive for only a fraction of what Warner Communication had bought it for over two decades earlier. Finally, in 2000, French software publisher Infogrames took over Hasbro Interactive, and the Atari brand was now no longer American.

The mid-1990s also saw another Japanese giant entering the gaming race, with the release of the Sony PlayStation. Once the PlayStation found success, Sony began working on the PlayStation 2, drawing developers away from the Windows platform. In 1998, four engineers from Microsoft's DirectX team put together a prototype for a gaming console, which they referred to as the DirectX Box. Microsoft accepted the idea, shortened the name to Xbox, and in November of 2001, the system was finally released, joining the PlayStation 2, released in 2000, and the Nintendo GameCube, released in 2001, in the sixth generation of console system technology. The Xbox was the first console to have a built-in hard disk drive, eliminating the need for memory cards, and the system was also known for its Xbox Live on-line gaming service. The Xbox was the first competitive home video game system to come from an American company in over a decade and a half, and soon Microsoft became one of the Big Three console producers along with Nintendo and Sony. The US was back in the gaming game.

By 2001, computer graphics were widespread in all areas of American visual media. Computer graphics had been used in Hollywood feature films in the 1970s and 1980s, and television commercials also provided the high budgets and hunger for novelty that computer graphics needed to advance. Film and television made companies providing these graphics feasible, and those companies' developments would find their way into video games. Home video games began using filled-polygon three-dimensional graphics around the mid-to-late 1990s, but they would always lag behind cutting-edge computer graphics due to games' need for graphics that were rendered interactively in real-time (some games used pre-rendered imagery, but were less interactive as a result). But even with lower polygonal resolution, flat lighting, and limited textures, three-dimensionally rendered computer-generated imagery brought video games closer to other media like film and television.

Soon after the World Wide Web went worldwide in 1993, the American game industry also launched the genre of massively multiplayer on-line role-playing games. The first game to be considered as an MMORPG was 3DO's *Meridian 59* (1995), but by the end of the 1990s, the Big Three MMORPGs with the most players were Origin Systems's *Ultima Online* (1997), 989 Studio's *EverQuest* (1999), and Turbine Entertainment Software's *Asheron's Call* (1999). On-line games grew in popularity into the 2000s, though 2002 saw the release of both *Ragnarok Online* and the free-to-play *MapleStory*, two South Korean MMORPGs that helped make South Korea a major player in the realm of MMORPGs.

Nostalgia, Retrogaming, and Preservation

By the mid-1990s, many of the members of "Generation X" who had grown up with video games were beginning to have children of their own, and they were also becoming nostalgic for the early games of their own youth. As home computers became more powerful, emulators for earlier game consoles began to appear, leading to the retrogaming movement and renewed interest in early games. Communities formed on the Web to collect and exchange old game information, and homebrewers even wrote games for older systems like the Atari 2600 and the Vectrex. Over the next decades, not only would older games be re-released in new forms for newer systems, but the old games would also prove to be good fodder for the tiny screens of cell phones and other mobile gaming devices, which, at the time, had neither the computational power nor the screen resolution to compete with contemporary home console games and home computer games.

Nostalgia not only calls attention to objects of the past, it also helps reveal the current state of their preservation. In the United States, video games were the object of study by hobbyists and journalists from the 1970s onward, discussed in such venues as the magazine *Popular Electronics*, which featured a multi-part essay by Jerry and Eric Eimbinder on the history of video games which appeared beginning in October of 1980. In the 1980s, entire magazines devoted to games appeared, such as *Electronic Games* (1981–1985), *Computer Gaming World* (1981–2006), *Atari Age* (1982–1984), *Commodore Power/Play* (1982–1985), *Amiga World* (1985–1995), *GamePro* (1989–2011), and others. During the 1980s, psychologists like Patricia Marks Greenfield also studied video games and their effects on youth, and in 1985, the first doctoral dissertation on video games, *Interactive Fiction: The Computer Storygame 'Adventure'*, was written by Mary Ann Buckles at the University of California, San Diego. Alongside the retrogaming movement, video games were gradually acknowledged as objects worth of preservation, with *Hot Circuits: A Video Arcade* as the first museum exhibit devoted to video games, which ran from June of 1989 to May of 1990 at the American Museum of the Moving Image in Astoria, New York.

Nostalgia was not limited to Americans, either, as video games had been around long enough in many countries for the retrogaming movement to appear in many areas around the globe. Games in general were no longer made only for domestic markets, but drew interest and profits from a much wider audience. Perhaps today more than ever, specific cultural content and influence from their cultures of origin may be what set games apart from others, allowing them to offer something which cannot be found elsewhere.

The Continuing Relevance and Development of American Video Games

Possibly attributed to the pioneer spirit, the desire to invent and innovate also has an entrepreneurial side, which business conditions in America tend to encourage. Applied to video games, we find that there are such a wide range of video games, along with their design styles, goals, and game content, that it becomes difficult to say anything in general that applies to all American video games. Here, for example, are screenshots from *Sneak 'n' Peak* (1982), *flOw* (2006), *Passage* (2007), and *The Stanley Parable* (2013) (see Fig. 1).

Sneak 'n' Peak is a game based on hide and seek, played in a simple house with extremely limited graphics, an odd idea for a game from a time when graphics were so limited. *flOw* is an abstract game in which the player controls an undersea creature which eats other organisms, growing and changing based on what is eaten, an open-ended game which continues as long as one wishes to play. *Passage* is an Art game, a deliberately low-resolution game which is not about winning or losing but rather a metaphor for the passage of a person's entire life, played on a horizontal strip of a screen that compacts on both ends but opens out in the middle where the player's character is moving. *The Stanley Parable* is a game known for its breaking of the rules and conventions that video game players expect, which is responsible for much of its charm and uniqueness.

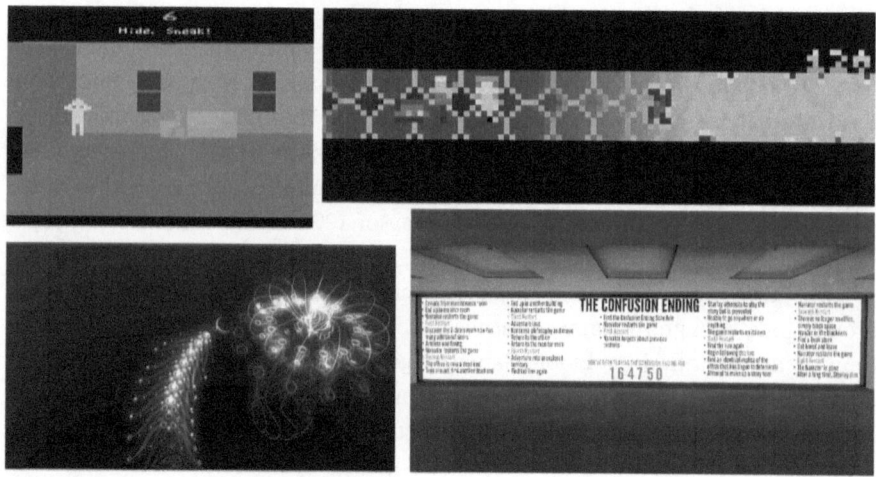

Fig. 1: Screenshots from *Sneak 'n' Peak* (1982) (top, left); *flOw* (2006) (top, right); *Passage* (2007) (bottom, left); and *The Stanley Parable* (2013) (bottom, right).

One can also debate where the line around "American games" should be drawn; while *flOw* was made by American game company thatgamecompany, the main design force behind the game was Jenova Chen, a Chinese immigrant who came to the United States to study at USC, where the game became his Master's thesis. How long must someone live in the US to be considered American? At the same time, the wide-ranging mix of immigrants and other cultures is itself a part of what made America what it is, and continues to be important.

Diversity can also be attributed to the fact that independents and small studios make up a large part of the American video game industry. The Entertainment Software Association's 2017 report, "Analyzing the American Video Game Industry 2016", provides the following statistics:

- There are 2,457 active game companies in the United States across 2,858 locations.
- Game companies are located in all 50 states and 83.70% of Congressional districts.
- There are an estimated 65,678 direct employees in America's video game industry.
- 99.7% of American-based game companies are small businesses.
- Video game industry growth is due to (1) the rise of independent video game developers, who in 2016 made up 98.10% of all company additions, and (2) the increasing amount of video game studies courses and programs offered across 940 American educational institutions of higher learning. (ESA 4)

The report also noted that 94.57% percent of the 2,457 companies were founded domestically (ESA 5), and that "96.55% of Congressional districts have either a video game company or a higher educational institution offering education in video game studies" (ESA 11). Most of the companies also publish their own games, and "70.80% of developers create content for computer and online distribution platforms" (ESA 23). Thus, the American video game industry is robust and widespread, and so it is naturally an arena where competition is vital.

It is perhaps not surprising, then, that competition-based games have become the dominant form of video gaming. It did not necessarily have to be so, and cooperative games could have become the dominant type; consider the mass popularity of cooperative MMORPGs in Asia, where culture tends to be more collective in nature than individualistic. Other genres, like adventure games that require navigation and exploration or puzzle games, or open-ended sandbox-style games, could have also become dominant; but they did not. Instead, one of the most popular genres is the first-person shooting game, the very name of which emphasizes an individual's first-person perspective on the world of the game.

American video game arcades from the early days of video game history provided an interesting combination of competition and individualism at the same time; many arcade games were played by a single player while others merely watched the performance, yet from *Asteroids* (1979) onward, many games featured personalized high-score tables where players could record their initials, making them able to compete with others for high scores, and even compete with their own high scores. The connection between video games and war has been present in American films like *Tron* (1982), *WarGames* (1983), *Cloak & Dagger* (1984), *The Last Starfighter* (1984), *Toys* (1992), *Ender's Game* (2013), and *Ready Player One* (2018). Typically in these films, the otherwise virtual activities within video games become tied to real world stakes and consequences, and the development of players' game skills become connected to some type of life-or-death military conflict. The American military has used video games in its training ever since Atari's *BattleZone* (1980) was retooled for the military as the *Bradley Trainer*, and of course countless video games have war and personal combat as their subject matter. There are so many connections between war and video gaming that it is difficult to even imagine that it might have been otherwise, until one considers the wide range of content in video games coming out in industries around the world.

Part of the reason for its continuing relevance is the industry's willingness to take risks; American companies have risked some of the highest budgets to ever be spent on video game development. According to statistics found on Wikipedia regarding on game development and marketing costs, American companies have published nine out of ten of the most expensive video games, with *Grand Theft Auto V* costing around $266 million.[7] The total cost of developing and marketing each of these games is over $100 million, which represents risks on a similar scale with big-budget Hollywood films. Of course, it should also be noted that Wikipedia's "List of commercial failures in video gaming" also contains a fair share of failed endeavors by American companies.

Of course, sometimes the expectations of industry can also go too far, and ask too much of employees. As production deadlines near and "crunch time" goes into effect to get games done by their release dates, workers can be asked to put in long hours, sometimes without the additional pay that usually comes with working overtime. For example, in 2004, Electronic Arts faced a class-action lawsuit, Jaime Kirschenbaum vs. Electronic Arts, which accused the company of not paying employees the overtime pay they deserved. It all began when a blogger claiming to be the spouse of an EA employee complained that graphic artists were treated unfairly and asked to work a typical week of 9:00 am to 10:00 pm, Monday through Saturday. The suit was finally settled a year later in 2005, with EA paying out $15.6 million. Months later a second lawsuit was filed, this time for overtime pay for programmers and engineers, which was later settled for $14.9 million (Surette). Four year after that, in 2010, the wives of workers at the San Diego branch of Rockstar Games complained about the working conditions endured by their spouses and threatened legal action, posting an open letter on *Gamasutra* from "Determined Devoted Wives of Rockstar San Diego Employees," after the "crunch mode" period required for the completion of *Red Dead Redemption* (2010) (Chalk). What is interesting in both of these cases is that it was the employees' spouses at home, not the employees themselves, who initiated these complaints, suggesting that the long hours are assumed to be a part of the internal culture of the industry.

Finally, there is one vast area of popular culture, advertising, which has cast its immense shadow on American video games and should be considered here. First, game advertisements very quickly framed video games as a product and family activity for the home, as something interactive and conducive to family-bonding as opposed to the relatively passive activity of watching television, helping it become an accepted part of American culture. Second, like all other media to come along before it, video games also became yet one more venue for advertising itself to reach an audience.

Advertisements were introduced into games beginning in the early 1980s. Atari's *Pole Position* (1982) used in-game roadside signs (see Fig. 2) to advertise real companies, and *Chase the Chuck Wagon* (1983), *Kool-Aid Man* (1983), and *Pepsi Invaders* (1983) were all essentially advertising.

Fig. 2: Roadside billboard advertising, in various ports of Atari's *Pole Position* (1982), the first game to feature in-game advertisements.

Some games came with the products they advertised, for example, Quaker Oats's *Cap'n Crunch's Crunchling Adventure* (1999) was released on a CD-ROM attached to cereal boxes. The companies most interested in advergaming, as it came to be called, tended to be those marketing food and drink to younger crowd: snack food and soda companies like 7-Up, Coca-Cola, Cheetos, and Pepsi, and fast-food restaurant chains like Burger King, McDonald's, and Domino's Pizza. Advergames could target adults as well; for example, car manufacturers including BMW, Toyota, and Volvo also produced advergames.

After the appearance of web-based games, advergames began appearing online, usually with links to companies' websites, allowing games to be more closely connected with their company and company information, and spreading the games digitally without additional cost, resulting in viral marketing. Services like The Massive Network can place ads into on-line video games through the use of software development kits that place advertising images onto in-game billboards, posters, and other surfaces, and can change these ads over time. Advertising, then, has become just another way of adding verisimilitude to the vast video game worlds that emulate the real one, and which, more than ever, are designed for consumption around the world.

Producing for a Global Market

By the turn of the millennium, video games were well-established in most countries around the world, with many strong national industries producing games for worldwide consumption, including console games, on-line games, computer games, and casual games. At the same time, the very notion of a national video game industry is itself becoming blurred and eroded. Major game companies like Sony, Nintendo, and Rockstar Games have offices in multiple countries, and it is not unusual for games to cross many borders during their production.

And today, it's easier than ever to start a video game company. The availability of off-the-shelf hardware and software tools for game design, coupled with the growing market for mobile games and the ease of their distribution and delivery, have reduced the overhead necessary for starting a company, making them possible even in economically-depressed parts of the world. Mobile games and MMORPGs quickly propagate far beyond their national origins, and hits like *Angry Birds* (2009), from Finland, and *Pou* (2013), from Lebanon, demonstrate that top-selling games can come from smaller national industries. Simultaneous worldwide releases offer the lure of greater profits, and increasingly multinational corporations are up to the task. Games like *Grand Theft Auto V* (2013), by multinational video game developer and publisher Rockstar Games, had a reported development and marketing budget of USD $266 million (Acuna) and made USD $800 million on its first day of sales. It reached USD $1 billion after three days, making it the fastest-selling entertainment product in history (Goldfarb, Thier, Westbrook). Only with the anticipation of a global audience—and the means for simultaneous worldwide release—are such successes possible.

Collaborations, company ownership, branch office locations, and franchised intellectual property (IP) are crossing national boundaries more than ever before. For example, The LEGO Group, a Danish company, hired Travellers' Tales, a British company now a subsidiary of the American Company Warner Bros. Interactive (itself owned by conglomerate Time Warner, Inc.), to produce LEGO-themed video games, and to do so, Traveller's Tales outsourced some of the work to the Argentine company Three Melons; the games were then programmed for systems from the US and Japan. Thus, the companies influencing the final form of the LEGO games are located in at least five countries on four continents. And this is not unusual; according to a 2008 *Game Developer* research survey, 86% of game studios used outsourcing for some aspect of game development ("Survey").

So just as many national video game histories are finally being written, the very concept of a national industry is being reconfigured by the growing shift toward transnational game development. What is more, such transnational exchanges also enrich the cultures they impact, while at the same time establishing video game conventions at a global scale, spreading influence and combining ideas until they can no longer claim a single country of origin. The cross-fertilization of ideas and influence has yielded a rich harvest of diverse designs and styles, form and content, transcending points of origin and opening to the further exploration of the possibilities that video game designers have yet to discover.

Works Cited

Acuna, Kirsten. "*Grand Theft Auto V* Cost More To Make Than Nearly Every Hollywood Blockbuster Ever Made." *Business Insider*, 9 Sep. 2013, www.businessinsider.com/gta-v-cost-more-than-nearly-every-hollywood-blockbuster-2013-9. Accessed 15 Jan. 2019.

Chalk, Andy. "'Rockstar Wives' Complain About Working Conditions." *The Escapist*, 11 Jan. 2010, www.escapistmagazine.com/news/view/97391-Rockstar-Wives-Complain-About-Working-Conditions. Accessed 15 Jan. 2019.

Eimbinder, Jerry, and Eric Eimbinder. "Electronic Games: Space-Age Leisure Activity," *Popular Electronics*, Oct. 1980, pp. 53–59.

Entertainment Software Association. "Analyzing the American Video Game Industry 2016." February 2017, www.theesa.com/wp-content/uploads/2017/02/ESA-VG-Industry-Report-2016-FINAL-Report.pdf. Accessed 30 Dec. 2018.

Goldfarb, Andrew. "*GTA 5* Sales Hit $1 Billion in Three Days." *IGN*, 20 Sep. 2013, www.ign.com/articles/2013/09/20/gta-5-sales-hit-1-billion-in-three-days. Accessed 15 Jan. 2018.

"List of most expensive video games to develop." *Wikipedia*. en.wikipedia.org/wiki/List_of_most_expensive_video_games_to_develop. Accessed 15 Jan. 2019.

Marks Greenfield, Patricia. *Mind and Media: The Effects of Television, Video Games, and Computers*. Harvard UP, 1984.

Surette, Tim. "EA Settles OT Dispute, Disgruntled 'Spouse' Outed." *Gamespot*, 26 Apr. 2006, www.gamespot.com/articles/ea-settles-ot-dispute-disgruntled-spouse-outed/1100-6148369. Accessed 15 Jan. 2019.

"Survey: Outsourcing in Game Industry Still on Increase." *Gamasutra*, 2 Apr. 2009, www.gamasutra.com/php-bin/news_index.php?story=23008. Accessed 15 Jan. 2019.

Thier, Dave. "*GTA 5* Sells $800 Million In One Day." *Forbes*, 18 Sep. 2013, www.forbes.com/sites/davidthier/2013/09/18/gta-5-sells-800-million-in-one-day. Accessed 15 Jan. 2019.

Westbrook, Caroline. "*Grand Theft Auto 5:* Game Smashes Records to Become 'Fastest Selling Entertainment Product Ever' after Passing $1bn Mark." *Metro News*, 21 September 2013, metro.co.uk/2013/09/21/grand-theft-auto-5-becomes-fastest-selling-entertainment-product-ever-after-passing-1bn-mark-4061933. Accessed 15 Jan. 2019.

Michael Fuchs, Michael Phillips, and Stefan Rabitsch
The end is nigh! Bring forth the Shepard!
Mass Effect, the Apocalypse, and the Puritan Imagination

The apocalypse is a foundational element of the American imagination and still influences the ways in which many Americans perceive the world, the course of history, and their providential role in it. Against this background, the image of America as a paradisal 'city upon the hill' contains a range of latent undercurrents that have placed "a persistent value strain" on American culture (Lipset 268). Indeed, the accompanying rhetoric of national self-confidence, sense of mission, and guaranteed redemption of a divine promise, first established by early Puritan settlers, has always been attended by a discourse of fear, doom, and failure.

Michael Wigglesworth's "The Day of Doom" (1662), which is often considered the first American bestseller, perfectly illustrates the darker undercurrent that permeates the 'Land of the Free.' As its title indicates, the 224-stanza poem revolves around Judgment Day and tries to justify God's wrath at the end of (human) time. Wigglesworth's underlying intent was to promote humanity's need for incessant regeneration and renewal of their covenant with God—in America's case, often through violent means (cf. Slotkin). This idea would later evolve into the irony-laden concept of America as a perpetually "unfinished country" (cf. Lerner) constantly chasing the ideals of continuous change and progress in pursuit of redeeming God's promise. The apocalyptic rhetoric epitomized by Wigglesworth's poem has reemerged in times of crisis, from the 'Great Awakening' of the 1740s through the Cold War threat of nuclear annihilation right up to 9/11 as a sign of the end of America's global leadership. However, while visions of the world's impending demise have been a consistent theme throughout American history, the means of disseminating these apocalyptic scenarios have definitely evolved.

In this context, Daniel Wojcik has stressed that "electronic media are especially valuable sources of information about the (...) expression of apocalyptic beliefs" in the current day and age. Film, television, the internet, and video games are frequently used to express "the concerns, feelings, and hopes of people who anticipate the end of the world" (17). In line with Wojcik's argument, the video game trilogy *Mass Effect* (BioWare, 2007–2012) presents an ideal artifact for examining the role of apocalyptic narratives in the early twenty-first century. Apart from its global reach and popularity, the game series' mythological im-

https://doi.org/10.1515/9783110659405-003

prints, which were enhanced by its unusual development history, make it a particularly fertile ground for cultural analysis.

When the final installment of the *Mass Effect* trilogy was released, fans of the series complained so vociferously about the narrative's conclusion that the developers ultimately added 'extended endings' months after *Mass Effect 3*'s launch. While some scholars have discussed this unusual development twist as representative of the shifting balance of power between 'consumers' and 'producers' in the digital age (cf. Jenkins, in general, and Ganzon with reference to *Mass Effect*, in particular), a closer analysis of the trilogy's multiple conclusions also offers a revealing look into the ways in which the game reinforces deeply ingrained American cultural narratives while simultaneously exposing uncomfortable specters that have haunted American culture since the Puritans.

In this chapter, we will argue that whereas *Mass Effect* originally had the potential to 'do' space opera differently (in part because of its self-proclaimed Canadian imprint[1]), market-driven decisions forced the sequels and thus the series' narrative to conform to a familiar adventure formula reminiscent of the Puritan Jeremiad.[2] Thus, faced with chaos and destruction of apocalyptic proportions, the player character, Commander Shepard, lives up to his or her[3] name by serving as a kind of *Nehemiahs Americanus* in space. He (and thus also the player) reenacts a divinely ordained role that Cotton Mather ascribed to the first governor of Massachusetts, John Winthrop, in *Magnalia Christi Americana* (1702), and which has since been attributed to a range of American prophet figures. According to the Judeo-Christian tradition, Nehemiah rebuilt the walls of Jerusalem. The Puritans, who believed in the interrelation between scriptural history and the real world, saw themselves and their works as an "errand into the wilderness"

---

1 Peter Kuling has discussed the ways in which the voice actresses' and actors' performances reveal a Canadian identity. However, as we will argue below, the narrative also taps into distinctly American national narratives.
2 For more on the use of the adventure formula in BioWare's digital role-playing games, see Fuchs, Erat, and Rabitsch.
3 Please note that we will use the masculine pronoun when referring to Shepard, as we have primarily experienced Shepard as a male character. While some minor details of *Mass Effect*'s story differ when playing a female Shepard, the larger narrative remains unchanged, which is why we believe that Shepard's gender has little impact on the larger cultural narratives we address in this essay (many of which are gendered). A thorough discussion of the game's complex gender (as well as ethnicity and sexuality) dynamics is beyond the scope of this essay. Readers interested in the game trilogy's gender dynamics may consult Carlen Lavigne's essay, in which she argues that despite the "signs of inclusiveness and flexibility, *Mass Effect* remains distinctly straight-male-focused. In particular, (...) the ad campaign for *Mass Effect 3* reveals how Shepard's feminist (or post-feminist) positioning appears primarily incidental" (318).

(cf. Miller) that would result in America becoming a New Canaan—a divine promise contractually guaranteed in their covenant with God. While the Puritans did not complete the New Jerusalem during their lifetime, God's promise entered the American national mythos in which redemption, while guaranteed, was perpetually deferred. This is why, as we will further argue, the backlash of American players in particular against the original endings of *Mass Effect* laid bare deeply rooted and usually unconfronted fears about the (perceived) failure to redeem God's promise. As Sacvan Bercovitch has reminded us, "[f]ailure [is] un-American (...). It was the secular mark of those whom the Puritans had designated as visibly not one of the elect" (xxxvii).

Mass Effect: Yet Another Errand

In terms of its narrative context and content, *Mass Effect* is a space opera set toward the end of the twenty-second century. While reminiscent of science fiction classics such as *Star Wars* and *Star Trek*, *Mass Effect* is likewise indebted to *Babylon 5*. Its vast, complex, and immersive storyworld, as well as its mythopoetic scope, were introduced in the first game and then developed in the subsequent two games, as well as numerous transmedia extensions (comics, novels, handheld games, an animated movie, and various online texts).

According to *Mass Effect*'s fictional history and mythology, human explorers first discovered traces of an ancient spacefaring civilization on Mars in 2148.[4] The artifacts, as Captain David Anderson puts it in the first game, "jumped [humanity's] technology forward two hundred years" and allowed human civilization to expand beyond the frontiers of the solar system. Only nine years later did humanity cross paths with the Turians, a martial culture seeking to police humanity's actions on Mars (where humans had unknowingly violated interstellar laws). Confronted with the seemingly belligerent aliens, humans shot first and asked questions later, thereby revealing humankind's xenophobic impulse to eliminate that which is unfamiliar. Despite the fact that this first human encounter with another advanced species fueled mistrust in humankind for decades to come, over the course of the next thirty-five years the human race became increasingly integrated into galactic politics.

Within this historical context, *Mass Effect* puts players in control of Commander Shepard, a human soldier whose gender, ethnicity, and personal

---

[4] For general introductions to fictional histories and mythologies in imaginary worlds, see Robertson and Alexander.

background can be customized before the beginning of the first game, while his sexual orientation and personality are performatively defined during gameplay. As the narrative unfolds, Shepard uncovers a cyclical historical pattern controlled by an ancient, sentient machine race—the Lovecraftian Reapers. This pattern, which repeats every 50,000 years, involves the "harvesting" of all advanced organic life forms, which makes possible the Reapers' evolution. Unsurprisingly, the cycle is about to end, and Shepard emerges as the individual upon whom "the fate of the galaxy depends," according to an insert in the opening moments of the third game.

At the start of the third game, Reapers are attacking the sprawling Vancouver-Seattle megacity in which Shepard resides. In the opening minutes, the player is confronted with a truly apocalyptic scenario. Against the backdrop of debris and fire, the gigantic squid-like Reapers move across the scene, systematically annihilating whatever stands in their way. The Old Machines descending from the skies leave trails of fire in the dust clouds emerging from the destruction on the ground level. These visuals evoke the *Book of Revelation:* "there came hail and fire mixed with blood, which was hurled down to the earth" (*New American Bible,* Rev. 8.7). As the Reapers move about, they make deafening sounds, recalling Wigglesworth's lines inaugurating the apocalypse: "Before his Throne a Trump[et] is blown, / Proclaiming th' Day of Doom." By employing these well-established tropes in its initial minutes, *Mass Effect 3* emphasizes its setting at a moment in time when not only the world but also the galaxy are teetering on the brink of destruction—the end times have clearly begun. However, this destruction is repeatedly delayed until the end of the game (and postponed even further in the game's extended endings). In the roughly forty hours of playing time between *Mass Effect 3*'s beginning and its conclusion, Shepard unites various species that had been in conflict with one another for centuries under the banner of humanity. Finally, as the end of the game approaches, the Reapers launch a large-scale attack on Earth, as numerous organic and synthetic species fight the enormous spaceships in a battle to decide the fate of the galaxy.

The fact that the various species living in the Milky Way join forces in order to fight for a common cause under humanity's leadership is merely one of several aspects that symbolically align humankind with the United States. Not only does the uniting of species echo America's national creed, "*E pluribus unum,*" it also bears the stamp of America's sense of mission, which shaped the course of global events for the better part of the twentieth and early twenty-first centuries in an attempt to enforce the hegemony of *Pax Americana*. In addition, *Mass Ef-*

Fig. 1: The third game's opening moments depict an apocalyptic scenario. Screenshot from *Mass Effect 3*, Xbox 360. *Mass Effect 3* © EA International, 2012.

fect projects the idea of Manifest Destiny into the interstellar sphere.[5] This exceptionalist discourse, which has been imprinted on the American cultural imagination since the early nineteenth century (if not since Winthrop's 1630 sermon "A Model of Christian Charity"[6]), feeds off two interconnected themes—one exemplary (i.e., America as a role model), the other evangelical (i.e., America's divinely ordained mission)—which reverberate in *Mass Effect*'s apocalyptic timbre.

Not coincidentally, the game's developers have stressed that Shepard's name was inspired by Alan B. Shepard, Jr., the first American to travel into space, a connection which evokes Cold War discourses and America's proclaimed mission to defend freedom in the face of the perceived Communist threat to democ-

---

[5] The ideology of Manifest Destiny pertains to the Westward Expansion and the Frontier myth. In this way, *Mass Effect* draws on a dominant trope in American science fiction. For example, in *Frontiers Past and Future* (2006), Carl Abbott concludes that the "theme of continental expansion," which is interconnected with "the advance of civilization through contests with nature, native peoples, and nasty out-laws," is possibly "the dominant national myth of the United States" (14). American science fiction which "deals with the outward spread of Earth-based peoples and cultures" taps into this theme of continental expansion (Abbott 14).

[6] Winthrop was a subject of the British crown throughout his life. Hence, he did not propagate 'American' exceptionalism the way it is commonly understood. However, his sermon provided the discursive building blocks which became key to the national project of the United States.

racy across the globe. What is more, the thinly veiled allusion between the player character's name and the 'shepherd,' a well-worn Judeo-Christian archetype, adds a potent layer of meaning. As Bercovitch has suggested, prophet figures such as the biblical Moses and John Winthrop are part of a narrative cycle that sees an oppressed and/or persecuted but chosen people embark on an exodus out of bondage and toward (New) Canaan (cf. 55–63).

By tapping into these American myths and symbols, the game text reinforces the idea that despite the continued existence of nation-states, in *Mass Effect*'s twenty-second-century reality, "the cause of America" has truly become "the cause of all mankind,"[7] to quote from Thomas Paine's elaborations on the American character (3–4). In fact, in *Mass Effect*, this American/human cause becomes the cause of the entire galaxy, as the advanced species fight for freedom from the "order" the Reapers seek to impose in an effort to end "the chaos of organic evolution."

The Crucible of *Mass Effect*'s Endings

This American ideological underpinning also comes to the fore in the series' original endings. In *Mass Effect 3*'s finale, Shepard confronts a literal *deus ex machina:* the Catalyst, a god-like artificial intelligence which, in its own words, "control[s] the Reapers," which are its "solution" to the "inevitable" annihilation of advanced organic life forms by synthetics. Since Shepard is the first organic being to confront the Catalyst, it concludes that its "solution won't work anymore" and presents three options to Shepard: destroying all synthetic life, controlling the Reapers, or "combin[ing] all synthetic and organic life into a new framework; a new DNA."

While the game text strongly suggests that synthesis is the preferred choice, for it "is the final evolution of life," the game series' conclusion lies in the player's hands—at least theoretically. In practice, the player's choice has little effect on the actual ending of the game and the series. No matter the choice, the Mass Relays, which are interconnected and make interstellar travel possible, explode, each one vaporizing the entire star system in which it was located (as the "The Arrival" add-on to the second game suggests). In other words, even though the

---

[7] Of course, *Mass Effect* is far from the first science fiction text to draw on this idea. Infused with post-Cold War triumphalism, science fiction blockbuster films of the 1990s make for obvious examples. In *Independence Day* (1996), for example, President Whitmore (Bill Pullman) unites the world "in our common interest," declaring that "the Fourth of July will no longer be known as an American holiday," but rather re-inscribes it as a global day of freedom.

Reaper threat may be contained, most of the galaxy is devastated, and what remains are insular planets unaffected by the large-scale destruction that occurs at the conclusion of *Mass Effect 3*. Thus, despite the galaxy-wide destruction, Shepard's crew (but not Shepard himself) ends up on a remote planet in most of the endings.[8] The visual depiction of the virgin planet, characterized by a lush, natural environment, seemingly untouched by civilization, evokes popular images of the Garden of Eden.

Fig. 2: In most of the original endings, Shepard's crew lands on a virgin planet. Screenshot from *Mass Effect 3*, Xbox 360. *Mass Effect 3* © EA International, 2012.

Wojcik has suggested that the second half of the twentieth century witnessed a move away from earlier interpretations of the end of days as "a meaningful, transformative, and supernatural event" toward "a meaningless apocalypse" (1). However, *Mass Effect* is not one of these "meaningless" apocalyptic stories. Indeed, the return to Eden at the end of the trilogy makes explicit that American apocalyptic tales do not simply envision the end of life; rather, the genre is built upon imagining a future by evoking an imagined golden age located in the past and a space deeply ingrained in the American national project. In the case of *Mass Effect*, this future is, in fact, a return to a simpler time. Of course, this nos-

---

[8] The crew dies if Shepard (the player) fails to complete enough missions to earn sufficient military support from the various galactic species. Since this ending effectively implies the player's failure, we have ignored it here.

talgic return to the past does not imagine revisiting any 'real' point in history but rather constructs an idealized image of the past. In a world in which biotechnology, second (or third or even n^{th}) lives, and virtual landscape design have essentially denaturalized nature, the nostalgic yearning for a harmonious existence with nature expressed in the trilogy's endings is, indeed, understandable. However, this nostalgia for a "lost referential" that never was but always could have been ensures that "what is lost is the original," which nostalgia "reconstitute[s] as 'authentic'" (Baudrillard 43, 99). Similar to the Puritans' belief that they were re-enacting and thus actualizing scriptural history (i.e., a past that never was), the imagined return to the simulacral past in *Mass Effect 3*'s concluding moments is equally an imagined future. In this way, the apocalypse guarantees a new beginning, whose perpetual repetition provides a central component of American mythology (cf. Martin).

This new beginning, founded on the ruins of the galaxy, is characterized by a simpler existence in a paradisiacal setting, the beauty of which emerges from a desire to escape the tumultuous and frightening present. However, as Maria Manuel Lisboa has astutely observed, "the deep structures of the new world often have inbuilt in them the prototypes of old errors repeatable indefinitely" (54). In *Mass Effect*, this inbuilt error is civilization's hubristic reliance on technology, most specifically in the form of synthetics and artificial intelligences. The Catalyst emphasizes that "the created will always rebel against their creators," and that without the Reapers' intervention, "synthetics would destroy all organics."[9] Tellingly, EDI (an artificial intelligence installed on Shepard's starship in *Mass Effect 2* which takes on a gynoid body in *Mass Effect 3*) 'survives' the apocalypse and is still part of the crew when they crash on the remote planet in the narrative's concluding moments. In fact, EDI's presence in the new Garden of Eden not only literalizes Leo Marx's notion of the machine in the garden, but also leaves players to wonder whether (and to what extent) the new civilization that is about to be established will be different from the one it has just replaced.

On a deeper, cultural level, for both American players and players who grew up with constant exposure to American cultural narratives in popular culture, the series' original endings evoke redemption and the concomitant fulfillment of a divine promise informed by the latent Calvinist belief in predestination, which undergirds American exceptionalism and the Puritan Jeremiad. However,

---

9 The fact that the Catalyst created artificial life in order to destroy all advanced organic life in order to stop artificial life from exterminating all organic life is, of course, circular logic and indicative of sloppy storytelling. So, too, is the fact that the Catalyst even highlights this "inevitable" clash if Shepard successfully reunites the Quarian people with their artificial creation, the Geth, after nearly 400 years of conflict.

since this narrative template does not come full circle in *Mass Effect*, the endings expose a specter that haunts the American promise—the inability to accept failure. In other words, the American belief in guaranteed success makes any situation that leads to (perceived) failure an identity-negating rupture; if the belief in and hope for a guaranteed success is taken away, American identity ceases to exist. Rather than developing mechanisms to cope with failure, American culture has relied on strategies to recode the anxieties attendant to a 'sacred' belief in guaranteed success whose fulfillment is perpetually deferred. For example, promoting hyper-individualism as an ideal, American culture deploys the individual as locus for any failure which, since it limits failure to the individual, does not jeopardize America's gospel of success. Even relatively simple rhetorical strategies (e.g. there are no 'problems' in everyday American discourse, only 'challenges') belie the deep-seated anxiety over—and inability to accept—failure.

This rejection of a foundational national myth arguably influenced players' responses to *Mass Effect*'s endings. Indeed, *Mass Effect*'s devotees did not receive the third game's conclusions favorably (to put it mildly). Supporters of the series expressed their disappointment in blog posts, YouTube videos, fan fiction rewrites, modifications of the game's endings, and various other means available to fans in the digital age. When upset fans established a movement called "Retake Mass Effect" and launched a fundraiser that generated more than 70,000 dollars on its first day, even the *Wall Street Journal* and *Forbes* took notice, commenting that "the game's most ardent fans were the ones getting mad" (LeJacq para. 7). Confronted with negative press from around the globe, but chiefly from the United States (cf. Bennett), the developers surrendered to fan and media pressure and made a free extended cut available as a downloadable content pack a little over three months after the game's release.

This extended cut 'fixes' some plot holes and clarifies, as the game's director Casey Hudson put it, "what the endings mean and what's going to happen next, and what situation (…) the characters [are] left in" (qtd. in Gaudiosi para. 11). Yet despite the addition of a fourth choice in the game's conclusion (namely refusing to pick any of the three options suggested by the Catalyst), the extended cut failed to—and, in fact, could not—address the most glaring critique of the conclusion: that players were deprived of any true influence on the story's end, as their actions were part of a prefabricated narrative from the get-go. For players, this lack of agency was particularly galling in light of the ambitious claims made earlier by the developers. Prior to the third game's release, they promised that since decisions from the first two games would be taken into account, *Mass Effect 3* would truly be a rhizomatic narrative "that diverges into wildly different conclusions based on the player's actions" (Wesrcks13, post #1). Of course, the agency video games afford players is ultimately nothing more than an illusion.

As Hans-Georg Gadamer has suggested, "all playing is a being-played. The attraction of a game (...) consists precisely in the fact that the game masters the players" (106). Since "playing a video game" thus implies "reflecting upon the very notion of authority" (Fassone 49), *Mass Effect*'s ending, in which all three (or four) choices lead to essentially the same result, offsets the hundreds of choices made before the final encounter. The game confronts players with the harsh reality that the course of events was essentially decided before they even picked up the controller. Following Johan Huizinga, one may argue that the video game itself thus became a spoilsport by "rob[bing] play of its *illusion*" (11; italics in original).

While such a pre-determined narrative arc is not so rare in video games, in most cases the attendant disappointment is mitigated by the emotional satisfaction of "conquering the game" by winning it, thus bringing the narrative to a satisfying conclusion. Interestingly, to this day, BioWare's official website guarantees that players will "[e]xperience the beginning, the middle and the end of an emotional story unlike any other, where the decisions you make completely shape your experience and your outcome" (para. 1). However, a moving story arguably requires a satisfying ending, which typically does not involve the death of the players' virtual double.[10] In the case of *Mass Effect*, the disturbance of the character's death is further exacerbated by the final 'challenge,' which comes in the form of a *deus ex machina* that completely dictates the outcome of the story in the last minutes of a narrative in which players have invested about a hundred hours.

Although the developers ultimately refused to implement the kind of wholesale alterations needed to resolve this problem, the small changes they made in the new endings did subtly alter the implied meaning of the textual events and provide some limited consolation to disappointed players. The new concluding videos emphasize that the Mass Relays were, in fact, not destroyed, but merely "severely damaged." The extended endings thus clarify that life across the galaxy is not wiped out and that by defeating the Reapers, Shepard has successfully averted the apocalypse.[11] However, in order to stop the end of the galaxy from

---

10 As Jesper Juul demonstrates in his book *The Art of Failure* (2013), failure is an essential component of the experience of playing video games. He suggests that the death of the main character may become meaningful if "it makes sense within the story of the game" (107). In *Mass Effect*'s case, however, many players felt that simply choosing one out of three (or four) options disagreed with what Shepard stood for.

11 Shepard even successfully averts the apocalypse if he decides to reject all options offered by the Catalyst—just not in the diegetic present, for the epilogue notes that "the information passed down" about Shepard's deeds will enable a future civilization to defeat the Reapers.

happening, Shepard needs to "g[i]ve up his life to become the one who c[an] save the many," as Shepard-turned-posthuman narrates in one of the extended endings. This point may not have radically changed from the original endings, but the fact that Shepard's death is no longer overshadowed by galaxy-wide annihilation ensures that he emerges as *the* victim of the Reaper War—which, in the next step, highlights Shepard's sacrifice.

In the revised endings, Shepard's sacrifice thus gains an added resonance. Georges Bataille has suggested that sacrifice is "a human action more significant than any other" (73), for it is a "noble death" that "endows the sacrificial object with sacrality and power" (King 41). Like Jesus, humanity's self-proclaimed shepherd (*New American Bible, John* 10.11), Shepard sacrifices himself for the renewal of humanity. Yet while there may be the promise of renewal, similar to the way in which the post-apocalyptic world returns to an earlier point in history, sacrifice tends "to restore (…) prior (imagined) states of unity and unanimity by whatever means necessary" (King 38). In the world of *Mass Effect*, this past was characterized by stability, which was disrupted by the Reaper invasion. Due to the Reaper's overwhelming technological superiority, symbols of power such as military force no longer mattered, and the balance of power could only be restored by a strong act of personal sacrifice. The added resonance of this noble sacrifice provides a more emotionally satisfying conclusion to the trilogy's narrative arc, assuring players that their virtual death was for a higher cause.

American Fears Assuaged, Please Restart the Game

Moving from the ludo-narrative to the allegorical level, the changes made to the endings reflect different reactions to the changing role of America in a globalized, post-9/11 world. Because 9/11 "made [Americans] aware of [their] mortality and that of [their] nation" (Manjikian 158), all of *Mass Effect*'s endings imagine a world that is safe and in which humanity's—therefore, America's—value system is restored. Both the original and the extended endings imagine utopian scenarios that express a desire for a simpler life far removed from the difficulties arising from the complicated, tension-filled present. That the realization of this utopian vision in the real world is unlikely (at best) is irrelevant. What matters is that *Mass Effect*'s endings project plausible (however improbable) futures built on the past and present that serve to support Americans' claim of utopia "as foundational to their official political authority" (Berlant 7).

However, there is a crucial difference between the original endings and the supplemental endings. Whereas the pre-Reaper galaxy featured various interplanetary organizations as well as trans-stellar networks and flows (of capital, labor, resources, bodies, etc.), the world imagined in the original endings is characterized by isolation. Mary Manjikian has diagnosed a similar theme in recent American apocalyptic narratives. As she stresses, "[b]y erasing the vestiges of capitalism and militarism and withdrawing from the interdependent, globalized world, 'Americans' are able to rediscover their innate goodness" (171). Although Shepard's crew may not entirely rediscover their own 'goodness' when they are stranded on an uncharted planet somewhere in the galaxy, the return to a more rudimentary life at the end of the game series pictures an existence without the complexities of a galactic (read: 'globalized') world. Add to this aspect the return to a pastoral past so often envisioned in the American imagination, and one can conclude that the game's ending suggests a kind of centripetal isolationism:[12] America should refocus on its foundational ideas and ideals to restore the strong, independent, unified nation that it believes it once was.

While this return to original principles is consistent with American exceptionalism, it deprives the nation of its imagined role as the indispensable leader of the free world. Perhaps the visions of the original endings, in which Shepard's sacrifice simply opened up an escape route from the complexities of an interstellar world, were not enough to assuage anxiety about the decline of American influence. In the extended endings, on the other hand, the galactic civilizations continue on a centrifugal path paved by humanity (read: 'America') and "build a future greater than any" individual species "could imagine." In this instance, although a galactic system had already been in place prior to the Reaper War, the newly emerging galactic system is, effectively, created by the human race. Allegorically speaking, this scenario suggests that America established the world system and is thus not required to adapt to changing realities in the global sphere, since it actively shapes said sphere. More polemically, *Mass Effect* seems to speak to America finally addressing its own position in a post-Cold War world—a project which was delayed by the triumphalism of the 1990s and subsequently exacerbated by the trauma of 9/11.

Thus, the new endings preserve the idea, so important to many Americans, that America holds a sacrosanct responsibility to serve as a leader and role

---

[12] While often glossed over in post-WWII discourse, isolationism is a key correlative to US exceptionalism. Over the course of the nineteenth century, isolationism (e.g. the Monroe Doctrine and its various corollaries) was the dominant foreign policy doctrine, which left an indelible imprint on the US-American worldview while its expansionist narrative played out across the continent.

model for the rest of the world. After all, therein lies the core meaning of America, but also its attendant irony—the process of renewal cannot be anything but perpetual. Ultimately, the final redemption of God's promise has to be deferred forever, lest American identity is radically changed, or, even worse, ceases to exist entirely. Accordingly, rather than "querying the hegemonic consensus regarding America's leading role in the world" (Manjikian 135–36), the apocalypse imagined (and averted) in these new endings removes any anxiety about the decline of the American empire and heralds a *novus ordo seclorum* that follows in the footsteps of pioneering America. And, consciously or not, the mere fact that a video game series produced in Canada offers these America-oriented interpretations only confirms America's soft power and further perpetuates American ideology in the industrialized Western world.

Works Cited

Alexander, Lily. "Mythology." Wolf, pp. 115–26.

Bataille, Georges. "The Jesuve." 1930. *Visions of Excess: Selected Writings, 1927–1939*, edited by Allan Stoeckl, translated by Donald M. Leslie, Jr., Carl R. Lovitt, and Allan Stoeckl, U of Minnesota P, 1985, pp. 72–78.

Baudrillard, Jean. *Simulacra and Simulations*. Translated by Sheila Faria Glaser, U of Michigan P, 1994.

Bennett, Collette. "Mass Effect, Indeed: How One Game Changed the Industry Forever." *Geek Out!* Blogs CNN, 5 Apr. 2012, geekout.blogs.cnn.com/2012/04/05/mass-effect-indeed-how-one-game-changed-the-industry-forever/. Accessed 15 Jan. 2019.

Bercovitch, Sacvan. *The Puritan Origins of the American Self*. Yale UP, 2011.

Berlant, Lauren. *The Anatomy of National Fantasy: Hawthorne, Utopia, and Everyday Life*. U of Chicago P, 1991.

BioWare. "Interactive Storytelling." *Mass Effect*, Electronic Arts, 2012, masseffect.bioware.com/about/story/. Accessed 15 Jan. 2019.

Fassone, Riccardo. "This is Video Game Play: Video Games, Authority and Metacommunication." *Comunicação e Sociedade*, vol. 27, 2015, pp. 37–52.

Fuchs, Michael, Vanessa Erat, and Stefan Rabitsch. "Playing Serial Imperialists: The Failed Promises of BioWare's Video Game Adventures." *The Journal of Popular Culture*, vol. 51, no. 6, 2018, pp. 1476–99.

Gadamer, Hans-Georg. *Truth and Method*. 1960. Continuum, 2004.

Ganzon, Sarah Christina. "Control, Destroy, Merge, Refuse, Retake: Players, the Author Function and the *Mass Effect* Ending Controversy." *Crossing Channels—Crossing Realms: Immersive Worlds and Transmedia Narratives*, edited by Natalie Krikowa and Shawn Edrei, Inter-Disciplinary Press, 2013, pp. 41–52.

Gaudiosi, John. "Exclusive: *Mass Effect 3*'s Director Addresses the Game's Controversies (Updated!)." *Digital Trends*, 13 March 2012, www.digitaltrends.com/gaming/exclusive-mass-effect-3s-director-addresses-the-games-controversies/. Accessed 15 Jan. 2019.

Huizinga, Johan. *Homo Ludens: A Study of the Play-Element in Culture.* Routledge & Kegan Paul, 1949.
Independence Day. Directed by Roland Emmerich, performances by Will Smith, Bill Pullman, Jeff Goldblum, and Mary McDonnell, 20th Century Fox, 1996.
Jenkins, Henry. *Convergence Culture: When Old and New Media Collide.* NYU P, 2006.
Juul, Jesper. *The Art of Failure: An Essay on the Pain of Playing Video Games.* MIT Press, 2013.
King, Claire Sisco. *Washed in Blood: Male Sacrifice, Trauma, and the Cinema.* Rutgers UP, 2011.
Kuling, Peter. "Outing Ourselves in Outer Space: Canadian Identity Performances in BioWare's *Mass Effect* Trilogy." *Canadian Theatre Review*, vol. 159, no. 2, 2014, pp. 43–47.
Lavigne, Carlen. "'She's a soldier, not a model': Feminism, FemShep and the *Mass Effect 3* Vote." *Journal of Gaming & Virtual Worlds*, vol. 7, no. 3, 2015, pp. 317–29.
LeJack, Yannick. "Why the Ending of *Mass Effect 3* Started a Furor." *The Wall Street Journal*, 26 March 2012, blogs.wsj.com/speakeasy/2012/03/26/why-the-ending-of-mass-effect-3-started-a-furor/. Accessed 15 Jan. 2019.
Lerner, Max. *The Unfinished Country: A Book of American Symbols.* Simon & Schuster, 1959.
Lipset, Seymour Martin. *American Exceptionalism: A Double-Edged Sword.* Norton, 1996.
Lisboa, Maria Manuel. *The End of the World: Apocalypse and its Aftermath in Western Culture.* Open Book, 2011.
Manjikian, Mary. *Apocalypse and Post-Politics: The Romance of the End.* Lexington, 2014.
Martin, Terence. *Parables of Possibility: The American Need for Beginnings.* Columbia UP, 1995.
Marx, Leo. *The Machine in the Garden: Technology and the Pastoral Ideal in America.* 1964. Oxford UP, 2000.
Mass Effect. BioWare, 2007.
Mass Effect 2. BioWare, 2010.
Mass Effect 3. BioWare, 2012.
Miller, Perry. *Errand into the Wilderness.* Belknap Press, 1984.
New American Bible Revised Edition. Biblica, 2011, *BibleGateway.com.* Accessed 15 Jan. 2019.
Paine, Thomas. *Common Sense.* 1776. *Common Sense, The Rights of Man and Other Essential Writings of Thomas Paine,* edited by Sidney Hook, Signet, 2003, pp. 3–68.
Robertson, Benjamin J. "History and Timelines." Wolf, pp. 107–14.
Slotkin, Richard. *Regeneration through Violence: The Mythology of the American Frontier, 1600–1860.* U of Oklahoma P, 1973.
Wesrcks13. "UNOFFICIAL *Mass Effect 3* HYPE Thread (56k of Reapers invading)." *GameSpot Forums*, CBS Interactive, 15 Jan. 2012, www.gamespot.com/forums/system-wars-314159282/unofficial-mass-effect-3-hype-thread-56k-of-reaper-28977118/?page=1. Accessed 15 Jan. 2019.
Wigglesworth, Michael. "The Day of Doom." *The Norton Anthology of American Literature Volume A: Beginnings to 1820*, 8th ed., edited by Wayne Franklin et al. Norton, 2012, pp. 239–54.
Wojcik, Daniel. *The End of the World As We Know It: Faith, Fatalism, and Apocalypse in America.* NYU P, 1997.
Wolf, Mark J.P., editor. *The Routledge Companion to Imaginary Worlds.* Routledge, 2018.

David Callahan
The Last of the US: The Game as Cultural Geography

This chapter constitutes a reading of the geographical locations in Naughty Dog's survival-horror, stealth action adventure game *The Last of Us*. To complete the game the player, in the form of protagonists Joel and Ellie, has to traverse a good portion of the United States in the classic East-West motion of American identitarian myths. The supposition is that the principal sites that the gameplay takes players through may be read as leveraging historical and cultural subtexts with respect to the progression of the characters and the player toward what resolution the game affords. While the first spatial location in the present of the game, Boston, may easily be apprehended as a form of commentary on the broken ideals of the establishment of a would-be morally pure settlement on the part of the early invader-settlers and/or the American Revolution against British control, the rest of the localities in which player actions occur are slightly or much less obviously legible. For example, the fact that the game does not take the protagonists to California and that its most westward point is Salt Lake City appears to interrupt the myth of westward motion and asks questions with respect to the cultural reference points which become staging grounds of the game's significant areas. As Dawn Spring claims in an article about how video games have the potential to be used as academically respectable iterations of history, "[t]he historical narrative and the video game both examine and form points of view about how cultures, economies, polities and societies function" (208). From the Austin, Texas, of the prologue to the Wyoming compound at the end, the locations in *The Last of Us*, as with most American places, may accordingly be read in terms of the accretion of meanings over the American landscape through competing cultural scripts evidenced in such discursive activities as education systems, public pronouncements, historiography, and creative work from poetry to, well, video games.

The basic scenario of the game is, in general terms, one in which social systems have broken down under the impact of a cataclysmic event. This event has been the spread of a virus which transforms human beings into rabid creatures who attack and bite any uninfected person they can, which transforms the bitten person into an infected one. The ability of a virus to take over human beings in such a manner is a well-established scenario in science fiction and dystopian narratives. Inspiration for the specifically-named virus, however, came from witnessing a David Attenborough program in which he explains the actions of an actual family of fungi, Cordyceps, which targets insects in certain tropical jungles (Lexzie). Each species of Cordyceps targets a particular host insect, taking over its brain, directing it to a location which will aid the Cordyceps in spreading its spores, and then bursting out of the host's body in the typical bulbous-headed shape of a fungus prior to sending out new spores to repeat the cycle. In *The Last of Us* a mutation of the fungus has targeted humans, progressively taking over its victims until they are grotesque and blind, their heads transformed into fungal growths, but always dangerous whatever stage they are at. Holger Pötsch offers a critical assessment of this narrative foundation when he argues that, "[b]y taking recourse to a sudden breakdown of order that is unequivocally connected to a clear external cause, the game loses its ability to meaningfully comment upon key tendencies in contemporary society and politics" (170). That is, narratives of social breakdown basically offer the possibility of dissecting systemic failures and highlighting what is wrong in the ways in which societies are currently organized. However, when the cause of social breakdown is a fungal mutation which has accidentally taken hold, no critique is supposedly being directed at those in power; the ways they have used their power have not been the cause of the disaster. Even that staple of infection narratives from Stephen King's *The Stand* to currently running television series *Z Nation* —the government or a company it has hired has been working on weaponizing a biological agent which has then escaped the laboratory—is not targeted in the game. Given that the Cordyceps fungus actually exists, and that mutation is a common phenomenon in all species, the infection could be quite unrelated to the ethical deficit of the military-industrial complex. The game does not tell us, and in this sense one opportunity to comment on socio-political phenomena is indeed absent.

However, disaster narratives tend to comment in two main ways on the deficient dedication of those in power to the welfare of their citizens. While one takes Pötsch's point, in the sense that it has not been social or political trends which have led to social breakdown, this is only one of those ways. The other is that in which the vision of the defective response of those in power to destabilizing events becomes a critique of the mechanisms and priorities of power, whatever the cause of the destabilization. This critique has indeed become the default narrative in contemporary US culture: those who wield power cannot be trusted to act in the best interests of their populations, horrifyingly revealed in real time in the lackluster and racially-inflected response to Hurricane Katrina in 2005. *The Last of Us* conforms to this second sedimented social script, and this establishes its central scenario in which individuals have to negotiate social breakdown without official help. Indeed, official power is quickly revealed in the Austin prelude featuring Joel, his daughter Sarah, and Joel's brother

Tommy, to be ruthlessly prepared to murder its own citizens. Citizens become a potential threat to be exterminated without any assessment of their condition, with the callousness of government instrumentalism highlighted in the killing of Joel's young daughter Sarah by a soldier under orders to shoot anyone attempting to flee the city.

In responding to this scenario of social breakdown and survival, *The Last of Us* does not appear to be set in random locations, to the extent that the spatial movement in the game also participates in the generation of meanings with respect to the game's possible commentary on American history and culture. Amy Green has drawn attention to the narrative of the game as passing through "the creaking, unstable, and rusted remains of all of humanity's progress," with America having "died as a culture and an ideal" (753). In a eulogistic review for *Eurogamer*, editor Oli Welsh pinpointed that the game was "the classic journey into the west, the pioneer's tale—but turned on its head, because this anti-Western isn't about the birth of a nation. It's about the death of one." My article expands on these general observations in order to suggest how highly attentive Naughty Dog has been to national history and its mythologies in the game's movement through types of national locations. Thus it is that at the beginning of the game's present-day, while social systems may have broken down under the rapid spread of the virus, the attempt at official social control has not, as was seen in Austin. The Boston of the beginning of the main game exists as an ironically overbearing and vicious attempt at official repression. Ironically, given the established narrative in which it was precisely overbearing British control of its citizens which led to the emigration of thousands of people into the New England region at the start of the colonial process, followed by overbearing British control of its colony in the Bay area which had to be shaken off for the nation of the free association of citizens to establish itself. Even though, as Bernard Bailyn has shown in his classic works on the demographics of early North America, the established narrative is reductive of the motives for emigration and the settlement patterns which ensued, the myth remains an active component of American cultural flows. In this myth, the initial settlement was likened to a biblical exodus, to the extent that, in Sacvan Berkovitch's words, "from the start, the colony was knit together, rhetorically, by a cultural 'errand' into the wilderness" (32). This could be applied to Joel and Ellie's trek across the country, except with a significant loss of optimism in the potential project which the "errand" might lead to.

Joel and Ellie's plight may thus be seen as a veiled commentary on the possibilities available to current Americans if placed in a loosely analogous situation to both the early wandering settlers and later colonists of western lands. No biblical script endorses their actions, and little sense of the possibility of a spiritually superior community animates the game's journey. Little, but not none: Joel's deracinated sense of life as solitude and survival is countered by the purpose of their quest to deliver Ellie to a laboratory at first imagined only as somewhere in the west. Being immune, Ellie may provide clues leading to a cure for the virus and therefore the potential to recover a functioning community or even nation. The vagueness of the destination at first parallels the unfocused hopefulness of the movement west in American history. Later, the destination becomes less significant than what happens there, and this also may be seen to loosely parallel what happened to many early wanderers: their optimism was tempered by encountering people with very different priorities—Indigenous nations—and material conditions that were uncomfortable and resistant. During Joel and Ellie's cross-country trek, in vaguely parallel fashion, almost all of the non-infected they encounter will try to kill them, and after leaving Boston in a beautiful New England Fall, the land will reveal itself to be progressively harsh, until, chastened, they encounter a version of a reduced promised land in the classic far west.

Boston and the Bay area, conceptualized as a fundamental origin point in America's sense of itself, accordingly provide a rich set of cultural meanings as the starting point of Joel and Ellie's traversing of most of the country. However, in the game the Boston which stands for the establishment of freedom is now a polity controlled violently by unelected and faceless authorities, whose response to the spread of the disfiguring virus is to turn the city into a police state. That this is the only location in the game's present in which any official authority remains underscores the irony of the failure of founding ideals. The perception that the knee-jerk reaction of authority to a socially disruptive event will inevitably be that of the suspension of legal rights and the imposition of violent tyranny has become a standard observation; the fact that this perception is so deeply-rooted in current beliefs about power speaks to a radical loss of belief in the social contract putatively represented in the state's institutions and practices. The use of Boston is surely not an innocent choice in this scenario, even if not as transparently flagged as in Bethesda's *Fallout 4* (2015), in which the sites of the American Revolution are clearly invoked in a commentary on the failed ideals of what the Revolution signified. Nevertheless, one important city location Joel and Ellie move through in their attempt to escape official control and set out on their quest references city institutions associated with power and official stories. This site is the building in which Joel's partner Tess is revealed to have been bitten in the doomed attempt to evade the military and leave the city. Just as this is revealed to the others and to the surprised player, official forces arrive, and Joel and Ellie are involved in a desperate escape involving the need to kill members of the military or be killed. Tess dies attempting to hold off the soldiers and buy the others time. The building in which this action unfolds is clearly modeled on the existing Massachusetts State House, the seat of government for Massachusetts and a site on Boston's most popular tourist destination: the Freedom Trail (whose site thefreedomtrail.org ironically refuses access to the Tor browser). Erected before the end of the eighteenth century, it represents not only official power but the hopes of the American Revolution itself. That it should become the setting for a firefight in which official forces are the enemy thus becomes one more significant statement in the game on the failed ideals of the US-American national project itself.

Fig. 1: Building modeled on Massachusetts State House

Another location in Joel and Ellie's escape from Boston also represents official stories in the form of a museum, although this has not been clearly identified with any real museum in the city. Amy Green speculates that it is "most likely a mimetic reimagining of Boston's Commonwealth Museum" (753), and even if this is a speculation, it fits well the thematic of the failure of official narratives. That both power and the representation of history have been lost specifically in Boston underscores the loss of the ideals of not merely the city or the state, but of the nation itself.

The hinterland of Boston embodied in the town of Lincoln is described by real-world location spotter Adam Clare as "just a generic small town in Massachusetts," even though there is a town called Lincoln not far from Boston. Clare's supposition that the town serves as an amalgam of typical towns of this size in Massachusetts seems accurate, but that still begs the question as to why the name of a real place was chosen if there is no attempt to represent even a small selection of real-world locations in the town. At first sight the key might be the name itself. "Lincoln" is an evocative name in American culture and history, through the iconic president Abraham Lincoln, who may be generally brought to mind as, like Boston, another crucial high point of American hopefulness. Whatever the complexities of Lincoln the man or his period in American history, Lincoln is perceived as a sign of progress, optimism, and the possibility of the perfectable society. For a town with his name, in a state once symbolic of such utopian hope, to be one more failed environment may continue the game's cultural commentary as well as providing opportunities for a visually-changed 'dungeon' based on suburban plots and individual houses after the claustrophobically urban Boston. One problem with this explanation is that the Massachusetts town of Lincoln is the only one of that name in the US which is not named after the President but after the city of Lincoln in England. It is, however, quite possible that this was unknown to the game's makers, and would definitely be unknown to all of the game's players, save those from Lincoln itself. Those from the town, however, would be aware that Paul Revere was captured by the British in Lincoln, another event which could be figured as the operation of brutal authority over the desires of local people. There is a further problem in the link between the town and the President, in that the game could have simply made a stop in a location in Lincoln, Illinois, the state for which Lincoln was a senator and a city named after him even before he became President. Despite these problems, the location of Lincoln at this point in the game works well, in that both Boston and Lincoln (the Presidential myth) serve as political and social ideals, so that their failure so close together reinforces the disintegration of key hopes in American history and culture.

Moreover, to the failure of the symbolically resonant name of Lincoln can be added the failure of the symbolically resonant small-town America. For many in American culture, inheriting Old Testament strictures against the iniquitous city as exemplified by Babylon, it might be no surprise that the city is a symbol of failure. Cities even equal failure in some conservative anti-urban myths. From quite different angles, also, cities have been equated with the imposition of "control, repression and confinement, detrimental to individual freedom and the welfare of the community," in Elsa Bouet's words, glossing Henri Lefebvre (51). In Nick Dyer-Witheford and Greig de Peuter's *Games of Empire*, even more bluntly, "[t]he city is a key site of Empire" (153). For some, social perfectability can supposedly only be found in the more human-sized small town, and the descriptor 'small-town America' retains its hopeful moral and organizational overtones in contemporary American culture. That this exemplar of a small town has no more been able to resist the breakdown of community and order than the Babylonian city and seat of power is one more in the game's relentless unpacking of a series of American associations of faith in almost all forms or sizes of social organization. The communal and healthy future which Abraham Lincoln was supposed to point to, which, in terms of the mixed motives associated with the Civil War, never ensued at any stage, have left this example of small-town America as the fiefdom of an embittered individual, Joel's contact Bill. As a result of the catastrophe, the inhabitants of the small town have not been able to band together any more communally or efficiently than the alienated city inhabitants of Boston. Even the smallest community of a couple has not been able to survive, not so much because Bill's partner Frank has committed suicide after becoming infected, but as suggested in his suicide note, in which he leaves behind the information that he had actually "hated [Bill's] guts" and "this shitty town." Many characters in *The Last of Us* are difficult to categorize simplistically, and this is one of the strengths of the writing of the game. Bill is crusty and aggressive, but he is also helpful and useful, which cannot be explained simply by the fact that he owes Joel favors. Given the level of breakdown among people, the non-payment of a debt would hardly be surprising.

The Last of Us's next major stop in Pittsburgh returns to a major US city, and one with a symbolically close connection to another key American myth: that of the Industrial Revolution, tied to Pittsburgh's central role in the industrial development of the US. Pittsburgh is known in American history in connection with the development of the iron industry in the eighteenth century, followed by the coal and steel industries in the second half of the nineteenth century. As the initial heart of the American Industrial Revolution, the second named revolution in American history, Pittsburgh already bears strong symbolic freight. That Pittsburgh, like Boston, has also become completely dysfunctional in the game can thus be read as an indication of the breakdown of the hopes and values of a society which came to be based upon a myth which to some extent replaced that of the building of a morally-righteous "city upon a hill," in the phrase associated with early Puritan divine John Winthrop (echoing Jesus's words as related in Matthew 5.14).

Moreover, Pittsburgh's industrial development, happening when it did, resulted in the city's being centrally implicated in perhaps the most powerful of American mythic histories, that of the westward expansion and colonization of Indian lands. For the iconic historian, not to say mythographer of the west, Frederick Jackson Turner, Pittsburgh was simply "the historic gateway to the West" (161). This is because the military, agricultural, and transport hardware necessary for American territorial and cultural aggression relied upon the iron and then the steel produced in Pittsburgh and distributed from there to points west. Pittsburgh's location situated it in the early eighteenth century and into the nineteenth century at the frontier between the more settled east and the as yet uncolonized west, so that it was well-placed to supply the advanced products the invading Americans needed to murder and oppress the land's Indigenous inhabitants, to farm and mine the land, to build railroads and all the structures of the modern world. Pittsburgh has been lost in the game to lawlessness and to the infected, but the game's visuals also strikingly render the city as being taken over by the plant and animal life whose destruction the Industrial Revolution so decisively heralded. The colonization of the city's urban structure by plants features more strongly than in Boston or even Lincoln.

Fig. 2: Overgrown Pittsburgh and the Fort Duquesne Bridge

One of Joel and Ellie's first sights is one of the city's iconic bridges, the Fort Duquesne Bridge, and when they flee the city they cross the similar Fort Pitt Bridge (both bridges are very close), Pittsburgh's bridges serving as powerful symbols of the city's conquering of nature through technology. The passage at one point through a control node in the city's underground water supply system can even conceivably be read as a passage through another iconic space in the establishment of the modern city through the wonders of technology, a space through which human beings established control over dirt and waste, enabling large numbers of people to live together without disease, but which in the game houses diseased bodies that can appear without warning. Further, the game recognizably shows the city's two tallest buildings, the US Steel Tower and the Mellon Center, monuments to the industrialization and the urbanization it encouraged, now wrecks.

Both Boston and Pittsburgh are easily deputized into a reading of the game as incorporating social commentary on the legacy of America's dreams of progress, however loosely anchored. Where such ingenuity could go with the narrative's passage through the invented University of Eastern Colorado, however, is less apparent. Only a sighting of a map of the campus provides the information that the university is in Boulder, Colorado, which is where the principal campus of the real University of Colorado is located (although in what may be an in joke on the part of the game's makers, the zip code on the map is that of Santa Monica, 90405). Given that Colorado was admitted into the Union in 1876, exactly one hundred years after the success of the American Revolution, the triumphalism associated with westward expansion may thus be symbolically represented by the state. Indeed, Colorado was the only new state to be admitted in 1876, with the University of Colorado also being founded in Boulder in the same iconic year. The renaming of the University in the game remains a puzzle, although one cannot discount nervousness over being sued whenever a named, existent entity is used in media representations, not to mention the ire of sharp-eyed fans and observers of popular culture who are all too ready to denounce failures of accuracy when real places are depicted. After all, the game is replete with named businesses and locations which do not reproduce the names of existing companies or entities. That this is not accidental might be gleaned from the in-game existence of the Rivers Café in Pittsburgh. A consultation of yellowpages.com reveals that, unsurprisingly, given Pittsburgh's location at the confluence of three major rivers, there are no less than six cafes in Pittsburgh with the name River Café, so that the presence in the game of a café with a slightly variant name indicates the extreme care with which Naughty Dog distributed named locations throughout the game: the names are true to the geo-historical realities of the city or town, but not identifiable as particular existing businesses or organizations (with the apparent exception of the Broadway Army Navy Surplus; cf. Taylor). There is a Rivers Casino, but this can hardly be confused with a humble café. Pittsburgh, more than Boston, has been the occasion for a good fan summary and analysis of the relation of the city in the game to the materially existing city (cf. Taylor; also skrutop).

Colorado serves well, then, as a representative of the westward colonialism of the US facilitated by the Industrial Revolution signified by Pittsburgh, and a university serves well as a representative of the failed promise of science and knowledge associated with that era. Among the failed knowledge implicit in the game is the crucially failed promise of the Enlightenment domination of Nature, so spectacularly apparent in *The Last of Us*, but also the failed promise of rational social organization associated with the very foundational period of the independent nation. What is not referenced, however, is what might be considered a "determinate absence" in Pierre Macherey's classic term (80), something that we might legitimately expect to be present in a text but which is not. That is, the place of Native peoples in the space and time of a game for which history and its myths of progress are so central. Boston, Pittsburgh and Colorado were all significant waystations in the nation's oppression and suppression of the land's original inhabitants. The moral scaffolding which supported this colonial and ruthless enterprise justification for the occupation of a different culture's territory could be sourced from anywhere within Western 'knowledge,' from scripture to philosophy to history to biology. By the time of the late-nineteenth-century massive push into western lands, the arguments had added Enlightenment rationalizations of 'progress,' muddied slightly by Romantic notions of noble savages and discomfort over the early-nineteenth-century Trail of Tears, but never enough to deflect the relentless movement of European peoples into American Indian homelands. In Native American memory Colorado features as the location of the infamous Sand Creek Massacre, one of the most heinous and savage acts of European hypocrisy in the nation's history. Both the state of Colorado and the University of Eastern Colorado as failed representatives of Western power and knowledge erected on top of Native American territories could serve well in a critique of this aspect of American history. However, American Indians are not alluded to in the game, and the reason it might be figured as a determinate absence relates to the game's focus on finding a place where mostly white people can be safe and holding on to it, in a modern-day version of a redoubt erected in Native territory.

Although an exact location is not specified in the game for the next area, the Lakeside resort sequence, also the town of Silver Lake, it is named on an information board as being in Colorado. There is a Silver Lake (not a town) in Colorado, but as it is in the southwest of the state, it is too far from even a fictional University of Eastern Colorado to serve as the original in this case. For most of this 'dungeon' we switch from playing as Joel to play as Ellie, which, in terms of my theme, intensifies the meanings of location even more. The sequence begins with a cutscene showing a rabbit hopping out of its burrow only to be killed by Ellie's arrow. Next she hunts a deer, and kills that too. The west is a location generally perceived as still containing large tracts of country which are wilder and supposedly more natural than most other locations in the country. Accordingly, it is a place potentially more available for Americans (more typically, white male Americans) to assert their fit with national ideals by making use of its resources freely. Animals are there to be hunted, the landscape to be roamed across on identity-affirming trails (and Native American scripts to be ignored ex-

Fig. 3: University of Eastern Colorado, Boulder

cept as colorful background). While at first it seems as if Ellie is simply owning the landscape via the birthright of all white Americans, ironically she soon becomes hunted prey herself. At the same time, the band of uninfected gathered around a new character, David, reveal themselves to be the most horrifying group encountered in the game thus far, in that they survive by eating people, and there is a suspicion that David keeps fourteen-year-old Ellie alive after she is captured because he wants to have sex with her. If the less urban and more natural environment of the west is figured symbolically in American culture as a location where human beings can live more physically and morally healthy lives, the abject failure of David's group to embody this is yet another of the game's surreptitious comments on yet another of the nation's failed cultural itineraries. In this, it takes its place in a pre-existing oppositional discourse exploding the Transcendentalist-inflected myth of living in 'Nature' as equaling moral superiority, most notoriously articulated in James Dickey's *Deliverance* (1970) and John Boorman's 1972 film of the same name.

The fact that the game reaches its most westward point in the ideologically complex site of Salt Lake City is only momentarily less easily co-opted into an analysis of the game in terms of the cultural significance of its geography. Salt Lake City, and the state of Utah in general, can in fact be closely twinned with Boston as sites of utopian mythologies and histories which have both collapsed in the game. Mormonism, the religion but also social system associated with Salt Lake City, is a mythology and a lived experience uniquely developed within the

US, an ultra-American cultural script, even if athwart most official practices and beliefs. The embattled nature of Mormonism can also be seen to clearly parallel the embattled position of the American patriots before the Revolution to establish local control, while the rhetoric and customs developed by the Church of Latter Day Saints in the effort to establish their version of a just society under God also echo some of the early exertions of the pilgrims in the Bay area. Before the Mormons established themselves in Utah they had been subject further east in the US to vicious persecution, violence, and even massacres, as highlighted by Patricia Limerick in her classic work of cultural analysis *The Legacy of Conquest: The Unbroken Past of the American West*. In a tidy parallelism, Boston and Salt Lake City can thus be bookended as sites where persecuted minorities attempted to establish religiously-regulated polities which diverged from existing societies, perceived as a falling off from authentic Christian values and behaviors. These new societies offered what Limerick sums up in the case of the Mormons as "certainty and community" (281). What we see in *The Last of Us*, however, is an America in which, under pressure from an extreme event, it is precisely certainty and community which are unable to be maintained.

The game ends with Joel and Ellie back at the remote redoubt of Joel's brother Tommy in Jackson County, Wyoming, which they had visited en route to Colorado. While there is no Jackson County in Wyoming, there is a town called Jackson in the west of the state. The town has not been named after Native American nemesis Andrew Jackson, associated with the removal of southeast Indian nations from their lands, but derives its name from a well-known traveler and trader of the early years of Europeans' initial encounters with the area (cf. Jackson). Such a figure serves as a representative of the hardy, self-reliant, land-claiming white pioneer associated with the west. In this light, Wyoming is one of the Pacific Northwest states associated with the so-called prepper movement of right-wing anti-authority groups ('prepper' from 'prepared'). Prepper ideologies hold that people need to prepare for social breakdown by learning survival and bushcraft skills, how to live without modern technologies and so on. While these may undoubtedly be useful skills, the movement draws its energies from a cocktail of cultural sources with deep roots in rejection of official authority, and one of these sources is Mormonism. Wyoming borders onto Utah, and the Mormon presence is strongly represented in a prepper movement which is also overwhelmingly white (only one African American is glimpsed the first time Joel and Ellie visit the redoubt). That the game deposits Joel and Ellie in this environment, represented as the only safe space in almost a crossing of the entire nation, appears to deny any suggestion of future communities as both mixed and mobilized by common projects which have evacuated divisive identities as a conflictive component of the daily staging ground of identity. This failure of a federative project is seen when passing through Pittsburgh if a particular Firefly note is found, in which we may read: "I don't agree with them wanting to take the fight to other cities (...) and I DEFINITELY won't take orders from some Firefly leader all the way on the other side of the country. This is our city. Our people. I don't see why we can't rule ourselves" (emphasis in original). Having the Firefly group which is operating on Ellie, in a procedure which will kill her, led by a black woman—indeed, Marlene is an obviously "mixed race" woman—constituted near the end of the game as the main enemy, and executed by Joel, may be seen as tantamount to an aggressive continuation of white control in the future. This is underlined by portraying a wilderness space in the west empty of all reference to Native Americans. TreaAndrea M. Russworm, in a very good article on the racial politics of the game, describes the elimination of Marlene as demonstrating "that the interpersonal project of building attachment and empathy between white characters must be protected and prioritized at all costs" (113). It is a project that cannot envisage the possibility of cooperation beyond the immediate group, and in which even positively represented outsiders fall by the wayside, such as African Americans Henry and Sam, encountered outside Pittsburgh and traveled with for a short time.

In this framework, the prologue in Austin, Texas becomes an intriguing part of the puzzle. Although in one iteration Texas and Mexican Americans, and indeed Mexicans as well, constitute one cultural-historical identity of the state, in another, Texas serves as a metaphorically aggressively white state in terms of narratives of entitlement and power. The state's very size becomes an emblem of this white power. Austin, however, site of the University of Texas, has come to be perceived as an enclave within the state which resists conservative hegemonic views and practices, despite being the state's capital. We do not see Joel's former life as participating in this cultural resistance, and the supposed realia we see and which might provide clues as to his socio-political leanings are not helpful. For example, the house's newspaper which Joel's daughter Sarah consults, the *Texas Herald*, does not exist. The game's narrative could hypothetically be read as beginning by destroying the presence of such anti-conservative enclaves as Austin in the American space, leaving only the type of enclave represented at the game's end in Wyoming, one in which self-governing survivalists have triumphed, government has been destroyed, and the land belongs to those mostly white people strong enough to hold onto it. No significant gaming choices exist for this not to be the end reached by all players.

Such a reading naturally does not constitute the "meaning" of the game, and concluding on this note would be a surprise to most players, if not an outrage. The game's final moments, with Joel and Ellie heading towards Tommy's community, are a peaceful, even elegiac coda to a violent quest across the nation.

The game appears to most players to be exploring the psychology of traumatized individuals rather than unpacking American myths of community and progress. James Berger sums up this common pattern at the end of "many science fiction post-apocalypses" as "what survives is some version of humanity in the midst of the inhuman" (10). *The Last of Us* seems more about knitting together than detaching the nation from its illusions of large-scale cooperation and nation-building across a continent. The mythic legacies of the different locations traversed are not mentioned by the characters, and experience is never ethnicized; that is, characters do not refer to their own or others' apparent ethnic identities during the game. Arriving in Utah does not stimulate Joel or Ellie to mention Mormonism, an association which is almost universal in America. Gareth Schott considers this to be a general condition of video games dealing with the aftermath of an apocalyptic event: players "encounter despoiled ravaged worlds that have left individuals morally contaminated. When players inhabit an original game character they too embody the amnesiac. Typically there is no history to be recalled or drawn upon as they deal with the ambiguity of the present and the future" (191).

As this article has argued, however, choices are never innocent even if they are unconscious, and despite the relatively recent founding of the USA, the massive repetition of (mostly white) American explorations of its history over time in all representative modes ensures that no place and no space in the country is without rich accumulations of symbolic resonance. The game may not direct us overtly to recall historical events or geo-social contexts, but players do not come to games unprovided with references. This definitely includes non-American players, given the global circulation and familiarity of the stories, images and myths of America. Whether a place is named, like Boston, or generic, like Silver Lake, American locations are replete with accompanying meanings. This means that while, in Bernard Perron's summation, "[t]he allegory of space in the videoludic realm is constructed around a relentless oscillation between danger and safety" (338), space as in-game maze or puzzle is not the only way in which it is experienced. Players are clearly able to operate within more than one discursive plane at the same time, regardless of Espen Aarseth's provocative strictures about not noticing Lara while playing as her (strictures well unpacked by Esther MacCallum-Stewart). The insistence with which the locations in *The Last of Us* reinforce a dystopian view of the breakdown not simply of social order but of several central mythic scripts in American cultural history can accordingly be construed as making it much more than a game of evading danger and reaching safety, or the story of two individuals surviving catastrophic national collapse. The absence of references to the rest of the world, even Canada, in the game intensifies the focus on the narrative and the gameplay as heralding not merely the last of us, but the last of the US as a historico-cultural project.

Works Cited

Aarseth, Espen. "Genre Trouble, Narrativism and the Art of Simulation." *First Person: New Media as Story, Performance and Game*, edited by Noah Wardrip-Fruin and Pat Harrigan, MIT P, 2004, pp. 45–55.
Bailyn, Bernard. *Voyagers to the West: Passages in the Peopling of North America on the Eve of Revolution*. Knopf, 1986.
Bailyn, Bernard. *The Barbarous Years: The Peopling of British North America: The Conflict of Civilizations 1600–1675*. Knopf, 2012.
Berger, James. *After the End: Representations of Post-Apocalypse*. Minnesota UP, 1999.
Berkovitch, Sacvan. *The Rites of Assent: Transformations in the Symbolic Construction of America*. Harvard UP, 1993.
Bouet, Elsa. "Architecture of Punishment: Dystopian Cities Marking the Body." *Cityscapes of the Future: Urban Spaces in Science Fiction*, edited by Yael Maurer Yael and Meyrav Koren-Kuik, Brill Rodopi, 2018, pp. 49–65.
Clare, Adam. "Real World Architecture and Locations in *The Last of Us*." *Reality is a Game*, 30 July 2013, www.realityisagame.com/archives/2070/real-world-architecture-and-locations-in-the-last-of-us/. Accessed 15 Jan. 2019.
Deliverance. Directed by John Boorman, Warner Brothers, 1972.
Dickey, James. *Deliverance*. Houghton Mifflin, 1970.
Engler, Craig, and Karl Schaefer, creators. *Z Nation*. Go2 Digital Media, 2014-.
Limerick, Patricia. *The Legacy of Conquest: The Unbroken Past of the American West*. Norton, 1987.
Dyer-Witheford, Nick, and Greig de Peuter. *Games of Empire: Global Capitalism and Video Games*. U of Minnesota P, 2009.
Fallout 4. Bethesda, 2015.
Green, Amy M. "The Reconstruction of Morality and the Evolution of Naturalism in *The Last of Us*." *Games and Culture*, vol. 11, nos. 7–8, 2015, pp. 745–63.
Jackson, John C. *Shadow on the Tetons: David E. Jackson and the Claiming of the American West*. Mountain Press Publishing, 1993.
King, Stephen. *The Stand*. Rev. ed. Doubleday, 1990.
Last of Us, The. Naughty Dog, 2013.
Lexzie. "*The Last of Us:* Inspiration Behind the Infected." *The Artifice*, 11 Aug. 2015, the-artifice.com/the-last-of-us-inspiration-infected/. Accessed 15 Jan. 2019.
MacCallum-Stewart, Esther. "'Take That, Bitches!' Refiguring Lara Croft in Feminist Game Narratives." *Game Studies*, vol. 14, no. 2, 2014, www.gamestudies.org/1402/articles/maccallumstewart. Accessed 15 Jan. 2019.
Macherey, Pierre. *A Theory of Literary Production*, translated by Geoffrey Wall, Routledge & Kegan Paul, 1978.
Perron, Bernard. *The World of Scary Video Games: A Study in Videoludic Horror*. Bloomsbury Academic, 2018.

Pötsch, Holger. "Selective Realism: Filtering Experiences of War and Violence in First- and Third-Person Shooters." *Games and Culture*, vol. 12, no. 2, 2015, pp. 156–78.

Russworm, TreaAndrea. "Dystopian Blackness and the Limits of Racial Empathy in *The Walking Dead* and *The Last of Us*." *Gaming Representation: Race, Gender, and Sexuality in Video Games*, edited by Jennifer Malkowski and TreaAndrea Russworm, Indiana UP, 2017, pp. 109–28.

Schott, Gareth. *Violent Games: Rules, Realism, and Effect.* Bloomsbury Academic, 2016.

Skrutop. "Comparing Pittsburgh in *The Last of Us* to the Real Thing." *giantbomb*, 22 June 2013, www.giantbomb.com/profile/skrutop/blog/comparing-pittsburgh-in-the-last-of-us-to-the-real/101577/. Accessed 15 Jan. 2019.

Spring, Dawn. "Gaming History: Computer and Video games as Historical Scholarship." *Rethinking History*, vol. 19, no. 2, 2015, pp. 207–21.

Taylor, Brian. "*The Last of Us* and Pittsburgh: Real Game Worlds." *Paste*, 17 Oct. 2013, www.pastemagazine.com/articles/2013/10/the-last-of-us-and-pittsburgh-what-place-is-this-p.html. Accessed 15 Jan. 2019.

Turner, Frederick Jackson. *The Frontier in American History.* U of Arizona P, 1992.

Welsh, Oli. "*The Last of Us* Review." *Eurogamer*, 31 July 2014, www.eurogamer.net/articles/2014-07-28-the-last-of-us-review. Accessed 15 January 2019.

Patricia Maier
Mobility and Choices in Role-Playing Games

The cultural analysis of video games must consider at least two intersecting dualities. First, it needs to recognize that both the code underlying the game—and therefore its rules—as well as the fictional world play an important role, as Jesper Juul shows in his seminal work *Half-Real* when arguing that video games consist of "real rules and fictional worlds," hence the title-giving "half-real" status of video games (Juul 1). Second, the cultural artifact of the video game includes both the cultural influences in and on the games themselves as well as the cultural context of the players. As Phillip Penix-Tadsen writes in his work on Latin American culture and video games, "[b]oth static code and subjective play have been shown to contribute to the process of meaning creation in games. But culture also comes into play, not only due to the particularities of the social contexts in which video games are produced and consumed, but also through symbolic, environmental, and narrative elements that contribute to meaningful in-game experiences" (1). For this paper, I will use his concept of culture, which he defines "in terms of the tokens, symbols and other devices that are employed in the context of specific semiotic systems (including but not limited to video games) in order to represent characteristics attributed to a group of individuals" (cf. 8–9). Penix-Tadsen puts an emphasis on the "commodified and negotiated nature" of this sense of culture, "while also accounting for the contrasting meanings that culture can take on depending on the semiotic systems and interpretive contexts in which its signification is generated" (9).

The role-playing game (RPG) is one genre of video game that bears especially close ties to mainstream US-American culture as its generic meaning-making is often tied to a major trope of Americanness: mobility. The concept of mobility will be explained in detail using Tim Cresswell's work, which in turn will provide the basis for introducing Ann Brigham's ideas on American road narratives. Analyzing these road narratives in terms of mobility, she includes the concept of incorporation to explain an exchange of ideas between the traveler and the place they are traversing. This concept bears close ties to that of Gordon Calleja, who uses it to find an alternative to the terms immersion and presence in video games. Relating these concepts to Michael Nitsche's work on video game spaces and Miguel Sicart's on morality in video games, they will form the basis for an analysis of an example in *The Elder Scrolls V: Skyrim*.[1] In this situation, the player's mobility and freedom is contrasted with that of one of the in-game "races," the Khajit. In the encounter with the Khajit, the player's status as special is revealed while the game also asks the player indirectly to make a moral decision regarding their engagement with the Khajit. As the player is free to ignore or engage with these choices, as is usual in open-world games, I claim that the freedom to choose is a direct result of the player's mobility, and the related possibility of acquiring new information and a new perspective is the basis for making moral choices in the fictional world.

To understand why mobility is such an important factor for the player of an RPG, a closer look at mobility as a concept in US-American culture as well as popular culture is necessary. "[M]obility is central to what it is to be human," Cresswell states in the introduction to *On the Move: Mobility in the Western World* (1), and indeed discussions on who moves and who does not, who should be allowed to and who should not, and where movement is wanted, have been and still are some of the major debates of our time. Cresswell puts it fittingly:

> Mobility, it seems, is also ubiquitous in the pages of academia. It plays a central role in discussions of the body and society. It courses through contemporary theorizations of the city. Culture, we are told, no longer sits in places, but is hybrid, dynamic—more about routes than roots. The social is no longer seen as bound by 'societies,' but as caught up in a complex array of twenty-first century mobilities. Philosophy and social theory look to the end of sedentarism and the rise of foundationless nomadism. Finally, but perhaps most importantly, mobility bears a number of meanings that circulate widely in the modern Western world. Mobility as progress, as freedom, as opportunity, and as modernity, sit side by side with mobility as shiftlessness, as deviance, and as resistance. (*On the Move* 1–2)

Furthermore, mobility is not only a concept but "[s]tories about mobility, stories that are frequently ideological, connect blood cells to street patterns, reproduction to space travel. Movement is rarely just movement; it carries with it the burden of meaning and it is this meaning that jumps scales" (*On the Move* 6–7); in other words, when people move not just physically but across scales, meaning is made (cf. 2). Because of the power relations inherent in these movements, Cresswell emphasizes that movement and mobility are not interchangeable. He defines movement "as abstracted mobility (mobility abstracted from contexts of power)," and it "therefore, describes the idea of an act of displacement that allows people to move between locations" (2). He thus relates movement to space while he sees mobility as "the dynamic equivalent of *place*" (3). Mobility in-

---

[1] Called *Skyrim* from here on. As the game is set in a place of the same name, *Skyrim* will denote the game, Skyrim the place.

cludes all the implications space is missing as place is tied to ideology and power, a "meaningful [segment] of space" (3).

While Cresswell writes about mobility in the Western world, freedom of movement has a particular historical relevance in American culture because "mobility as a right—as a geographical indicator of *freedom*—has been most forcefully intertwined with the very notion of what it is to be a national *citizen* —to be American" (*On the Move* 151). Mobility in the sense of freedom to move where and when one wanted is therefore ingrained in American culture, and it is not surprising that free and unhindered movement in and exploration of a vast game world is an important, if not *the* major selling point for RPGs on computers and game consoles. Trailers and marketing material of games such as those of the *Elder Scrolls*, *Dragon Age*, or *Fallout* series focus on the expansive game worlds and the freedom the player will experience in traversing and exploring them. Games initially developed for the American market unsurprisingly put such stock in the willingness of players to spend hours upon hours traveling through landscapes.

This is also tied to another concept: the idea of going 'on the road,' whether by foot or car, symbolized escape for the American traveler, a "flight from that which constrains us—society, self, the family, the past, or the familiar" (Brigham 6). This is, as Ann Brigham notes, one of the major traits scholars have identified in American road narratives in literature and film (cf. 6). It is related to a notion that had a strong influence on what Brigham calls the Euro-American national identity: the "promise of mobility: the freedom to go anywhere and become anyone" (3). Therefore, the road trip as the quintessence of mobility "is not merely the means but the actual manifestation of an authentic American experience," and the road narrative "reasserts the American as a mobile subject" and "mobility as an American subject" at the same time (Brigham 3).[2] Mobility and being on the road therefore stand for possibilities, for the chance to free oneself from the bonds of home and society. Traveling on the road holds the promise of escaping from anything that would hamper the individual, be it other people, work, or something less specific. It is hence seen as an "escape of tensions" (Brigham 6) as well as "read in terms of familiar binaries: home/away, domesticity/mobility, conformity/rebellion, stasis/movement, confinement/liberation" (Brigham 8). Brigham sees this in a negative light as mobility on the road may be seen as

---

[2] While Brigham focuses specifically on road trips, mostly by car, her ideas about mobility across physical space and conceptual spaces also apply to video game spaces and the traversal of their fictional worlds even though the player is on foot most of the time. As the player can keep running without a pause in most games, the relatively quick traversal of space similar to real-life driving or biking is a given in games.

fixed, "self-evident," and universal, while in truth mobility is constantly changing (cf. 6). The above-mentioned binaries are not applicable to road narratives either as they do not grasp the depth of the conflicts and engagements in them. This is due to the opposition of the mobilities presented in Brigham's examples toward the 'mainstream' idea of mobility in American thought:

> Mobility does not function as an exit from society/home/the familiar, but instead emerges as a dynamic process for engaging with social conflicts. This makes sense because road stories themselves are plotted around unsettling processes: the crossing of borders, the courting and conquering of distance, the reinvention of identity, and the access, negotiation, and disruption of spaces. The road introduces an otherness that is both spatial and social, and so mobility becomes a process for working out the fact of difference. (Brigham 8)

These conflicts and "unsettling processes" the traveler is presented with and takes part in lead to a transformation of their subjectivity while simultaneously transforming the space they travel in as they are confronted with "an otherness." The engagement with these conflicts hence means that the road narrative is not just about dealing with conflict in general but also about incorporation (Brigham 8). The traversal of space, be it across, through, or over space, is about being included—incorporated—into something different than the entity one belongs to. This 'something' may be a social group, a town, or an idea or concept. As Brigham writes, it is about "joining with an entity larger than the self" (8). This "joining" happens due to the change in the traveler's location, not just in the sense of physical location but also on other levels such as the social realm. "The tensions of incorporation, that is, the joining of, to, or with another, are expressed spatially with the movement between and across scales," Brigham states. "Road narrative protagonists leave home, cross state lines, and search for America. Often their journeys develop as a change in the scale of identification" (10). Changing location therefore gives the traveler a new perspective, enabling them to incorporate new ideas into themselves (Brigham 8). According to Brigham, being on the road shows the link between the ideas of moving and becoming, of how movement across material space also leads to movement across immaterial lines such as social or sexual boundaries, among others. Road trips have therefore come to infuse popular culture as "a quintessential expression of Americanness" (Brigham 3), not just the ability to move freely but to "become" someone else by incorporation. How this looks in video games becomes apparent in the work of Gordon Calleja. In *In-Game: From Immersion to Incorporation* he introduces incorporation as "*the absorption of a virtual environment into consciousness, yielding a sense of habitation, which is supported by the systemically upheld embodiment of the player in a single location, as represented by the avatar*" (169). What he means by this is that the player incorporates the game world by traversing and acting in it. At the same time, the avatar the player controls incorporates them in this world.

However, being on the road not only offers the chance of incorporation, it also "makes transitions between scales explicit; thus, its importance derives from its connection to, not detachment from, various scales" (Brigham 10). Analyzing this movement in particular helps dismiss what Brigham calls "the cultural romanticization of the road" in the US-American context while illustrating this romanticization's origins and how certain "meanings and identities" are seen as bound to specific scales (Brigham 10). Drawing on geographical concepts, Brigham argues that "scale affects the possible forms that identity and social interaction may take, and these forms can enforce or challenge the status quo" (11). An important point about these scales is that they are not in any way natural but instead socially and culturally constructed. Scales are *made*, and mobility is one of the factors in creating them (cf. Brigham 11–12). Movements across scales hence makes apparent how those scales work in influencing culture, and they therefore "trouble scale," as Brigham writes: "If social order is produced and sustained, in part, through specific structurings of geographical scale, then troubling scale serves to challenge the social order that scales support" (12). Mobility can create this troubling as well so that it is not simply a way to flee the constraints of the traveler's life but also to build and criticize scales (cf. Brigham 12–13).

Thus, as Brigham makes clear, narratives of people on the road are also always about 're-creation,' meaning the destruction and re-building of ideas about mobility by bringing into focus different mobilities and how the mobilities of people of a different "class, race, ethnicity, gender, sexuality, culture, geography" stand in contrast to the mainstream concept of American mobility and identity (cf. Brigham 4). Therefore, "mobility is not a method of freeing oneself from space, society, or identity but instead the opposite—a mode of engagement. Indeed, this genre's significance emerges in its demonstration of the ways mobility both thrives on and tries to manage points of cultural and social conflict" (Brigham 4). While mobility is usually seen as positive and often transgressive, this stands in contrast to the issues "of spatial and social otherness," and the traveler may either incorporate that otherness or place themselves in opposition to it by "consolidating identity through the shoring up of sameness and exclusion of difference" (Brigham 9–10). This is especially important in RPGs, as the game worlds are usually recognizable to the player but not set in 'realistic' circumstances. Therefore, even if the player may feel a certain familiarity with in-game places, groups, or persons, this sense cannot be as strong as in real-life, and there is always a certain negotiation between the known and the unknown. As Robert Baumgartner writes, different fantasy worlds will be known or recognizable to the player to varying degrees (cf. 96–101), and this is due to game designers using "a culturally coded gamespace" to "add dimension to semiotic and narrative elements by contextualizing them within a specific environment with its own particular manners of conveying meaning" (Penix-Tadsen 175). The player will be aware of certain cultural connotations while seeing others as strange and different (cf. Baumgartner 97–98).

However, being on the road and encountering new ideas is not only about incorporation of the traveler but about incorporating something new into the world of the traveler in turn. In the road narratives Brigham analyzes, the process of travel incorporates new spatial or social concepts into a preexisting concept of America that can contain them. This boils down to the question of who and what America is, and who is included and excluded in the definition (cf. Brigham 9). Not only does the traveler question how to define America, but the road narrative offers the possibility of incorporation on both sides. The new is incorporated into America and America is being given shape. Brigham describes this process: "Because the idea of 'America' is also always a projection of an ideal, road narratives reveal the ways that abstract ideas (Americanness) and physical places (America) are in constant need of having their 'shape' substantiated" (Brigham 9). In parallel, a player therefore not only incorporates new ideas about the game world but at the same time substantiates it. By acting in it, the player confirms or denies the fictional world, similarly to road narratives showing how America and Americanness have to be constantly defined and redefined. Even before the player acts, the fictional worlds of RPGs may for example be initially substantiated by NPCs who are stating and repeating information and opinions and thereby explaining the world's rules to the player. The player then substantiates the game world by acting in it and by adhering or not adhering to the ideas presented within (Sicart 12–13). In video games, this is most apparent in a player's acceptance of the rule that killing an attacker/bandit/enemy is not necessarily murder in the statistics of the game, or at least is not penalized by the game.[3] This is the most obvious of the rules a player would generally not accept in real life.

The player's actions are therefore vital to the game world, but to substantiate it, the player needs to understand it and how their choices will be interpreted in its context. Michael Nitsche describes this process of making sense of a fictional world in his book *Video Game Spaces*. According to him, "game worlds depend on representation and sign systems," but "[g]ame spaces are approached not as

---

[3] In *Skyrim*, the player can look up a list of their deeds that only includes the killing of friendly NPCs such as city inhabitants or guards as murder. Enemies are furthermore tagged as such by attacking either on sight or as soon as the player moves too close to their stronghold, thereby offering self-defense as a potential excuse for the killings.

foregrounded spectacles based on visual cues such as perspective and parallax but as presented spaces that are assigned an architectural quality" (3). The player does not engage the game world as they would a piece of art or picture. Instead, the space bears the same connotations as real space since the player recognizes its "architectural quality," for example that a door may be entered, and acts accordingly. The player therefore engages with the game world according to the signs presented to them in the game world. By interpreting the visual cues, they can act accordingly if given the choice by the game. The player's avatar will act as the player commands as "a surrogate body replete with powers and limitations" (Gee 18). However, their understanding alone will not influence their actions. For these actions to have a moral component, they need not only to understand but to become complicit in the game world.

Miguel Sicart writes about how video games can influence and challenge a player's ideas of the world, specifically moral ones. He states that "creators of aesthetic experiences that deal with morality must be aware of their audience as an ethical and moral force that receives and constructs experiences" (21). Based on this premise, he develops his own concept of player complicity in which he claims that games ask players to adhere to "the logic of the ethical systems that structure the gameworld" in order to make sense of what the decisions they have to make will have in the game world (22). According to Sicart, this also means that players are aware that there is a moral component to those decisions and in turn will influence the game world accordingly (22). However, this idea gives little importance to player complicity or non-complicity in the game world when it is not so tied to major decisions as in games such as *The Walking Dead* or the *Mass Effect* series. In the minor decisions that are not specifically presented as such, the player still acts according to a moral code, be it their own, that of the game world, or an arbitrary one for the duration of the game. Furthermore, this code may be informed by advantages and disadvantages in terms of gameplay.[4]

Sicart's description indicates that these decisions are not meaningless:

> Player complicity means surrendering to the fact that actions in a game have a moral dimension. Players use their morality to engage with and adapt to the context of the game. When playing, players become complicit with the game's moral system and with their own values. That capacity of players to accept decision making in games and to make choices based on moral facts gives meaning to player complicity. (23)

---

4 See Sicart's *Beyond Choices* for his own description of how he made decisions in *The Walking Dead* according to characters' usefulness (cf. 22–23).

This complicity is closely related to the player themselves. As James Paul Gee claims, a player's "avatar is also an *identity* that a player inhabits," and this identity is shaped by what the player as the avatar can do, their skills, and their history and reasons for acting (18). Therefore, the player's actions carry weight when undertaken in what Penix-Tadsen calls a "multimodal game *environment*" (176–77) that offers reaction to input.

An example is the world of the *Dragon Age* series. Mages in this world are seen as dangerous and therefore locked in so-called "Circles" for life. These Circles are, for example, a tower on an island or an old prison complex at the edge of a city, and they are run and guarded by the armed section of the major religious organization in the game series. Mages trying to live outside the Circles are branded as "apostates" and hunted. If the player starts a new game in the first installment of the series, *Dragon Age: Origins*, and chooses a mage as an avatar, the 'origin story' they play involves helping a friend escape the Circle. The player can either help or report on the friend to the authorities of the Circle. At this point, the player is not yet aware of how mages are ostracized in this fictional world. In the course of the game, the player will encounter the people of the fictional world as well as other mages (even one apostate who joins the player's party). The player is now confronted with the decision to accept the fictional world's judgment of mages as dangerous and untrustworthy or take a different view to the mainstream fictional opinion and act accordingly by, for example, accepting quests from a society of mages secretly living in freedom. At the end of the game and in subsequent playthroughs, the player's knowledge, awareness, and ability to interpret the situation due to new information will have been enhanced. Regardless of a change in their opinion about a choice, the player's understanding will have been changed due to new knowledge and the awareness that the choices they make matter.

To briefly return to Penix-Tadsen's point that games react to input: the player's actions are also meaningful because the game needs this input for anything to happen, for changes to occur. Nitsche explains why this contributes to meaning-making. Spaces in video games, and virtual spaces in general, are human-made and not directly connected to other spaces as the rules and needs of those 'real' spaces do not apply. They are missing "geographical, zoological, and most physical dependencies that heavily impact real-world locations" (Nitsche 191). As "a universe of coordinates" they are "spatial but not a place" (Nitsche 191). To add meaning to those spaces and thereby turn them into places, the player needs to interact with them:

> In order for these data visualizations to become meaningful, they [the spaces] have to be engaged by the player. Through the active work of the player, through comprehension

and interaction, the masses of polygons can transform into places. A genius loci is often defined by subjective experience of the location. (Nitsche 191)

The world is therefore shaped according to the player's deeds, which are themselves shaped by how they understand the game world. In more linear games, decisions usually have an immediate result, and the player keeps playing in this newly changed world. On the other hand, RPGs in particular change with the player. In *Skyrim*, for instance, if the player kills an NPC, that character remains dead and the player can encounter their family or friends mourning their demise. If the player kills someone in sight of a peaceful citizen (or horse, as it were), a bounty is set and the player cannot traverse a part of the game world (the county in which they incurred the penalty) without paying a fine, going to jail, or fighting their way to their next destination. These decisions are not vital to further the story of the game nor are they enforced, but they still do force the player to "live" in and face the fictional world they both encounter and form at the same time (Baumgartner 88).

While Sicart focuses mostly on games that specifically offer important choices, an example from *Skyrim* will illustrate how comprehension and complicity with the game world confront the player with more subtle choices but force the player to apply their knowledge and values in a fictional world without a clear guide to right and wrong or an initial awareness of the importance of their choices. The analysis will show how the interplay of the fictional world with the game rules and the player's ability to actually act according to (or against) their beliefs offers a deeper understanding of how rich an experience video games offer.[5]

In the fictional world of *Skyrim* and the *Elder Scrolls* series in general, the player can play as—and encounter—what are styled as different "races," among them humans and elves as well as people who have the fur and face of cats (Khajit) or the scales and face of lizards (Argonians). These two races are already set apart as different by their looks, and they have specific abilities that the player can use if the character is chosen accordingly. The Khajit have the ability to see in the dark while Argonians can breathe underwater. It is not only their looks that set them apart, however. While the player may hear verbal abuse aimed at them as many of the other "races," it is more frequent if an elf, Khajit or

---

[5] See Sicart 94–95 on how the "tension between the procedural and the semiotic levels" of a game can influence players to think morally outside a binary of right and wrong, and Sicart 104–05 for an appeal to designers to curb information to players so their choices have a larger impact. My example will show how Sicart's two general concepts are specifically tied to mobility in *Skyrim*.

Argonian is chosen. Furthermore, the player hears about the two "races," especially the Khajit, that the inhabitants of Skyrim do not trust them. A citizen of Whiterun, Ysolda, explains when questioned that the townspeople do not trust the Khajit because of a few Khajit who turned to thievery and cheating. The Khajit, who are encountered as traveling merchants, are therefore not allowed to enter the cities of Skyrim, so they move from city to city and are forced to camp outside the city walls while they sell their wares. The placement of these camps not only physically places them outside the city, but also outside the city's society. As Tim Cresswell states, "[i]mplied in these terms is a sense of the proper. Something and someone *belongs* in one place and not in another. What one's place is, is clearly related to one's relation to others" (*In Place* 3). The relation of the Khajit is clearly as outsiders, both physically and psychologically.

In the encounter with the Khajit the player is confronted with some of the very few people who move around the game world themselves (albeit on predefined paths) and yet do not do so because of a privileged position but because they cannot settle in Skyrim. The juxtaposition of the player's freedom of movement, which is seen as positive, and the distrust of Skyrim's inhabitants directed against the mobility of the Khajit, exposes the game inhabitants' underlying (mainstream) values. Building on Cresswell's description of how this way of being too mobile has always been connected to deviance, Brigham states that claiming someone is out of place also "differentiates between kinds of places" instead of seeing place "as a moral world existing in clear-cut opposition to immoral mobility. Instead, certain spaces—in this case, the global—are perceived as dangerously mobile, capable of infiltrating other spaces like the nation-state and thus threatening an 'authentic' national identity" (Brigham 7). The Khajit as obviously "foreign" to Skyrim, as well as too mobile, carry real-life connotations. They are the "global" of the world of *Skyrim*. Excluding and ostracizing the Khajit, who hail from a far-away realm and are mobile across the racial and ethnic territorial lines of the game world, is easily connected to real-life instances of marginalization. The player will therefore recognize the behavior of the townspeople and will understand that the way they are situated marks them as other. That the Khajit are expected to stay outside the walls corresponds to Cresswell's statement that "expectations about behavior in place are important components in the construction, maintenance, and evolution of ideological values" (*In Place* 4). The player will understand how the Khajit are treated due to real-life counterparts. In the game, there are no rules to deny players interaction with the Khajit. Furthermore, due to their status as merchants, the Khajit are an important resource for the player to sell their inventory. As the player, especially in the later stages of the game, is usually encumbered with a variety of high-value items that they will have problems selling due to a cap on money available to merchants, the Khajit offer additional persons to sell to and amass fortune. If the player decides to ignore the Khajit like the rest of the population does, they would have to stick to the cities' merchants. Furthermore, the Khajit merchants are some of the rare merchants that sell "moonsugar," a drug and an alchemical ingredient in the game. Hence the gameplay advantage of trading with the Khajit stands in contrast to their 'racial' condemnations within the game world.

Furthermore, the encounters also reveal the player as the one who is able to trouble scale, being the only privileged person allowed to travel. With the player able to go anywhere and become anyone, troubling scale is in their hands. As Michael Nitsche writes, the player as the hero of the game encounters "quests as processes of personal growth and maturing" (59). This is especially apparent as the player's mobility is not curbed even if they play as a Khajit. The player, as they expect to be, is allowed to enter the cities, a fact that sets them apart from the Khajit. Due to their importance to the game, the player belongs where the Khajit do not. In many games, the player's movements are curtailed up to a certain point, so that they can not immediately reach every area of the game world. However, for the player it is always implied that if a certain task is completed, a stage is reached, or enough time has passed, they will be allowed to enter the entirety of the game world. Thus in-game work such as finishing quests or helping others enables the player to move forward while the Khajit remain static. This is not only due to their being NPCs but because they are images of a world in which Khajit do not have the option to move upward across scales. While they are moving due to their trade, they have no possibility of finally entering the cities or moving up the social ladder unless they happen to be the chosen one (the implication being that there is only one). They move farther than most other NPCs in the game but do not gain by it. The situation of the Khajit in comparison to the player therefore enhances the player's status as special. The game's rules that demand the player move freely can here be taken as the reason why the player has more freedom. If they play as anyone other than a Nord, who are native to Skyrim, they should, according to the fictional world, not be allowed to move as freely as they do. This conforms to Juul's suggestion that parts of a game's fiction can be explained by the game rules if they clash with the interpretation of the game world (130). The ability of the player to move as a Khajit can therefore be related to their status as the player and the need for them to move freely.

The important point to make about the encounters with the Khajit is that the player does not have to engage them. There are no major disadvantages in gameplay or story, so the player's decision for action will be based on interest, curiosity, morality, or even greed. The freedom to choose is the main reason why the encounter has a stronger impact than a decision in, say, the first three games of the *Mass Effect* series that clearly tells the player if a decision is considered good or bad, going so far as to color-code certain answers in conversations to indicate the option's direction.[6] Instead of quickly clicking through the requisite answer to develop their avatar in the preferred direction within a clear moral binary, the player has to make decisions out of the blue and without further comment from the game. *Skyrim*, on the other hand, produces an atmosphere that makes most choices seem possible. As Markus Engelns writes in his essay on the game, *Skyrim* goes to great lengths to envelop the player in different atmospheres in different guilds and situations and therefore facilitates an atmosphere of murder in which no decision can be traced back solely to the player (cf. 149–50). This is especially important considering the free choices the player can make. They can accept to follow the rules of the game world, i.e. shun the Khajit or support a side in the ongoing civil war. According to Engelns, the game does not endorse the murders the player commits, but it offers a potential for tension (*Spannungspotential*) in the clash of gameplay, atmosphere, and morals that leads to a unique player experience (cf. 150). It is that interplay that not only influences the atmosphere of murder, as Engelns calls it, but which also influences the whole experience of the game as the rules and morals of the game world stand in contrast to the need to think strategically for gameplay advantages while considering the player's own moral code. Connecting this to Brigham's idea of incorporation, the clash and *Spannungspotential* between the player's values in real life and in the game world become apparent to the player.

This brief analysis of *Skyrim* has shown that the player's mobility in the game is tied to a freedom of action and a freedom to change. On the road, the player will be faced with situations that demand their contemplation of both the moral and gameplay aspects of the game. Due to the overlap of the values of the player with those of the game world—similar to the incorporation in the road narratives Brigham analyses—the player is confronted with their own values. This, however, is only possible because *Skyrim*, and RPGs in general, offer the player a freedom of movement and choice that more linear games do not. The advantages that come with the mobility the player experiences come with possibilities of encountering and dealing with the other, especially as the player's mobility is contrasted with that of NPCs in the game. This idea of mobility is intimately tied to an American cultural context that considers it as both blessing and threat. Given the large American share in the production of the most prominent games on the market, the tools developed by the field analyzing this cultural discourse are vital to understanding these titles. The richness and

---

[6] Sicart calls this type of design "instrumentalizing play" (66–67).

potential of video games can only come to the fore if an analysis treats them as both a game and a cultural artifact that says as much about its contexts as novels and films do. As my brief exemplary analysis has shown, the trope of the road narrative, in particular, opens up a vast research potential in this regard, and it will find ample material in video games as it will find ample methodological tools in the theoretical repertoire of American Studies.

Works Cited

Baumgartner, Robert. "Ankunftsmomente: Die Vermittlung von Atmosphäre in Rollenspielen am Beispiel der *Elder Scrolls*-Reihe." Huberts and Standke, pp. 71–113.
Brigham, Ann. *American Road Narratives: Reimagining Mobility in Literature and Film*. U of Virginia P, 2015.
Calleja, Gordon. *In-Game: From Immersion to Incorporation*. MIT Press, 2011.
Cresswell, Tim. *In Place/Out of Place: Geography, Ideology, and Transgression*. U of Minnesota P, 1996.
Cresswell, Tim. *On the Move: Mobility in the Modern Western World*. Routledge, 2006.
Dragon Age: Origins. Electronic Arts, 2009.
Engelns, Markus. "Vom Helden zum Mörder? Zur Herstellung einer 'Atmosphäre des Mordens' in *The Elder Scrolls V: Skyrim*." Huberts and Standke, pp. 117–152.
Fallout 3. Bethesda Softworks, 2008.
Gee, James Paul. *Unified Discourse Analysis: Language, Reality, Virtual Worlds, and Video Games*. Routledge, 2015.
Huberts, Christian, and Sebastian Standke, editors. *Zwischen/Welten: Atmosphären im Computerspiel*. Verlag Werner Hülsbusch, 2014.
Juul, Jesper. *Half-Real: Video Games between Real Rules and Fictional Worlds*. MIT Press, 2005.
Mass Effect. Microsoft Game Studios and Electronic Arts, 2007.
Mass Effect 2. Electronic Arts, 2010.
Mass Effect 3. Electronic Arts, 2012.
Nitsche, Michael. *Video Game Spaces: Image, Play, and Structure in 3D Game Worlds*. MIT Press, 2008.
Penix-Tadsen, Phillip. *Cultural Code: Video Games and Latin America*. MIT Press, 2016.
Sicart, Miguel. *Beyond Choices: The Design of Ethical Gameplay*. MIT Press, 2013.
The Elder Scrolls V: Skyrim. Bethesda Softworks, 2011.
The Walking Dead. Telltale Games, 2013.

Dietmar Meinel
Playing the Urban Future: The Scripting of Movement and Space in *Mirror's Edge* (2008)

From *Pong* (1972) to *Pac-Man* (1980), from *Space Invaders* (1978) to *Donkey Kong* (1981), movement in virtual space has been one core mechanic of most video games. As computers and consoles became increasingly more powerful, both the digital representation of space and of movement in space became more elaborate, most notably in games such as *Super Mario Bros.* (1985), *Sonic: The Hedgehog* (1991), *Prince of Persia* (1989), or *Metal Gear Solid* (1998).[1] Yet while navigating a digital world continues to be an essential feature of modern-day first-person shooters, open-world games, competitive fighting games, or MMORPGs, movement in space mostly functions as an appendage to other game mechanics. A rare exception, *Mirror's Edge* (2008) puts players in the shoes of a female courier runner and asks them to sprint, jump, glide, and climb through a dystopian high-tech metropolis in order to deliver information. Players enter individual stages or levels after a comic-style cutscene and are tasked to move from one point in the city to another. They control their character, Faith Connors, from a first-person perspective and have to rush through a particular part of the level as they are being chased by police officers or are chasing after other characters themselves. These speed sections alternate with platforming sections in which players attempt to find a path, for example into an office building or out of the urban sewer system. Here, players are less in danger from the police and need to find their way vertically rather than traversing the landscape horizontally. Eventually, mastering (fast) movement through the urban landscape mechanically will challenge the surveillance state narratively.

---

[1] In "Allegories of Space" (2007), Espen Aarseth defines the experience of "spatiality" in video games as their main purpose—even as he omits any reference to movement in space as the main practice to experience most digital environments: "The defining element in computer games is spatiality. Computer games are essentially concerned with spatial representation and negotiation, and therefore the classification of a computer game can be based on how it represents or, perhaps, implements space. More than time (which in most games can be stopped), more than actions, events and goals (which are tediously similar from game to game) and unquestionably more than characterization (which is usually nonexistent), games celebrate and explore spatial representations as a central motif and raison d'être" (44).

https://doi.org/10.1515/9783110659405-006

Since movement in an urban world is the essential ludic feature of *Mirror's Edge*, this paper examines its production of space.[2] In the spirit of Henri Lefebvre's *The Production of Space* (1991), I particularly explore the various ways in which the video game mediates urban environments with the help of its architecture, its visuals, and its level and world design. Yet, *Mirror's Edge* not only offers insights into the signs and symbols of the (digital) "representations of space" (Lefebvre 33) as its interactive nature also invites questions about the ways in which the game scripts urban experiences in the act of playing. The notion of "scripting," to borrow from urban literary scholars Barbara Buchenau and Jens Martin Gurr, indicates a horizon of possible interactions with and within an urban environment. In their conceptualization, scripts function "as powerful unconscious or semi-conscious guides of individual and collective human behavior" ("Textuality" 136). Although many daily practices, such as a restaurant visit, prescribe social interactions, Buchenau and Gurr are particularly interested in the various ways the infrastructure of urban environments and the "detailed guidelines about proper usage of standard urban commodities and amenities (...) script what urban dwellers do and don't do" ("Textuality" 136). Just as architectural and urban scripts may "initiate various sets of action" ("Textuality" 148), the urban environments in *Mirror's Edge* similarly script interactions with its digital spaces and places. Encouraging players to frantically traverse the top of skyscrapers or race through the local sewer system, however, the video game suspends the "detailed guidelines about proper usage of standard urban commodities" and instead proposes novel scripts for the experience of its environments.

In particular, *Mirror's Edge* re-scripts expected behavior in urban space by explicitly borrowing from Parkour. This subcultural practice of moving through an urban environment at high speed by finding unexpected pathways necessitates a re-reading of the city and its architecture. In the eyes of Elizabeth Freitas, such subcultural re-scripting constitutes "a subversive practice that *transforms* the built environment" (emphasis in original, 210). Since Parkour runners, or *traceurs*, defy the prescriptive uses of urban spaces, Michael Atkinson maintains that Parkour is "an innovative form of anarcho-environmentalist resistance (...) [and] a political *re-appropriation* of commercial urban spaces" in which "[b]uildings, parks, walkways, dumpsters, steps, and practically any edifice is viewed as an obstacle to be used for spiritual and physical development and site for disrupting the order of technocapitalist space" (emphasis mine, 183). Where most

---

[2] In linking mobility to urban space, this paper follows urban theory in conceptualizing mobility as "constitutive of urbanism" (Söderström 198).

of us may see walls and other obstacles, *traceurs* as well as players in *Mirror's Edge* are asked to see opportunities to arrive at seemingly unreachable destinations seizing ledges, tubes, or vents. In drawing on Parkour, *Mirror's Edge* undermines established urban movement scripts as players use everything but the sidewalk to traverse the digital metropolis.[3]

In re-scripting movement in urban environments, *Mirror's Edge* simultaneously implements novel scripts of traversing its unnamed metropolis. Such guidelines about the usage of space, as this paper aims to show, are not only shaped by the game world and the level design but by their aesthetic mediation as well as the gameplay mechanics. Eventually, *Mirror's Edge* appropriates the subversive potential of everyday practices for its story about a dystopian urban future. However, while the video game converts "non-places," to use a term from urban studies scholar Marc Auge, such as rooftops and sewers into sites of urban spectacle, the organization of the world into separate levels segregates the city into playgrounds of entertainment and thereby undermines the narrative of subcultural resistance, female agency, and political liberation the game aims to tell. Ultimately, the production of space in *Mirror's Edge* follows a neoliberal urban script.

Consequentially, this paper draws from the long-standing tradition in American Studies to explore the role of mobility and space in the making (not only) of US culture. From the first white colonists arriving in North America to the displacement of Native American cultures and the transportation of enslaved African men and women, movement and mobility have been at the heart of American experiences. Writing in *American Mobilities* (2016), for example, Julia Leyda understands mobility as "a key feature in American culture from the settlement of the original colonies to the nation's expansion toward new territories. Even after the closing of the frontier in 1890, Eastern populations continued to spread westward in search of property and prosperity" (11). Indeed, the (in)famous essay "The Significance of the Frontier in American History" (1893) by Frederick Jackson Turner described the process of becoming a US American as a practice of westward movement into the space of 'the frontier.' Writing from and about a white Eurocentric perspective (even as he hoped to substitute the former with a white US American perspective), Turner was not the first and would not be the last scholar to link the westward movement of settlers and colonists to particular spaces. Well into the twentieth century, notions of a "wilderness," a "virgin land," a "garden," the "frontier," or a "city upon a hill" continued to indicate

---

[3] In many game sections, landing on the sidewalk actually leads to the death of the player character, regardless of the height of the fall.

the centrality of spatial conceptions of the United States in American Studies.[4] Even as numerous scholars from Gloria Anzaldúa to Patricia Limerick have challenged such views to highlight the countless experiences of multi-directional mobility, their work also introduces novel spatial conceptions of North America and the United States as a contact zone, borderland, or transnational site, thereby exemplifying the persistence of a spatial language.[5] In recent decades scholarship in American Studies has increasingly interrogated the imperial and neocolonial features of the geopolitics of movement and space to draw attention to their legacies in the present. Spatiality, as Klaus Benesch asserts in his introduction to *Space in America* (2005), is "perhaps the most important single driving force not only to build a new nation but to imagine one" (18). Yet, such notions of space are not only shaped by geographical and physical experiences of movement.

When Leyda reminds us that "American national identity has always concerned itself with movement—into the wilderness, across the continent, into middle and upper classes, into outer space" (18), she also highlights the social

---

[4] I am particularly thinking of Henry Nash Smith's *Virgin Land* (1950), Perry Miller's *Errand into the Wilderness* (1952), Leo Marx's *The Machine in the Garden* (1964) and Richard Slotkin's *Regeneration through Violence* (1973).

[5] In *The Legacy of Conquest* (1987), Patricia Limerick challenges not only the Turnerian notion of the frontier as a "civilizing" process but the entire idea of Westward movement as progress. For Limerick, Turner and his frontier thesis "had arbitrary limits that excluded more than they contained. Turner was, to put it mildly, ethnocentric and nationalistic. English-speaking white men were the stars of his story; Indians, Hispanics, French Canadians, and Asians were at best supporting actors and at worst invisible. Nearly as invisible were women of all ethnicities. Turner was also primarily concerned with agrarian settlement and folk democracy in the comparatively well watered Midwest. Deserts, mountains, mines, towns, cities, railroads, territorial government, and the institutions of commerce and finance never found much of a home in his model" (21). Limerick therefore prefers to understand the American West as "an important meeting ground, the point where Indian America, Latin America, Anglo-America, Afro-America, and Asia intersected" (27) and were shaped by the pursuit of conquest. In *Borderlands/La Frontera: The New Mestiza* (1987), Gloria Anzaldúa similarly shifts perspective by detailing the history of movements on the North American continent from early human settlement to the present. Anzaldúa places the numerous experiences of movement (and displacement) of indigenous and Mexican people at the heart of that history. Borders do not separate two irreconcilable opposites as Western historians tended to rationalize European colonial and imperial conquest, but are products of cultural, economic, political, and social struggles for Anzaldúa. As a consequence, indigenous and Mexican people (not only) in the US-American South have been and continue to inhabit a borderland: "a vague and undetermined place created by the emotional residue of an unnatural boundary [that] is in a constant state of transition" (Anzaldúa 3). With this shift in perspective away from a white Anglo-centered history, Anzaldúa connects the hope of fostering a "mestiza way" (82).

facets of space and mobility. Spatial movement also connotes social movement most prominently in the much ballyhooed American Dream. While for some "westward movement had always implied progress, development, and opportunity, and thus been linked ideologically with upward class mobility" (Leyda 12), for many physical movement did not translate into social (upward) mobility. From the Black Atlantic to Native American removal in the past to the policing of African Americans and people of color today, mobility is still highly contested as (the control of) movement and space continue(s) to shape everyday experiences. Likewise, the detention centers at US borders exemplify correspondingly what Maryemma Graham and Wilfried Raussert describe in their introduction to *Mobile and Entangled America(s)* (2016) as "an understanding of culture and cultural contacts that is based upon mobility's being entailed in, and in turn (re)producing, *geographic and social immobilities* and concepts of territory(ialit)y" (emphasis mine, 5).

The extent of spatial or social (im)moblities today is intimately tied to modern technology. Whereas present-day means of transportation allow for the ever-expanding global flow of goods and people in the physical world, contemporary means of communication enable the immediate travel of information and ideas at the palms of our hands in the digital word. In his introduction to *Culture and Mobility* (2013), Benesch acknowledges that "[t]hanks to the new mobile communication technologies we can 'go places' even while standing in line at a ticket counter, waiting at a street light or being stuck in a traffic jam," and he concludes that "[w]e are all in motion, constantly" (2). Though one may interject that travel writing and particularly American road narratives would also have their readers "go places," technology does offer novel ways of experiencing space, movement, and mobility. The interactive experience of three-dimensional video game spaces, in particular, provides players with the possibility of traveling to places either beyond the reach of their personal means or into historical pasts, imagined futures, and the fantastic. It is in this light that the following passages examine *Mirror's Edge*, a game also demanding that players be "in motion, constantly." Keeping in mind both the liberating and debilitating qualities of geographical and social mobility, this paper explores the ludic pleasure of movement in space and its simultaneous production of a neoliberal urban script.

Neoliberal Rationales in Video Games

At first glance, *Mirror's Edge* possesses none of the in-game mechanics most scholars have read as perpetuating neoliberal rationales. For example, in "Governmentality, Neoliberalism, and the Digital Game" (2009), Andrew Baerg focuses on the freedom of choice in connection with the fixation on numerical values in video games to describe their "potential to reproduce procedural rhetorics linked to neoliberal political rationalities" (125). Video games "potentially legitimize and naturalize" neoliberal rationales by favoring "free choice" in their "stress on player choice" combined with a "calculative rationality applied to risk management" ("Governmentality" 125). Whether it is through the possibilities of developing a particular player avatar, the necessity to constantly make choices, or the weighing of risk-reward scenarios, video games ask players to evaluate their options and manage risk by rendering all the necessary information for their decision process as numerical entities, for example when developing an avatar's attributes, tracing their progress with experience points, or measuring their damage output. Numbers quantify risks and choices through discourses of calculation (cf. Baerg "Neoliberalism").[6]

Whereas Baerg probed into role-playing and sports-managing games, Oliver Perez-Latorre and Merce Olivia extend their examination of neoliberal rationales into the game mechanics of (first-person) action adventures with role playing elements (cf. 15). Analyzing *BioShock Infinite* (2013), they describe the ability to customize an avatar, the amassing and consumption of in-game items for character improvement, the narrative of the "individualist epic," and the competiveness within an incentive-driven system as (potentially) following a neoliberal logic (cf. 11–14). Particularly when experienced together in a single game, these features foster a neoliberal individualism in which "[c]ollective wellbeing should be achieved through the sum of the actions (free and autonomous) of individuals and companies who try to maximize their own wellbeing" while advocating "the dismantling of public policies" (Perez-Latorre and Olvia 11).[7]

Since players cannot accumulate in-game items, earn experience points to optimize their character, or manage their risk of moving through a hostile environment according to numerical values, *Mirror's Edge* may seem devoid of neo-

---

[6] Baerg further describes the neoliberal logic of personal risk management via numerical value calculation as an (in)voluntary feature of gaming: "In being deployed in digital games, the numbers become an indicator of both potential risk and how well a gamer may be managing risk. In weighing the risks of a choice against its potential benefits, all against the backdrop of quantitatively inflected variables, gamers become responsibilized to minimize risk in keeping with a neoliberal calculative rationality. Certainly users are not forced to make the most prudent choices, but failing to act responsibly inevitably leads to a failure to win or potentially a failure to enjoy the digital game experience and accrue the benefits that derive from victory and/or participation. The rational gamer aims to successfully confront the virtual world from a calculative perspective and, in doing so, responsibly manages risk" ("Governmentality" 124).

[7] Such game mechanics, as Perez-Latorre and Olivia emphasize, extend beyond any single game or genre (cf. 15–16).

liberal game mechanics. Because the video game scripts its urban environment akin to segregated sites of entertainment, its production of space nonetheless follows a neoliberal rationale. The notion of a 'progressive neoliberalism' will eventually provide a framework to think through such ambiguities. In the following, I will first explore the ways in which a fractured urban environment and fluid movement—instead of accumulation, consumption, and risk management—model a neoliberal rationale of mobility.[8]

Scripting Urban Environments in Digital Media

With its focus on frantic running, jumping, and climbing, *Mirror's Edge* draws on a host of earlier platforming games but faces the challenge to provide adequate information for a smooth and seamless movement across its chaotic environments. Particularly its first-person perspective immerses players in a dystopian world yet complicates a quick reading of urban space. Since most platforming titles utilize a third-person perspective, they often allow players to control the camera angle to provide a better view of a particularly challenging section. Although *Mirror's Edge* plays from the narrower first-person perspective, no such options exist.[9] Instead, the opening section of most levels offers a moment of orientation when little or no action has been initiated and players may tentatively sketch a path toward their distant objective. Since unforeseen obstacles can appear at any moment, players sometimes need to chase other characters, or the setting simply moves from rooftops to underground or indoor sections, one can hardly plan the fastest route before beginning the level properly. The moment players step from the starting platform, they have to quickly respond to shots fired from police officers, sudden obstacles in the environment, or new in-

---

[8] Although mobility and movement are often used interchangeably, this paper understands mobility as distinct from movement in that the former "encompasses different types of movement and their interrelations" (Söderström 198). In this sense, movement may connote the geographical, spatial, or physical change of place while mobility refers to "the capacity to be mobile" and therefore functions as "a specific form of 'spatial capital'" (Söderström 198).

[9] In an interview with *mtv.com*, senior producer Owen O'Brien explains the design decision behind the game's first-person perspective: "the camera in our game does quite a lot of clever things. It's simulating your eyes rather than your head. I think what a lot of people have done in the past is they've stuck a camera in the person's head and they move around like robots (…) The field of view is very important. A lot of first-person games have a very claustrophobic point of view, usually to create tension or scares. We've got a very wide field of view which gives you much more peripheral view of the city. And you get much less disoriented" (qtd. in Totilo).

formation from other characters. The plethora of visual information, the in-game sounds as well as the controller feedback further immerse players in the game world. *Mirror's Edge* thereby scripts movement in its urban environment as fast, frantic, and empowering (when successful) as players scramble to find the quickest path away from gunshots and toward safety. Such a scripting of movement in urban spaces at high velocity, however, necessitates the curbing of sensory information.

As players receive visual as well as sonic and sensory information, strategies of curating that information seem particularly pertinent in video games not least because players simultaneously provide input into the medium. Photographers and filmmakers, for example, choose perspectives, compose shots, and crop images in post-production to organize information.[10] To ensure playability, games borrow or remediate these practices yet also provide simplified means of reading the game world such as in-game maps, radars, and dotted lines to orient players. *Mirror's Edge* refrains from using such established mechanics and instead opts to curate its information primarily via its gameplay, its aesthetics, and its structuring of urban spaces.

Such design decisions not only shape the immediate playing experience but also contribute to the overall composition of the game world. The urban environment of *Mirror's Edge* eventually "shape[s] a player's particular understanding of a larger set of spatial ideologies inherent to the game" (Magnet 143)—to adopt Shoshana Magnet's analysis of the role of digital landscapes in her essay "Playing at Colonization" (2006). As the virtual environments are not "static objects 'to-be-looked-at,' but are dynamic and require the active involvement of the player in their construction" (143), Magnet draws from the work of Henri Lefebvre and W. H. K. Chun to conceptualize the production of these spaces, or "gamescapes," as the result of "repetitious (...) spatial practice of gameplay" (147). Ultimately, the reduction of possible interactions with the game environment and sensory information not only enables players to maneuver through the game world fast and efficiently but also contributes to the production of a desolate (albeit stylized) urban environment in the act of playing.

---

10 In *Video Game Spaces: Image, Play, and Structure in 3D Game Worlds* (2008), Michael Nitsche explores the parallels (and dissimilarities) between the cinematographic work in film and its adaption in video games. He argues that "[t]he plane of the mediated space is part of the interactive system in video games, but it quotes many visual traditions from cinema. In order to keep the mediation legible, 3D games have lined themselves up in the tradition of the moving image, and it is not surprising that a remarkable amount of effort has gone into the use of cinematic visualization techniques in video games" (79).

Although the setting of *Mirror's Edge* is a vast and sprawling metropolis, interaction with the world is limited to a handful of button prompts. As players move from the top floors of a skyscraper to the underground sewers, the gameplay stays the same throughout all levels: running, a lot of jumping, and occasional climbing. Since the jump button also doubles for grabbing objects and pulling the character onto platforms, the game makes only partial use of the controller layout. In addition to scripting a small set of interactions with the environment, *Mirror's Edge* also provides only a partial urban experience. Neither driving a vehicle nor going shopping or enjoying a coffee are part of that experience. Similarly doors are usually not opened but kicked in, and elevators appear to have only an up and a down button.

The spatial design of the urban environment as well as of interior spaces exhibits similar constraints. Urban spaces are generally kept in a sleek white to give the city a futuristic touch. At closer inspection, the architecture of many buildings and the surfaces of objects, however, are kept simple. Crates, tubes, doors, or house fronts, for example, have very little detail. As graphical assets are continuously re-used, the exterior spaces and buildings may deviate in height and arrangement but rarely in surface, color, or design. Indeed, as white cubes dominate the urban landscape, the metropolis in *Mirror's Edge* brings architectural scale models to mind. The interior spaces appear even more generic. The metropolis in *Mirror's Edge* has an uncanny visual conformity because of the extensive use of white and the relative absence of details. Thematically fitting for a dystopian urban future, the minimal design also assists and immerses players in the world of an urban courier runner.

In addition to the gameplay and the visual representation of the urban environment, *Mirror's Edge* helps orient players with its "runner's vision" mechanic. Because of the unfamiliarity of the environment, the unforeseeable gaps between buildings, or the spontaneous appearance of enemies, players cannot predesign their way to the end of a level. Similarly, I found myself often misjudging distances, choosing the wrong path, and thereby falling to my death or losing momentum. *Mirror's Edge* aims to circumvent these complexities of its urban environments—and frustrating game experiences—by highlighting single objects in red which players may use to their advantage. Available in easy and normal mode, this "runner's vision" simulates the ability to see unconventional paths Faith developed from years of experience and the player may be missing. Similarly, should players feel completely lost, pressing a single button lets Faith look into the general direction of her destination. *Mirror's Edge* hence organizes the complexity of urban environments by visual cues that script possible paths through its urban gamescape; its "set of spatial ideologies" (Magnet 143) further aim to contribute to a narrative about challenging a totalitarian surveillance state.

Running the Digital City

As players learn the fastest paths through the individual levels, their playing or running of the urban maze becomes a mode of reading the digital urban environment and a subversive practice within the story. In light of the disciplining power urban spaces exert in "determining conditions of social life," urban scholar Michel de Certeau contends, everyday practices become "individual mode[s] of reappropriation" (96). Particularly walking in urban spaces possesses the potential to "elude discipline without being outside the field in which it is exercised" (de Certeau 96), or—as Deborah Stevenson explicates in her reading of de Certeau— walking "take[s] place within existing (imposed) regulatory frameworks but manage[s] to avoid the nets of surveillance, policing and discipline" (67).[11] In the future city of *Mirror's Edge*, that kind of walking is painstakingly hard to experience as Faith immediately falls into a quick stride at the slightest push of the controller. Nonetheless, physical movement possesses a similar potential to undermine urban disciplinary frameworks because the completion of an in-game section of the metropolis, albeit in the form of running, functions as a subversive practice within the narrative logic. The more often players speed through a level, the faster the seemingly chaotic gamescape becomes readable as Faith successfully "eludes the surveillance, policing, and discipline" of the state. Since players are encouraged to enter individual sections repeatedly to compete for faster completion time, they will eventually master the game mechanically and thereby expose the evildoings of the totalitarian regime narratively. Running the city, players challenge the dystopian police state.

The scripting of movement in an urban environment not only serves to elude discipline in *Mirror's Edge*. In drawing on Parkour, the game appropriates a subculture which similarly subverts the everyday practices of movement in urban space. Elizabeth Freitas, for example, describes Parkour as a transformation of the built environment that "speaks back to the dominant spatial practices prescribed therein" (209). Similarly, for Michael Atkinson, Parkour provides an experience of freedom and thereby "challeng[es] dominant social constructions of (…) urban environment as sanitized corporate space" (170). In loping, vaulting,

---

11 Historically, the notion of the act of walking in de Certeau corresponds to the ascendancy of the urban planning paradigm of the automotive city in the twentieth century.

or scaling the urban architecture, *traceurs* appropriate and re-script the "determining conditions" de Certeau sees at work in urban spaces. Atkinson even draws parallels to the nineteenth-century *flâneur* as he asserts that both "deliberately call attention to the late modern city's spatial organization and its environmentally sterile, commercial policing" (174). Seen from this perspective, the practice of Parkour "eschew[s] the totalitarian technocapitalist enframing of the late modern city" as *traceurs* inscribe into (local) urban spaces "their physical, emotional, and psychological needs as urbanites" (Atkinson 178, 180). Leaving the question aside whether the late modern city can be described exclusively as "technocapitalist," *Mirror's Edge* adapts the subversive aspects of Parkour into a story about a surveillance state but shifts its narrative critique from commercial to governmental policing.

In centering on Faith Connors, *Mirror's Edge* furthermore constitutes one of the rare instances of a playable female and Asian American protagonist, as both continue to be utterly underrepresented in Western video game development to this day. Tom Farrer, one of the game's producers, spoke about the ambition "to get away from the typical portrayal of women in games, that they're all just kind of tits and ass in a steel bikini. We wanted her to look athletic and fit and strong [enough] that she could do the things that she's doing. We wanted her to be attractive, but we didn't want her to be a supermodel" (qtd. in Ashcraft). For players and game critics, the developers have succeed with their aspiration as Faith "manages to be athletic, stealthy and attractive without relying on suggestive camera angles or physically impossible cleavage" and is "dressed for success, wearing clothes runners actually don while hopping through parking garages" (Elston). Not surprisingly, Faith continuously appears on lists ranking the "Most Inspirational Female Characters in Game" (*GamesRadar*), the "Greatest Video Game Heroines" (*SFGate*), the "Greatest Heroines in Video Game History" (*Complex*), or "Kick-Ass Women in Videogames" (*Entertainment Weekly*). She is even hailed as "[o]ne of the strongest women in the modern gaming landscape" (Vance). Such widely-shared appreciation for the playable heroine in *Mirror's Edge* seem to further foreground the progressive politics of a narrative about civil disobedience by having players run in Faith's shoes.[12]

Whereas *Mirror's Edge* links the empowerment of a marginalized citizenry to the fast-paced movement of a female protagonist through space, Andreas Höhne

---

[12] In this context, the first-person perspective further contributes to this sense of giving voice and empowerment to Faith via the player. Although players do not acquire weapons or in-game abilities in *Mirror's Edge*, Nitsche's statement about first-person shooters still applies: "[t]he view stays consistent, but the dramatic position of the hero changes from victim to killer" and *"the game space changes from threat to familiar and mastered ground"* (emphasis mine, 105).

reminds us that "we must be careful to not simply bestow fluidity and mobility with positive connotations while perceiving immobility as a sign of exclusion and marginalization" (161). Höhne draws from the field of mobility studies and its insights into "the doctrines at the very core of (neo)liberal ideology of being mobile, flexible, and connected" (161–62). Indeed, *Mirror's Edge* constantly incentivizes players to stay on the move as the narrative, the dialogues, or the mission design foster a permanent urgency to progress.[13] Seen from this perspective, the scripting of high-speed urban mobility complicates the narrative framing of empowerment in the game as slowing down and actually walking along the tops of the metropolis would constitute a subversive practice within the spatial logic of *Mirror's Edge*. However, not only does the immediate experience of movement in a single level adhere to a neoliberal logic of mobility, *Mirror's Edge* also scripts all of its mediations of the urban environment as a postmodern space of late capitalism.

The Urban Script of Progressive Neoliberalism

In spite of the possibilities to explore the city of *Mirror's Edge*, the urban environment becomes only partially readable because of its fractured mediation. While players see most of the metropolis through a first-person perspective, the game depicts the city in two additional ways, thereby scripting a neoliberal experience of urban space. First, players actually enter the urban environment via the starting screen. Here, they can choose to replay completed levels or continue with the main story. As players select a particular section of the city, they also receive a visual approximation of the entire metropolis. Although only depicted as a three-dimensional urban planning model of various white cubes, its skyline of skyscrapers brings to mind contemporary megacities such as New York or Shanghai. This urban vista draws from high modernist planning ideas and the notion of the Vertical City in particular. Inspired by the work of Le Corbusier and his rigorously geometrical principles, the high-rising architecture was "underpinned by a modernist concern with efficiency, rationality and simplicity" and "had façades and interiors that were relatively free from 'unnecessary' ornamentation and references to the past" (Stevenson 82–83). This high-modernist style appears a suitable choice for a dystopian gamescape in which, as Faith explains in the

---

[13] The time-trial mode further contributes to such a reading. After finishing a level players may choose to replay the section in a timed mode and compete for the fastest completion time with other players on a global online score board.

opening scene, the expansion of the police state succeed slowly as most citizens "didn't realize, or didn't care, and accepted" the curbing of civil rights in favor of leading "a comfortable life" (*Mirror's Edge*). The minimalistic design and simplistic layout of the map, however, contribute little to the overall understanding of the spatial organization of the city acquired in the individual levels.

Similarly, after the completion of every level, the game provides a cutscene narrating the main story. Presented in an anime style, the scenes introduce major and minor characters to tell the game's story of a city-wide conspiracy. Here, the perspective shifts from a first-person view to an external camera. Spatially, these scenes are often situated in locations never visited by the player and not highlighted on the map screen. For example, Faith meets a police informant in an underground garage the location of which remains opaque since players never arrive at the garage at the end of a level and the game offers no geographical indication on the map screen. By having players race the individual levels, interact with the map screen, and watch cutscenes, *Mirror's Edge* thus scripts its experience of urban space as an assemblage of three distinct perspectives.

In the eyes of Frederic Jameson, such unreadability is an essential quality of postmodern spaces. The assemblage of a multitude of often contradictory referents, Jameson diagnoses, renders postmodern spaces "illegible" (156). In the postmodern aesthetics of *Mirror's Edge*, players do possess the capacity, in contrast to Jameson's assertion, to "map [their] position in a mappable external world" (43). Even as the fragmented depictions of urban space—the first-person perspective, the map screen, and the cutscenes—preclude a coherent reading of the metropolis, that assemblage never inhibits or completely deters a comprehension of the game world. What seemed disorienting about space in the late 1980s and postmodernism in general has come to designate, as many scholars have noted since, an established and readable feature of contemporary (urban) aesthetics (cf. Patton 112–24). Similarly, the fragmentation of a video game into individual levels which are accessible through the larger game world (or from a map screen) is also an established mode of in-game world design. In this sense, *Mirror's Edge* draws on postmodern aesthetics to offer ludic pleasure to players running and reading a fractured urban space; its assemblage of assorted spatial experiences thereby exemplifies "the cultural dominant of the logic of late capitalism" (Jameson 46). Thanks to its scripting of the game world, *Mirror's Edge* produces a spatial experience scholarly literature refers to as 'neoliberal urbanism.'

In his contribution to *Urban Theory: New Critical Perspectives* (2017), Ugo Rossi describes the neoliberal commodification of cities as an obliteration of "the publicness of contemporary cities through myriad process of enclosure" (217). Neoliberal urbanism or urban segregation, in his view, is driven by "the urbanization of creativity" (the widespread policies catering to a "creative class") and "the mobilization of culture for urban regeneration purposes" (Rossi 215). Particularly the latter sees tourism as an opportunity for expanding the local and regional service industry sector. While neither creativity nor tourism figure prominently within *Mirror's Edge*, its urban experience also hinges on a "process of enclosure" to foster the ludic pleasure of frantic movement as players only traverse those sections of the metropolis that provide speed, tension, and challenge (avoiding all other areas through cutscenes and the map screen). The fragmentation of the metropolis into meticulously designed and conveniently accessible sites of entertainment lets players consume the city as a present-day tourist.

Rather than a tourist, however, *Mirror's Edge* stylizes its protagonist as a subcultural revolutionary. In combining subversive narrative elements with scripting a late-capitalist experience of urban space, *Mirror's Edge* exemplifies what Rossi describes as the "co-optation of alternative subjectivities (…) and the spectacularization of social and cultural diversity" (214), and what Nancy Fraser concisely labels "progressive neoliberalism." The combination of a female Asian American protagonist challenging a totalitarian political system thanks to her extensive spatial mobility bears close resemblance to what Fraser describes as "an alliance of mainstream currents of new social movements (feminism, anti-racism, multiculturalism, and LGBTQ rights), on the one side, and high-end 'symbolic' and service-based business sectors (Wall Street, Silicon Valley, and Hollywood), on the other." As progressive movements and ideas joined modern forms of capitalism in this seemingly unexpected partnership, "the former lend their charisma to the latter [as] [i]deals like diversity and empowerment, which could in principle serve different ends, now gloss policies that have devastated manufacturing and what were once middle-class lives" (Fraser). Similar to the experience of urban space, the subversive potential of Faith's "individualistic epic" eventually contributes to a neoliberal rationale in *Mirror's Edge*.

Conclusion

All games, even the *GTA* or *Assassin's Creed* series with their sprawling open worlds, script the complexity of urban environments. Since *Mirror's Edge* particularly constricts its dystopian world to a narrow set of mostly non-places players often need to traverse at high speed, this paper has concentrated on the production of urban space via movement. To mediate its spatial experience, *Mirror's Edge* appropriates the subculture of Parkour to tell a story about civic disobedience against total surveillance. As players learn to read the unnamed metropolis by dashing through the levels, *Mirror's Edge* toys with the idea of the subversive potential of everyday practices.

At the same time, the game uses not only in-game world design but also cinematic cutscenes and a map screen to assemble its metropolis from a variety of divergent perspectives. Although such a scripting of urban space complicates a coherent reading of the city, in tune with postmodern architecture or fiction, the fragmentation of the urban environment actually contributes to the pleasure of the game as its initial unreadability prefigures its subsequent mastery. Indeed, the fragmentation of urban space further enhances *Mirror's Edge*'s ludic pleasure by minimizing the need to traverse longer stretches of urban spaces without any meaningful interaction. Yet the ludic pleasure of the fragmented urban environment in *Mirror's Edge* thereby also curates a ghettoized urban experience in which only the privileged few—extensively trained, able-bodied, and highly mobile—experience the city as a spectacle of entertainment. In letting players run in the shoes of a female Asian American courier, the game eventually mediates a neoliberal urban space in the spirit of a 'progressive neoliberalism.' Instead of subverting the dystopian status quo in a narrative about the political oppression of a vulnerable citizenry and individual revolt, the seamless accessibility of curated sites of entertainment lets players consume the city akin to urban tourists.

Works Cited

Aarseth, Espen. "Allegories of Space: The Question of Spatiality in Computer Games." von Borries, Walz, and Böttger, pp. 44–47.

Anzaldúa, Gloria. *Borderlands/La Frontera: The New Mestiza*. Aunt Lute Books, 1987.

Ashcraft, Brian. "Faith Is Not a 12 Year-Old With A Boob Job." *Kotaku*, 26 Nov. 2008, www.kotaku.com/5099050/faith-is-not-a-12-year-old-with-a-boob-job. Accessed 15 Jan. 2019.

Atkinson, Michael. "Parkour, Anarcho-Environmentalism, and Poiesis." *Journal of Sport and Social Issues*, vol. 33, no. 2, 2009, pp. 169–94.

Auge, Marc. *Non-Places: Introduction to an Anthropology of Supermodernity*. London, Verso, 1995.

Baerg, Andrew. "Governmentality, Neoliberalism, and the Digital Game." *Symploke*, vol. 17, no. 1–2, 2009, pp. 115–127.

Baerg, Andrew. "Neoliberalism, Risk, and Uncertainty in the Video Game." *Capital at the Brink: Overcoming the Destructive Legacies of Neoliberalism*, edited by Jeffred R. Di Leo and Uppinder Mehan, Open Humanities Press, 2014, pp. 186–214.

Benesch, Klaus. "Culture and Mobility: An Introduction." *Culture and Mobility*, edited by Klaus Benesch, Universitätsverlag Winter, 2013, pp. 1–8.

Benesch, Klaus. "The Concept of Space in American Culture: An Introduction." *Space in America: Theory, History, Culture*, edited by Klaus Benesch and Kerstin Schmidt, Rodopi, 2005, pp. 11–24.

Boron, Dariusz Jacob. "A Short History of Digital Gamespace." von Borries, Walz, and Böttger, pp. 26–31.

Buchenau, Barbara, and Jens Martin Gurr. "City Scripts: Urban American Studies and the Conjunction of Textual Strategies and Spatial Processes." *Urban Transformations in the USA.: Spaces, Communities, Representations*, edited by Julia Sattler, transcript, 2016, pp. 395–420.

Buchenau, Barbara, and Jens Martin Gurr. "On the Textuality of American Cities and Their Others: A Disputation." *Projecting American Studies: Essays on Theory, Method, and Practice*, edited by Frank Kelleter and Alexander Starre, Universitätsverlag Winter, 2018, pp. 135–54.

de Certeau, Michel. *The Practice of Everyday Life*. U of California P, 1984.

Elston, Brett. "The Top 7...Tasteful Game Heroines." *Gamesradar+*, 10 Nov. 2009, www.gamesradar.com/the-top-7-tasteful-game-heroines/2/. Accessed 15 Jan. 2019.

Fraser, Nancy. "The End of Progressive Neoliberalism." *Dissent*, 2 Jan. 2017, www.dissentmagazine.org/online_articles/progressive-neoliberalism-reactionary-populism-nancy-fraser. Accessed 15 Jan. 2019.

Freitas, Elizabeth. "Parkour and the Built Environment: Spatial Practices and the Plasticity of School Buildings." *Journal of Curriculum Theorizing*, vol. 27, no. 3, 2011, pp. 209–20.

Graham, Maryemma, and Wilfried Raussert. "Introduction: Just a Small Step: From Jamaica Kincaid's *A Small Place* to Mobile and Entangled America(s)." *Mobile and Entangled America(s)*, edited by Maryemma Graham and Wilfried Raussert, Routledge, 2016, pp. 1–12.

Höhne, Stefan. "An Endless Flow of Machines to Sever the City: Infrastructural Assemblages and the Quest for the Metropolis." *Thick Space: Approaches to Metropolitanism*, edited by Dorethee Brantz, Sasha Disko, and Georg Wagner-Kyora, transcript, 2012, pp. 141–64.

Jameson, Frederic. *Postmodernism, or, The Cultural Logic of Late Capitalism*. Duke UP, 1991.

Jayne, Mark, and Kevin Ward, editors. *Urban Theory: New Critical Perspectives*. Routledge, 2017.

Lefebvre, Henri. *The Production of Space*. Blackwell, 1991.

Leyda, Julia. *American Mobilities: Geographies of Class, Race, and Gender in US Culture*. transcript, 2016.

Limerick, Patricia. *The Legacy of Conquest: The Unbroken Past of the American West*. New York, W. W. Norton, 1987.

Magnet, Shoshana. "Playing at Colonization: Interpreting Imaginary Landscapes in the Video Game *Tropico*." *Journal of Communication Inquiry*, vol. 30, no. 2, 2006, pp. 142–62.

Nitsche, Michael. *Video Game Spaces: Image, Play, and Structure in 3D Game Worlds*. The MIT Press, 2008.

Patton, Paul. "Imaginary Cities: Images of Postmodernity." *Postmodern Cities and Spaces*, edited by Sophie Watson and Katherine Gibson, Blackwell, 1995, pp. 112–24.

Perez-Latorre, Oliver, and Merce Olivia. "Video Games, Dystopia, and Neoliberalism: The Case of *BioShock Infinite*." *Games and Culture*, 10 Oct. 2017, DOI: doi.org/10.1177%2F1555412017727226. Accessed 15 Jan. 2019.

Rossi, Ugo. "Neoliberalism." Jayne and Ward, pp. 205–217.

Söderström, Ola. "Mobilities." Jayne and Ward, pp. 193–204.

Stevenson, Deborah. *Cities and Urban Cultures*. Open UP, Philadelphia, 2003.

Totilo, Stephen. "*EA Discusses Mirror's Edge Sickness Concerns, Lack of Color Green.*" *MTV.com*, 3 July 2008, www.mtv.com/news/2456471/ea-discusses-mirrors-edge-sickness-concerns-lack-of-color-green/. Accessed 15 Jan. 2019.

Vance, Alyx. "The Wednesday 10: Gaming Heroines." *IGN.com*, 8 July 2009, www.ign.com/articles/2009/07/08/the-wednesday-10-gaming-heroines. Accessed 15 Jan. 2019.

von Borries, Friedrich, Steffen P. Walz, and Matthias Böttger, editors. *Space Time Play: Computer Games, Architecture and Urbanism: The Next Level*. Birkhäuser Verlag, 2007.

Martin Lüthe
Playing on Fields: Seasonal Seriality, Tele-Realism, and the Bio-Politics of Digital Sports Games

On July 17, 1994, a soccer ball took flight in the midday heat of summer in California and traveled beyond the crossbar of the goal. Roberto Baggio, *Il Divin Codino*, "the godly ponytail," recipient of the *Ballon d'Or* for the best player in 1993, had brought a soccer world cup to an end in an unprecedented manner: with his decisive fifth penalty miss against Brazil, he would become the first and only player to date to miss the final shot in a penalty shoot-out in a world cup final. Baggio's decisive miss came at a crucial historical conjuncture in the global and globalizing marketing of real life action sports, as the entire FIFA world cup in 1994 can best be understood as a strategic response to the Olympic games in Barcelona in 1992, which had—for the first time in the history of the event—featured a US-American basketball team of professionals, stylized as the Dream Team, in an effort to further popularize the major outlet of competitive professional basketball in North America, the National Basketball Association (NBA), with new global audiences. David Stern, the commissioner of the NBA, where all of the members of the Dream Team competed against one another from season to season, had set out to give the professional sports of soccer a run for its money in global sporting marketplaces.

While professional digital sports, or e-sports, as we know them now, had not yet been institutionalized in the early and mid-1990s, digital sports games arguably stood at the beginning of the modern 'franchise era' of sports. After all, *John Madden Football* by Electronic Arts (EA), first released in 1988, had changed its name to the slicker *Madden NFL* in 1993, cementing EA's commitment to the game of American Football and to the *Madden* franchise *as* franchise. At the same time, Renegade looked like it might be able to establish a digital soccer franchise with its title *Sensible Soccer* (serialized as *Sensible World of Soccer*) on the Amiga. Arguably, then, the early 1990s marked the first time in which sports games for digital machines could be conceived of as becoming serial franchises in the first place, thanks in large part to the increasing technological efficiency and the resurgence of the digital gaming markets roughly a decade after the crash of 1983 (cf. Pursell 150–52).

In its most abstract, I hope to make a twofold contribution in analyzing digital sport fields here: to think digital gaming critically in the larger cultural history of 'real-life action' sports by means of the complexities of digital seriality and embodiment, and also to salvage digital sports gaming itself as a frequently marginalized genre/form of digital gaming culture so as to instead establish it as a meaningful object of inquiry at the nexus of Game Studies and American Studies. Especially the body and its production or reproduction in digital games provides one example of a meaningful site where Game Studies and broader Cultural Studies scholarship can enter a transdisciplinary dialogue. As Ella Brians reminds us: "Historically, cyber discourses have been characterized by a desire to transcend the perceived limits of materiality, which inevitably means transcending the body," and that "while versions of cyber discourse that argue for taking embodiment seriously have emerged, the fantasy of escaping the flesh persists" (118).

In what follows I briefly outline the entangled histories of professional real-life action sports and their digital gaming imprints, exemplified here in the cross-franchise competitions of *Madden* and *NFL2K* (digital American football) and the *FIFA* and *Pro Evolution Soccer* (*PES*) franchises (digital soccer). I then introduce two analytical prisms for the study of digital sports game series, namely 'seasonal seriality' and 'tele-realism.' With the help of these concepts, I hope to critically assess the histories of serial production and dissemination of digital sports games in the United States and globally, before I turn to my final topic that combines seasonal seriality, tele-realism, and physical embodiment. I argue that the simulations at hand play with and interrogate the limits of physicality (in sports) much in line with how bodies function in diverse genres of digital gaming, while they simultaneously reproduce cultural anxieties of the digital era regarding the fragility and volatility of the human body in general, and the (white) male sporting/slouching body specifically.

Placing the Fields: Historicizing Digital Sports Games

In "To the White Extreme: Conquering Athletic Space, White Manhood, and Racing Virtual Reality" David J. Leonard observes that "[t]he sports gaming industry is the crown jewel of the video games world" (110). It comes as no surprise that sports as widely televised, watched, and played in the world as soccer and American football played a meaningful role in the development and further popularization of digital gaming. Accordingly, as soon as programmers could program complex code to simulate a complex set of rules and some graphic elements to move across a playing field representing a soccer pitch or football field, soccer and football games became available for almost any of the early digital gaming consoles and computers, even though the histories for each branch of digital sports game remain different, especially in light of their respective results. Arguably, both digital soccer and digital football games went through an early period of experimentation on the side of developers, especially in the Nintendo NES and Commodore era.

Commodore's C64 featured the game *International Soccer* as early as 1983, its successor, Commodore's Amiga 500, had the popular *Kick-Off* and its influential sequel *Kick-Off 2*, while the Nintendo Entertainment System (NES) and the Gameboy showcased *Nintendo World Cup* in 1990, a decisive year in digital soccer history, partly because of the real-life world cup hosted by Italy in 1990 and the resulting awareness of soccer in global sports cultures. Accordingly, an increasing number of digital soccer games were released around this time, giving soccer and gaming aficionados permanent input and the possibility to choose rather freely between various digital soccer games.[1]

However, while the real-life event of the world cup in Italy might have stirred soccer excitement on the sides of producers and consumers in the digital market, the first watershed moment in the history of digital soccer games came with the production and release of the aforementioned *Sensible Soccer* and its even more popular sequel *Sensible World of Soccer* (*SWOS*) by Sensible Software, which was marketed by Renegade. *SWOS* gained an unprecedented popularity when compared to any digital soccer game, even those of the pre-2000 and pre-sixth-generation console era. As a consequence, a list of the ten most important digital games of all times, compiled by Henry Lowood of Stanford University, featured *SWOS* as its only sports game (Chaplin E7). Even though any list of that kind must be treated with skepticism, it is striking that the five experts put *SWOS* in the company of games such as *SimCity*, *Tetris*, *Super Mario Bros. 3*, *Zork*, and *Doom* as the only sports game on the list. No tennis, basketball, baseball, or American football game ranked among these games that have supposedly shaped the history of digital gaming. In many ways, then, it is partly the success

---

[1] For a number of reasons, the sixth generation marks an important moment in console history as the economic powerhouse Microsoft entered the console market and Sony released its Playstation 2, the bestselling gaming console to date. For a brief, concise history of the history of digital gaming, see Garrelts, "Introduction" 1–19; for a discussion of the nexus of capitalist globalization and digital gaming, see Dyer-Witheford and de Peuter. Some of the original digital soccer games still have fan followings on the internet, and digital gamers can still compete regularly for trophies and recognition in some of them; for example, the website www.kickoff2.com features dates and results of contemporary competitions in Germany and seeks to provide players with a network of other aficionados. Of course, a 'cult following' of such nature is common for many of the earlier games in digital gaming history. For another history of digital sports games, see Baerg, "It's in the Game."

and respect that *SWOS* gained which further solidified soccer as a crucial element in digital gaming cultures. Crucially, however, the mini-franchise *Sensible Soccer* did not make the transition to the fifth console generation and was devastatingly impacted by Commodore's bankruptcy around the same time in the early 1990s.[2]

As early as 1991, however, Japanese publisher Konami released a soccer game for the Super Nintendo Entertainment System that would provide the foundation for the *International Superstar Soccer* (*ISS*) franchise, which itself was revamped as *Pro Evolution Soccer* in Europe and *Winning Eleven* in North America, starting with the sixth console generation. Konami thus maintains the role of the sole competitor to EA Sports' *FIFA* series, which was originally published in 1993 as *FIFA International Soccer* by the Canadian EA studio and has since been able to uphold its status as the leading global soccer game across consoles and PCs (cf. Baerg, "It's in the Game"; Vincent; "EA Sports FIFA Is the World's Game"). Additionally, EA Sports has been responsible for one of the most successful digital gaming franchises in North America in their *Madden* series ("Fans Are Going Mad for MADDEN"). In fact, Madden has been so successful a franchise that it now practically has the monopoly in digital American football gaming; the process during which competitors eventually stopped producing American football games for consoles or the PC arguably marks the major difference between the state of digital soccer and digital American football today. Ever since Visual Concepts produced and released *NFL 2K* for a final time in 2005 for the Dreamcast console, EA Sports' Madden franchise has only been competing with other, previous installments of itself. It is here that the notion of seasonal seriality serves as a helpful concept in dissecting the logic behind the specific seriality of digital sports games.

Towards Digital Seasonal Seriality and Tele-Realism

I consider what follows an extension or specification of Shane Denson's and Andreas Sudmann's arguments pertaining to the "digital seriality" of sports games. In the course of their insightful exploration they point out that "[t]he history of digital games is above all a history of popular series: it is the story of countless

---

[2] The history of Commodore not only speaks to the different histories of digital gaming technologies in North America, Europe, and Asia, but also to the complex interrelationship between digital gaming consoles and the emerging notion of a so-called personal computer.

sequels, prequels, remakes, hacks, mods, copies, updates, and franchises" (262). Denson and Sudmann carefully analyze the multiple ways in which processes of serialization inform and make digital games, not only – but also – in the obvious processes of the kind of franchise serialization outlined above in my history of the digital sports game. What appears more crucial to Denson and Sudmann is the fact that since at least the 1980s games "had begun introducing the mechanism of save points, thus ordering gameplay itself as an episodically segmented but continuing serial activity" (262). Consequently, to Denson and Sudmann gaming as practice becomes decisively serial, adding to the narrative logic of games in their deployment of levels and the serialized logic of gaming industry production in installments or series. Digital sports games, I argue, produce a specific, seasonal form of seriality. Structurally, the season informs digital sports games in three interrelated, yet slightly distinct ways: firstly, in that the release of digital American football and soccer games happens annually in the fall season, which secondly—of course—corresponds with the seasonal logics of the real-life sports themselves; and thirdly, the intradiegetic season marks a crucial and distinctive formal feature of the 'narrative' of digital sports gaming, resembling the save point or the level as ordering principles of the gaming experience, while maintaining its own distinct quality.

Even though my observation regarding the meteorological season might seem equally arbitrary and obvious, the sports season reinforces the meteorological season as a structuring principle of modern and contemporary life. The obvious point to make here pertains to the summer as a time of vacationing and breaks and the fall as the time to go back to work—this is even more true with regard to the pre-season, season, and post-season structure of American football, which features stretches of crucial decisions from December through mid-February. For digital gamers, the seasonal logics might be even more obviously relevant, with fall and winter featuring the release of new games, emulating to some degree the idea of the winter holiday blockbuster and the Xmas movie, and allowing for cozy autumn days in front of the digital interface. Additionally, though, with trading and transfer windows closing in late summer in the professional sports I am interested in here, the games logically have to follow a similar rhythm of release. As a consequence, the discussions and speculations among users about upcoming installments of the respective franchise naturally intensify in the weeks before the release, which puts these discussions in sync with the flow of news pertaining to the real-life pre-season period, which is marked by transfer rumors (soccer) and draft and trade speculations (American football), and also the general murmurs regarding strengths and weaknesses of teams in the upcoming season (cf. Buehler 4–5). With regard to digital games, the speculations often revolve around questions of licensing, the changes in the 'narrative' modes of the games, and—crucially—about the new features producers use to market each new installment of their franchise to the gamers.[3] I would maintain that the bottom line in the seasonal marketing usually entails the promise to further increase what I would call the 'tele-realism' of the upcoming installments, a concept I will elaborate on in the following. Here, the demise of *NFL 2K* exemplifies a central tenet of the digital sports gaming franchise era: namely that a perceived gap in the 'tele-realism' of two competing franchises poses a threat to the continuation of a profitable franchise.

Tele-realism marks the effort of the producers of digital sports games to re-create the televised live event of the respective sports in the digital game on at least three levels: firstly, the level of graphics and visuals, ranging from the televisual logic of the camera as the organizing principle of the games' aesthetics to the motion-capturing of key players (and the atmosphere of a live event filmed in a stadium). Secondly, the level of licenses, meaning the inclusion of original team and player names, pre-ranked by the producers in accordance with their collective and individual levels of skill, but also featuring the voices and commentary of broadcasting personnel of the TV stations televising the real-life leagues and competitions featured in the games; thirdly, the level of the assumed realism of the gameplay and the overall physical reality of the digital game version of the sport at hand. Figure 1 below encapsulates how tele-realism is deployed in marketing and historicizing the *Madden* franchise.

As holds true for the fierce competition regarding the rights to broadcast certain sports competitions nationally and globally, the second point raised above, that of licenses and copyrights, mostly depends on economic prowess and business strategy on the side of the producers of digital games. Accordingly, when EA Sports was able to gain the exclusive rights to the NFL (including team and player names), Visual Concepts could have only continued to produce a game of American football featuring a fictionalized professional league with fictional players that—depending on what "exclusive" here designated exactly—could not have been programmed to resemble real-life NFL stars. Similarly, Konami's

---

[3] What I call narrative modes here are the so-called "career" modes of digital sports games, in which you typically play multiple individual soccer or football matches while managing a club of your choice. Here, too, the games simulate and celebrate the seasonal structure of real-life professional sports: long seasons feature intermissions of transfer and draft periods and—much in line with story modes of other games—the teams you chose typically increase progressively in overall ability (as does the competition) as the central narrative feature of the modes. Recently, Brendan Buehler has convincingly pointed to the ways in which these "career" modes further blur the distinction between (white-collar) work and play in truly neoliberal fashion, and Andrew Baerg has pointed to the workings of temporalities in these modes ("It's Game Time").

Fig. 1: "Fans Are Going Mad for MADDEN"

PES franchise has never featured a version of the German Bundesliga nor a fully licensed English Premier League.[4] Even though the question of licenses seems crucial for gamers playing digital sports games, gameplay and the overall physical reality of the games arguably remain the most contested issue in discussions online (and equally crucial to the perceived tele-realism of the games); as a consequence, the studios have placed great emphasis on the tangible physical realness of the recent installments of *PES* and *Madden*, respectively.

In the following, I analyze this aspect in particular by tracing the significance of corporeality for recent installments of Konami's *PES 2019* and *Madden 19* in three intersecting ways: firstly on the level of avatar creation and the body, secondly on the in-game level of physicality, and thirdly on the level of how EA and Konami have marketed the tele-realism of their games via the (corpo)reality of the digital simulations. Here I argue that both franchises reproduce anxieties

---

4 As the complex of licenses and copyrights is not the focus of this contribution, I will not further explore the different developments in terms of licenses in each installment of the respective digital soccer games; suffice it to say that the issue of licenses figures very prominently in the discussions among users online and often serve to explain why they prefer one game over its competitor. See, for example, the following thread on Konami's choice to limit the number of licensed in-game second divisions: twitter.com/PESCommunityit/status/1031131458910474240; last retrieved 22 Oct. 2018.

and concerns regarding (white) male physicality and the 'athletic body' as part of larger cultural concerns in our contemporary digital era of 'slouching.'

Offsides: Digital Seriality and Bodily Complexities

With regard to physicality and the meaning of the in-game body, both *PES* and *Madden* have tried to (re-)produce an increasingly realistic physical world—in terms of both in-game physics and corporeality. The movements of bodies on the virtual playing field, the impact of physical contact and interaction between players, and the range of creating soccer and American football players' bodies in the edit modes of both games have been improved year after year. Not surprisingly, then, both franchises have frequently marketed recent releases by also explicitly advocating the improved production of the physical bodies of the players in the game. As Konami has put it on their promotional website of the game for the 2013 installment:

> Such is the level of graphical finesses that you can see players sweating, their neck muscles tensing as they call for the ball and bark orders to each other, and the muscles in their mouths and around their eyes contort to show the emotions the players are experiencing.

Of course, while this quote speaks mostly to the general efforts in current digital game production to achieve photo- or telerealistic graphics in most gaming environments, K o n a m i here p l a c e s the emphasis decisively on a specific hard masculine physicality through the signifiers of "sweating," "neck muscles tensing," and especially the deployment of the "bark" as an ascription of animalistic physicality onto the virtual players' bodies. The text thus reveals the presumed significance of the production of the body for the level of realism and fun the game could evoke. Similarly, the E3 reveal trailer for *Madden 19* features a voice-over of a deep male voice, typical of the cinematic trailer for sports or war movies, as it takes the viewer right into the middle of the action beginning with the first shot:

Much like the quote, the still frame below illustrates a steadily growing awareness of the importance of the production of bodies in the course of the game. Such an awareness might have existed in the early days of gaming consoles but could not realistically be understood as crucial for the fun of gameplay, as in-game athletes were pixelated abstractions and looked very much alike (except for the color of their hair), and physical contact could at best be graphically alluded to. The opening shot of the trailer not only takes the viewer into the midst of the

Fig. 2: *Madden 19* reveal trailer, opening shot, still frame

virtual action with the usual caption that claims the shot to feature "game engine footage," but it also features a low shot of the action with the in-game camera seemingly placed on the ground of the field; in such instances the developers play with the very notion of tele-realism in creating a sense of embeddedness that navigates the border between the telecast sports event and the participation in the event as player, in both senses of the term.

This strategy has at least two effects: on the one hand it displays the tele-realistic graphics from close range (as well as the licenses), while on the other hand it emphasizes the high physical intensity of the game with the ball-carrying New York Giants player breaking No. 93's tackle while the audio features sounds of bodies colliding and of men grunting and moaning. Here, EA chose the feat of breaking a tackle near the line of scrimmage as the most suitable representation of what the game has to offer—tele-realism with an extra-dosage of physical proximity. Similarly, a trailer for *Madden 16* had already featured real people in the uniforms of well-known NFL stars stepping out of the shadows until their faces were half-lit under the helmet, with the added tag-line "Be the playmaker," to underscore the potential to physically enter the game-world. This idea of physically entering a digital space, often referred to as virtual reality, has of course been informing digital sports game marketing (as it has arguably functioned as a cultural obsession since at least the mid-eighties). Consequently,

> [a]s digital games have become more technologically advanced, the possibilities for interaction within the world of a game have also exponentially increased. The result is that while early games could be easily discussed and studied, it is much more difficult to discuss and study recent games because the 'played game' is different depending on who is doing the playing. (Garrelts 3)

One of the crucial ways for players to interact with the game world of digital sports game is through the creation of avatars. This feature has become increasingly more refined from installment to installment and marks one way for players to further enhance the tele-realism of the games they play by creating more life-like players who might not be licensed for the game at hand. Avatar creation, of course, puts the body center-stage, as the player 'programs' the facial features, hairstyles, physical movement, the height and weight, and the skillset of player avatars into the game.

In addition to underscoring the meaning of the digital bodies that players move across the digital playing fields, avatar creation and physical digital bodies in *PES* reproduce and affirm some of the pervasive neocolonial and racist rhetoric of sports broadcasting in Europe and the US, most notably in the way *PES 2019* still portrays black physicality as a colonial-racist fetish. As a consequence, in-game African nations often excel in the categories of speed, stamina, and strength, while they lag behind their European counterparts in regard to tactics and organization. And, unlike FIFA's more recent installments, the gaming world of PES 2019 is still and exclusively that of male competitive soccer.[5]

Whereas the reproduction of ideologies of gender and race intersect in the games' deployment of physicality, it is the production of the body in the games' core element of simulating a game of soccer or American football that I find most complex. Evidently, sports are by definition dependent on a specific utilization of physical expertise, and while the significance of the mind in soccer, for example in the realm of tactics and analyzing an opponent, can and have been simulated with an astonishing degree of realism, certain physical aspects of the game seem still harder to simulate. For digital sports games this arguably provides the most problematic part regarding an actual simulation of real-world sports; as Andrew Baerg argues, both optimistic and pessimistic discourses regarding the (ir)relevance of the physical body for digital sports gaming are of importance for the cultural study of digital gaming, and

> these kinds of discourses become important to consider in thinking about the material nature of bodies in real-world sport as they become translated into new media and how this translation shapes the experience of sport. ("Fight Night" 329)

Accordingly, it is the process of translating real-life and digital gaming experiences of physicality, beginning with the creation of avatars, that provide the most critical potential for fruitful analyses of corporeality and/in digital gaming.

---

5 I have dwelled on this point elsewhere; cf. Lüthe.

In *PES 2019* and *Madden 19*, as in other sports games, certain elements of physical reality are simulated very convincingly and in accordance with the gamers' expectations; the most notable example being the simulation of fatigue and stamina. *PES 2019* enhances its prequels in the representation of fatigue and stamina in a yet more meaningful way: a player whose stamina has been exhausted, as indicated by an emptied gauge under the player's name on screen, shows clear symptoms of fatigue and will not at all resemble the player's actual skillset. Once the player's gauge is completely empty, controlling the player becomes less immediate and the player's maximum speed, hardest shots, and accuracy noticeably decrease. The effect of fatigue can also lead to avatars cramping on the field (with the commentator pointing it out to the player).[6] In *PES 2019*, the in-game treatment of stamina is at its most dynamic: players (and their gauges) show signs of fatigue in response to a long sprint across the field or in response to heightened physical demands, for example after tackles and running duels, and they will place their hands on their knees and take deep breaths, or even hold their legs due to cramping, as figure three illustrates.

I conceive of such emphasis on endurance and fitness as a reproduction of current medico-scientific discourses on health and aging, which frequently emphasize the correlation between physical activity or fitness and living a healthy and long life. Said perspective has come under critical scrutiny in the field of fat studies, which questions some of the parameters, premises, and truisms of contemporary health discourses and reads them in the context of a specific neoliberal emphasis of an individual's responsibility for their own health and fitness to be and remain productive. The sharp drop in players' on-field abilities strikes me as almost hysterically emphasizing these conventionalized truths and thus as expressing a cultural anxiety of the slouching, gaming body of the avatars' Other at the same time. Kathryn Morgan, for example, rightly conceives of a neoliberal biopower at work in these concerns regarding the body as an object of governmentality. While players controlling avatars deal with fatigue management on-screen, they also deal with "weight management" in front of it by being measured

---

[6] However, some in-game regeneration is possible by limiting sprinting with an already tired player and during the half-time break. Also, resting players becomes necessary when managing a team through a tight season schedule, , because permanently maxing-out the players' fitness negatively impacts their overall mood and thereby their form on game day. The worse the form, the sooner players tire, as the form also impacts the absolute stamina of the players. The second gauge, smaller and presented below the bigger stamina gauge, indicates a process of physical strain or fatigue and increases as stamina decreases. While players that are not fully rested tire sooner, players that display increasing fatigue are more likely to get injured during a game and to stay injured for a longer period of time after the match.

Fig. 3: In-game footage of player's cramps in *PES 2019*

by a "carnal governmentality" against the backdrop of "a vigilant community of disciplined and (self-)disciplining, compliant individuals—totalized (...) by being weight and measured into discrete categories of normalcy and hierarchies of obesity-pathology" (Morgan 197). Here, contemporary public discourse is quick to connect obesity as a disease with the lack of physical activity of (young) people who play digital games. Here, the emphasis that digital sports games place on stamina and fitness thus repeats a current cultural concern with a body politic in the digital age. These games thus simultaneously evoke the bodily ideal of the fit male body and its inherent fragility in an age of neoliberal weight management and of widespread slouching.

Beyond fatigue and stamina, physicality is most obviously simulated in the control over a given player's body on the field at any given moment of a game. The way players are controlled, then, most powerfully contributes to the simulation of corporeality in the games at hand. Game Studies scholars generally agree that there are at least two kinds of controlling in-game/on-screen bodies in digital games: symbolically and iconically. Said distinction refers to the relationship between the motion performed on the controlling device and the one reacting to it in the game (cf. Baerg, "Fight Night" 339). The typical example of a symbolic transformation is that of shooting or passing, in which pressing a specific button generates the complex movement of shooting or passing a ball through digital space. The complex muscular motion a soccer or American football player has to perform in order to shoot or throw is being visualized in its complexity, but it is only symbolically brought about by pressing a button on the control pad.

Some of the tricks and most of the movements in space, however, follow an iconic logic of translating movement via the interface into the digitalized world of the game.

The one-on-one situation is where in-game physicality really comes to the fore: body contact among players in the game, sliding tackles (soccer), full-body tackles (American football), and the performance of physically demanding tricks when in possession of the ball most powerfully exemplify the complexity of the body in digital sports games. In their recent installments the producers and programmers of *PES* and *MADDEN* have developed and marketed a number of strategies and options to increase the level of excitement especially with regard to these intense one-on-one situations. In the context of digital soccer and American football, three of these strategies appear especially meaningful with regard to the production of physicality I examine here: firstly, the tackling options for players not in control of the ball, secondly, the trick, shield, or spin options for players in control of the ball, and thirdly, the simulation of instant replays after harsh fouls and the subsequent writhing in pain of the potentially injured player. Taken together, all of these actions underscore the complexity of physicality and bring cultural assumptions regarding sporting and non-sporting bodies to the cultural fore, especially in the way that they simultaneously emphasize physical fitness and physical violability in the games.

It is thus not surprising that digital sports games have represented injuries and pain with an increasing attention to detail, often by simulating the broadcasting strategy of instant replays and/or through filmic intermissions in cut-scenes. Instant replays in sports gaming as well as in televised sports narratively structure the event at hand. Arguably, the broadcasting director's decisions of which scene demands or deserves instant replays could be regarded as his or her central concern for the most powerful tool to impact how the television audience perceives a televised sports event; accordingly, the same holds true for the programmers and producers of digital sports games.

The filmic sequences of an in-game player writhing on the ground simulates the real-life sports practice of players performing pain in order to increase the likelihood of referees to implement draconic measures against the offender, as holds more immediately true for soccer and less commonly in American football. Furthermore, the sequences of players in pain keep the gamer in suspense as to whether or not the player can continue playing or needs to be substituted as a result of an injury. If the player was mildly injured, he can still continue to play, even though his physical abilities are noticeably impeded and the sequence of a subsequent substitution of the player will show him limp off the field, his face contorted with pain.

Much in line with the logics of fatigue, I read the noteworthy visual attention to injuries as serving two rather different purposes: firstly and superficially, these cut-scenes serve the purpose of creating and recreating the appearance and appeal of the live sports broadcast audiences are familiar with;[7] secondly, however, I believe that something else is at stake when we move those bodies swiftly across the pitch and then they get stopped rigorously and painfully by opposing defenders. Here, I think, the body emerges as something problematic, a site of vulnerability, and it enters a meaningful relationship with the body of the gamer on the other side of the interface. After all, the conventionalized split between the bodies across the interface has recently emerged as an issue in cultural discourses of our digital age. We find that split hardly anywhere more pronounced than between the athletic, sporting body of the digital sport game and the presumably slouching, passive body of the gamer. The tropes of the dysfunctional and misshaped gaming body of the digital age have recently entered and dominated discourses about young people (and the generation of digital natives) in the United States and Western Europe, especially in the context of an alleged decline in real-life athletic abilities (see for example Lindemann).

Thus, the trope of the male injured body, of male bodies in pain, in digital sports games not only evokes a long tradition in US cultural production and especially as part of the Hollywood imaginary; it furthermore condenses the current incitement to discourse of the "gaming body" onto the digital field in the figure of the injured, pained, and exhausted male body. Corpo-realities are at stake here, in the interface and the transition into what some consider a 'gamified' age: in an almost paradoxical manner, these young, athletic, male bodies on the screen make our current anxieties vis-à-vis a generation of "slouching bodies" visible —on any given Sunday, in any given season, on any given field.

---

[7] It appears that it is during these situations that the game's demands materialize in the gamers' bodies in that the virtual reality of a tight space and looming one-on-one results in a physical tenseness, sometimes a cringe, on the gamers' side. Recent psychophysiological research, which transcends the tiring debate concerning the relationship between video gaming and adolescent violence, also seems to indicate that the virtual pressure on a player in a game could very possibly sometimes be displaced into or shared by the gamers' bodies (Ravaja et al. 344–46; Shinkle). Even though the gamers do not find themselves confronted with the physical stress and challenges of a real-life soccer game, then, there is a chance that they still experience a measurable level of physical stress in the act of controlling the on-screen bodies on the field.

Works Cited

Baerg, Andrew. "Fight Night Round 2: Mediating the Body and Digital Boxing." *Sociology of Sport Journal*, vol. 24, no. 5, 2007, pp. 325–45.
Baerg, Andrew. "It's in the Game: The History of Sports Video Games." *American History through American Sports: From Colonial Lacrosse to Extreme Sports*, edited by Danielle Sarver Coombs and Bob Batchelor, vol. 2, Praeger, 2013, pp. 75–90.
Baerg, Andrew. "It's Game Time: Speed, Acceleration, and the Digital Sports Game." *Temporalités*, vol. 25, 2017, https://journals.openedition.org/temporalites/3655. Accessed 15 Jan. 2019.
Brians, Ella. "The 'Virtual' Body and the Strange Persistence of the Flesh: Deleuze, Cyberspace and the Posthuman." *Deleuze and the Body*, edited by Laura Guillaume and Joe Hughes, Edinburgh UP, 2011, pp. 117–43.
Buehler, Brendan. "White-Collar Play: Reassessing Managerial Sports Games." *Velvet Light Trap*, vol. 81, 2018, pp. 4–17.
Chaplin, Heather. "Is That Just Some Game: No, It's a Cultural Artifact." *The New York Times*, 12 March 2007, p. E7.
Denson, Shane, and Andreas Sudmann. "Digital Seriality: On the Aesthetics and Practice of Digital Games." *Media of Serial Narrative*, edited by Frank Kelleter, Ohio State UP, 2017, pp. 261–83.
Bryce, Jo, and Jason Rutter. *Understanding Digital Games*. Sage, 2006
Davidson, Drew. *Well Played 2.0: Video Games, Value, and Meaning*. ETC Press, 2010.
DeCastell, Suzanne, and Jennifer Jenson. *Worlds in Play: International Perspectives on Digital Games Research*. Peter Lang, 2007.
Dyer-Witherford, Nick, and Greig Peuter. *Games of Empire: Global Capitalism and Video Games*. U of Minnesota P, 2009.
"EA Sports FIFA Is the World's Game." *Businesswire.com*, 5 Sep. 2018, www.businesswire.com/news/home/20180905005646/en. Accessed 15 Jan. 2019.
"Fans Are Going Mad for Madden." Businesswire.com, 13 Aug. 2018. https://www.businesswire.com/news/home/20180813005649/en. Accessed 15 Jan. 2019.
Garrelts, Nate. *Digital Gameplay: Essays on the Nexus of Game and Gamer*. McFarland, 2005.
Garrelts, Nate. "Introduction: Negotiating the Digital Game/Gamer Intersection." Garrelts, pp. 1–19.
www.kickoff2.com. Accessed 15 Jan. 2019.
King, Lucien. *Game On: The History and Culture of Video Games*. Laurence King, 2008.
Kline, Stephen, Nick Dyer-Witherford, and Greig Peuter. *Digital Play: The Interaction of Technology, Culture, and Marketing*. McGill-Queens UP, 2003.
Lindemann, Thomas. "Videospiele machen schlau—und fett." *Die Welt*, 20 Aug. 2008, www.welt.de/wirtschaft/webwelt/article2325745/Videospiele-machen-schlau-und-fett.html. Accessed 15 Jan. 2019.
Lüthe, Martin. "(Re-)producing the Body: Motion Capture and the Meaning of Physicality in Digital Soccer Games." *Build 'em Up—Shoot 'em Down: Körperlichkeit in digitalen Spielen*, edited by Peter Just and Rudolf Inderst, Verlag Werner Hülsbusch, 2013, pp. 25–41.
Leonard, David J. "To the White Extreme: Conquering Athletic Space, White Manhood, and Racing Virtual Reality." Garrelts, pp. 110–28.

Morgan, Kathryn Pauly. "Foucault, Ugly Ducklings, and Technoswans: Analyzing Fat Hatred, Weight-loss Surgery, and Compulsory Biomedicalized Aesthetics in America." *International Journal of Feminist Approaches to Bioethics*, vol. 4, no. 1, 2011, pp. 188–220.

PES Community. twitter.com/PESCommunityit/status/1031131458910474240. Accessed 15 Jan. 2019.

Pursell, Carroll. *From Playgrounds to Playstation: The Interaction of Technology and Play.* Johns Hopkins UP, 2015.

Ravaja, Niklas, et al. "Phasic Emotional Reactions to Video Game Events: A Psychophysiological Investigation." *Media Psychology*, vol. 8, 2006, pp. 343–67.

Shinkle, Eugenie. "Corporealis Ergo Sum: Affective Response in Digital Games." Garrelts, pp. 21–35.

Valentine, Rebekah. "FIFA 18 sells over 24 million copies." *Gamesindustry.biz*, 5 Sep. 2018 www.gamesindustry.biz/articles/2018-09-05-fifa-18-sells-over-24-million-copies. Accessed 15 Jan. 2019.

Stefan Schubert
Narrative and Play in American Studies: Ludic Textuality in the Video Game *Alan Wake* and the TV Series *Westworld*

The study of US popular culture has long focused—mostly implicitly—on a particular symbolic form: narrative. Popular crime-fiction or science-fiction novels, movie blockbusters, big-budget television shows, comic books or graphic novels, and many other types of texts and media that make up popular culture, while diverse in their specific aesthetic and medial properties, share a fundamental focus on telling a story. In contrast, other symbolic forms, understood as ways of meaning-making and making sense of experience, have often been sidelined in popular-culture studies, and in American Studies as well. I contend, however, that the study of US-American popular culture should more strongly recognize and be opened up to another symbolic form in particular: play. Methodologically, this focus on symbolic forms shifts attention away from the medium of (diverse) texts. Consequently, a video game may be understood, in terms of its symbolic forms, as predominantly play yet including many narrative elements as well. Likewise, there are texts and media traditionally understood as (only) narrative that also exhibit ludic aspects. Such a fusion of narrative and play, in fact, is most visible in contemporary US popular culture (roughly from the late 1990s onward), as I will show.

Aligning myself with the call to recognize and make use of the general affinity between the methods of American Studies and the subject of video games that Sascha Pöhlmann has outlined in the introduction of this volume, I want to take a conceptual step back to suggest that there is an even larger link connecting these two areas of inquiry, the one between narrative and play. More specifically, I suggest that applying the methods of American Studies to video games also allows for an investigation of the interplay of narrative and play. In turn, I argue that such an investigation makes visible a particularly prominent trend in contemporary US popular culture to engage in what one could call 'ludic textuality,'[1] a fusion of play and narrative that has achieved particular popularity and cultural salience in recent years. While this is a fusion of forms most readily visi-

---

[1] This conception follows research conducted as part of my dissertation on 'narrative instability,' in which I understand the infusion of play into narrative as one of the ways in which the narrations of contemporary US popular-culture texts become destabilized (cf. Schubert).

ble in video games, it is actually a trend that works across media and extends to texts one would not usually consider a 'game,' such as a film like *Inception* (2010), a TV show like *Westworld* (2016-), or a novel like Mark Z. Danielewski's *House of Leaves* (2000).

In the following, I will thus first outline a few theoretical and methodological considerations on the intermingling of narrative and play, understood as symbolic forms. Subsequently, I will specify these links by examining how contemporary popular culture interweaves these elements, arguing to understand both the video game *Alan Wake* (2010) and the TV series *Westworld* as 'narratively liminal' texts that exhibit ludic textuality. I will conclude with some implications for how American Studies could conceptualize and think about play and narrative given this contemporary dominant in popular culture.

Video Games and Ludic Textuality: Narrative and Play

I suggest we should understand narrative and play as symbolic forms that cannot necessarily be neatly separated from each other.[2] Lev Manovich prominently uses the term 'symbolic form' in his call to consider database as a different form than narrative, as a "new way to structure our experience of ourselves and of the world" (81). Manovich traces this use to Erwin Panofsky's discussion of perspective as a symbolic form, which in turn builds on Ernst Cassirer's theories, as Panofsky advocates that perspective "may even be characterized as (to extend Ernst Cassirer's felicitous term to the history of art) one of those 'symbolic forms' in which 'spiritual meaning is attached to a concrete, material sign and intrinsically given to this sign'" (40–41). Slightly moving away from Cassirer's philosophy of symbolic forms and instead embracing Manovich's rather loose use of the term (at times used interchangeably with 'cultural form'), I understand symbolic forms as distinct ways of meaning-making, of "structuring" and making sense of "our experience" (Manovich 81). These different forms, consequently, also entail different pleasures, aesthetics, affordances, and user experiences, which can be studied as elements that characterize a symbolic form.

---

2 Many of the following ideas and theoretical considerations have been formed during discussions and collaborations as part of the research network "Narrative Liminality and/in the Formation of American Modernities" (www.narrative-liminality.de), funded by the German Research Foundation.

Manovich initially replicates the humanities' predominant focus on the symbolic form of narrative when he claims that "narrative [is] the key form of cultural expression of the modern age" and that narrative has "traditionally dominated human culture" (80), but then he moves on to say that database has now emerged as a new, ubiquitous form. In order to 'see' and recognize this, one first needs to be aware of narrative as another such form, not just as *the* (universal or standard) form of meaning-making. Somewhat similarly, early 'ludological' scholarship in the field of game studies constructed narrative as an antagonist from which video-game scholarship needed to separate and emancipate itself, where a theoretical interest in studying narratives in video games was suspected of finding narratives even where there are none (cf., e.g., Eskelinen). Partly, this over-emphasis on narrative even on the part of those who seek to distance themselves from it is a result of the 'narrative turn' in much of the humanities and beyond (cf. Punday 1–20), prompting disciplines like history, political science, or psychology to productively consider questions of narrativization and the narrative constructedness of experiences (Czarniawska 2–3). Yet a flip-side of that innovative focus, and of the at times "imperialist tendencies" of literary studies (Pöhlmann 5), has indeed been an often implicit tendency threatening to identify all kinds of texts or other phenomena as (only) narrative. While I want to sideline this larger 'ideological' discussion in this article,[3] I deem it crucial to recognize the fact that other symbolic forms, other ways of ordering meaning and experience beyond narrative, do exist, among them play, data, ritual, the lyrical, performance, spectacle, and a host of others.[4]

Focusing particularly on play and narrative as connected yet distinguishable symbolic forms necessitates an exploration of how they process meanings and structure experiences in different ways. Such an endeavor naturally entails certain generalizations, yet particularly for the study of narrative, it seems productive to consider narrative not as a 'given,' as a (culturally) 'unmarked' category but as 'marked' as well—as not necessarily a 'neutral' way of processing information but as one that comes with certain biases or preconceptions. Similar to other

---

[3] In terms of the ludology-narratology debate, Ian Bogost offers a particularly compelling analysis of the underlying formalist questions that characterize both approaches. In contrast, my interest does not concern the question of what video games are (play *or* narrative?) but, rather, the more functionalist question of what this means, of how exactly video games might work as fusions of play and narrative, and what that can tell us about US culture.

[4] This is not, of course, an exhaustive list, but many of these forms have been studied as part of the work in the aforementioned research network on "Narrative Liminality." In previous scholarship, these have rarely been considered or called 'symbolic forms' but have still been examined along similar lines, for instance in Diane Taylor's discussion of ritual.

marked/unmarked pairs, this status of narrative becomes (more) visible in comparison and in contrast to other symbolic forms. Accordingly, and in no way claiming exhaustiveness, I would name as characteristics of narrative, in particular, a certain coherence, order, and causality of the depicted events (cf. Nünning and Nünning 66), a focus on 'linearity' in representing these events,[5] and a drive toward closure and finality. This, however, would be a kind of 'prototypical' narrative, when in actuality many narratives violate some of these principles, for instance by foregoing closure or complicating an ordered or coherent retelling of the events.[6] The fact that narrative is so amenable to variation and modification speaks to its pull as a symbolic form, and texts that test the limits of narrative do not refute these more general characteristics but are evidence that they exist in the first place. Accordingly, within the methodological framework I outline here, whenever a specific text strays from these narrative principles, it can be considered to abandon the foothold of narrative as a symbolic form and to become narratively liminal.

In contrast, I see play—in an equally generalized manner—as characterized by interactivity, agency, nonlinearity, and iteration (among others): games have to be actively (and often physically) interacted with in order to 'work' (cf. Aarseth 1–2), an interactivity that also implies familiarity with the rules of a game, a central focus of many ludological takes on video games (cf. Aarseth; Juul; Frasca).[7] Play provides options and decisions to players between which they can choose, fueling the agency players might feel they have (cf. Murray 126–53). These

---

[5] However, with 'linearity,' I do not mean to refer to chronological narration. Narratives can, of course, be told achronologically, with analepses and prolepses. Instead, narrative can be understood as linear in the sense that *non*linearity denotes that there "is not simply one fixed sequence of letters, words, and sentences but [that] the words or sequence of words may differ from reading to reading because of the shape, conventions, or mechanisms of the text" (Aarseth 41). Nonlinearity thus entails the "ability to vary, to produce different courses" (Aarseth 41–42), which is more typical of play than it is of narrative. For example, in the video game *Heavy Rain* (2010), the choices the players make for the four protagonists can lead to vastly different narrative outcomes, including the aspect whether each of them survives or dies. When players finish the game, they will have witnessed one particular "sequence" or "course" of the narrative events, in Aarseth's terms, yet if they play again and make different choices, their gaming experience can "produce different courses." In a 'traditional,' linear novel, nonlinearity in this sense usually does not exist—there are, however, ways to imitate this ludic nonlinearity and to engage in a similar aesthetic, which I will discuss below.
[6] This general tendency is also one of the principal ways in which such narratives become, in my terminology, narratively unstable (cf. Schubert).
[7] Additionally, next to an engagement with the game, interactivity also entails a social component, most notably in cooperative or online games that depend on other players, which in turn raises competitiveness as an element of many instances of play.

choices, in turn, can lead to different experiences and outcomes, and this constitutes the nonlinearity of games. Finally, because of this, many games encourage repeated playthroughs or repetitions of individual sequences, establishing the iterative nature of play. These elements also combine to create (narrative) openness rather than closure. As with narrative, not all instances of play are characterized by all of these aspects equally, which speaks to an understanding of play (and other forms) as gradual rather than absolute. Particular acts of playing, be they a game of chess, playing hide and seek, or the video game *Grand Theft Auto V* (2013), might offer different amounts of agency and choice to their players, they might entail very different ways of interacting with them, or they might encourage repeated engagements in pronounced ways or not at all. Consequently, these differences would make them more or less ludic in this fluid understanding.

Significantly, unlike Manovich's oft-quoted dictum that "database and narrative are natural 'enemies'" (85) or some ludologists' insistence that play and narrative are fundamentally different, I do not understand narrative and play as strictly separated. Instead, they differ in their characteristics as symbolic forms, but more importantly, they frequently intermingle, since they share a rather symbiotic relationship, as Henry Jenkins seminally proposed in "Game Design as Narrative Architecture." Actual pop-culture texts will frequently exhibit characteristics of multiple symbolic forms, overall constituting their liminality with regard to any of them. While I understand video games as predominantly a combination of play and narrative (whereas other scholars might emphasize other forms), individual games or even larger genres of games can differ significantly in the emphasis they lay on these particular elements. While a game like *Pong* (1972) or *Tetris* (1984) consists almost exclusively of ludic elements and virtually no narrative ones, a so-called 'walking simulator' like *Dear Esther* (2012), while a video game in terms of medium, exhibits a very low number of ludic aspects and relies almost entirely on narrative for how it structures meaning and experience. Most video games, however, are located somewhere in the middle of this spectrum from narrative to play, and popular games like the *Grand Theft Auto*, *Assassin's Creed*, or *Call of Duty* series want to both be played/interacted with and tell some kind of story.

In these games, then, narrative and ludic elements coexist: individual ludic elements, like the player having to make a choice, are frequently connected to narrative aspects (and vice versa), for instance by narratively motivating that choice (cf. also Manovich 83). Additionally, many of the seemingly contradictory elements of the two forms can be effectively combined in order to create a pleasurable text: narrative's drive towards closure, for example, will tend to compel players of a choice-heavy game like *Heavy Rain* or *Detroit: Become Human*

(2018) to bring the story to a close, in turn increasing their investment in the choices they can make to affect that ending, as these games offer multiple possible outcomes as part of their nonlinearity, which does not by itself entail closure.

While understanding video games in this way is not necessarily a very novel idea, I suggest to consider other pop-culture media/texts besides video games as such fusions of narrative and play as well—for instance so-called gamebooks (choose-your-own-adventure stories), 'twist' or 'mindgame' films (cf. Elsaesser), novels like *House of Leaves* or Salvador Plascencia's *People of Paper* (2005), or TV shows including *Lost* (2004–2010), *Westworld*, or *Dark* (2017-). I realize that proposing such a vast array of media and text types as potentially ludic invites disagreement, but importantly, with this characterization, I do not intend to make any ontological claims: *House of Leaves*, for instance, is still a novel and not a game like *Heavy Rain*, yet I am interested in how it can still be characterized as ludic or playful. Instead of making an ontological claim, I suggest that such texts entail pleasures, make use of aesthetics, suggest certain affordances (cf. Levine 6), or provide an overall user experience that are associated more with play than with narrative. This does not have to extend to all of the characteristics I mentioned above, depending on how (more or less) ludic such a text might be understood. For instance, in *House of Leaves*, the numerous footnotes(-within-footnotes) frequently refer to a later footnote or a later chapter, which readers can—but do not have to—skip to, and once there, they can equally decide if they want to return to the original footnote or continue reading the later chapter. These two generalized decisions thus also create two different experiences of the text, and while, looking at the 'materiality' of the novel compared to that of a video game like *Heavy Rain*, this is not exactly the same as in the game, the pleasures this formal characteristic offers to readers are very similar. It mimics interactivity by providing readers with agency, since a meaningful choice in the text has to be made.[8] 'Meaningful,' in this context, relates back to how this

---

[8] This perspective also helps specify my understanding of interactivity, which complicates Aarseth's notion of ergodic texts mentioned above. On the one hand, interactivity is not a binary category for me, and instead, certain texts, activities, or artifacts can be more or less interactive—arguably, for instance, *Tetris* is less interactive than *Minecraft* (2011) because of both the quantity of potentials to interact with the game and the quality, the impact that such interactions have on it. On the other hand, such interactivity does not only extend to the physical realm—a choice one can make in a game might be difficult on a physical level, because of the gameplay (e.g. by necessitating a complicated sequence of buttons), but it also usually includes a mental effort, to different degrees. Choosing between dialogue options in *Heavy Rain* or footnotes in *House of Leaves* is not very interactive on a physical level, but it can be a challenging and demanding decision narratively, taking into account the effects this choice may have on

choice is narrativized—it is one that requires thinking within the storyworld. *House of Leaves* thus affords being read nonlinearly, affecting the sequence of the narrated events as they are experienced by a reader, similarly to player choices in the narrative of *Heavy Rain*. Both texts thus suggest pleasure in the combination of ludic (nonlinear choices) and narrative (eventual closure) elements. Overall, probing into what these diverse media and texts share can help elucidate what the borderlands of narrative and play, i.e., what ludic textuality looks like.

Narrative and Play in Contemporary Popular Culture: *Alan Wake* and *Westworld*

Next to historical examples demonstrating the fusion of narrative and play in US culture, I contend that ludic textuality plays an especially prominent role in contemporary popular culture, where it works to engender mainstream popularity through particular textual pleasures. This understanding relates to and accentuates other scholarly takes on recent popular culture, which characterize the contemporary period, for instance, as a time of convergence culture (cf. Jenkins, *Convergence*), of widespread remediation and transmediality (cf. Bolter and Grusin; Thon), or of (narrative) complexity (cf. Mittell; Kiss and Willemsen). While these paradigms frequently work together, they rarely acknowledge one aspect that simultaneously drives the movements towards convergence, transmediality, and complexity: the fusion of narrative and play, which brings together different media in narratively more 'complex' ways. Overall, while these different studies tend to approach such connections along media lines, I instead propose to understand them as a productive synthesis of symbolic forms.

However, recognizing such media differences, the development towards ludic textuality is evident in two larger areas: video games, as fundamentally ludic media, remediate elements of novels, films, and TV series for how they engage in narration. In turn, these other, traditionally more narrative media are increasingly influenced by video-game aesthetics, inserting ludic elements into the way they tell their stories. Thinking strictly on the level of symbolic forms, play becomes more narrative, and narrative becomes more playful. Such ludic textuality in contemporary US popular culture has achieved considerable main-

---

the experience of the text. The more potentially impactful this effect is, the more nonlinear the text can be, and the more agency can be given to players/readers, highlighting how closely interactivity, nonlinearity, and agency are connected to each other.

stream popularity—forming part of what some have called a 'ludification' (cf. Frissen et al.)—which can be partly explained by the pleasures that the combination of narrative and ludic elements affords. For instance, the decisions and choices one can make in a video game are a significant source of pleasure in themselves, yet they become more meaningful if they are narrativized, and the feeling of agency they can create largely depends on the success of convincing players that their choices have a narrative impact as well. Likewise, a movie that places particular importance on an unforeseen narrative event—such as a twist film—can increase its ludic appeal if it encourages and narratively rewards rewatching specific scenes closely with additional hints toward a twist ending, aesthetically mirroring the iterative experience of play. I will further elucidate the contemporary salience of ludic textuality through two brief exemplary readings, of the video game *Alan Wake* and the TV series *Westworld*.

Alan Wake

Released in 2010, *Alan Wake* casts players in the role of the eponymous Alan, a best-selling crime and horror writer who has recently been suffering from writer's block and, as a potential remedy, goes on vacation to a town called Bright Falls. The game's basic narrative premise finds Alan trapped inside his own story, a story he cannot remember writing but from which he constantly finds manuscript pages detailing events that are still about to happen. He also repeatedly witnesses somebody on TV screens that looks exactly like him and is talking to himself, and he is frequently addressed by another writer called Thomas Zane, somehow communicating with Alan without a physical form and suggesting how he can manipulate the world by 'writing' himself and a variety of objects into scenes.

Alan Wake is an action/adventure game in which players control Alan throughout Bright Falls and shoot supernatural enemies conjured by the Dark Presence haunting the small town. In terms of its medium, *Alan Wake* is clearly a video game (released for Xbox 360 and in 2012 for PCs), and its most fundamental elements all take a ludic form: players have to navigate the digital space, choose where to go and what to interact with, pick up useful items along the way, use a flashlight and various weapons to defend Alan against the Dark Presence, solve a few environmental puzzles to advance to the next area, and so on. Many of these choices, however, are explicitly narrativized: trying to find the optional manuscript pages from Alan's novel, for instance, does not help players to defeat the game's enemies or to advance through the levels. Instead, it offers a narrative reward, as Alan reads out the individual pages, which flesh out the game's narrative background or offer hints towards solving its narrative mysteries.

Overall, on the spectrum of ludic textuality, I would classify *Alan Wake* as more narrative than play, an emphasis that, curiously, manifests itself through an awareness of media (and not symbolic forms) in the game itself. While the game generally displays a high degree of textual self-awareness toward its own storytelling capabilities, it renders this through references to other media, specifically traditionally narrative ones. Its more intricate narrative setup does not just feature such particular elements but also a concern with narrative (and text) itself. The manuscript pages, for instance, point to the game players are experiencing as a fictional artifact as well, while some specific pages display the metatextual link between the game and the pages of this novel, foreshadowing events that are still about to happen or that are happening right in the moment of reading the page. This self-awareness of the game trying to tell a story is thus processed through the narrative medium of the novel. In comparison, at least on a surface level, there are almost no explicit references to *Alan Wake* being a game. Instead, there are myriad examples of characters referring to what they experience as a story, to Alan talking about how this mirrors a novel, to parallels between the events players witness and a TV show that Alan had been writing years earlier, etc. For all of the game's overall self-awareness, however, there are no overt references to Alan being trapped inside a video game. Instead, within *Alan Wake*'s storyworld, an awareness of the game's own narrativity and textuality appears through explicit references to other media. The game itself thus is torn between the symbolic forms of narrative and play, a dialectic that it negotiates through media differences within its own storyworld.

For instance, in regard to television, these aspects come together especially well in scenes when the Alan players control sees the other Alan, who is writing in the cabin, through a television set. These TV sets are spread throughout the game, but in each occurrence they present a distinct metaleptic narrative structure. In the first such scene, as players approach a TV inside a gas station, it switches on and shows Alan sitting in a cabin, talking to himself about the need to continue writing the story of the Alan controlled by players. The TV switches off again, and Alan's voice-over says: "I don't believe this. It'd been me on the TV, talking crazy. Was I losing my mind?" Cabin Alan, writing the novel that Player Alan is featured in, is on a higher level of narration, yet through the TV, players are able to see and witness that higher level from Player Alan's hypodiegetic level—usually a narrative impossibility, which thus pinpoints the game's pervasive use of metalepses and highlights its own narrativity. Moreover, the scene points to the general difficulty of positioning Alan's voice-over narration. Usually, it is suggested that the voice-over is a representation of Alan's current thoughts (part of his internal focalization), but the setup in this scene also hints at the possibility of the voice-over actually being part of the narrator's passages in the novel Alan is writing in the cabin. This blurring is evident in the tense shift in the quote, which begins with what could be considered Alan's current thoughts in present tense ("I don't believe this") but then goes over to the past tense typical of narration ("Was I losing my mind?").

Importantly, the television set that links these two narrative levels also references the game's general awareness of other media and its own medialization and narrativity. The narrative 'conflict' between the different Alans is thus presented as a struggle between what is considered 'old' and 'new' media.[9] The game itself is also narratively structured with storytelling devices from a TV show, as it is separated into six individual chapters (similar to TV episodes), each of which ends with a cliffhanger and an outro song and begins with a "Previously, on Alan Wake" segment, a storytelling device that—in a video game that, for the most part, was not released episodically—mirrors an aesthetic of seriality nowadays known especially from Netflix's practice of releasing all episodes of a TV show's season at once.

Alan Wake, then, does not only feature relatively typical elements of trying to inject narrative into play, such as narratively motivated choices, settings, and characters, but it also is an example of a video game, a form of play, that displays an explicit and metatextual interest in storytelling. Rather than develop this interest along the narrative peculiarities of video games, it instead renders them through references to other media. In turn, however, this also explains why *Alan Wake* is relatively linear and thus, on many accounts, more aligned with narrative than play: the game mimics a (traditionally linear) television show, it is reluctant to recognize its own status as a game, and, perhaps most importantly, it suggests that what players experience is part of a novel Alan has written—an Alan whom players, however, do not control, severely reducing their agency over the unfolding narrative. Specifically, the few choices in optional exploration that the game does include have no effect on the overall narrative outcome. Hence, *Alan Wake*'s resemblance to the two traditionally linear narrative media of the novel and television holds back the game's ludic aspects, offering relatively little agency and nonlinearity and ultimately suggesting pleasure rather through the disentangling of a complex and mysterious story than via its (relatively basic and repetitive) gameplay. This penchant ultimately speaks

---

9 Additionally, players looking at their avatar through a TV or a computer screen adds yet another metatextual level to these scenes, alluding to a breaking of the fourth wall (cf. Gonzales).

to the game's own unease as a ludic text, metatextually transferring Alan's ontological and epistemological anxieties (cf. Fuchs) to the game itself.

Westworld

I propose using a similar approach for studying ludic textuality in media that are not obviously 'games'—or play—as well, and to that extent, the TV show *Westworld* may serve as an example. The science-fiction series is set in an undisclosed futuristic time, in which a theme park called Westworld offers a kind of alternate reality in a Western setting, replete with android 'hosts' catering to human visitors. In terms of medium, *Westworld* is obviously a TV show (inspired by the 1973 film of the same name), featuring a serialized narrative over two seasons (at the time of this writing) with ten episodes each.[10] However, the form in which it makes sense of experience, and overall the cultural work it does, can be better grasped as an instance of ludic textuality, a story whose telling is characterized by a number of 'playful' elements.

On the one hand, the show makes a number of references directly to video games as a medium (rather than to play as a symbolic form), particularly in reference to the depiction of the Westworld theme park. For instance, numerous characters, and particularly the Man in Black, repeatedly describe visiting and experiencing the park and the search for the maze as a "game" whose "deeper level" needs to be found (e. g. S1E1, S1E2, S1E4, S1E8, S1E9). This experience is also similar to that of controlling an avatar in a video game, an aspect highlighted when William is shown to be able to choose his wardrobe before entering Westworld (S1E2), mirroring character-creation screens in many role-playing video games. Other such smaller elements include references to difficulty settings and "level[s]" by Logan (S1E1, S1E5), (side) quests as found in many games (S1E2), references to an "Easter egg," a gimmick hidden in video games (S1E4), or loot found off the corpses of bandits (S1E4). Larger gaming and playing principles are also implied, such as multiple evocations of rules that structure the Westworld park (S1E5, S1E9, S1E10) and the central competitiveness of many video games, which the Man in Black evokes in his philosophy that "winning doesn't mean anything unless someone else loses" as part of his zero-sum attitude to experiencing Westworld (S1E1).

On the other hand, I suggest that beyond these mere references to video games, there are aspects of the show's narration that mirror forms of play,

---

10 My focus here is on the show's first season, aired in 2016.

which is most notable in its iterative narrative structure. This is generally evident in a number of references to loops and reboots throughout the series (cf. Kanzler 58–64), for example in the multiple times that the daily routine of Dolores, one of the park's androids, is shown: waking up, leaving the house, and riding to the nearby town of Sweetwater. The first season depicts the image of Dolores dropping a can of milk on the streets of Sweetwater multiple times, establishing that depending on who picks up the can (Dolores, another host called Teddy, or a human guest), the rest of Dolores's routine will differ. Accordingly, the repetitive nature of her daily cycle includes potentials for agency, and for diverging paths, that establish a nonlinearity typical of play. While this nonlinearity exists only within the storyworld (i.e. for the characters), it thus leads to an iterative narrative structure for the viewers. Another example of a ludic kind of narration invokes the video-game mechanic of 'quickloading' and 'quicksaving': Dolores's ability to remember her memories very clearly and to tap into their 'reality' is discursively presented according to a similar logic as the ability to save in a video game, attempt a difficult passage, fail, and reload in order to try again. When Dolores is shot by a person yelling at her to "[g]et back here," the camera shows her holding her hands over the bleeding wound (S1E3). Then, the same person is heard yelling again, and Dolores's wound is suddenly gone. This time, with the knowledge of what is about to happen, she can react quickly and runs away. The scene thus is presented as if Dolores pushed the 'quickload' button in order to replay the same sequence and act in a different way. Overall, these more subtle similarities to play add to the more overt references to video games and thus characterize *Westworld* as an example of how contemporary popular culture is increasingly 'ludified.'

In addition to this focus on iteration and agency,[11] *Westworld* also frequently evokes the trope of the maze as an enigma that both Dolores and the Man in Black pursue (cf. Kanzler 64–68). Using the maze as a way of metaphorizing what it is that both some hosts and most guests in the park seek accentuates elements of play involved in interpretation, an interaction and 'playing' with meanings in the form of a narrative puzzle that has to (and can be) 'solved.' On a metatextual level, the show thus suggests to take pleasure in its narrative

---

[11] On a different, purely thematic level, how Dolores thinks about agency also mirrors the way choices—as part of interactivity, nonlinearity, and agency—are often depicted in video games. Initially, Dolores believes that "[t]here's a path for everyone" (S1E1), a particular phrasing repeated multiple times, yet later she wonders "if in every moment, there aren't many paths. Choices, hanging in the air like ghosts" (S1E5). This idea of multiple choices for specific decisions is referenced via the video-game logic of branching paths, whereas the existence of only one 'path' implies linearity and little potential for agency.

by understanding it, partly, as a form of play, at least in the sense of a narrative 'puzzle' or 'maze' to be solved. In turn, the show's reception demonstrates that this suggested pleasure in the fusion of narrative and play seems to have resonated, since *Westworld*'s openly insinuated mysteries were prominently discussed week by week in online articles, blog entries, forums, and on social media. Viewers predicted some of the narrative revelations by looking closely at specific scenes, rewatching episodes, and contextualizing later episodes with previous ones, all of which mirrors practices that aesthetically resemble the interactive and iterative nature of playing.[12] Part of the metatextual parallels *Westworld* draws between the visitors of the park, its hosts, and viewers of the show thus also entails engaging the narrative that it tells as a form of play or a kind of game, self-consciously positioning itself between the aesthetics of traditional stories and newer media like video games. Whereas *Alan Wake*'s narrative, though sophisticated in its telling, becomes atypically linear for a video game because of its draw to media like the novel and television, *Westworld* infuses its storytelling with ludic elements. It does not, of course, offer the same kind of interactive potential that a video game might, but in its narrative, it affords pleasures for how to actively engage with the text that aesthetically mirror activities inherent in acts of play.[13]

Taken together, these brief glimpses of analysis point to how two ostensibly very different texts—in terms of medium, genre, themes, etc.—share elements of

---

[12] As just one such example, a thread on the website Reddit correctly speculates on a number of larger narrative revelations in the show (OthoHasTheHandbook). It was posted on October 25, 2016, after only the first four episodes of the show had been broadcast. Simultaneously, there were also, of course, other ideas and fan 'theories' that later turned out to be incorrect, so the existence of these more accurate predictions does not imply that everybody already knew about *Westworld*'s later twists by the fourth episode. Yet more importantly than whether these speculations turned out to be accurate or not, they point to the pleasure that actively 'investigating' and working with the text's formal aspects can entail, similar to an enjoyment of the "operational aesthetics" in the role of "amateur narratologists" that Jason Mittell describes for complex television (51–52). As the Reddit user remarks at the beginning of their post: "It's just fun to speculate, even if I'm completely off the mark" (OthoHasTheHandbook). Overall, by inviting such a form of reception and encouraging active interpretation through narrative openness, *Westworld* offers similar pleasures and tries to mirror the iterative and (interpretively) interactive nature of play.

[13] This fusion of narrative and play seems to have been less successful in the second season of the show, where multiple timelines blend seamlessly into each other. This also mirrors the non-linearity of play—or, for instance, skipping back and forth between multiple pages in a novel because of footnotes leading one there—but, judging from the less enthusiastic reception of the season, does not seem to have offered enough coherence in the end, nor enough of a narrative payoff.

both narrative and play to different degrees. A video game like *Alan Wake*, which in terms of its medium might be assumed to thoroughly embrace play, demonstrates how narrative can structure and curtail the 'ludic-ness' of the medium. *Westworld*, in turn, evidences that more traditional narratives can be innovated and experimented with through ludic aesthetic principles, fostering agency and 'interactivity' on the audience's side by encouraging interpretative communities and highlighting narrative and interpretive openness (instead of closure) by mimicking games' nonlinearity, advocating multiple possible outcomes, and embracing ambivalence. Despite all their material and ontological differences, the way these texts want to be engaged with—the uses and experiences that they afford—and the pleasures that they offer share certain similarities. Accordingly, how audiences engage with many video games and certain contemporary pop-cultural texts can also similarly be described as understanding them partly as narrative, partly as ludic. Hence, while *Alan Wake* and *Westworld* make different use of ludic textuality, they both demonstrate how moments of fusion seem to foster particular pop-cultural pleasures. Additionally, both use their references to other symbolic forms as part of larger self-reflexive discussions of textuality and narrativity, displaying a metatextual awareness of the borderlands between narrative and play that they occupy.

Conclusion

Throughout this brief argument, I have attempted to demonstrate the methodological value in considering narrative and play as distinct yet related symbolic forms. In particular, I have argued how a fusion of narrative and play—which I call ludic textuality—is particularly characteristic of contemporary US popular culture, visible both in video games like *Alan Wake* exhibiting especially strong narrative ambitions and in traditionally narrative media like the TV show *Westworld* with its ludically infused narrative discourse. Taking a step back, these propositions have a number of implications for the study of video games in American Studies: first, the focus on ludic textuality helps contextualize other paradigms of studying contemporary US culture, such as convergence culture or narrative complexity. Second, it also sharpens our understanding of popular culture and popular pleasures in the contemporary US, where the fusion of narrative and play emerges as a driver of innovation and popularity (and commercial viability). Similar trends have existed in US culture before, but the prominence of ludic textuality in contemporary popular culture points to an embrace both of the narrative turn and of an ongoing 'ludification' of culture. Additionally, this focus illuminates some of the pleasures that video games and play in general afford, for instance a dialectic between narrative closure and nonlinearity or openness and an active engagement with the formal aspects of a text. In turn, some of these pleasures complicate monolithic understandings of popular culture, since they would traditionally only be associated with 'high' culture, such as the enjoyment of texts' operational aesthetics or of their pronounced metatextual dimension. Third, American Studies' interest in texts' cultural work and in their textual 'politics'[14] lends itself to deliberations of play as well, in turn helping to transcend more formalist engagements in some approaches from game studies.

Finally, fully embracing video games and, more generally, the symbolic form of play could entail potentially productive transformations for American Studies as well. The field is already interested in diverse kinds of media (and other types of texts), and studying video games transmedially accentuates their medial peculiarities. Something similar would be true for an embrace of play and narrative as symbolic forms, comparatively sharpening the contours of both. While the fusion of the two forms might be most visible in video games, from there, American Studies might recognize similar instances of narrative liminality in other media as well. This would both broaden the field's horizon beyond an implicit focus on narrative and facilitate a better understanding of narrative itself—in contrast to other symbolic forms—as well. In fact, a certain kind of indeterminacy implied in (narrative) liminality, and particularly the unstable looseness between play and narrative, connects with a healthy "skepticism toward its own object of research" inherent in the field of American Studies (Pöhlmann 14). Revisiting and extending our understanding of contemporary US (popular) culture by more thoroughly taking play into consideration thus promises to productively complicate and renegotiate understandings that have been implicit in the field's strong interest in narrative, an undertaking best started by analyzing video games but one that should also be applied beyond medial boundaries.

Works Cited

Aarseth, Espen. *Cybertext: Perspectives on Ergodic Literature*. Johns Hopkins UP, 1997.
Alan Wake. Remedy Entertainment, Microsoft, 2012.

---

14 Both are aspects that are highly relevant for *Alan Wake* and *Westworld* too, even though I could only vaguely allude to them in this paper. Specifically, it seems particularly interesting how these texts' politics are affected by their formal properties—their fusion of narrative and play—as well, be that in their metatextual deliberations or in the discourses surrounding gender, whiteness/blackness, and (narrative) power with which both the game and the TV series engage.

Bogost, Ian. "Videogames Are a Mess." *Ian Bogost*, 3 Sept. 2009, www.bogost.com/writing/videogames_are_a_mess.shtml. Accessed 15 Jan. 2019.
Bolter, Jay David, and Richard Grusin. *Remediation: Understanding New Media*. MIT P, 2003.
Cassirer, Ernst. *The Philosophy of Symbolic Forms: The Phenomenology of Knowledge*. Yale UP, 1953.
Czarniawska, Barbara. *Narratives in Social Science Research*. SAGE, 2004.
Elsaesser, Thomas. "The Mind-Game Film." *Puzzle Films: Complex Storytelling in Contemporary Cinema*, edited by Warren Buckland, John Wiley and Sons, 2009, pp. 13–41.
Eskelinen, Markku. "The Gaming Situation." *Game Studies*, vol. 1, no. 1, 2001, www.gamestudies.org/0101/eskelinen/. Accessed 15 Jan. 2019.
Frasca, Gonzalo. "Simulation versus Narrative: Introduction to Ludology." *The Video Game Theory Reader*, edited by Mark J. P. Wolf and Bernard Perron, Routledge, 2003, pp. 221–35.
Frissen, Valerie, et al. *Playful Identities: The Ludification of Digital Media Cultures*. Amsterdam UP, 2015.
Fuchs, Michael. "'A Horror Story That Came True': Metalepsis and the Horrors of Ontological Uncertainty in *Alan Wake*." *Monsters and the Monstrous*, vol. 3, no. 1, 2013, pp. 95–107.
Gonzales, Racquel M. "'This Must Be a Bad Movie': Genre and Self-Reflexivity in *Alan Wake*." *Flow*, 30 July 2010, flowtv.org/2010/07/this-must-be-a-bad-movie/. Accessed 15 Jan. 2019.
Jenkins, Henry. *Convergence Culture: Where Old and New Media Collide*. NYU P, 2006.
–––. "Game Design as Narrative Architecture." *electronic book review*, July 2004, www.electronicbookreview.com/thread/firstperson/lazzi-fair. Accessed 15 Jan. 2019.
Juul, Jesper. *Half-Real: Video Games Between Real Rules and Fictional Worlds*. MIT P, 2005.
Kanzler, Katja. "'This Game Is Not Meant For You': *Westworld* an der Schnittstelle von Narrativ und Spiel." *Mensch, Maschine, Maschinenmenschen: Multidisziplinäre Perspektiven auf die Serie* Westworld, edited by Brigitte Georgi-Findlay and Katja Kanzler, Springer, 2018, pp. 53–70.
Kiss, Miklós, and Steven Willemsen. *Impossible Puzzle Films: A Cognitive Approach to Contemporary Complex Cinema*. Edinburgh UP, 2017.
Levine, Caroline. *Forms: Whole, Rhythm, Hierarchy, Network*. Princeton UP, 2015.
Manovich, Lev. "Database as Symbolic Form." *Convergence: The International Journal of Research into New Media Technologies*, vol. 5, no. 2, June 1999, pp. 80–99.
Mittell, Jason. *Complex TV: The Poetics of Contemporary Television Storytelling*. New York UP, 2015.
Murray, Janet. *Hamlet on the Holodeck: The Future of Narrative in Cyberspace*. MIT P, 1998.
Nünning, Ansgar, and Vera Nünning. "Conceptualizing 'Broken Narratives' from a Narratological Perspective: Domains, Concepts, Features, Functions, and Suggestions for Research." *Narrative im Bruch: Theoretische Positionen und Anwendungen*, edited by Anna Babka et al., Vandenhoeck and Ruprecht, 2016, pp. 37–86.
OthoHasTheHandbook. "[THEORY] Dolores' Conversations Are with ARNOLD, Not Bernard." *Reddit*, www.reddit.com/r/westworld/comments/59bwvd/theory_dolores_conversations_are_with_arnold_not/. Accessed 15 Jan. 2019.
Panofsky, Erwin. *Perspective as Symbolic Form*. Zone Books, 1991.

Punday, Daniel. *Narrative after Deconstruction*. SUNY P, 2003.
Schubert, Stefan. *Narrative Instability: Destabilizing Identities, Realities, and Textualities in Contemporary American Popular Culture*. Winter, forthcoming.
Taylor, Diana. *The Archive and the Repertoire: Performing Cultural Memory in the Americas*. Duke UP, 2003.
Thon, Jan-Noël. *Transmedial Narratology and Contemporary Media Culture*. U of Nebraska P, 2016.
Westworld. Created by Jonathan Nolan and Lisa Joy, HBO, 2016–2018.

Andrei Nae and Alexandra Ileana Bacalu
Toward a Reconsideration of Hypermediacy: Immersion in Survival Horror Games and Eighteenth-Century Novels

Probably more than ever, our contemporary media ecology is engaged in an immersion race that calls for the constant upgrading of each medium's capacity to create the illusion of medial transparency. Although the aesthetic goal of erasing mediation can be traced back to the arts of the Renaissance, the push toward heightened realism and immersion has not dwindled, despite the critique mounted against it by postmodern thought.[1] The aesthetics of realism still enjoys a dominant position in contemporary mainstream fiction, and cinema is already normalising its 4DX technology as a standard film-watching practice, while gaming platforms are trying to integrate virtual reality gear into the average gameplay experience. Furthermore, the ideal of medium transparency that has driven art from the Renaissance onward has in the past decade exceeded the boundaries of art and entertainment and become an ideal of any communication technology, as best exemplified by the smartphone. What was at first a technology based on a symbolic control of the device that enabled the user to shuffle through menus using buttons has now turned into a seamless device that presents itself as an independent artificial world whose objects can be physically manipulated by the user via a symbiotic control scheme.[2]

However, as Ian Bogost points out, highly immersive technologies are very effective in concealing their ideologies (cf. 112–13). Immersion is such a strong and pervasive cultural value that we tend to regard technologies of immersion as politically neutral artefacts. Even more so, the assumption of political neutrality leads to a naturalization of the ideology implicit in these cultural products. This naturalization does not only concern the more obvious conservative ideol-

---

[1] We are mainly referring to critics such as Jean Baudrillard and Frederic Jameson, who maintain in their different ways that in the postmodern age representation has become more real than the object of representation.
[2] According to Gordon Calleja (63), control in video games oscillates between two poles: a symbolic pole whereby the physical manipulation of the controller does not reflect the movement of the playable character or entity, and a symbiotic one in which case the physical movement of the player maps the movement of the playable character or entity. This account of the control in video games is relevant for understanding interaction in other digital technologies as well, such as the smartphone.

https://doi.org/10.1515/9783110659405-009

ogies pertaining to race, class, and gender that have to do with the represented (or simulated, in the case of interactive media) content, but also the ideologies embedded within the media's very means of representation and simulation (cf. Hayse 445).

In order to target a global audience, AAA video games usually fall back on many pre-established narrative settings which are familiar to this target group. These settings, some of which have already been popularized by other media such as comic books or the cinema, are either explicitly or implicitly linked to the United States. Whether it is a real historical setting such as the American Revolution in *Assassin's Creed III* (Ubisoft Montreal, 2012), a counterfactual historical one as in *Wolfenstein II: The New Colossus* (MachineGames, 2017), or a fictional setting in the real USA, as it is the case with the eponymous town in *Silent Hill* (Konami, 1999), America seems to occupy a privileged position in the world of video games. Consequently, AAA video games cue players to construct a mental storyworld that is strongly indebted to the players' knowledge of the US, but which at the same time plays an active role in shaping players' understanding of the American context and its cultural identities. Games achieve this by providing players with a seamless gameplay experience that naturalizes these American identities and obfuscates the ideology behind them.

In the present article we hope to show that seamlessness is not the sine qua non condition of immersion, and that hypermediacy, too, can lead to immersive experiences. For example, survival horror video games reject the game design norms of more conventional action-adventure games and employ hypermedial formal features such as a highly fragmented visual representation, counterintuitive control schemes, and unpredictable game mechanics in order to immerse the player. We additionally show that these formal aspects contribute to the simulation of versions of masculinity that challenge the conservative gender construct of AAA video games which primarily cater to an intended American male audience. This alternative immersion strategy, which relies on hypermediacy rather than immediacy, is not new and can be found in another, well-established genre, such as the eighteenth-century novel, which relies heavily on digression, fragmentation, and metatextuality in order to similarly create the illusion of realism and authenticity. In making these arguments, we hope to productively complicate the dominant position held by the erasure of mediation as the means to achieving immersion, thus showing how (sub)cultures of immersion can connect across centuries.

Emri and Mäyrä's Account of Immersion in Video Games

Especially in the visual arts, immersion is associated with immediacy, i.e. the tendency of modern arts to erase their mediation (cf. Bolter and Grusin 5–6). While immediacy has been a guiding principle for modern arts ever since the Renaissance (cf. Bolter and Grusin 21), it has also been accompanied by a tendency that, instead of erasing mediation, seeks to highlight it, namely hypermediacy (cf. Bolter and Grusin 6).[3] Although hypermediacy is seen as inimical to immersion, survival horror games seem to prove the opposite. But before looking into what specific means these games employ to immerse the player, a more general account of immersion in video games is required. Because video games are an interactive and a narrative medium, a mere consideration of the realism of its visual representations does not do justice to their complexity. In order to fully account for the affordances of video games, in this chapter we will be relying on the theoretical model proposed by Lara Ermi and Frank Mäyrä.

According to them, immersion in video games is buttressed on three components: sensory, challenge-based, and imaginative immersion (cf. 7–8). The concept of sensory immersion is coextensive with that of immediacy because it designates video games' capacity to use big screens and headphones to isolate the player's senses from external stimuli and to provide her with realistic visual, aural, and, in the case of controllers, kinaesthetic input (cf. 7). Challenge-based immersion takes into consideration video games' capacity to confront players with a variety of challenges that keep them mentally engrossed in game world (cf. 7–8). Although Ermi and Mäyrä do not explicitly refer to game mechanics and controls, these play an important part in maintaining a high level of challenge-based immersion. Easily learnable and predictable controls and efficient game mechanics facilitate the immersion of the player, while the opposite leads to the player's disengagement with the video game. Finally, imaginative immersion refers to the ability of video games to absorb players into complex storyworlds that manage to add narrative meaning to the ludic goals of the game (cf. 9).

---

[3] Both immediacy and hypermediacy are to be construed from a historical perspective (cf. Bolter and Grusin 67). Formal traits of media and aesthetic norms of genre may fluctuate between immediacy and hypermediacy across time. For example, one might argue that while in Michael Haneke's *Funny Games* (1997) the breaking of the fourth wall is a metacomment on the narrative formula of horror films, in *Deadpool* (2016) the same aesthetic choice does not seem to dispel the illusion of immersion.

In what follows we would like to show that, although in terms of sensory and challenge-based immersion survival horror video games would not qualify as immersive, they manage to compensate for the hypermediacy of the aural and visual representation and the cumbersome gameplay by evincing a high degree of imaginative immersion. This is mainly achieved through a process of narrativization (cf. Fludernik 25) which presupposes that players are encouraged by the storyworld to invest incoherent ludic or diegetic elements with a narrative meaning. In the particular case of survival horror games, the mechanics that fragment and encumber gameplay are narrativized as consequences of the protagonist's vulnerability.

The Hypermediacy of Survival Horror Video Games

Survival horror games are action-adventure games that balance combat with puzzle solving. In opposition to more conventional representatives of the action-adventure genre,[4] survival horror games feature a set of ineffective and clunky core mechanics that are governed by cumbersome control schemes. This already complicated simulation is further obstructed by a highly fragmented representation of the game world. One of the first hypermedial elements of the games that players are faced with is the movement mechanic. Most survival horror games such as *Alone in the Dark* (Infogrames, 1992), *Resident Evil* (Capcom, 1996), *Dino Crisis* (Capcom, 1999), *Silent Hill* and others employ tank controls. This control scheme presupposes that playable characters can move only forward and backward and that, in order for the direction to be changed, the playable character must be turned to the left or the right before the forward button is pushed. While such a control system may be functional and intuitive in a first-person view or a third-person view with a tracking camera (as it is the case with *Resident Evil 4* (Capcom, 2005), or *Gears of War* (Epic Games, 2006)), this is not the case when used in combination with fixed camera angles. All the games mentioned above (with the exception of *Silent Hill* during some parts of the game) use fixed cameras that cut to a new angle when a new room or location is accessed. The angles do not only vary but are also placed in positions that make movement counterintuitive (cf. Rouse 23): often the camera is positioned in

---

[4] In keeping with Chris Crawford's distinction of video game genres based on the player skills required (*The Art of Computer Game Design*), survival horror games can be subsumed to the more encompassing action-adventure genre.

front of the playable character in a medium or even close shot, sometimes the camera is placed on one of the sides, and it is only very rarely that the camera is placed behind the playable character in the intended direction of movement. The variation which characterizes the use of angles has an important bearing on challenge-based and sensory immersion.

As far as the former is concerned, the angles and cuts make movement counterintuitive and unpredictable. The player's p-actions[5] are no longer in keeping with the player's intention, thus leading to a thwarting of the player's sense of extended embodiment (cf. Gregersen and Grodal 67). This affects the game's balance in the sense that apparently simple tasks (judging by the standards of mainstream action-adventure games) such as defeating a first-level adversary become abnormally difficult. The confrontations of survival horror games usually take place in small rooms and tight corridors filmed in close and medium shots which leave the player's adversaries off-screen. Due to the scarceness of ammunition and the ineffectiveness of the shooting mechanics, the player must often evade her adversary once it appears on-screen. This task is hampered by the absence of an evasion mechanic and by the counterintuitive movement controls, which can make the player unwittingly move directly into the arms of the adversary instead of moving away from it.

Challenge-based immersion is also obstructed by the inefficient shooting mechanics. Survival horror games differ from more conventional third-person shooters in that the aiming system does not rely on the movement of the mouse which maps the movement of the gun's aim in the game world. Instead, survival horror games either employ a manual aiming system that does not graphically mark the gun's direction, or an automatic aiming system.[6] In both cases, however, the aiming and shooting mechanics are not very functional. The manual system is once again encumbered by the camera angles, the close/medium shots, and tank controls. Not only is it difficult for the player to establish where the adversary is, but the unconventional third-person view makes it difficult for the player to point the gun in the desired direction. Furthermore, in a manner similar to the problem of moving, determining the right button to push in order to move the gun's aim can become a real challenge because of the tank controls and the camera angles. Issues of functionality are characteristic not only of the manual aiming system but also of the automatic one. Contrary to the player's expectation, by pressing the 'aim' button the playable char-

---

5 P-actions are the actions made by the player in the real world in order to control the playable character (cf. Gregersen and Grodal 70).
6 Some games allow the player to choose the aiming system, for example *Resident Evil Remake* (Capcom 2002).

acter does not always aim toward an adversary, as it is the case with *Silent Hill*. Although there is an adversary in the playable character's proximity, Harry Mason (the protagonist of the game) does not always aim in the required direction, which leads to the wasting of precious ammunition.

Sensorial immersion and challenge-based immersion are also impeded by the system used by survival horror games to manage the items carried by the playable character. If more conventional action games use the heads-up display in order to enable players to select a particular weapon or item, survival horror games employ an inventory which, when accessed, pauses game time and switches to a new screen. This new screen resembles that of a menu and offers important ludic information such as the level of health, and it allows players to equip weapons and investigate or combine items. Although this mechanic is more functional than other core mechanics, it fails to contribute to the immersion of the player. In the case of sensorial immersion, the seamlessness of the aural and visual input is fragmented, thus adding to the segmentation of the gameplay experience determined by the use of fixed camera angles. As far as challenge-based immersion is concerned, the fact that any change or equipping of an item has to be operated in the inventory has significant consequences for the simulation of combat. Action games require that players show good hand-eye coordination in order to quickly react to approaching threats. Players must swiftly move, aim, and shoot any potential danger present in the game world. In order for this to be achieved, a continuous representation of the game world is necessary so that players may always know where the threat is. Although survival horror games have a strong emphasis on combat, the inventory can further complicate the already cumbersome gameplay generated by their clunky combat mechanics. As if the close shots, sight-limiting camera angles, and inefficient combat mechanics were not enough, on some occasions the player must also exit the screen and access the inventory during combat. This can be determined by the player's need to switch weapons, combine ammunition clips, or restore health. During battle, these changes of screen further disorient the player and make it more difficult for her to successfully deal with her assailants.

Survival horror games seem to do their best to prevent players from being immersed in their respective worlds. While most action-adventure games strive to offer the players a seamless gameplay experience, survival horror games prompt the player with a fragmented and frustrating one. Nevertheless, in the next paragraphs we would like to show that, in spite of all of the above, survival horror games do manage to immerse the player by narrativizing the otherwise hypermedial elements of their game designs. Therefore, instead of relying on sensorial and challenge-based immersion, these games focus on imaginative immersion in order to diegetically salvage their encumbered gameplay.

Immersing the Player through Narrativization

The relationship between game mechanics and the storyworlds of video games has been discussed by Jesper Juul, who distinguishes three types of relation:
1. Fiction implemented in rules: The most straightforward situation, where the game rules are motivated by the game's fiction. [...]
2. Fiction not implemented in game rules: When fiction suggests a possibility that is not accessible to players. [...]
3. Rules not explained by fiction: When rules are difficult to explain by referring to the game's fiction. (175)

In the case of survival horror games, it is the first kind of relationship that is foregrounded. These games manage to assign a narrative role to game mechanics that might otherwise be considered a result of bad game design and technological limitation. Survival horror games simulate the experience of vulnerable male or female characters who, in opposition to the protagonists of more conventional action-adventure games, are disempowered and incapable of summarily defeating their foes. This is why the protagonists of such games are usually American (or Japanese) everymen and -women who lack the skills of the genetically engineered supersoldiers so often encountered in the leading roles of AAA action-adventure games.[7] The helplessness of these characters narrativizes the counterintuitive controls and inefficient core mechanics as manifestations of their vulnerability.

When playing video games, players extrapolate their knowledge of the real world and apply it to the storyworld of the game, with the exception of those aspects where the conventions of the genre and the particularities of each storyworld prompts them to do otherwise (cf. Ryan 51). As a result, after the game has begun, it is easy for the player to infer from the identity of the characters that they are unlikely to be capable of efficient melee and firearm combat. In games such as *Silent Hill*, *Fatal Frame* (Tecmo, 2001), *Haunting Ground* (Capcom, 2005), *Clock Tower III* (Capcom, 2003), *Outlast* (Red Barrels, 2013), *Resident Evil 7: Biohazard* (Capcom, 2017), and others, the playable characters are average middle-class men or women, and the core mechanics confirm the expectation of helplessness raised by the name of the genre and the identities of the protagonists. For example, in *Silent Hill*, the male protagonist is governed by a set of

---

[7] This is not to say that there are no soldiers or other such characters whose identities are consistent with the norms of the action genre. However, in this case survival horror games undermine the stereotypical representation of action characters and end up yielding a parodic effect.

highly unpredictable core mechanics that, even when activated, lead to a set of moves and combos that are nowhere near the action spectacle that video games often borrow from action films. In *Clock Tower III*, the female protagonist is almost never capable of fighting her opponents, while *Resident Evil 7*, which departs from the classical formula and uses first-person shooter mechanics, features a set of aiming and shooting mechanics that are below the standards of average first-person shooters.[8]

By means of narrativization, the disruptive game mechanics that fragment representation and gameplay become congruous with the storyworld of the game, and instead of thwarting immersion they become constitutive of it. The alternative means used to achieve immersion seem to tie in with a set of alternative identity politics. While AAA action-adventure video games usually pay tribute to conservative gender politics that reassert the supremacy of white masculinity, survival horror video games immerse players into a verisimilar interactive storyworld which is populated by alternative versions of white masculinity. In a manner similar to representations of masculinity in crisis in cinema (cf. Chaudhuri 106), these versions of masculinity distort the conservative gender construct of the active, heroic white man.

Besides the clunky mechanics and controls, the storyworld of survival horror games sometimes feature elements which are apparently incoherent with the rest of the narrative and have the potential of breaking the sense of realism and immersion. Therefore, in order to maintain a high level of imaginative immersion, narrativization in survival horror games also functions on the level of the scripted narrative, whereby implausible pre-established events are turned natural and made consistent with the rest of the events. For example, the storyworld of *Silent Hill* is a supernatural one that demands of players to suspend a part of their knowledge of the real world in order to be able to immerse themselves into the game. However, one of the endings manages to naturalize the otherwise supernatural elements of the game. *Silent Hill* simulates the story of Harry Mason who, while driving with his daughter beside him, has an accident near the town of Silent Hill. After regaining consciousness, he realizes that his daughter has disappeared and goes into the town to look for her. In his attempt to find his missing daughter, Harry Mason faces a series of supernatural challenges in the form of monsters and a town that sometimes takes a nightmarish shape which makes the protagonist's progress more difficult. The game's 'bad' ending manages to naturalize the supernatural elements of the storyworld by playing a

---

8 This difference is particularly conspicuous when playing the DLC mission "Not a Hero" in which the player assumes control of Chris Redfield, who, unlike Ethan, is a professional soldier.

cut-scene that shows Harry Mason in his derelict car with a bloody wound to the head. This suggests that the events of *Silent Hill* are, in fact, the hallucinations of the dying protagonist who has never left his car in the first place.

Similar strategies are employed by other installments of the franchise such as *Silent Hill 3* (Konami, 2003) and *Silent Hill: Homecoming* (Double Helix Games, 2008). *Silent Hill 3* begins with the daughter of Harry Mason, Heather, entering the otherworld version of Lakeside Amusement Park. After a few minutes of gameplay, the game coerces the player to walk up along a rollercoaster track where the playable character is inevitably killed. The inability to avoid death defies the expectations that players have with respect to video games (which, no matter how difficult, should offer the player at least one way to win), yet this aspect of the game is soon naturalized by a cut-scene that shows the protagonist waking up from a dream. This cues players to interpret the previous events as unreal relative to the fictional storyworld, thus rendering the inability to avoid death natural and consistent with the norms of video games.

Silent Hill: Homecoming uses both strategies of narrativization in order to frame events that may encumber the player's suspension of disbelief. The game begins in medias res with Alex Shepherd, the protagonist, being carried around on a stretcher in an insanitary hospital where the patients are submitted to a variety of torture methods. As in *Silent Hill 3*, Alex Shephard's attempt to escape the hospital ends with him being killed in an elevator, upon which the game cuts to a scene of Alex suddenly waking up in the passenger seat of a truck. The game narratively frames the hospital level as the protagonist's nightmare and, in doing so, resolves its puzzling setting and events. However, like *Silent Hill*, *Silent Homecoming* uses one of its endings in order to render the events of the game as figments of the protagonist's imagination. The game's 'bad' ending features the protagonist strapped to a stretcher in the same hospital of the initial dream and being subject to shock therapy. This ending reverses the initial narrative framing: the hospital scene had been real all along while the rest of the events had been a fantasy of the protagonist under shock treatment.

The emphasis on imaginative immersion compels survival horror games to make their storyworlds as realistic as possible, which is why these games attempt to narrativize potentially disruptive elements. This tendency, however, also yields important aesthetic results in the sense that survival horror games end up relativizing the status of the world in which the playable character finds himself or herself. When playing survival horror games, players can never be sure whether they are immersed in the storyworld's reality or in the vision/hallucination/dream of a traumatized character.

The Redundancy of the Level Design

Despite the efforts of art and entertainment to fully immerse their audience, the immersion ideal is yet to be reached. Even those media that are considered the most immersive feature a set of artificial traits that make it hard for the user to suspend her disbelief. In the case of survival horror video games, we have shown how formal aspects that defy the dominant norms of the action-adventure genre are, in most cases, deliberate aesthetic choices that have the role of reflecting the vulnerability of the often white middle-class male protagonists. However, not all formal traits lend themselves as easily to narrativization. While the inefficient core mechanics governing the player's control over the playable character can easily blend into the storyworld, players may find it difficult to narrativize the redundancy of the level design.

In order for games to be immersive, they must prompt players with ever new challenges so that the player may remain cognitively engrossed in the game (cf. Murray 126). Despite featuring difficult combat and complex puzzles, survival horror games also require players to repeatedly backtrack through many previous locations whose challenges have already been solved. While initially the need to revisit the same location was a strategy aimed at prolonging game time due to the limited data storage capacity, after the turn of the millennium this became more of an aesthetic choice than the result of a technological limitation. For example, the designers of *Resident Evil Remake*, which was released in 2002 for the Game Cube and later for other consoles and platforms, were making a game for platforms that were significantly superior to the PlayStation (the first console for which the first *Resident Evil* released). Nevertheless, instead of adding more variation to the gameplay, the remake coerces players to revisit previous locations more often than the original did.

The novelty responsible for this additional backtracking is the crimson head. Unlike in the original *Resident Evil*, in the remake zombies do not die immediately after being killed. After a while they rise again, but this time in a faster and stronger version called the crimson head. Because crimson heads are more difficult to kill than average zombies, the best way to prevent their appearance is to burn the zombies shortly after they have been killed. However, in order to do so, the player must carry a fuel canteen filled with gasoline and a lighter. Given the limited inventory slots, players must repeatedly travel back and forth to item boxes, where the player stores her items, to pick up the canteen and the lighter. Additionally, if the canteen is empty, the player must make her to way to another room where it can be filled. All this wandering around the mansion amounts to a very repetitive gameplay that involves revisiting over and over again the same rooms that have already been cleared of any danger.

Similar examples of repetitive level design can be found in *Silent Hill 4: The Room* (Konami, 2004) and *Forbidden Siren* (Sony, 2003). In the former, the player must go through each level twice and, in-between levels, return to his apartment through the hole in his bathroom. In the latter, the player must complete each mission at least twice, but with different playable characters. This type of redundant tasks affects not only challenge-based immersion, since familiarity with the level makes it easier for the player to progress, but also imaginative immersion. By walking the player through the same levels repeatedly, survival horror games undermine the sense of progression that is relevant both from a ludic and a diegetic perspective. Players can be confused by the apparent formlessness of the games and, in light of their previous experience of games and narratives, can no longer tell whether they are actually making progress, or if they are regressing to previous stages and locations. This confusion subverts the perception of sequentiality which is a prototypical feature of any narrative (cf. Herman).

Although this aspect of the game design is contrary to the dominant conception of narrative as a sequence of events, it can, nevertheless, be narrativized in keeping with the norms of the horror genre in the sense that the redundancy of the level design contributes to the sense of entrapment that is exploited by horror across media. Under the influence of cinema, conventional action games often set their events in a variety of exotic and lavish locations that offer the player voyeuristic pleasure, which accompanies the ludic pleasure drawn from gameplay. Through the use of large angles and wide spaces, these games offer players the illusion of freedom of movement, which encourages them to explore the surroundings, do side quests, and gather resources. In opposition to conventional action games, survival horror games set their events in twisted, narrow, maze-like environments that engender a sense of claustrophobia and entrapment (cf. Kirkland 64). In survival horror games, exploration is not encouraged by the enticing scenery but rather by the need to gather resources, which are generally very scarce. The protagonist of such games is overwhelmed by the complexity of the maze, which ties in with the sense of helplessness and vulnerability simulated by the controls and mechanics.

So far we have argued that survival horror games employ an alternative immersion strategy that manages to turn fragmentation, a cumbersome control of the playable character, confusing aspects of the scripted narrative, and the repetitive nature of the level design from hypermedial elements to immediate ones. Survival horror games herald an aesthetic discourse that contests the dominant view in contemporary arts and entertainment according to which seamlessness lies at the heart of immersion. As evinced by the success of many of the games referred to in this chapter, this alternative aesthetics has obtained social validation in a gaming subculture that deems survival horror games to be valuable and their methods capable of achieving immersion. In what follows, we would like to show that this alternative aesthetic code is not new, and that it can be linked to the aesthetics of realism endorsed by the eighteenth-century novel, a genre which immerses the reader by using a series of means which, judging by the dominant standards of novel writing and novel reading from the nineteenth century onwards, would count as hypermedial.

Hypermediacy and Realism in the Eighteenth-Century Novel

Only a brief look at the early English novel of the eighteenth century reveals a tension between the pursuit of realism and immediacy, on the one hand, and ever-increasing self-reflexivity and experimentation with convention, on the other. Although the early novel departs considerably from the anti-mimetic genre of the romance,[9] it goes against the readerly expectations that have since been established in reference to the paradigmatic nineteenth-century realist novel and its tradition of narrative effacement, transparent representation, or stylistic objectivity. Perhaps unexpectedly for readers accustomed to this dominant realist tradition, the early novel exhibits a vast array of formal features and narrative strategies that we normally associate with hypermediacy. Any attempt at neatly classifying these is not only thwarted by the variety of sometimes diverging novelistic innovations at this time, but also by the overwhelming increase in printed materials that were involved in the 'rise' of the new genre.[10] Nevertheless, several salient directions can be traced. Our focus is on two of these, derived from the last couple of features that Paul Hunter includes in his definition of the early novel, namely: 1) "self-consciousness about innovation and novelty" and 2) "inclusivity, digressiveness, fragmentation" (*Before Novels* 24–25). The former can also be related to Michael McKeon's discussion of the self-reflexive impulse involved in the epistemological attitude shared by many early novels, which he identifies as "extreme skepticism" (cf. 47–64). These, we argue, represent the main contributors to the early novel's hypermedial quality.

---

9 On the question of eighteenth-century romance-novel dialectics, see McKeon 25–64.
10 For an early account on the rise of print and the many "pre-texts" that informed the novel genre, see Hunter, *Before Novels* 167–356.

The first of these sets of features may be broadened to include all forms of self-reflexivity and metatextual commentary that the early novel engages in, promoted not just by the ongoing critique of the emerging genre and its need to acquire legitimacy,[11] but also by the age's ideals of sociability and polite conversation,[12] which warranted direct address to the reader. Such self-referentiality can be found primarily in the novels of the mid-century onwards, with Henry Fielding and Laurence Sterne coming to mind first. We may think of the narrator of *Tom Jones*, who constantly comments upon the literary devices that he employs. The title of chapter six, for instance, informs its readers that "Mrs. Deborah is introduced into the Parish with a Simile" (*Tom Jones* 62), which is followed by the narrator clarifying his intentions and explaining the device. It goes without saying that *Tristram Shandy* constitutes an even more robust example of the early novel's penchant for commenting upon and overturning its own emerging conventions. One need only recall the Shandean dash or the notorious black page to get a sense of such strategies. Nevertheless, unlike previous work conducted by Christina Lupton and Peter McDonald on the parallels between eighteenth-century novels and contemporary video games (cf. 158), our interest does not lie with their mutual reliance on metatext as a means of interrogating or simply poking fun at their own artificiality. Rather, we would like to emphasize the second body of hypermedial features[13] and stress that, although it might seem counterintuitive, these work in such a way as to enhance the novel's realism and its immersive effects. In other words, we will explore the ways in which some of the features included under this second head support "the air of complete authenticity" (Watt 24) or "the claim to historicity" (cf. McKeon 45–47) that is prevalent in eighteenth-century novels—the claim that these represent collections of authentic documents that have been found and published by various editors with little, if any, emendation. We thus join the efforts of Watt and McKeon, who have shown how many defining features of the new genre are directly designed to strengthen this claim. We add that these are hypermedial fea-

---

[11] For a brief discussion of eighteenth-century distrust in the novel, see Hunter, "The Novel" 24–28.
[12] For instances of the early novel's approach to reading as conversation, see Fielding, *Joseph Andrews* 23–25 and Sterne 47–51.
[13] This is not to say that the first traits we have discussed, namely the use of metatext and other self-reflexive strategies, might not serve to strengthen the eighteenth-century novel's claims to realism and authenticity or coexist with the second group of features. However, we have chosen to focus on the second set of novelistic characteristics in order to depart from existing studies and focus on a relatively neglected commonality between early novels and video games.

tures which can be equally used to subvert or enforce claims to realism and immersion.

This second group of traits has to do with the early novel's display of its own medial or generic specificities and limitations, which often lead to its perceived formlessness and fragmentation. As has already been argued by critics of the 'rise' of the novel, this tendency primarily stems from the romance-novel dialectic and the latter's rejection of the traditional literary conventions represented by the former, in terms of both style and plot (cf. Watt 9–34; Hunter, *Before Novels* 22–28; McKeon 25–64). Thus, the regularity and predictability that such conventions entail no longer finds its way in the emerging genre. Instead, the sense that the early novel lacks structure and cohesion is generated by a wide range of recurring features: the almost indiscriminate abundance of physical and factual details (cf. Watt 15–25), its constant slippage into digression (cf. Hunter, *Before Novels* 24), or for instance its generic heterogeneity and inclusiveness which sees the novel draw on a variety of both fictional and non-fictional writings, such as letters, diaries, memoirs, periodicals, natural histories, conduct manuals, and so on (cf. Hunter, *Before Novels* 167–356). To this we may also add features related to the novel's materiality, such as the occasional inclusion of graphic particularities, maps, diagrams or sketches inside its pages, not to mention its often unprecedented length. In order to explore these features and illustrate the manner in which they strengthen the early novel's claims to realism, we shall briefly examine the diary episode of Daniel Defoe's *Robinson Crusoe*. Our choice is guided by several considerations: the paradigmatic status of Defoe's novel, its early publication that prevents a metatextual questioning of the genre's not yet established conventions, and its well-documented reliance on the genres of history and natural history, which speaks of its engagement with epistemological questions.[14] At the same time, we may also think of certain thematic similarities between a novel like Defoe's and contemporary survival horror video games, which similarly stage ordinariness and vulnerability.

The first third of the Defoe's novel, which precedes the diary episode, takes the shape of a retrospective first-person narration which provides the reader with the protagonist's biographical details and recounts his first travels at sea, his capture by pirates and subsequent escape, his brief success as a plantation owner in Brazil, and finally his shipwreck on the island. The narrator, Crusoe, then recalls his initial despair and fear of death, the days in which he salvaged the many goods left on the ship and built a raft for this purpose, as well as the time he spent constructing his shelter, fence, and first tools. It is at this point that

---

14 On this latter feature, see McKeon 65–89; Sill 69–106; Mayer 158–226; Corneanu 183–95.

Crusoe informs his readers that he was also able to start a diary by finding ink and paper on the ship, and the novel briefly and somewhat abruptly assumes the shape of his private journal.

The first thing to notice is that the former half of Crusoe's diary has little narrative use and does not do much to help drive the story forward. The first pages of the diary spanning roughly from September 30 to January 3 merely recapitulate what was narrated before, from the shipwreck to the erection of the fortress, in succinct diary form. Some of the entries even make use of the same vocabulary or sentence structure of the preceding corresponding paragraphs, mirroring them almost exactly at times. The only new information that the reader is offered amounts to additional circumstantial detail joined to previously narrated events. The following is a brief example of such mirroring paragraphs:

> When I wak'd it was broad Day, the Weather clear, and the Storm abated, so that the Sea did not rage and swell as before: But that which surpris'd me most, was, that the Ship was lifted off in the Night from the Sand where she lay, by the Swelling of the Tyde, and was driven up almost as far as the Rock which I first mention'd [...]; (42)

> Oct. 1. In the Morning I saw to my great Surprise the Ship had floated with the high Tide, and was driven on Shore again much nearer the Island, which as it was some Comfort on one hand, for seeing her sit upright, and not broken to Pieces, I hop'd, if the Wind abated, I might get on board, and get some Food and Necessaries out of her for my Relief; (61)

Thus, on account of the diary, the main events that follow Crusoe's shipwreck are narrated twice in similar wording, thus resembling the repetitive structure of survival horror games. Crusoe himself warns his readers that "in it will be told all these particulars over again" (60) but does not do anything to avoid it. What is more, the literature on Defoe's novel has recorded several inconsistencies and contradictions between the first part of the narrative and the diary. McKeon, who notes this recapitulation, also gestures at a number of discrepancies between the two versions that have to do with time sequence (cf. 315–18). One of the examples that he provides is that, in the first version, the rain stops after Crusoe's first night on the island, while in the second it continues several days after (cf. 316). Another one of the inconsistencies he points out is that the second version inverts the narrative chronology of two events, the completion of the chair and the construction of the shelter (cf. 316). Only the latter half of the diary, which details the sprouting of the barley, the hurricane, Crusoe's sickness, his dream and subsequent conversion moves on to events that have not been previously related.

Another feature of Crusoe's diary to examine is the frequent intrusion of digressions. In fact, the diary is even introduced by means of a parenthesis. Crusoe tells his readers that he did not take up his private journal until after his first few days on the island, since he was extremely distressed and occupied with gathering and making provisions. Otherwise, he claims, his diary would have been "full of many dull things" (60), yet he still insists on digressing and providing his readers with an example of what his first entry would have sounded like. Needless to say, the imagined sample that he provides rehearses yet another previous passage, in which he recounts the desperate cries and confused motions he made during his first day. However, the digressions do not stop there. As McKeon also points out (317), while reading Crusoe's entries we discover that this is not in fact a rough copy of the initial diary he penned on the island, but an edited version that includes annotations, clarifications, and digressive sequences which serve to retrospectively complete the narrative or make sense of events in terms of punishment and providence. Many entries are overtaken by such lengthy retrospective digressions without any notice, and the unaware reader is informed of this only at the very end of the parenthesis, through Crusoe's many repetitions of "But I return to my journal" (78). The following is an example of such a retrospective note that is much longer than the diary entry itself:

> Jan. 3. I began my Fence or Wall; which being still jealous of my being attack'd by some Body, I resolv'd to make very thick and strong.
> N.B. This Wall being describ'd before, I purposely omit what was said in the Journal; it is sufficient to observe, that I was no less Time than from the 3d of January to the 14th of April, working, finishing, and perfecting this Wall, tho' it was no more than about 24 Yards in Length, being a half Circle from one Place in the Rock to another Place about eight Yards from it, the Door of the Cave being in the Center behind it. (65–66)

These frequent digressions and intrusions make it increasingly difficult for the reader to follow the diary, make out the sequence of events, and distinguish between the distinct styles of the original journal and Crusoe's retrospective comments.

In addition to the mere inclusion of repetitions and digressions, it is worth noting that these do not seem to follow any consistent pattern. Although Crusoe does warn his readers that his diary will repeat some of the events he has already narrated and provides annotations claiming that he has omitted some sections in order to avoid this, as we have noticed, most of his journal remains a mere recapitulation. Moreover, there is no apparent rule as to the balance, proportion, or sequence of old and new information. At the same time, we have seen that the diary section is highly fragmentary and eclectic. Not only does it combine two related yet distinct genres, i.e. the memoir and the diary, but it abruptly and insidiously alternates between original diary entries, retrospective digressions, and notes. It is not clear what the principle that guides Crusoe's choice between the latter two is, since both seem to serve a similar purpose.

Even if we take into account the new genre's use of simple and strictly denotative language, its rejection of opaque literary conventions, or the disappearance of the heavy typographical ornamentation that used to overwhelm the pages of books (cf. Keymer 17–18), novels still found ways of challenging the sense of seamless transparency and immediacy. In her recent study, Natalie M. Philips has shown that, in fact, many later eighteenth-century novels labored to encourage complicated modes of attention and distraction in their readers, thus dismantling the flawed narrative of readerly absorption that we associate with the age (cf. 1–28). In our case, the fragmentation and inconsistency present in Defoe's novel and heightened during the diary episode emerge as vexing, poses difficulties of reading and comprehension, and draws attention to the act of writing and its medial and material constraints. After all, the shape(lessness) and brevity of Crusoe's diary is accounted for by the frequently asserted fact that he had only found a limited amount of ink on the ship that would soon run out, which manages to narrativize the formal traits of the dairy but, at the same time, sheds light upon the book's complicated materiality and the fact that we are dealing with a mediated narrative. Yet these strategies, together with the metatextual commentaries that often accompany them, are not designed to stress the artificiality of the acts of writing and reading and to subvert the novel's realism. On the contrary, all the features we have examined are in fact aimed at strengthening "the claim to historicity" that is famously found in Defoe's preface. Rather than striving to reveal the artificiality of representations that are mediated through one's consciousness and the impossibility of circumventing this, the novel attempts to faithfully capture Crusoe's individual subjectivity, which, as we have seen, is confused, digressive, and constantly struggles to scrutinize his experience on the island for signs of grace and salvation. As McKeon states: "And yet in the first-person narration of Defoe, the effect is less to throw the historicity of the travels themselves into question than to sensitize us to the personalized veracity of Robinson's experience, which is all the more authentic for having this subjective volatility" (317). It is telling that the diary episode occurs at the beginning of Crusoe's isolation on the island and precedes his conversion. Scholars have argued that *Robinson Crusoe* shares the generic conventions of the age's treatise on the passions, aimed at diagnosing and prescribing cures for maladies of the soul (cf. Sill 69–85; Corneanu 183–95). The novel's survey of the disordered and passionate state Crusoe finds himself in just after the shipwreck and during his sickness can thus be understood as a brief natural-philosophical inquiry which aims at epistemic accuracy and has an authenticating role.

In light of these observations, even a novel like Sterne's *Tristram Shandy*, which is often anachronistically said to predict postmodernist metafiction, can in some respects be understood as improving upon the authenticating techniques used by Defoe. If historical Lockean notions of selfhood lie at the basis of Sterne's project, then the novel's profuse digressions and constant use of metatextual commentary can be understood as reflections of a distracted and irregular psyche dominated by the laws of association and, most importantly, by the inherently self-reflexive nature of consciousness.[15] This dimension of the novel can very well coexist with other, satirizing uses of metatext.

Conclusion, or, toward a Pluralization of the Concept of Immersion

In this chapter we have analyzed two genres, survival horror video games and the eighteenth-century novel, in order to challenge the dominant status enjoyed by the erasure of mediation as the cornerstone of immediacy and immersion. The two genres discussed adopt similar aesthetic codes which, despite their rejection of seamlessness, present themselves as alternative means of achieving immersion. Both genres make their reception difficult for the player/reader in the sense that, while gameplay in survival horror is hampered by counterintuitive control schemes and unreliable mechanics, in eighteenth-century novels the events are often conveyed by a disorganized and digressive narrator who constantly comments on his or her own technique. Although such formal aspects stress the materiality of the two media, in both cases they end up contributing to the immersion of the player/reader. In survival horror games, the cumbersome gameplay can be construed as a simulation of the vulnerability of the protagonist, who is usually an average white middle class American man with no experience in combat. In eighteenth-century novels, the digressiveness and fragmentariness of the narration become signs of authenticity which strengthen the genre's realism. In the particular case of *Robinson Crusoe*, the narrativization of these formal traits is aided by the protagonist's vulnerability, which sanctions the digressions and inconsistencies of the novel as the manifestation of a distempered mind which has to survive under extreme conditions—shipwrecked on an island in the middle of the ocean.

Our investigation of the two genres has pointed out that hypermediacy is not necessarily inimical to immersion, and that across modernity various aesthetic discourses pertaining to various genres have managed to accommodate hypermediacy within immersion. The eighteenth-century novel and survival horror

---

15 On Lockeon consciousness and its reliance on self-reflexivity, see Weinberg 26.

games pay tribute to a conception of immersion that defies the centrality of seamlessness. In doing so, these genres question the dominant status of the erasure of mediation as the only means of achieving immediacy and call for a reassessment of the idea of hypermediacy as the marginal aesthetic other of immediacy.

Works Cited

Baudrillard, Jean. *Simulacra and Simulation*. Translated by Sheila Faria Glaser, U of Michigan P, 1995.
Bogost, Ian. *Persuasive Games: The Expressive Power of Videogames*. The MIT Press, 2007.
Bolter, Jay David, and Richard Grusin. *Remediation. Understanding New Media*. 1999. The MIT Press, 2000.
Calleja, Gordon. *In-Game. From Immersion to Incorporation*. 1991. The MIT Press, 2011.
Capcom. *Clock Tower III*. Capcom, 2003.
Capcom. *Dino Crisis*. Capcom, 1999.
Capcom. *Haunting Ground*. Capcom, 2005.
Capcom. *Resident Evil 4*. Capcom, 2005.
Capcom. *Resident Evil 7: Biohazard*. Capcom, 2017.
Capcom. *Resident Evil Remake*. Capcom, 2002.
Capcom. *Resident Evil*. Capcom, 1996.
Chaudhuri, Shohini. *Feminist Film Theorists*. Routledge, 2006.
Corneanu, Sorana. "Devout Affections: Theology, Medicine, and the Novel." *Imitatio-Inventio. The Rise of 'Literature' from Early to Classic Modernity*, edited by Mihaela Irimia and Dragoş Ivana, Institutul Cultural Român, 2010, pp. 179–97.
Crawford, Chris. *The Art of Computer Game Design*. McGraw-Hill/Osborne Media, 1984.
Defoe, Daniel. *Robinson Crusoe*. 1719, edited by Thomas Keymer, Oxford UP, 2007.
Double Helix Games. *Silent Hill: Homecoming*. Konami, 2008.
Epic Games. *Gears of War*. Microsoft Game Studios, 2006.
Ermi, Laura, and Frans Mäyrä. "Fundamental Components of the Gameplay Experience: Analysing Immersion." *Changing Views: Worlds in Play. Selected Papers of the 2005 Digital Games Research Association's Second International Conference*, Edited by Suzanne de Castell and Jennifer Jenson, 2005, pp. 15–27.
Fielding, Henry. *Joseph Andrews*. 1742. Könemann, 1998.
Fielding, Henry. *Tom Jones*. 1749. Penguin Books, 1985.
Fludernik, Monika. *Towards a 'Natural' Narratology*. 1996. Routledge, 2001.
Gregersen, Andreas, and Torben Grodal. "Embodiment and Interface." *The Video Game Theory Reader 2*, edited by Bernard Perron and Mark J.P. Wolf, Routledge, 2009, pp. 65–84.
Haneke, Michael, director. *Funny Games*. Concorde-Castle Rock/Turner, 1997.
Hayse, Mark. "Ideology." *The Routledge Companion to Video Games*, edited by Mark J. P. Wolf and Bernard Perron, Routledge, 2014, pp. 442–50.
Herman, David. *Basic Elements of Narrative*. Blackwell Publishing, 2009.

Hunter, J. Paul. *Before Novels: The Cultural Contexts of Eighteen-Century English Fiction*. W.W. Norton, 1990.
Hunter, J. Paul. "The Novel and Social/Cultural History." *The Cambridge Companion to the Eighteenth-Century Novel*, edited by John Richetti, Cambridge UP, 1996.
Infogrames. *Alone in the Dark*. Infogrames and I*Motion, 1992.
Jameson, Frederic. *Postmodernism, or the Cultural Logic of Late Capitalism*. Duke UP, 1997.
Juul, Jesper. "On Absent Carrot Sticks. The Level of Abstraction in Video Games." *Storyworlds across Media: Toward a Media-Conscious Narratology*, edited by Marie-Laure Ryan and Jan-Noël Thon, U of Nebraska P, 2014, pp. 173–92.
Keymer, Thomas. "Novel Designs. Manipulating the Page in English Fiction, 1660–1780." *New Directions in the History of the Novel*, edited by Patrick Parrinder, Andrew Nash, and Nicola Wilson, Palgrave Macmillan, 2014, pp. 17–49.
Kirkland, Ewan. "Storytelling in Survival Horror Videogames." Perron, pp. 62–78.
Konami Computer Entertainment Tokyo. *Silent Hill 3*. Konami, 2003.
Konami Computer Entertainment Tokyo. *Silent Hill 4: The Room*. Konami, 2004.
Konami Computer Entertainment Tokyo. *Silent Hill*. Konami, 1999.
Lupton, Christina, and Peter McDonald. "Reflexivity as Entertainment: Early Novels and Recent Video Games." *Mosaic: An Interdisciplinary Critical Journal*, vol. 43, no. 4, 2010, pp. 157–73.
MachineGames. *Wolfenstein II: The New Colossus*. Bethesda Softworks, 2017.
Mayer, Robert. *History and the Early English Novel: Matters of Fact from Bacon to Defoe*. 1997. Cambridge UP, 2004.
McKeon, Michael. *The Origins of the English Novel, 1600–1740*. Johns Hopkins UP, 1987.
Miller, Tim, director. *Deadpool*. 20th Century Fox, 2016.
Murray, Janet H. *Hamlet on the Holodeck. The Future of Narrative in Cyberspace*. The MIT Press, 1997.
Perron, Bernard. *Horror Video Games, Essays on the Fusion of Fear and Play*. MacFarland & Company, Inc., 2009.
Phillips, Natalie M. *Distraction. Problems of Attention in Eighteenth-Century Literature*. Johns Hopkins UP, 2016.
Red Barrels. *Outlast*. Red Barrels, 2013.
Rouse, Richard III. "Made in Hell: The Inevitable Success of the Horror Genre in Video Games." Perron, pp. 15–25.
Ryan, Marie-Laure. *Possible Worlds, Artificial Intelligence, and Narrative Theory*. Indiana UP, 1992.
SCE Japan Studio, Project Siren. *Forbidden Siren*. Sony Computer Entertainment, 2003.
Sill, Geoffrey. *The Cure of the Passions and the Origins of the English Novel*. Cambridge UP, 2001.
Sterne, Laurence. *The Life and Opinions of Tristram Shandy, Gentleman*. 1759–67. Oxford UP, 2009.
Tecmo. *Fatal Frame*. Tecmo, 2001.
Ubisoft Montreal. *Assassin's Creed III*. Ubisoft, 2012.
Watt, Ian. *Rise of the Novel. Studies in Defoe, Richardson and Fielding*. U of California P, 1957.
Weinberg, Shelley. *Consciousness in Locke*. Oxford UP, 2016.

Doug Stark
Ludic Literature: *Ready Player One* as Didactic Fiction for the Neoliberal Subject

> There is no way out of the game of culture
> — Pierre Bourdieu, *Distinction* 6

Digital cultures are dynamic transmedia ecologies with access to vast cultural reserves. Modern technologies facilitate the coming together of styles, media, platforms, and peoples to form a network of communication and exchange. Products of this "convergence culture" (Jenkins), from *Harry Potter* fan fiction to *Pokémon Go*, often combine the form and content of existing cultural artefacts—old and new. Drawing from cyberpunk literature and digital games, the video game novel is an exemplary product of convergence culture.[1] Labelled both "ludic" (Kuehl, Detweiler, Condis) and "gamic" (Jupin) fiction,[2] the video game novel tells stories within video game worlds or about video game playing while using the components of games—specifically their rules and boundaries—to entertain and communicate. Not only does the video game novel concern game playing but it can "also *require* game-playing and puzzle-solving of readers" (Condis 2). To fully comprehend novel heterocosms (cf. Hutcheon xxiv)—their storyworlds—which extend beyond bound pages, readers must traverse a variety of media formats (cf. Jenkins, *Convergence* 93–130) including online forums, Alternate Reality Games (ARGs), music and video streaming sites, and video game emulators.[3] While it is common for literary texts to include intertextual references, certain video game novels such as the one I am concerned with here, Ernest Cline's *Ready Player One* (2011), are notable in their ability to motivate and *train* readers to navigate and even discuss its referents in a particular way. Essentially, Cline's novel invites its reader to *play* the game of literature according to its own

---

[1] Cyberpunk precursors of the video game novel include William Gibson's *Neuromancer* (1984), Orson Scott Card's *Ender's Game* (1985), and Neal Stephenson's *Snow Crash* (1992).
[2] John Kuehl, Robert Detweiler and Megan Condis use "ludic fiction" in reference to cyberpunk literature and its derivatives. Condis also refers to "ludic fiction" as a kind of "meta-geek fiction." Tanner Jupin's "gamic fiction" refers to novels about video games and their deployment of forms and techniques usually found in video games.
[3] This non-trivial effort required to traverse the heterocosm of the video game novel is what celebrated game scholar, Espen Aarseth, refers to in relation to cybertexts as "ergodic" (1). We might, therefore, conceptualize these print video game novels as cybertexts as their narrative extends into cyberspace and across media.

rules and boundaries. To take part, all you need is the book and access to an internet connection.

So, what is a video game novel and, more important still, what does it *do*? This essay proffers an answer to this question by reading *Ready Player One* as a didactic novel which harnesses ludic techniques to teach its readers about 1980s video game culture through play. *Ready Player One* is both a story about games and a game itself, which makes it an exemplary video game novel, as does its critical and popular success that was only increased by the recent big-budget film adaptation. A dystopian novel set in 2044, *Ready Player One* is actually a thinly veiled homage to the age in which Cline grew up, and it is full of references to 1980s film, music, and video games. For all that, the young adult novel is not a pure a nostalgia trip for those of Cline's era, as critics have frequently suggested.[4] Instead, I argue that Cline's novel is a gamer primer that should be understood in the tradition of didactic writing—a genre in which "instruction [is] a primary element or tendency" (*OED*). Didactic writing refers to a diverse number of texts in a variety of periods and traditions such as the moral instruction of Aesop's tales and William Langland's *Piers Plowman*, eighteenth-century women's conduct material including *The Female Tatler* and *The Female Spectator*, nineteenth-century novels exemplified by Jane Austen's *Northanger Abbey*, and even twenty-first century self-help and entrepreneur fiction/non-fiction. This perspective reveals references in Cline's novel as key touchstones with which to educate the reader about 1980s gamer culture. In order to fully comprehend Cline's novel, to 'get' all the references, the reader must be prepared to learn. Cline's comment in the "Acknowledgments" at the end of the novel are indicative of this goal. He writes:

> Finally, I want to thank all of the writers, filmmakers, actors, artists, musicians, programmers, game designers, and geeks whose work I've paid tribute to in this story. These people have all entertained and enlightened me, and I hope that—like Halliday's hunt—*this book will inspire others to seek out their creations* [emphasis added]. (374)

---

4 Reviewers that had lived through the 1980s appreciated the cultural references on a personal level. For example, Patrick Rothfuss writes: "This book pleased every geeky bone in my geeky body. I feel like it was written just for me" (qtd. In Cline, *Ready* back cover). Paul Malmont praises Cline for "somehow manag[ing] to jack into the nervous system of some great warm collective geek-dream nostalgia of the '70s and '80s" (qtd. in Cline, *Ready* front matter). John Scalzi describes the book as a "nerdgasm" (qtd. in Cline, *Ready* back cover), and Christopher Farnsworth describes the novel as "Pure geek heaven. . . . A story that will resonate in the heart of every true nerd" (quoted. in Cline, *Ready Player One* front matter).

The contents of the novel's intertextual syllabus are taught using both narrative and games. "[S]eek[ing] out [these] creations" and arriving at 100% completion of the novel—getting all the references—is motivated in three ways. First, the novel catalyzes the reader's motivation by reifying gamer communities as progressively countercultural with a narrative that positions gamers as societal saviors. Like much contemporary sci-fi, *Ready Player One* proposes that the future of humanity rests upon the ethical implementation of technology. Significantly, *Ready Player One* identifies gamer communities as arbiters of ethical technology implementation in resistance to the tyranny of corporations. It thus contributes to the myth that gaming communities are somehow inherently subversive to authority despite being the foundation of a multi-billion dollar industry that mostly panders to white men.

Second, the novel catalyzes motivation by providing a model for gamer conduct. Events in the narrative and interactions between the characters illustrate a system of exchange and self-fashioning that extends beyond notions of "cultural capital" (Bourdieu) toward a "gaming capital" (Consalvo) in keeping with so-called neoliberal subjectivity. Indeed, I read *Ready Player One* as inherently imbricated with trends and practices identified by critics as neoliberal. I will provide exposition on my use of "neoliberal" in due course, but for now we can characterize the twentieth-century liberal to neoliberal shift as a resurgence of *laissez-faire* economics, a further withdrawal of the state intervention in favor of governance by market logics, and a ubiquitous assimilation of both institutional and individual common sense with economic rationality. Notably for the task at hand, economists often mobilize games to explain neoliberal practices. Contemporary reflections on game theory argue that the pedagogy of games—exemplified by the Prisoners' Dilemma—have been integral to the formation of neoliberal subjectivity, with game playing being "interchangeable with contemporary paradigmatic instrumental rationality" (Amadae 61). In other words, the pursuit of financial gain is analogous to the win-at-all-costs attitude prevalent in meritocratic, non-cooperative game worlds—earn points and ignore the virtual (and sometimes real) consequences. Money, as "the medium of all value" (Amadae i), is gamified; neoliberalism is an intensification of capitalist logics, where financial accumulation is a means to an end in itself, a game played for the sake of the game. In arguing that the novel provides a conduct model for the neoliberal subject, I build on these economic analyses by proposing that *Ready Player One* speaks to a gamification of value that extends beyond traditional forms of financial capital; Cline's novel speaks to a desire for unmitigated accumulation in all cultural spheres that are themselves economized and, therefore, gamified. A gamer primer, *Ready Player One* helps the budding neoliberal subject self-fashion in gaming communities by indicating valuable markers (Cline's canon of references) and providing a conduct model to acquire and display "gaming capital"—an aggregation of gaming skill, knowledge, and experience. Though in the storyworld "gaming capital" has clear moral connotations (saving the world) and financial connections (winning a trillion dollar company), gamer value markers are clearly intrinsic to the formation and curation of character identity and worth. Seeking out the references and performing gamer knowledge may well be pleasurable means unto themselves, but this essay suggests that the joys of ludic accumulation and gamer self-fashioning via value markers profoundly resonates with market rationality and the seductive power of neoliberalism. In short, *Ready Player One* isn't just a game for fun, it's a game that instructs a gamer ethic—a mutation of Weber's Protestant Ethic—with auspicious parallels to neoliberal practices.

Third, the novel motivates the reader to emulate the characters' conduct and gamer ethic by not only being about their competition but also by being a competition itself—it replicates the Easter Egg hunt of the story world in the real world. Starting with an encoded URL hidden in the text, players are led to embody the fictional hunt by completing a series of challenges. Simultaneously, this leads to the formation of an online community of egg hunters comparable to the "gunters" (short for "egg hunters") in the novel. Further ARGs, forums and websites such as Cline's blog consolidate this community.

Over the years, critics have taken gaming communities to task over abhorrent exclusionary practices.[5] Cline's novel received similar treatment. Undoubtedly, in exploring what is essentially the creation of gamer history, questions about representative source selection and identity inclusion are important (cf. Condis). The conclusion that Cline's novel, in its reference to mostly white, male artists and focalization through a white, male subject position, contributes to the hegemony of heterosexual, cis white men in gaming cultures strikes me as irrefutable (cf. Nakamura). Taking such critiques of the novel as given, I want to highlight two of its other important implications. The first concerns how a twenty-first century print text harnessed the power of a transmedia ecology to create a community. In doing so, *Ready Player One* formed not only an historical consciousness about 1980s video game culture but also inspired a high degree of popular engagement with its intertexts; the novel actually inspired people to watch, listen to, and play 1980s cultural products. To explore the instructional capacity of *Ready Player One* is to consider how the novel form can affect change

---

5 For a summary of feminist approaches to game culture, a delineation of the infamous #GamerGate, and a reminder of the persistent violences perpetrated by men against presenting female gamers and game critics, see Shira Chess and Adrienne Shaw's "A Conspiracy of Fishes, or, How We Learned to Stop Worrying About #GamerGate and Embrace Hegemonic Masculinity."

in the digital age. Second, to read *Ready Player One* as a didactic novel is to consider how members of communities hailed as subcultural[6] fashion themselves. Cline's novel is a primer that not only educates the reader in 1980s gaming culture but also provides a fan culture code of conduct for gamers young and old. Indeed, for those that were video game players in the 1980s, the novel is still an important selective remembrance imbuing certain cultural artifacts with value—delineating the "right" kind of nostalgia. The phenomenon of *Ready Player One* expresses—that is, represents and contributes to—an important aspect of gamified, neoliberal digital culture: self-fashioning of identity and worth by incessantly accruing value markers such as Likes, Upvotes, Follows, and other forms of validation (cultural literacy, peer affirmation) as means unto themselves. This essay does not intend to enact a comprehensive discussion of self-fashioning in fan communities, a project which would require further case studies, but offers an important foray. To do so, it draws upon two main thinkers: Wendy Brown to set a working definition of neoliberalism and value, and Byung-Chul Han for his concept of the "project" or "achievement-subject." Together, they allow me to explain how even apparently subcultural modes of self-fashioning are not easily disaggregated from market logics—gamer conduct being precisely the kind of ethic required for navigating (and perhaps playing) the regime of neoliberalism. As a book about a game composed of a series of smaller games about knowing games that is itself a game that teaches the reader about games and how to play games within a gamer culture that is also one big game... *Ready Player One* is a paradigmatic literary artifact for the milieu of gamification. In moving beyond moralizing discussions of online communities, *Ready Player One* reveals what is both compelling and frightening not only about the culture of games but, in the prescient words of Pierre Bourdieu, "the game of culture" (6).

---

[6] I use no transcendent heuristic for identifying a subculture. As "subculture" is a dynamic, shifting term, only the act of hailing a group as subcultural provides a consistent definition. In other words, that which is called a subculture is a subculture. I use the term in this essay to identify those taste cultures which do not align with perceived mass culture from a media perspective. Geek and gamer communities have been consistently referred to by the media as subcultures or subcultural (cf. Thornton).

Gamers Rise Up: Reifying the Gamer as Countercultural

Set in 2044 urban America, *Ready Player One* begins after ecological and economic collapse has forced country dwellers across the US to migrate to the outskirts of major cities in search of jobs and internet access. In the subsequent build-up of towering "stacks" of mobile homes, we meet the novel's teenage protagonist, Wade Watts. Through Wade we learn how the dire state of dystopian existence has driven many people to seek solace in the O.A.S.I.S. ("Ontologically Anthropocentric Sensory Immersive Simulation") (48). The O.A.S.I.S. is "a massively multiplayer online game that (...) gradually evolved into the globally networked virtual reality most of humanity (...) [use] on a daily basis" (1).

Early in the novel, Wade reveals that the creator of the O.A.S.I.S., video game designer James Halliday, has passed away leaving no heirs. Upon his death, Halliday released a video challenging the entire population of the O.A.S.I.S. to find an Easter Egg buried deep within the game. The first person to progress through the series of challenges and clues that lead to the 'egg' inherits both Halliday's vast fortune and control of the O.A.S.I.S. Along with this message, Halliday released documents chronicling his life and 1980s pop culture obsessions as clues to the kind of knowledge players would need to succeed. Thus "a new subculture was born, composed of the millions of people who now devoted every free moment of their lives to searching for Halliday's egg. At first, these individuals were known simply as 'egg hunters,' but this was quickly truncated to the nickname 'gunters'" (8). Wade, whose O.A.S.I.S. user name is Parzival, is part of this gunter assemblage along with best friend Aech and love interest Art3mis.

The villains of the novel are a "global communications conglomerate" called "Innovative Online Industries" or "IOI" (33). IOI abuse their monopoly over many goods and services in the 2044 United States to produce circumstances equivalent to debt slavery. To 'pay off' these never-ending debts, people must work virtually in the O.A.S.I.S. for IOI. IOI's ultimate ambition is to expand their empire to full control of the real and virtual worlds. To do this, they must win Halliday's hunt within the same rules and boundaries as the gunters. While the gunters want to maintain the freedom of the O.A.S.I.S.—which currently provides not only free access to play but also education—IOI intends to monetize the virtual universe through advertising and subscription fees. If the gunters are the chivalric knights of this tale who play by the rules,[7] then IOI are the unfair deviants

---

7 Susan Aronstein and Jason Thompson argue in their essay "Coding the Grail: *Ready Player*

that break the "magic circle." IOI aggregate their collective performance to find the Easter Egg by hiring both players and researchers, spending huge amounts of money (which can be transferred to in-game finances) and threatening opponents in real life. Notably, IOI transgress the boundaries of the virtual game by uncovering Wade's identity and trying to assassinate him. In short, the gunters', and ultimately Wade's, victory over IOI to maintain Halliday's vision of a free O.A.S.I.S symbolizes a triumph of the individual over a faceless corporation, a free internet over a monetized one, teamwork over cheating and, above all, a game well played.

Ready Player One's O.A.S.I.S resonates with monopolistic digital platforms like Google whose services are used ubiquitously. On the one hand, the O.A.S.I.S. functions as essential societal infrastructure that provides a utopian escape from economic and ecological collapse, but on the other hand it is a continuous revenue stream for corporations and an advanced method of oppression via data tracking and immaterial labor. Contrary to early cyberpunk fiction such as William Gibson's *Neuromancer*, which fears an effacement of human agency in the face of the determinism of digital spaces,[8] *Ready Player One* depicts humans as in control of the future implementation of technology. The novel is optimistic about the possibility of an ethical implementation of platforms, suggesting it just takes the right leadership. Consequently, it is only by harnessing the power of technology that the future of humanity can be guided in the right direction. Clearly, corporations cannot be trusted to do this job because their ethics are clouded by their money-grabbing propensities. The stakes are high and the message is clear: that the gamers—as representatives of the young and tech-savvy—are society's saviors. In the repackaging of the classic tale of corporation vs. counterculture, the narrative reifies gaming communities as antithetical to the tyranny of corporatism.

This is the first and most superficial component of the novel's didacticism: an instructive myth teaching the reader that gaming culture is marginal and opposed to evil powers trying to take away fun and freedom. Simplistic but evocative, the novel appeals to the liberal proclivity to uphold the rights of man and resist domination by identifying gaming culture with an ethos of transgression. The moral of the story is: gamers are anti-corporate, gamers are good, be a gamer.

One's Arthurian Mash-Up" that Wade's choice of username, Parzival, is significant and connects the novel to a lineage of interpretations of Arthurian legend.

[8] For more on late-twentieth-century perspectives on technological determinism, see Raymond Williams's *Television: Technology and Cultural Form*, particularly pages 3–7.

Achievement-Subjects: Neoliberalism and the Person as Project

In a time where tech-entrepreneurs like Elon Musk are venerated as today's intellectuals and video game streamers like Ninja become celebrities, the geek-as-outcast and geek as antithetical to 'mainstream' or 'dominant' culture becomes an unworkable paradigm. *Ready Player One's* myth, therefore, needs to be distilled by theorizations of subjectivity that cut across supposed cultural boundaries for it to have any purchase on reality. Under the regime of neoliberalism, cultural distinctions become irrelevant: all is subsumed into the flows and circulation of capital. As everything is economized, individuals become less like disciplined subjects and more like faux-free "projects" under the illusion that they are idiosyncratically self-fashioning (Han 1). In reality, the "free" individual marches to the beat of market logics.

But what is neoliberalism and why should it transform our notions of social and cultural distinctions? As Wendy Brown explains: "Neoliberalism is commonly understood as a set of economic policies promoting unrestricted actions, flows, and accumulations of capital by means of low tariffs and taxes, de-regulation of industries, privatization of formerly public goods and services, stripped out welfare states, and the breakup of organized labor" (61). In his lectures on *The Birth of Biopolitics*, Foucault argues that neoliberalism should also be grasped as a governing rationality that forms new modes of subjectivity, conduct, and social relation. It is thus distinct, Brown argues, from ideology—"a distortion or mystification of reality"—in being both productive and world-making: its economization of "every sphere and human endeavor" forms a society based not on a "justice-producing social contract" and merely organized around markets but, instead, a state oriented by market requirements (62). Neoliberal rationality becomes common sense and its principles govern not only the state but also suffuse all other institutions and expressions of public and private life—including those groups hailed as subcultural. In this way, traditional notions of freedom —often conceptualized as a life devoid of necessity, subjugation, and external compulsion—become impossible. Freedom, too, is submitted to market logics, as it is equated entirely with the unregulated pursuit of private ends and is exercised to "enhance the value, competitive positioning, or market share of a person or firm" (62). The concept is thus stripped of any political valency; even the act of opposing 'dominant' institutions becomes another type of competitive positioning in order to enhance one's value. The community, too, is subsumed. Far from self-realization with others, what Marx defines as freedom—"Only in community [with others does each] individual [have] the means of cultivating his gifts in all directions; only in the community, therefore, is personal freedom possible" (*The German Ideology* 83)—the community is merely a set of parameters for self-interested competition, just like a game. As the unwitting "genital organs of Capital" (Han 4), relations between human actors amounts to the "relation of capital to itself as another capital, i.e., the real conduct of capital as capital" (Marx, *Grundrisse* 650). This faux-freedom amounts to what critics, following Gilles Deleuze's "Postscript on the Societies of Control," identify as a new form of governmentality. As Brown elucidates:

> [N]eoliberalization in the Euro-Atlantic world today is more often enacted (...) through 'soft power' drawing on consensus and buy in, [rather] than (...) violence, dictatorial command, or even overt political platforms. Neoliberalism governs as sophisticated *common sense*, a *reality principle* remaking institutions and human beings everywhere it settles, nestles, and gains affirmation [emphases added]. (*Undoing the Demos* 35)

As I will expand on shortly, it is already evident how this neoliberal reality principle—ubiquitous self-affirmation via competitive value accumulation in line with market rationality—has profound ludic resonances.

For now, the consequences of this neoliberal terrain for communities in the digital age are clear. Identifying and engaging with a so-called subculture is not to take-up a stance antithetical to the establishment, nor does it necessarily escape the logic of the neoliberal regime. Instead, the person merely occupies a position in another market with its own metrics of accumulation. The self-interested person—in this case someone who identifies with a subset of gamer culture, the *Ready Player One* fanbase—seeks to enhance their value in this new market. But what *is* value?

Conceptualizing the slippery term 'value' in the study of digital communities under the neoliberal regime is complex. Current scholarship on video game culture largely defers to Pierre Bourdieu's delineation of "cultural capital" in their discussions of value. Typically, we understand capital as a financial asset. For Bourdieu, however, cultural capital is something that improves the standing of those who possess it within a purportedly afinancial system of social exchange in which that thing is valued. Cultural capital refers to the performance of possessing markers—such as having read certain books or recognizing certain music —that allow their possessors access to the privileges of higher classes (Bourdieu 1–2). The historical purpose of, for example, literary study was to provide students with linguistic capital—in the form of "Standard English" as the preferred dialect of upper class communication—and symbolic capital, which gives the student the ability to impress others with their knowledge of canonical literature and thus demonstrate their good taste (cf. Guillory ix). In this way, literary study might advance a student's social standing in facilitating a display of certain knowledges equated with an upper-class lifestyle. The catch, of course, is that such knowledge is often predicated on access to certain types of education and experience. Therefore, existing financial and class privileges manifest themselves in the form of other symbols in Bourdieu's delineation of cultural capital. Indeed, the very purpose of the markers of this form of capital could be conceptualized as a gatekeeping method that manifests itself socially and allows the identification and exclusion of those not from similarly privileged backgrounds. Indeed, Nicholas Garnham and Raymond Williams have argued that what ultimately defines cultural capital as capital is its 'convertibility' into economic/financial capital (cf. 123).

Unfortunately, transposing Bourdieu's notion of cultural capital onto systems of value in the neoliberal regime is problematic, as it relies upon types of class stratification or, at least, meaningful distinctions between high and popular culture that no longer exist. This does not mean, however, that Cline's novel does not contain residual assumptions about the alignment of alternate canon formation and an ethos of political transgression. Henry Jenkins's analysis of internet communities epitomizes such an optimistic theorization. Jenkins argues that the formation of alternate canons and the production of user-generated content is a subversive feature of convergent, participatory cultures. "With relatively low barriers to artistic expression and civic engagement [and] strong support for creating and sharing creation" members of participatory cultures "believe their contributions matter and feel some degree of social connection with one another" (Jenkins, *Confronting* 5). Communities that engage in these practices typically transgress culturally dominant standards of "good taste" by constructing a seemingly non-hierarchical system of exchange (cf. 16). In the same vein, *Ready Player One* portrays its system of knowledge exchange as radically egalitarian. All players with access to the O.A.S.I.S. have access to *Anorak's Almanac* —a document released by Halliday on his death to serve as a guide to all his 1980s' obsessions. Purportedly, therefore, everyone has a chance to be a winner. We can therefore understand both the fictional gunter community in *Ready Player One* and the community that emerges around the novel as examples of a participatory culture: members are valued for their knowledge of Halliday's/Cline's 1980s canon, their video game skills, and their ability to contribute to the community.

This narrative of emancipation—that creating alternate systems of exchange subverts or escapes the neoliberal regime—obfuscates the two important aspects of value circulation. First, alternate systems of value exchange remain economized. Even in these subcultural internet communities, people function as self-interested accumulators. They are not breaking out of neoliberal world-making practices. Second, accumulation of markers does not signify social/cultural bracket access as with Bourdieu's cultural capital. That is, the accumulation of these markers does not cease to be relevant once the threshold for membership is reached. Instead, these markers are effectively monetized and continue to be currency accrued as a means unto itself. Inverting Bourdieu, rather than accumulating markers to enter a community, we might say that attaining community membership is desirable only insofar as that community facilitates accumulation.

To understand what monetized markers mean for gaming communities, it is helpful to consider value in digital culture more broadly. The neoliberal regime enmeshes subjectivity with accumulation practices as if, as Byung-Chul Han forwards, the neoliberal subject were not a subject at all but a project (cf. 1). For Han, "the project subject is a new, *more efficient kind of subjeçtivation and subjugation* (...). As a project deeming itself free of external and alien limitations, the *I* is now subjugating itself to internal limitations and self-constraints, which are taking the form of compulsive achievement and optimization" (1). Also referred to as the "achievement-subject," the project is more complex than *homo economicus*, a caricature of rational man who attempts to maximize profit and utility as producer and consumer, and it is less clearly related to financial capital than can be understood through the lens of human capital—knowledge, habits, and personality attributes that are ultimately embodied in the ability to perform labor and produce economic value. Instead, the project compulsively accumulates in order to improve itself. Wendy Brown draws similar conclusions when she states that the neoliberal regime produces "a creature who has to manage its value, whether through Facebook or Twitter, or interning for free, or selling its forehead as advertising space. It has to manage its value but it does this for itself. If it doesn't have any assets, anything it can capitalize or with which it can attract investors, then it becomes not just fungible but disposable" (80). But this is not purely a sterile, rational desire. Brown notes that

> there's much about financialisation and neoliberalism that's emotionally and affectively appealing. It's very, very seductive, and I don't just mean people are tricked. I'm not talking about false consciousness. I mean it's exciting and delicious in many ways to think about how to enhance the value of various bits of your self, how to brand yourself, how to attract investors, how to get more likes on Facebook, how to get re-tweeted, how to self-invest and get others to invest in you. ("Feminism, Law, and Neoliberalism" 83)

Indeed, with the emphasis on market logic, neoliberalism's mobilization of the excess of affect and emotion should not be obscured.

As already noted in identifying the co-emergence of game theory and neoliberal governance (cf. Amadae), there are profound resonances between the seduction of neoliberalism and the joy of playing games. Foucault's ludic economy analogy provides a lucid corroboration:

> In short, both for the state and for individuals, the economy must be a game: a set of regulated activities (...) in which the rules are not decisions which someone takes for others [but] (...) a set of rules which determine the way in which each must play a game whose outcome is not known by anyone. The *economy is a game* and the legal institution which frames the economy should be thought of as the rules of the game [emphasis added]. (173)

For Foucault, the neoliberal institution does not order subjects through discipline, it sets the parameters for the apparent contingency of free competition. This faux-freedom of the individual is analogous to the player in a game where all play is within set boundaries and is ultimately subsumed into the flows of capital; any activity ultimately becomes part of the game (of capitalism) itself. Tellingly, game theorists frequently compare life to a game or a series of games, sometimes in harrowing ways (cf. Amadae 61).[9] In brief, economized spheres are gamified spheres. And if, as Brown argues, all spheres of life are economized under neoliberalism, then all spheres of life are gamified. To be clear, I am extending this observation beyond the financial economy and arguing that the acquisition of alternate value markers—set by the parameters of a given community—is a practice indicative of and embroiled in the neoliberal "common sense" or "reality principle" that prioritizes market rationality (Brown *Undoing* 35). *Ready Player One*, therefore, can tell us something about the fatal attraction of neoliberalism. I believe it has something to do with why we like games so much. As Dana Smith writes of *Candy Crush Saga*: "Initially, the game allows us to win and pass levels with ease, giving a strong sense of satisfaction. These accomplishments are experienced as mini-rewards in our brains, releasing the neurochemical dopamine and tapping into the same neuro-circuity involved in addiction, reinforcing our actions." Might, as Brown notes, adhering to neoliberal metrics of valuation, the economization of everything, provide a similar sense of satisfaction? Might acquiring market value be analogous to playing games and accumulating dopamine hits? Might the ethic of neoliberalism *be* the gamer ethic? Such questions are unanswerable here but provide a generative context for the ensuing analysis.

Turning now to a definition of 'gaming capital' and its textual representation, Brown and Han's theorizations of neoliberal subjectivity serve as touchstones for understanding the project's notion of value and the connection be-

---

[9] As Ken Binmore muses: "suppose (...) the game of life is the infinitely repeated Prisoners' Dilemma" (96).

tween self-fashioning and an incessant drive for value acquisition. Moving beyond the superficial counterculture/mainstream binaries and reification of gamer identity delineated as the novel's first didactic move, Cline's novel illustrates how projects go about value accumulation. This is the second key component of the novel's didacticism—providing a model for gamer conduct and therefore a guide for achievement-subjects looking to invest in the currency of gaming communities.

Gaming Capital: The Economization of Play

Video games are clearly meritocratic. In the act of play, the trajectory of acquisition is clear to the project: win more games, earn more experience points, acquire more items, etc. It is less obvious how value circulates beyond the player's private experience of the game. The term 'gaming capital' helps explain how forms of accumulation and exchange in and around video game communities occur. Coined by Mia Consalvo, the notion of 'gaming capital' is intended to "capture how being a member of game culture is about more than playing games or even playing them well. It's being knowledgeable about game releases and secrets, and passing that information on to others. It's having opinions about which game magazines are better and the best sites for walkthroughs on the Internet" (18). Since Consalvo's use of the term, other critics have developed 'gaming capital' to signify the intersecting "cultural, economic, social and symbolic forms of capital that are embodied through the knowledge, skills, and dispositions of the bodily habitus within local sociologies of gaming" (Walsh and Apperley 2). In other words, being a good gamer is not just about being good at video games, it is about being engaged in the community and performing an in-depth knowledge of games and their paratexts[10]—other media and texts that exist alongside games and players. Essentially, gaming capital is a way of measuring the value of activities in the communities that emerge around gameplay.

In *Ready Player One*, the most obvious relationship between gaming and capital is the direct conversion of O.A.S.I.S. money to real-world money. Winning contests, performing virtual labor, and acquiring and selling items in the O.A.S.I.S. accrues in-game money which can be used to purchase products in

---

[10] Taken from Gérard Genette, Mia Consalvo uses the term 'paratext' in an expanded sense to signify "multiple elements involved in the larger game industry" such as magazines, forums, walkthroughs, and advertising (3).

meatspace. Conversely, money earned in the real world is spent on hardware to increase in-game effectiveness (such as more sensitive haptic gloves or a faster internet connection) or on virtual objects and services like weapons and transportation. The consequences of this equivalence are present in the novel with IOI drawing upon their vast resources to aid their cause in the Hunt and with wealthy Aech giving poor Wade money so they can virtually adventure together. But the devastation of translating real into virtual money is staged all the more dramatically in Spielberg's 2018 film version. Here, in the attempt to win a game, Wade's aunt's abusive partner, Rick, splurges all his money on virtual armor upgrades and weapons only to be gunned down in the heat of battle. The real-world consequences are violent. Rick reveals that he has spent the family savings and proceeds to release his ire on aunt Alice and Wade. On an institutional level, the equivalence of virtual and real money also leads to corporate oppression as people in debt to IOI must pay their dues indentured in a small booth performing work online in the O.A.S.I.S. Neither of these examples in *Ready Player One* are distant from our lived relationship with digital technologies abundant with microtransactions and virtual sweatshops. Indeed, the exchangeability of virtual and real money reveals a central paradigm of neoliberalism: not only the economization of games but the gamification of everything.

Within the novel's universe, knowledge about Halliday's life and interests also become gaming capital with a direct translation into financial capital, as it brings players closer to winning Halliday's fortune and having control of the O.A.S.I.S. In acquiring the keys to pass through the gates that eventually lead to finding the Easter Egg, players decipher clues and complete challenges. For example, the first challenge of the novel pits players against a non-player character in a game of *Joust* (1982). The player must be good enough to beat this difficult opponent whom one can only face every twenty-four hours. This skill is only developed by having practiced the game before the challenge. Another example is the "Flicksync" where players must recite, word for word, the lines of a character in a movie (112). For one challenge, Wade plays the role of Matthew Broderick's David Lightman in *Wargames* (1983) and, in another, a character in *Monty Python and the Holy Grail* (1975). These performative games require the player to deliver the correct dialogue at appropriate moments; they are awarded bonuses for chaining together correct responses and mimicking the gestures and inflection of the original films. Once again, this is not a game scenario where players can learn by repetition: they must prepare for these tests. To acquire this knowledge and move closer to victory in the hunt, one must study the "canon" (39) constituted by Halliday's favorite works.

The rules and boundaries of this gunter game of culture are thus set by Halliday's journal, *Anorak's Almanac* (Anorak being the name of Halliday's avatar).

These texts are treated with an almost religious reverence that imbues them with value above their ludic and aesthetic merits. Many of Halliday's favorite games come from his childhood in the 1980s, so, relative to 2044, as Wade describes, "these games were outdated digital dinosaurs that had become museum pieces long before [he] was born" (13). Far from "low-res antiques," Wade sees these relics from the 1980s as "hallowed artefacts. Pillars of the pantheon" (13). Knowledge of the canon is thus significant currency and, as Wade explains, "gunters loved to play the game of one-upmanship and were constantly trying to prove they had acquired more obscure knowledge than everyone else" (43). Here, the self-interested project's drive for accumulation is most clear. Competition with other gunters reveals how social interactions are codified as arenas in which to take stock of a project's market share. These interactions introduce an affective dimension to accumulation, as knowledge of the canon has an immediate emotional pay-off: praise and a sense of belonging. In the O.A.S.I.S., possession of gaming capital—in the form of knowledge and game skill—demonstrates worth not only to others but also to the self. There is certainly something comforting about having a primer—*Anorak's Almanac*—on how to make yourself worthy.

Ready Player One thus provides a model for conduct in the gamer game of culture: there must be clear markers of value or 'gaming capital'—in this case set by Halliday's journal, and there must be a system of exchange that provides some kind of affective validation of this value—the competitive games of one-upmanship. Together, the prospective currency is first circulated and then minted by a collective human capital investment of time and labor—an investment motivated in the novel by the promise of Halliday's massive fortune and control of the O.A.S.I.S. With these rules and boundaries set, emulating the gunters, the reader/project can begin to collect the markers of value. However, there is one problem with direct emulation: in the real world, a significant component of this system is missing. There is no massive fortune motivating the accumulation of capital. So why would a reader bother to seek out the constituents of Halliday's canon? The answer lies in *Ready Player One's* transmedia paratexts, which indicate the full force of the novel's pedagogy.

Teaching Games with Games: *Ready Player One* as a 1980s Gamer Education

The multi-trillionaire founder of the O.A.S.I.S. has entirely dictated the rules and limits of this game of culture. Halliday has used his power to create an Easter Egg hunt incentivizing an affinity with texts he values. Regardless of whether we read Halliday as a social progressive or a lonely man forcing others to share his nostalgia, his institutional position in control of a powerhouse digital platform is timely. Corporate magnates and superstar tech-entrepreneurs are venerated not just for their inventions or market achievements but as bastions of life advice and resources for self-help. Truly, the economization of all spheres under the neoliberal regime means that leading a life of success transcends occupational boundaries and splits between the public and private. From Steve Jobs to Warren Buffet, people want to know when they wake up, what books they read, how much sugar they have in their coffee: people want to know how they live. Essentially, the project asks: how do they accumulate better than me? How can I emulate their methods? Certainly, the memoirs of these success figures are examples of modern-day didactic literature as they are placed alongside self-help texts on bookstore shelves. Such texts and figures are important components in the maintenance of neoliberal worldmaking practices by emphasizing the trials of the self-interested individual and the telos of compulsive accumulation: fame and fortune. It goes without saying that a corporate oligarch's easy transposition from hedge fund manager to social, cultural, and even psychological instructor is a frightening prospect. Despite the ostensibly egalitarian aims of the O.A.S.I.S. in providing free use, education, and a platform for employment, *Ready Player One* provides a clear parallel to these real-world developments in Halliday's transition from introverted tech-entrepreneur to cultural dictator.

As the *Ready Player One* fiction bleeds into reality, a similar pedagogical ploy reveals itself: Cline educates his readership in 1980s gamer culture, the era of his childhood. But Cline is no corporate oligarch, nor, like Halliday, does he offer up the control of a trillion dollar company. Instead, ludic tactics with their own reward structures are mobilized to motivate engagement with his gamer primer and its intertexts. This is the third and final component of the novel's didacticism: teaching games with games.

Learning is enabled by easy access to internet search engines. A similar flattening of learning to the gunters'—in which all users can access the same information—has occurred in the contemporary reading process, only that, instead of the *Almanac*, we have Google. After Mia Consalvo's *Cheating*, we can understand how some reader/players might find value in traversing *Ready Player One*'s intertexts as an end in itself: different players have different ethics of engagement with a game. Just as one group of players might value completing just a video game's story mode, another group might aim to gather all collectibles and beat all challenges for a 100% completion rating. Similarly, there are different levels of completion for Cline's novel from just skimming the book to following all the references. For example, readers might search for and play *Joust* on an emulator or watch *Wargames* after reading about it. Here, the project accepts "Halliday's egg hunt, and by extension Cline's novel (...) as a classroom wherein student-readers learn about the origins of gamerdom" and begins to accumulate markers "Cline identifies as foundational to gamer culture" (Condis 3). For evidence of this reader engagement, we need look no further than Google once again. A quick search for *"Ready Player One* references" leads to multiple wiki sites, articles and forum threads documenting all the intertexts in the novel.[11] Similar lists have also been compiled for the film adaptation. In discussion threads on Reddit, for example, this *Ready Player One* knowledge is most clearly economized. Users disseminating the most obscure knowledge or theories tend to be upvoted the most—the value of gamer capital is quantified numerically.

Claiming that this kind of user engagement came into being without cultivation would, however, be inaccurate. If the canon of references is the *Ready Player One* syllabus then Cline's pedagogy is decidedly ludic. Indeed, Cline motivated readers to engage with the 1980s references by creating two new games for players to take part in. The first, which Cline released in 2012 on the novel's anniversary, was a real-world Easter Egg hunt ARG (Alternate Reality Game), starting within the text. Here, the reader/player was invited to search the novel for an encoded URL—http://anoraksalmanac.com/—that would begin a journey through a series of gates, clues, and challenges, just like in the story. Users deciphered the URL by combining misspellings in English print editions of the novel. This led to a game made about the *Ready Player One* novel called *Stacks* and unlocked a QR code: a clue to the next challenge. The second challenge, no longer available, was a Facebook game called *Ultimate Collector: Garage Sale* in which players had to collect the parts to build a DeLorean (of Back to the Future fame). The final challenge of the Easter Egg hunt required the player to set a world record on a select classic arcade game: *Pac-Man, Joust Arcade, Joust* Atari 2600, *Black Tiger,* or *Robotron 2084.* The prize? A DeLorean, of course. Cline used his well-followed blog to disseminate updates on the challenges and to celebrate player successes. Undoubtedly, this platform of fame via Cline's *Ernie's Blog* added another degree of prestige to the competition, another affirmation of gaming capital's value. In the end, Craig Queen was the first to make his way through all the gates and complete the final challenge.[12] In the process, therefore, players had to close-read the novel, play games that engaged with the novel's narrative

---

11 See *"Ready Player One* Wiki." *Fandom.* http://readyplayerone.wikia.com/wiki/Ready_-Player_One. Accessed 15 Jan. 2019.
12 cf. "The Grand Prize DeLorean at its New Home!" in *Ernie's Blog,* 2 September 2012.

and intertexts, and ultimately prove their gaming skills by setting a world record (verified by the organization *Twin Galaxies*) on a classic arcade game.

In December 2012, in a hat-tip to the foundation of the in-text O.A.S.I.S., Cline revealed the release of another game that allowed users to role-play within the *Ready Player One* universe via a chat-interface: the O.A.S.I.S. Multi-user Dimension. The M.U.D. has since been shut down, but similar user communities emulating its role-playing formula have replaced it. At the time of writing in 2018, *Reddit* is hosting forums where users refer to themselves as 'gunters' and search for Easter Eggs in the film adaptation. Once again, significant amounts of knowledge about *Ready Player One* and its intertexts are required in order to effectively engage in the gunter fantasy.

Ready Player One and the games within and around it have therefore spurred not only a community of avid followers but a great deal of participation. As a result, player/readers have built themselves into the novel's heterocosm by taking part in their own Easter Egg hunts and developing their own narratives in RPGs. Simultaneously, users have contributed to the expansion of the novel's heterocosm by producing artistic representations of characters, cosplaying, and writing fan fiction. One such product, "Lacero" by Andy Weir—a short story exploring chief bad guy Sorento's background—is now considered a canonical addition to the novel's plot. Such responses are indicative not only of the mutability of the parameters of this participatory community but also of the success of Cline's pedagogy in spreading his subcultural 1980s canon.

Conclusion

At the start of this essay I asked, what does the video game novel do? I have argued that one function of video game fiction is education, teaching readers about the beginnings of gaming culture in the 1980s, how to conduct oneself in gaming communities, and, ultimately, implicating player/readers in a literary game. It seems that *Ready Player One* has achieved the goal lain out in its "Acknowledgements"—to get readers to go out and play, listen to, and watch 1980s cultural products. But the novel reveals something more complex than a cause for celebrating the persistent power of print fiction. Indeed, as Angela Nagle notes in *Kill All Normies* (2017), academic discourse has (should have) moved well past the uncritical appraisal of so-called countercultural products:

> Half a century after the Rolling Stones, after Siouxsie Sioux and Joy Division flirted with fascist aesthetics, after *Piss Christ*, after *Fight Club*, when everyone from the President's fanboys to McDonalds are flogging the dead horse of 'edginess,' it may be time to lay the very

recent and very modern aesthetic values of counterculture and the entire paradigm to rest. (103)

After all, counterculture too is subsumed into the mutable regime of neoliberalism. In this way, *Ready Player One* merely depicts and comprises another economized sphere with its own metrics of accumulation. The self-interested project craves the accumulation of value, be it in the form of upvotes, high scores, or knowledge of Halliday's canon. Here, the didactic novel and the neoliberal subject/project intersect. For the projects who constantly seek to fashion themselves, to increase their market worth, pedagogic novels like *Ready Player One* are gamer primers—they function as practical conduct guides teaching readers what and how to accumulate in gaming culture.

It is easy to dismiss the neoliberal regime as a total oppression, as many have done after Gilles Deleuze's "Postscript on the Societies of Control." Yes, all modes of production including the immaterial are subsumed into the machinations of capitalism. Yes, digital technologies facilitate new, unseen forms of monitoring and oppression. Yes, traditional forms of creative expression, political action, even freedom all lose their valency. But what is often obfuscated by these analyses is what is so attractive about neoliberal world-making. I have gestured throughout this essay toward the appeal of clear methods and metrics to acquire value—whatever that may mean in a given context—and increase self-worth. *Ready Player One*, as primer, forwards a mode of self-validation through its clear delineation of value markers (gaming capital) and code of conduct (the gamer ethic). By connecting the beginnings of neoliberalism explicitly to games and game playing, I have proposed that, more than exemplary, *Ready Player One* may well be a paradigmatic phenomenon for the milieu of neoliberal gamification. To return to an earlier question: might the ethic of neoliberalism *be* the gamer ethic? The two certainly correspond in interesting ways. To claim, as McKenzie Wark does, that now "the form of the digital game is an allegory for the form of being" (171) would be too strong, however—not all things are gamified, suffering remains and resists. The comparison between pervasive market rationality and the game form is generative, though, for thinking the pleasures of being neoliberal. There is something about the compulsion to accumulate that is devoid of idealism but strangely comforting at the same time: it is not toward anything, it is almost playful—*Candy Crush*'s dopamine hit. In this way, the economization of games comes hand-in-hand with the gamification of the economy and social relations. But there is no game over, no victory clause, no control over the O.A.S.I.S. on the horizon—it is a game without winning. Truly, as Bourdieu writes, there is no way out of "the game of culture" (6).

Notably, even five years after the announcement of the Easter Egg hunt, when everyone had lost hope in finding, let alone passing, the first stage of the Hunt, Wade and friends continued to rigorously train in preparation. It is easy to imagine that, had Wade not happened upon the Copper Key, the gunters would have persisted to compulsively accrue gaming capital for the rest of their lives (9). Here, perhaps, lies part of the seduction of ubiquitous economization: at least infinite accumulation stuffs a void of meaning.

Works Cited

Aarseth, Espen. *Cybertext: Perspectives on Ergodic Literature*. John Hopkins UP, 1997.
Amadae, S. M. *Prisoners of Reason: Game Theory and Neoliberal Political Economy*. Cambridge UP, 2016.
Aronstein, Susan, and Jason Thompson. "Coding the Grail: *Ready Player One*'s Arthurian Mash-Up." *Arthuriana*, vol. 25, no. 2, 2015, pp. 51–65.
Bourdieu, Pierre. *Distinction: A Social Critique of the Judgment of Taste*. Translated by Richard Nice, Routledge, 1984.
Brown, Wendy. "Neoliberalism's Frankenstein: Authoritarian Freedom in Twenty-First Century 'Democracies.'" *Critical Times*, vol. 1, no. 1, 2018, pp. 60–79, ctjournal.org/index.php/criticaltimes/article/view/12/7. Accessed 15 Jan. 2019.
Brown, Wendy. *Undoing the Demos: Neoliberalism's Stealth Revolution*. Zone Books, 2015.
Cline, Ernest. *Ernie's Blog*. www.ernestcline.com/blog. Accessed 15 Jan. 2019.
– – –. *Ready Player One*. Arrow Books, 2011.
Condis, Megan Amber. "Playing the Game of Literature: *Ready Player One*, the Ludic Novel, and the Geeky 'Canon' of White Masculinity." *Journal of Modern Literature*, vol. 39, no. 2, 2016, pp. 1–19.
Consalvo, Mia. *Cheating: Gaining Advantage in Videogames*. MIT Press, 2007.
Cruz, Katie, and Wendy Brown. "Feminism, Law, and Neoliberalism: An Interview and Discussion with Wendy Brown." *Feminist Legal Studies*, vol. 24, no. 1, 2016. https://link-springer-com.libproxy.lib.unc.edu/article/10.1007%2Fs10691-016-9314-z, pp. 69–89.
Deleuze, Gilles. "Postscript on Societies of Control." *October*, vol. 59, 1992, pp. 3–7.
Detweiler, Robert. "Games and Play in Modern American Fiction." *Contemporary Literature*, vol. 17, no. 1, 1976, pp. 44–62.
Foucault, Michel. *The Birth of Biopolitics: Lectures at the College De France 1978–1979*. Edited by Michel Senellart, translated by Graham Burchell, Palgrave, 2008.
Garnham, Nicholas, and Raymond Williams. "Pierre Bourdieu and the Sociology of Culture." *Media, Culture and Society: A Critical Reader*. Edited by R. Collins et al., Sage, 1986, pp. 116–30.
Guillory, John. *Cultural Capital: The Problem of Literary Canon Formation*. U of Chicago P, 1993.
Han, Byung-Chul. *Psycho-Politics: Neoliberalism and New Technologies of Power*. Verso, 2017.
Hutcheon, Linda, with Siobhan O'Flynn. *A Theory of Adaptation*. 2nd ed., Routledge, 2013.
Jenkins, Henry. *Confronting the Challenges of Participatory Culture: Media Education for the 21st Century*. MIT Press, 2009.

Jenkins, Henry. *Convergence Culture: Where Old and New Media Collide.* New York University Press, 2006.
Jupin, Tanner J. *Gamic Fiction: The Intermediation of Literature and Games.*, University of California, Davis, 2014, Dissertation.
Kuehl, John. "The Ludic Impulse in Recent American Fiction." *The Journal of Narrative Technique*, vol. 16, no. 3, 1986, pp. 167–78.
Marx, Karl. *Grundrisse: Introduction to the Critique of Political Economy.* Translated by Martin Nicolaus, Vintage, 1973.
Marx, Karl, and Friedrich Engels. *The German Ideology, Part One.* Edited by C. J. Arthur, International Publishers, 2004.
Nagle, Angela. *Kill All Normies: Online Culture Wars From 4chan and Tumblr to Trump and the Alt-Right.* Zero Books, 2017.
Nakamura, Lisa. "Queer Female of Color: The Highest Difficult Setting There Is? Gaming Rhetoric as Gender Capital." *Ada: A Journal of Gender, New Media, and Technology*, vol. 1, no. 1, 2012, n.pag.
OED Online. "didactic, n. and adj." Oxford University Press, 2014, www.oed.com/view/entry/52341. Accessed 15 Jan. 2019.
"Ready Player One Wiki." *Fandom*, readyplayerone.wikia.com/wiki/Ready_Player_One. Accessed 15 Jan. 2019.
Smith, Dana. "This is What *Candy Crush Saga* Does to your Brain." *The Guardian*, 1 Apr. 2014, www.theguardian.com/science/blog/2014/apr/01/candy-crush-saga-app-brain. Accessed 15 Jan. 2019.
Thornton, Sarah. *Club Cultures: Music, Media and Subcultural Capital.* Polity Press, 2003.
Walsh, Christopher, and Thomas Apperley. "Gaming Capital: Rethinking Literacy." *Changing Climates: Education for Sustainable Futures. Proceedings of the AARE 2008 International Education Research Conference*, 30 Nov – 4 Dec 2008, Queensland University of Technology, 2009.
Wark, McKenzie. *Gamer Theory.* Harvard UP, 2007.
Williams, Raymond. *Television: Technology and Cultural Form.* Routledge, 2003.

Sebastian Domsch
Strategies against Structure: Video Game Terrorism as the Ultimate American Agency Narrative

This chapter will investigate how, within what I call the "Terrorist Narrative," video game rules, affordances, and valorizations create narrative archetypes. In terms of the relation between games and narrative, the approach sketched here is a departure both from theories regarding games as either being or containing narratives, and also from my own earlier investigation into how game structures are semanticized. As I have argued elsewhere about the relationship between gameplay and narrative, a marked phenomenon in players' interaction with game systems is what we might call a process of semanticization, since

> players constantly increase or decrease the semantics they associate with the structures they encounter, (…) they ascribe additional meaning to them (creating what we might call a semantic surplus), or chose to ignore potential meaning attached to them. It is this process that leads to the potential experience of a game system as gameworld, as a fictional world with its own self-contained meaning and rules. (Domsch 18)

What happens is that players are charging game mechanics with meaning:

> Many games can be played successfully in a purely abstract way, that is, by taking into account nothing but the rule structure as a self-contained system referring to nothing outside of itself. But one thing that almost inevitably happens when human beings play games is that they will start to invest the elements of the game and its structure—and consequently their own actions and decisions—with meaning that is not reducible to gameplay functions. (Domsch 19)

In the following, I would like to go one step further and, instead of focusing on how the player processes the choices and actions that are derived from the rules, look at the way that the specific nature of specific rules themselves enables the emergence of narrative forms. As we will see, this happens on a much more abstract level than the concrete and specific semanticizations that happen all the time in playing, and in which players identify elements that they encounter in gameplay as existents in a more or less coherent storyworld. The narrative forms that emerge out of repeated experiences with rule structures are located on a higher level of abstraction and are much less diverse than concrete semanticization, which is why we might call them narrative archetypes.

The notion of archetypal images and narratives has been analyzed repeatedly across the disciplines, from comparative religion studies and anthropology to psychoanalysis and literary and cultural studies, particularly in the first half of the twentieth century. The earliest approaches looked at archetypes as indications of shared mythologies, as exemplified in James George Frazer's monumental study *The Golden Bough: A Study in Comparative Religion* (first edition published in 1890, final edition 1915). One of Frazer's central observations was that different cultures that were very unlikely to have been in contact with each other throughout their history nevertheless featured stories with remarkable similarities in their mythologies. A few years later, the Swiss psychoanalyst C. G. Jung looked at archetypes in connection to what he had termed 'the collective unconscious.' Jung's hypothesis was that indeed any direct influence was unnecessary, that the similar mythologies were merely differing manifestations of structures deep in the human unconscious. It was these structures that Jung termed archetypes; they manifest themselves not only in myth and in dreams but in the finished art of cultures like our own. Thus we could say that for Jung, archetypes were expressive of psychological affordances. Maud Bodkin, one of the first scholars to apply Jung's ideas to literature, rejected this notion that archetypes are "stamped upon the physical organism" or "inherited in the structure of the brain," (Bodkin 4), but the notion of archetypal forms and narratives was very productively appropriated by literary scholars, with Northrop Frye as the most prominent example, both through his essay "The Archetypes of Literature" (1951) and his landmark monograph *The Anatomy of Criticism* (1957). Jung had laid the foundation for this through his interest in how archetypes manifested themselves not only in dreams, but also in myths, fairy tales, and other cultural productions.

What all of these approaches have in common with each other and with my own is that they look at the content of narrative, yet they are less interested in the concrete manifestations than in structures that emerge out of the comparison of a lot of individual narratives. Where they—and I—differ is largely in their explanations for the reasons why specific forms reoccur so frequently and become so pervasive within our attempts at making sense of the world. The focus of the following will therefore be on how narrative archetypes might be following directly out of rule structures (without a necessary connection to the semantic surplus) and also on their (subsequent) interrelation with society and culture. It could, for example, be argued that they also function as meta-narratives or *grand récits* that make attempts at world-understanding through narrative constructs.

Video games have developed a number of distinct archetypal narrative structures that are specific to this medium because of the way that they interact with gameplay elements, particularly the rule structures. These narrative archetypes emerge because of specific gameplay demands, affordances, and limitations, while at the same time working to integrate gameplay mechanics into a coherent fictional world. Thus, they are (relatively) independent of the concrete game semantics: though they are enforced by the specific details and proper names of the individual fictional narratives, they work in a much more general sense.

First of all, they are certainly below the level of fictional meaning or diegetic presentation of a game. It is of course on this level that narrative content is most frequently and most extensively written into the game—or rather, onto the game, like a skin or covering, which can often be exchanged with little to no effect on the way that the game works as a game. This can be seen best in serialized games that stick to a core set of gameplay mechanics while widely varying the game's diegetic presentation, like the *Far Cry* or *Assassin's Creed* games. While the diegetic representation of *Far Cry 3* (2012) suggests that the game is set in the present on a Pacific island, and that of *Far Cry 3: Blood Dragon* (2012) in a weird, 1980s-themed retro-future, both games as games are remarkably but unsurprisingly similar, given that they are based on the same game engine.

But while being relatively independent of the presentation level of a game, these narrative archetypes are also "above" any purely abstract formulation of game mechanics. They cannot be reduced to the mere rule structure. Instead, they are located in that conceptual space where game rules cannot be made sense of without any semantically charged reference. These are usually rules about values that hold in the context of a game, but also its particular affordances.

To get a better understanding of this, we need to look at the interplay between rules, affordances, and valorizations. All of these terms are different approaches to the fact that games usually contain an understanding of what players, can, cannot, and should do, and that this understanding is distinct from what pertains to the real world. In some games, we can fly but cannot open a door without a lock or jump over a knee-high fence, or we should steal money or even kill someone. The concept of rules is a set of instructions or commands, which is explicitly embodied in the game's code, but often only partly visible to players. The notion of affordances, on the other hand, rather looks at the elements of the game that the player encounters through actual gameplay and at the actions that these elements make possible or exclude—what they afford to the player. The idea of affordances was popularized in design theory by Don Norman in his *The Design of Everyday Things*. According to Norman,

> [t]he term affordance refers to the relationship between a physical object and a person (or for that matter, any interacting agent, whether animal or human, or even machines and ro-

bots). An affordance is a relationship between the properties of an object and the capabilities of the agent that determine just how the object could possibly be used. (Norman 11)

To expand from a consideration of mere rules to the broader and less strict consideration of affordances seems apt with a view to the growing complexity of games and particularly the growing emphasis of many genres on the player's freedom to act, as is exemplified in the trend toward open-world structures or *paidea*-oriented games such as *Minecraft*.[1] Another difference between rules and affordances is that while rules can be thought of as a property of games, "affordance is not a property. An affordance is a relationship" (Norman 11).

Game rules are straightforward and unambiguous in theory, providing concrete limitations and affordances to players, but they are only communicated to the player to a very limited degree. In fact, it is one of the features of digital games that they can neglect the direct communication of their own rules to the players because they can enforce them. Players can simply try out what is possible and what is not, and the game will let them know—something that does not work with a physical chess board.

Games therefore rarely come with an instruction manual nowadays. Instead, because game designers also do not want players to endlessly and frustratingly learn about the gameplay through trial-and-error, games use what Norman has called "signifiers": "To be effective, affordances and anti-affordances have to be discoverable—perceivable. (…) If an affordance or anti-affordance cannot be perceived, some means of signaling its presence is required: I call this property a signifier" (11–12). To the extent that games are simulations and therefore representations of aspects of the real world, these in-game signifiers are combined with what is supposed to act as signifiers in the real world. The image of a door with a doorknob presents the signifier that this door is meant to be opened— though within the game, the door might not have this function at all (similarly, William Gaver further distinguishes affordances into perceptible, hidden, and false).

The player therefore constantly needs to negotiate these two systems of affordances/signifiers, gradually coming to an understanding of "what is to be done" in the game. "Playing a game means, in most cases, to develop our avatar further, to learn to control the game, and to adapt our actions to the affordances of the game software" (Wenz 313). Both real-world reference and fictional meaning are helpful in communicating information about the affordances: "In ab-

---

[1] For another use of affordance in video game analysis, see Dan Pinchbeck's essays "Counting Barrels" and "An Affordance Based Model for Gameplay."

stract games, gameplay can provide a type of interest that is independent of narrative, while at the same time the fiction of most contemporary video games helps players understand the affordances of the underlying rule system" (Juul 432).

A further distinction to be made concerns the difference between those rules of a game system that describe what a player can or cannot do in any given situation from those that describe what she should do. As I have argued in *Storyplaying*,

> all games that belong to the *ludus* category also contain at least one rule that defines the *valorisation* of the outcomes. This valorisation is not the same as the fact that outcomes might have different values, such as the rules that attribute different numerical values depending on where a dart hits a dartboard. It is only the valorisation that determines whether it is actually the higher, or the lower number that is 'better.' (150)

I want to argue that valorization rules play a role in the negotiation of gameplay affordances that they do not in relation to the affordances of objects in real life. In reality, affordances are amoral, unconcerned with how things should be used. An AR-15 rifle is not very good for hunting or for personal protection, since it is relatively unwieldy and cannot be concealed. It might have been designed with military confrontation in mind, and it affords this usage, but it also affords to be used in a mass shooting. There might be ethical considerations involved in the creation of these affordances, but these are not applicable to the object itself, since there is no "cosmic rule" that creates a need to use it. This should not be confused with a pre-existing need, in relation to which the object then might serve a purpose or not. Being hungry would be such a need, to which I might then relate the AR-15, finding in the process that it does not afford eating, that it does afford hunting to a limited degree, and that it does afford holding a whole restaurant hostage. But there is usually no need to use an object that is inherent in the object itself, in its mere presence in the world. We might be inclined to understand the presence of an object as an invitation to use it, but this is not objectively justifiable.

This becomes more understandable when we compare it to the situation in a video game. In a variation of the principle of Chekov's gun (if a gun is present on the stage in the first act of a play, it 'should' go off at some point later in the play), players will assume by default that a game's rules, and particularly its affordances, will have a purpose. Because of the controlled and fabricated nature of game systems, they can get around the is/ought problem (also known as Hume's guillotine, the fact that it is impossible to derive an *ought* from an *is*). The attitude of a player is usually: "If I *can* do this, it must mean that I *should* do this." This means that specific affordances, choices, actions, and their consequences gain a significance that is both cultural and narrative (for a related account, see Ian Bogost's concept of "procedural rhetoric").

Theoretically, the specific fictional framework—the semantic presentation of a game—could work to subvert or deconstruct such archetypal narratives, but as they are so intimately connected to the gameplay and its imperatives, this has rarely happened so far. Take an example from the area of navigation: the existence of navigable space in video games can be understood to mean that spatial movement, navigation, and exploration are valued in themselves. Mastering the game space by moving through it has been one of the core challenges in video games since their beginning, so if players encounter a space, they will assume that it is "good" to explore it—because why else would the designers have created it? This is also true if the game semantics, the diegesis, at the same time (seemingly) discourage spatial exploration. For example, in the game *The Path* (2009), developed by Tale of Tales, the player controls the character of one of six sisters, who is in a forest and on a path. The instructions that appear on the screen say: "Go to Grandmother's house and stay on the path." Yet if the player follows this order and refrains from exploring the forest in any way, she will miss most if not all of the game, and will be unable to finish it. Another very nice example, first released in 2015, is the aptly titled *Please, Don't Touch Anything*, in which the player is, of course, expected to disregard exactly this request.

There are a number of narrative archetypes that can be found to emerge out of different interplays between game rules, affordances, valorizations, and semantic presentations, among them *navigation* (the "colonial narrative"), *survival* ("memento mori"), *accumulation / attrition* (the "capitalist narrative"), and *destruction* (the "terrorist narrative"). These have not been described or formalized in any way so far, though they provide a rich area of analysis.

"Capitalist narrative," for example, is a (slightly polemical) term suggested for the pervasive success of motivation through accumulation in video games and the introduction of a virtual work ethic into gameplay. The basic assertions of this narrative are "more is better" and "effort equals gain." This can either be in a non-competitive context (as exemplified by most incremental games of the infamous *Cookie Clicker*-variant), or in a zero-sum framework, in which one player's loss is another's gain.

The main aspects that contribute to the development of the "memento mori" (survival) archetype are the frequently antagonistic nature of games, the vulnerability of the player character, and the limitation of his resources, which lead to strategies of evasion, the hostility of an environment that needs to be crossed in order to reach safety, the illusiveness of the environment, often conveyed through maze-like structures and limited illumination, and the isolation of the player character within the environment and in relation to other players. Opponents are not understood as executing parts of a larger organization, but as individual carriers of a principle directly threatening the player.

And finally, the narrative archetype that emerges out of the gameplay affordance of destruction leads to what I have (again somewhat polemically) called "the terrorist narrative." More neutrally, it could be described as the story of individual agency destabilizing a restrictive or limiting system or structure. Many gameplay features regularly found in video games are conducive to the forming of this particular archetype. In fact, it is tied to one of the core affordances of video games as dynamic game systems, namely that they are better suited than most other game systems for single-player playing. In video games, the game system itself can take on the role of opponent. Because of their dynamic nature, video games can do two things that other, non-dynamic media cannot: they can enforce the rules by which they are to be engaged, and they can initiate processes that are unrelated to the user's input, but that can still be "intercepted" by the player.

This is why only dynamic media such as digital systems can create successful single-player games that do not rely on the player's cognitive limitations. Single-player modes mean that individuals are not pitted against each other but one player against the game, and since games are often presented as a simulation of the or a world, the player is consequently also often pitted against "the world" (or the system). In game design, this is usually called player versus environment (PvE), as opposed to player versus player (PvP). In such cases, the player is invited to regard the environment, its elements, and particularly its structural makeup not merely as a visual display to be enjoyed aesthetically, or a space to be explored by navigation, but as a potential enemy and therefore as something that can and possibly should be destroyed or controlled. Indeed, the destructibility of elements with the gamespace has become an important aspect for game design at least in some genres.

Many games today contain physics engines that model the correct physical behavior of objects in the gamespace, which means that changes to the environment (particularly through the influence of physical force, such as gunshots or explosions) are not just pre-programmed in a fixed way (as in arcade-style shoot-'em-ups), but are generated procedurally. The result is that objects react in a contingent but physically consistent way: structures collapse, but they do so depending on the impact, and the results are highly varied—and therefore entertaining to experience. Games like the *Angry Birds* franchise have very successfully built their whole gameplay around the challenge and joy of toppling physical structures. An important principle for this gameplay is that even large structures have weak points, and that relatively small causes can lead to large effects through faithfully rendered chain reactions. In this, the conceptual parallels to the way that terrorism conceives of the opposition of agency to structure should become apparent, and if it sounds far-fetched when dealing with cute cartoon birds being thrown into toy towers, games like the *Red Faction* and *Just Cause* franchises spell it out much more precisely, since in both the player is cast as some kind of subversive oppositional agent up against a sinister political power, and the physical structures that are being gleefully destroyed with everything from a sledgehammer to carefully placed bombs model (relatively) realistic buildings.

Another relevant aspect is the use of violence as a communicative strategy. Video games are often filled with non-player characters (NPCs) that the player can interact and communicate with. Most of the communication is indeed scripted, i.e. it is based on pre-existing text, with the player's (and through the code also the NPC's) only activity a selection between a finite set of options. To procedurally generate communication is much more difficult and rarely attempted —with the exception of the "communication" that emerges out of violence. Indeed, if one accepts that violence is communication in the sense that it communicates meaning, it is one of the "communicative strategies" most easily reproducible through gameplay. This connects it particularly to terrorism as communication. Alex P. Schmid and Janny de Graaf have pointed to the instrumentalization of violence as communication with particular reference to terrorism, claiming that "terrorism cannot be understood only in terms of violence," since "terrorism does not murder to kill somebody, but to obtain a certain effect upon others than the victim. Terrorism, by using violence against one victim, seeks to persuade others." Therefore, they argue, "terrorism can best be understood as a violent communication strategy. There is a sender, the terrorist, a message generator, the victim, and a receiver, the enemy and/or the public. The nature of the terrorist act, its atrocity, its location and the identity of its victim serve as generators for the power of the message" (Schmid and de Graaf 14–15).

To reiterate: This is not about the concrete semantics of any given game. It is therefore not about the fact that some games like *Rainbow 6* or *Splinter Cell* represent terrorism, or even, like *America's Army*, *Modern Warfare 2*, and *Medal of Honor: Warfighter*, enable the player to act as a terrorist. In "Being a Terrorist: Video Game Simulations of the Other Side of the War on Terror," Marcus Schulzke analyzes the latter three games with regard to whether they enable the player to better understand terrorism and its contexts and motivations, concluding:

> popular games ultimately deliver experiences of terrorist subjectivities that have virtually no content and that leave terrorists almost indistinguishable from the games' heroes. The

terrorists whose viewpoints are shown are portrayed as people who engage in senseless acts of violence that are disconnected from motives or grievances. This leads the games to confirm the overarching War on Terror narrative that terrorists are irrational and evil enemies who are unworthy of respect. (1)

This is, in a way, exactly my point: the game mechanics and game rules can and will often be in contradiction to what the game seems to "be about." The reason for the notion of a "terrorist narrative" archetype rather lie in the way that one can conceive of this antagonism between agency and structure in general terms, particularly with a reference to sociological theories of agency.

In its most rudimentary definition, agency is the capacity of an actor to act in a given environment. It is a term that is prominent in philosophy, particularly in moral philosophy and investigations of determinism and free will, but it is also a central term within both sociology and game studies. In video games, agency is an important term that should, for clarification's sake, be clearly distinguished from interactivity. While interactivity in most definitions merely marks the ability to influence something reciprocally, while disregarding the level of significance of the action and reaction, the question of agency as it is here understood weighs on the potential (narrative) consequence of a player's decisions and actions. Janet Murray has used the term agency in this sense in her concept of interactive storytelling. For her, "[a]gency is the satisfying power to make meaningful action and to see the results of our decisions and choices" (126). The appeal of video games lies in their promise of agency, in the promise of an openness that is dependent on the player and her choices. Creating the experience of (player) agency is one of the primary goals of game design, particularly in single-player games.

PvE games routinely put the player in a position of restricted agency, putting obstacles against spatial movement or choices. In addition, the experience of player agency is heightened by creating the impression that the player is up against a force greater than herself (often when the game is not imitating an opponent that is basically identical to the player, as in a chess game). This impression is sometimes expressed in the number or size of the enemies. The fact that they appear in endless waves surely suggests a sender who is "greater" than the individual enemies. But this impression usually entails the understanding that the enemies are part of a larger organization, system, or structure, and that it is the structure that must ultimately fall for the waves of individual enemies to end.

This ties in with sociological discussions of agency that are concerned with its relation to the wide-ranging and occasionally "nebulous" concept of "structure" (Elder-Vass 1), which has become the favored term for the sociocultural context in which agency exists. Structure can be seen as the recurrent patterned arrangements that influence or limit the choices and opportunities available. In this sense, structure can refer to systems of social organization, such as the class system, but also to institutions and all forms of the organization of social or political power. It is the set of rules that organize and guide the social networks that bind us together, and ultimately the whole range of social norms that shape our individual behavior as well as the behavior of larger social units.

How the interaction between individual agency and structure works and how both are to be evaluated is highly contested in social and political theories. In general, agency can be seen as an opposition to structure, a symbiotic confirmation of structure, or a result of structure. Already in Hobbes, structure and agency are ambivalently related, in that structure, in the form of the state (Leviathan) takes away individual agency but also enables it by limiting that of others in the war of all against all. There is a tradition of critiques of social structures as opposed to individual agency, ranging from Marx and Engels through Louis Althusser to Michel Foucault.

One can look at the agency/structure relationship in different forms of (antagonistic/violent) power relations: in the state of anarchy, there is no structure, and every individual agency is up against each other's (this is the Hobbesian motif of *homo homine lupus*, or in video game terms a battle royale mechanic like in *Fortnite*). In most social contract theories, individual agency is limited by structure, sometimes voluntarily and sometimes involuntarily. In conventional warfare, two structures compete with each other while leaving the idea of structure untouched. In guerrilla warfare, individual agency is used against structure, usually with the aim of setting up a new structure. Mao Zedong, one of the most prominent proponents of guerilla warfare, was careful to note the point at which this type of warfare must be given up so as not to endanger one's own structure-building (cf. Dyer 399).

Terrorism, finally, tends toward a pure assertion of anti-structure. As Jürgen Habermas has stated: "Global terrorism is extreme both in its lack of realistic goals and in its cynical exploitation of the vulnerability of complex systems" (Borradori 34). In this context, it can also be understood as at least an implicit celebration of (individual) agency. Right from its conceptual beginnings, terrorist ideology emphasized the agentic over discursive, as in Johann Most's "Action as Propaganda" from 1885: "we preach not only action in and for itself, but also action as propaganda" (qtd. in Kemp 48).[2] This is where the structural affinities lie

---

[2] Cf. also Sergey Nechayev: "far from everything that is nowadays called a deed is a deed (...). We term real manifestations only a series of actions which destroy something absolutely: a per-

with video games in general, who are all about emphasizing and celebrating (the player's) agency, and gameplay features in particular that afford the chain reaction scenarios in which David is repeatedly able to topple Goliath by finding the right weak spot.

To call this narrative archetype the "terrorist narrative" is certainly not meant to imply that video games in some ways argue in favor of terrorism or create training situations for would-be terrorists, not least since that would mean to regress back to the level of semantic presentation. Celebration of agency means that the player is conceived of as an agent in the philosophical or sociological sense, not necessarily as an agent of the CIA (as in *Just Cause*). As the use of the term "archetype" implies, the phenomenon is more abstract than concrete individual realizations, though it can be observed through its manifestations in specific cases. The preceding allusion to David and Goliath already indicated that the narrative archetype is much older than both video games and terrorism as it emerged since the late nineteenth century. The archetypes sketched out in the preceding have rarely been identified or described in this way because it is only by approaching them through gameplay structures that they can be made visible. As the experience of playing video games becomes more pervasive in contemporary society, they will create, solidify, or modify the human repertoire of archetypal narratives, thereby showing yet another way in which video games partake in the formation of a shared cultural mythology.

Works Cited

Bodkin, Maud. *Archetypal Patterns in Poetry*. Oxford UP, 1934.
Bogost, Ian. *Persuasive Games: The Expressive Power of Video Games*. MIT Press, 2007.
Borradori, Giovanna. *Philosophy in a Time of Terror: Dialogues with Jürgen Habermas and Jacques Derrida*. U of Chicago P, 2003.
Clymer, Jeffory A. *America's Culture of Terrorism: Violence, Capitalism, and the Written Word*. U of North Carolina P, 2003.
Domsch, Sebastian. *Storyplaying: Agency and Narrative in Video Games*. De Gruyter, 2013.
Dubbelman, Teun. "Narrative Game Mechanics." *Interactive Storytelling: 9th International Conference on Interactive Digital Storytelling, ICIDS 2016, Los Angeles, CA, USA, November 15–18, 2016, Proceedings*, edited by Frank Nack and Andrew S. Gordon, Springer, 2004, pp. 39–50.
Dyer, Gwynne. *War: The Lethal Custom*. Rev. ed. Carroll & Graf, 2004.

---

son, a thing, or an attitude which is an obstacle to the liberation of the people. (...) We have lost all faith in the word" (qtd. in Clymer 14).

Elder-Vass, Dave. *The Causal Power of Structures: Emergence, Structure and Agency*. Cambridge UP, 2010.
El-Shamy, Hasan M., and Jane Garry, editors. *Archetypes and Motifs in Folklore and Literature: A Handbook*. M. E. Sharpe, 2005.
Gaver, William W. "Technology Affordances." *CHI '91 Proceedings of the SIGCHI Conference on Human Factors in Computing Systems*. The Association of Computing Machinery, 1991, pp. 79–84.
Juul, Jesper. "Narrative." Encyclopedia of *Video Games. The Culture, Technology, and Art of Gaming*, edited by Mark J.P. Wolf, vol. 2, Greenwood, 2012, pp. 430–33.
Kemp, Michael. *Bombs, Bullets and Bread: The Politics of Anarchist Terrorism Worldwide, 1866–1926*. McFarland, 2018.
Murray, Janet H. *Hamlet on the Holodeck: The Future of Narrative in Cyberspace*. Cambridge UP, 2001.
Norman, Don. *The Design of Everyday Things*. Basic Books, 2002.
Pinchbeck, Dan. "Counting Barrels in Quake 4: Affordances and Homodiegetic Structures in FPS Worlds." *DiGRA 2007 Conference Proceedings*, www.digra.org/digital-library/publications/counting-barrels-in-quake-4-affordances-and-homodiegetic-structures-in-fps-worlds. Accessed 15 Jan. 2019.
Pinchbeck, Dan. "An Affordance Based Model for Gameplay." *DiGRA 2009 Conference Proceedings*, www.digra.org/dl/db/09287.31155.pdf#_blank. Accessed 15 Jan. 2019.
Richter, David H., editor. *The Critical Tradition: Classic Texts and Contemporary Trends*. 3rd ed., Bedford/St. Martin's, 2007.
Schmid, Alex P., and Janny de Graaf. *Violence as Communication: Insurgent Terrorism and the Western News Media*. Sage Press, 1982.
Schulzke, Marcus. "Being a Terrorist: Video Game Simulations of the Other Side of the War on Terror." *Media, War & Conflict*, vol. 6, no. 3, 2013, pp. 207–20. doi:10.1177/1750635213494129. Accessed 15 Jan. 2019.
Wenz, Karin. "Death." *The Routledge Companion to Video Game Studies*, edited by Mark J.P. Wolf and Bernard Perron, Routledge, 2014, pp. 310–16.

Jon Adams
Why We Play Role-Playing Games

Why do we play role-playing games? A number of answers to this question have been proposed. The most obvious answer is that we play role-playing games because they are fun. Creating a game that is fun is the first principle of game development (cf. Rollings and Morris 38). In a game like *Diablo*, this fun is the constant and immediate positive feedback of defeating mobs, exploring the map, and finding treasure. A somewhat less obvious answer is that games provide a challenge. This challenge offers the cognitive pleasure of learning a complex system with problem-solving structures (cf. Gee 3). In a game like *Ark*, for example, a player uses problem solving to learn how to survive in a world inhabited by dangerous creatures. There are perhaps more answers to why we play role-playing games, but I want to propose one that is not at first obvious: we play role-playing games to prepare for the future. Specifically, we play games to prepare for a future dominated by algorithms. Some observers claim that this future has already arrived, that we already live "in the age of algorithms" (Domingos 1). Because algorithms are everywhere: they are in our computers, in our cell phones, in our cars, and even in our thermostats. Algorithms are changing our lives, often without us being fully aware of it. The problem is not to stop the proliferation of algorithms. That's not possible. Rather, the problem is one of awareness, of acquiring a certain level of algorithmic literacy (cf. Rainie and Anderson). This is a problem that role-playing games are in a position to deal with because what a player in such a game does is confront algorithms. It is what role-playing games are about.

Machines

Algorithms are used everywhere because they do things. They do things that help us in various ways, but they also do some things that are troubling. For example, if you have a passport photo, your "face has been turned into an algorithm" (Clare Garvie qtd. in Scola). This use of algorithms is troubling because we didn't anticipate it and we can't control it. I want to briefly point out three general ways in which algorithms are having an impact on our lives.

First, algorithms are beginning to replace us as workers. Robot-controlled algorithms are already replacing manual workers in many tasks. PricewaterhouseCoopers estimates that machines are likely to take over more than one-third of the jobs in America and Germany by the year 2030 (cf. Dennin). Such ma-

https://doi.org/10.1515/9783110659405-012

chines are not only poised to take over routine work, such as customer service and data processing, they are also threatening to take over such professions as medicine and law (cf. Susskind and Susskind). For example, Ross is a machine powered by IBM's Watson technology that serves as a legal researcher. It sifts through thousands of legal documents and delivers a ranked list of the most relevant ones. When it is asked a legal question, Ross replies with a few paragraphs summarizing the answer and a two-page explanatory memo. The results are indistinguishable from the work of a human lawyer, except that it is much faster (cf. Lohr, "A.I.").

In another example, machines are widespread in banks and wealth management companies. BlackRock uses Aladdin, a machine for investment management; Goldman Sachs uses Kensho, a machine for financial research; and UBS and Deutsche Bank use Sqreem, a machine for financial crime protection. These machines are different from earlier rule-based models; they are the next generation that use deep learning techniques (cf. Crosman).

Second, algorithms are beginning to collect more and more data about us. We all know that algorithms track us on the Internet. Most of us are probably familiar with cookies and know that we can delete them. But there are other tracking algorithms that don't use cookies. An algorithmic technique known as fingerprinting can identify unique features of our browser, give it an identifying number, and know when we return to the site (cf. Hill).

We can also be tracked even if our data is anonymous. There are laws against selling personally identifiable data in the US, such as a person's name, Social Security number, and medical condition. But if the data is scrubbed of personal information, then it is considered "anonymized," and it can be legally sold and publicly transferred. But there is so much publicly available information about us online that, combined with powerful algorithms, it is possible to re-identify a person's "anonymized" data. This means scrubbed data can now be traced back to the individual user to whom it relates (cf. Lubarsky).

Third, algorithms are beginning to make decisions not only for us but also about us (cf. Lohr, *Dataism*). For example, when we apply for a job now, algorithms are used to review our resumés. Human resource managers rely on these algorithms so much that they let the algorithms screen out over 70% of the job applicants without a human ever reviewing them (cf. Mann and O'Neill).

In another example, a man in Wisconsin was sentenced to six years in prison in part based on the analysis of a machine called Compas. Using data about the defendant, Compas reported that he had a high risk of violence and a high risk of recidivism. The defendant challenged the judge's sentencing because neither he nor the judge was able to examine the algorithm that produced the Compas report. The defendant's challenge was denied because the algorithm is a trade secret (cf. Liptak). In 2015, a California Appeals Court upheld this decision that a trade secret is privileged evidence to prevent disclosure of an algorithm's source code, even from the defense. This decision, "People v. Chubbs," is now being cited across the country to deny defendants access to trade secret evidence (cf. Wexler).

I don't think I'm overdramatizing the growing impact of algorithms. Others have suggested that algorithms are going to completely replace us (cf. Harari). At the moment, this seems a little extreme, but it is clear that algorithms are changing our lives and that we should at least be aware of their nature.

Games

With most algorithmic systems, the user requests information. There is interactivity between the user and such systems, but it is rather basic. The user sits outside the system and queries it, whether the system is the Internet or a doctor's diagnostic machine. A role-playing game is also an algorithmic system, but the player doesn't sit outside the system. The player enters the system, the game world, and explicitly confronts the algorithmic system. Lev Manovich pointed this out almost two decades ago: "as the player proceeds through the game, she gradually discovers the rules that operate in the universe constructed by this game. She learns its hidden logic—in short, its algorithms" (222). When we enter a game world, we learn to play the game, we learn about its algorithmic system, what the algorithms do and what they don't do. We learn this by playing the game, by doing things in the game world, because algorithms themselves do things. They are procedural; they are processes for making decisions. When we play a role-playing game we do the same thing: we make decisions and we do things in the game world. But in order for us to do this successfully, we have to understand the game world's algorithmic system. For example, the basics of any role-playing game consists of how to equip and move the player character, how to negotiate the map, and how to survive, either through combat or stealth. These are some of the simple mechanics of a game, and these mechanics are a system of algorithms.

Even a casual video game player learns a couple of general features of algorithms. For example, they learn that algorithms aren't perfect, and that they sometimes have errors, exploits, and unintended consequences. Our player characters, for example, used to fall through the map rather frequently, and getting stuck on the map still happens now and then. An unintended consequence in *Planetside* still sticks in my mind. *Planetside* was a massively multiplayer online game that had friendly fire. You could kill your own team members and they could kill you. As a result, there was a player who liked to drive a heavy truck and run over other players on his own team. There was some modeling glitch that made it nearly impossible to dodge the truck, so that even a near miss was fatal. Many players complained bitterly in-game and on the forums about this maniac truck driver, but since the mechanics of the game allowed it, he continued to run over his teammates.

Another general feature of algorithms is that they form a closed systems. The player can do anything the game or algorithmic system allows, but what the game allows is limited. In *Fallout 4*, for example, the player can craft a house, but he can't craft a bicycle, a car, or a boat. At first an open game world like *Fallout 4* may seem vast, but that's mainly because it is new and unexplored. A player can easily walk from one end of the map to the other, but he can't walk beyond the map. Algorithmic systems are limited not by what they do but what they don't and can't do.

Perhaps the most important general feature of algorithms is that they create systems that are a world apart, a world that is not only independent of our world but completely indifferent to it. Algorithms demand that they be dealt with on their terms, not ours. They don't adjust to us, so we have to adjust to them. In the classic role-playing game *Morrowind* many of the NPCs change their location and then stand in such a way that they block the movement of the player character. In the entrance hall of the mages' guild in Vivec there are two particularly irritating mages that tend to position themselves so that they block the doorway leading to the interior of the guild. The point is that the player has to deal with the problem and find a workaround. The mages, or the algorithm that controls their pathing, are completely indifferent to the player's concern. When the player character bumps into one of the mages, it doesn't move; instead he says, "What do you want, Outlander?"

Confrontation

Many features of algorithms appear in various types of video games, not just role-playing games. But in terms of confronting algorithms, role-playing games have an advantage because the player doesn't play against other players but against the environment, that is, against the algorithmic system of the game world. The importance of this aspect of role-playing games becomes clear when we remember that, unlike most video games, a player at the beginning of a role-playing game doesn't know all the rules that govern the game world. The player has to figure out what to do, how to play the game. The player has to "probe the game's logic" (Johnson 42).

One of the most important features of algorithms that a player learns in confronting the game system is that the player controls the situation, because nothing happens until the player enters the sphere of a mob's algorithmic system. For example, when the player meets the first boss in *Dark Souls 3*, the boss is on one knee with a sword in its side. The confrontation doesn't begin until the player pulls the sword out. This first boss in *Dark Souls 3* is considered a tutorial, a boss fight that teaches a new player the basics of boss fights in the game. What the player also observes is that the boss, as an algorithmic entity, has specific properties. For example, when a player character dies, respawns, and then returns for another attempt to defeat the boss, the boss has returned to a position in the center of the arena. This is a general feature of algorithms: they have an initial or default setting. And after a number of attempts to defeat the boss, the player will begin to notice a pattern, depending on whether he keeps his character close to the boss or away from it. In other words, the player learns that the boss, as an algorithmic entity, is predictable. And when the player finally defeats the boss, it despawns and the gate opens to the next zone. The boss, as an algorithmic entity, has reached its final state.

In his various attempts to defeat the first boss in *Dark Souls 3*, the player learns another lesson: the purpose of a game world is to retard or block a character's progress. This suggests that the game has no intrinsic purpose independent of the player. The player's motivation to play the game, his motivation to master the game world, gives him a certain control over the game world. When the player confronts the game world, it simply reacts. It is the player who has the task to change the game state, to invoke some algorithms and eliminate others. For example, the boss remains in its initial state until the player appears, then the boss enter its combat state. The algorithm, in other words, needs the player's input. This is what empowers the player in a game world: the player gives algorithms purpose.

Character

Another important advantage that role-playing games have over other games is that the player uses an algorithmic entity to confront the algorithmic system of the game world, for the player character is an algorithmic entity. The player uses his character in two ways: in the strategy he uses to approach the game and in the tactics he uses to implement his strategy. A major aspect of a player's strategy consists in how he configures his character. For example, in *Dark Souls 3* the player may decide to favor magic and speed over strength and armor, so he ignores attributes that support strength and armor in favor of skills that support magic and speed. During the game, each time the character gains a level, the player has to decide which skills to increase to support the way he plays his character. And each time the player defeats an enemy that drops armor or a weapon, he has decide whether he wants his character to use it. While on the surface these are strategic decisions that the player makes about how to use his character, at a deeper level these decisions are about how to configure an algorithmic entity to confront the algorithmic system.

Based on his strategy, the player uses his tactics to confront the game world. For example, when facing a mob like a Ringed Knight in *Dark Souls*, the player keeps his character at range and burns the Knight down with magic. More difficult mobs and bosses require kiting and dodging, which is where speed becomes important, but the tactic is similar. In role-playing games, tactics are a combination of what the player decides to do and the character executing that decision. If the player decides to throw a fireball or roll away from an incoming attack, it is the character that does the actually throwing and rolling. This means that the player works intimately with his character, with his algorithmic entity, in confronting the game world.

Using a character in a role-playing game allows a player to learn a number of specific features of algorithms, features that define what algorithms do and don't do:

1. Game worlds count everything. As a player guides his character across the map of a game world, walking, running, turning, sometime jumping, the game world appears to be an analog system. But as soon as the character confronts an enemy, in a game like *World of Warcraft*, numbers begin to flash on the screen because the outcome of the encounter is measured in numbers. The outcome is measured in how much damage a character can absorb and how much she can produce, and at the same time, how much damage the enemy can absorb and how much it can produce. Algorithms are very good at numbers because binary is their native language. In fact everything is measured in numbers: the map of the game world is a grid and a character's movements are measured on that grid. The only thing that is not measured in numbers is the player's decisions about what to do. In encountering a sabretooth tiger in *Ark*, for example, the player can decide to fight or, because the sabretooth runs in packs, he can decide to flee.

2. Game worlds are not realistic. Games like *Everquest* and *Star Wars*, with their fantasy and science fiction settings, aren't intended to be realistic, but even in a game like *Ark*, which tries to be as realistic as possible, there are game conventions that override any sense of realism. For example, the player character and mobs in a role-playing game have a health bar. On the one hand, this is part of measuring how much damage a character or mob can absorb, but on the other hand, the visual symbol of the health bar is an algorithmic

representation of "health." What the player learns is that algorithms may imitate biological entities but they are made up of numbers not organic cells.

3. Game worlds need to specify everything. Azeroth, the game world in *World of Warcraft*, is a fantasy world. Players can ride flying horses and tame spiders to fight for them. But even a fantasy world needs some consistency so as not to appear completely irrational. Yet in many dungeons in the *World of Warcraft*, a group's tank hits the boss with her sword to maintain threat, but when the boss begins to perform a power move, the tank can avoid the attack by just walking through the boss. This inconsistency in collision detection is part of the game world's non-rationality, but it also reveals the specificity of algorithms. This specificity defines the player's sword as having collision detection but the character herself as not having it. For algorithms to function, every feature of every object needs to be specified.

4. Game worlds have immaterial space. Space is a major feature of role-playing games, and it is one of a main reasons we talk about game worlds and why maps are important. Many of these maps in role-playing games are quite large, which in the past led to the problem of a character having to walk or run from one place to the next, often over and over again. To avoid the tediousness of walking everywhere, most games have a fast travel feature. A character can use a ring in *World of Warcraft*, a carriage in *Skyrim* or a bonfire in *Dark Souls* and move from one location in the game world to another location without traversing any of the locations in between. This travel is instantaneous. Algorithms are not bound to the spatial physics of our world.

5. Game worlds are arbitrary. For example, in most games the player character has an inventory, but the inventory is often implemented differently in different games. In *World of Warcraft*, the character's inventory is limited to the number of slots she has in her bags. In *Fallout*, the character has a seeming unlimited number of slots, but she is limited in the amount of weight she can carry before becoming encumbered. In *Elex*, the character has an unlimited number of slots and no weight limit. Notably, time in game worlds is also arbitrary, and a game world may or may not have a time structure. *Everquest* has a rapid day and night cycle. *Dark Souls* has no day and night cycle, but in some zones it is dark and in others it is not. *World of Warcraft* has a day and night cycle that has changed over the years since 2005.

Players understand these algorithmic features of role playing games. We see illustrations of this on the forums when players discuss the technical issues of a game. For example, in a discussion of how to play a tank in *World of Warcraft*, a player introduces the basic features of the threat algorithm.

> Threat is a means of measuring the level of animosity a mob has towards a specific player. Each mob has a threat table, and every person who performs hostile actions towards that mob is put on that table.
>
> There are two important actions which generate threat: dealing damage and healing. Other actions, such as casting a buff or debuff also generate threat, but in very small amounts which are not worth discussing.
>
> Normally, threat is generated at a 1:1 ratio with damage done to the mob, and a 1:2 ratio with healing done. However, in order to facilitate tanking, tanks generate far more threat from their damage. ("Tanking Guide")

As we can see from this description, threat is an algorithm that determines which character in a group a mob attacks. It is an algorithm that uses a measurement that is recorded in a table. This threat table is a data structure in the threat algorithm. If you are in a group in *World of Warcraft* you need to know this. And if you are the tank, then you need to know how to stay at the top of a mob's threat table, that is, you need to understand how the threat algorithm works.

Conclusion

We are facing what Shawn DuBravac calls a "digital destiny":

> The point is that in 2025 electronic devices connected to the Internet and equipped with powerful sensors will be ubiquitous, surrounding us at all times, acquiring and analyzing data, not only to give us what we need the moment we need it, but to acquire more information on our true identity. (118)

The point that I have been trying to make is that a user who has played role-playing games will not be a passive victim of these ubiquitous algorithms. First, he will know that he is confronting an algorithmic system, and he will look for ways to use the system to his advantage, just as he did in role-playing games, for example, when he learned to kite mobs and use line-of-sight to avoid taking damage. We already have a name for this: it's called gaming the system. Next, I think a user who has played role-playing games will look with some suspicion at the idea that algorithms gather data about his "true identity," because such a user will be familiar with an identity formed by algorithms. Such an identity will look very much like a player character in a role-playing game. Once a user sees this, he won't leave this algorithmic identity to the complete control of the algorithms. A user who has played role-playing games will want to configure his algorithmic character, to manipulate it to his own advantage because he will be familiar with configuring player characters. And he will know that an algorithmic system doesn't really care what he does, as long as he appears to being playing the game.

Works Cited

Ark: Survival Evolved. Studio Wildcard, 2016.
Crosman, Penny. "Beyond Robo-Advisers: How AI Could Rewire Wealth Management." *American Banker*, 5 Jan. 2017, www.americanbanker.com/news/beyond-robo-advisers-how-ai-could-rewire-wealth-management. Accessed 15 Jan. 2019.
Dark Souls 3. FromSoftware. Bandai Namco Entertainment, 2016.
Dennin, James. "Here's How Many US Jobs Could be Automated – and Why Robots Threaten American Workers Most." *Mic*, 24 March 2017, mic.com/articles/172071/how-many-us-jobs-could-be-automated-and-why-robots-threaten-american-workers-most-mnuchin#.c5B0kEPFE. Accessed 15 Jan. 2019.
Diablo 3: Reaper of Souls. Blizzard Entertainment, 2014.
Domingos, Pedro. *The Master Algorithm: How the Quest for the Ultimate Learning Machine Will Remake Our World.* Basic Books, 2015.
DuBravac, Shawn. *Digital Destiny: How the New Age of Data Will Transform the Way We Work, Live, and Communicate.* Regnery, 2015.
Elex. Piranha Bytes. THQ Nordic, 2017.
Everquest 2. Sony Online Entertainment, 2004.
Fallout 4. Bethesda Softworks, 2014.
Gee, James. "Games and Learning: An Interview Overview." *Good Video Games + Good Learning*, 2nd ed., Peter Lang, 2013.
Harari, Yuval Noah. *Homo Deus: A Brief History of Tomorrow.* Vintage, 2016.
Hill, Simon. "How Much Do Online Advertisers Really Know About You? We Asked an Expert." *Digital Trends*, 27 June 2015, www.digitaltrends.com/computing/how-do-advertisers-track-you-online-we-found-out/. Accessed 15 Jan. 2019.
Johnson, Steven. *Everything Bad Is Good for You.* Penguin, 2005.
Liptak, Adam. "Sent to Prison by a Software Program's Secret Algorithms." *The New York Times*, 1 May 2017, www.nytimes.com/2017/05/01/us/politics/sent-to-prison-by-a-software-programs-secret-algorithms.html. Accessed 15 Jan. 2019.
Lohr, Steve. "A.I. Is Doing Legal Work. But It Won't Replace Lawyers, Yet." *The New York Times*, 19 March 2017, www.nytimes.com/2017/03/19/technology/lawyers-artificial-intelligence.html. Accessed 15 Jan. 2019.
Lohr, Steve. *Dataism: Inside the Big Data Revolution.* Oneworld, 2015.
Lubarsky, Boris. "Re-Identification of 'Anonymized' Data." *The Georgetown Law Technology Review*, April 2017, www.georgetownlawtechreview.org/re-identification-of-anonymized-data/GLTR-04-2017/. Accessed 15 Jan. 2019.
Mann, Gideon, and Cathy O'Neil. "Hiring Algorithms Are Not Neutral." *Harvard Business Review*, 9 Dec. 2016, hbr.org/2016/12/hiring-algorithms-are-not-neutral. Accessed 15 Jan. 2019.
Manovich, Lev. *The Language of New Media.* MIT Press, 2001.

Morrowind. Bethesda Softworks, 2002.
Planetside. Sony Online Entertainment, 2003.
Rollings, Andrew, and Dave Morris. *Game Architecture and Design*. New Riders, 2003.
Rainie, Lee, and Janna Anderson. "Code-Dependent: Pros and Cons of the Algorithm Age." *Pew Research Center*, 8 Feb. 2017, www.pewinternet.org/2017/02/08/code-dependent-pros-and-cons-of-the-algorithm-age. Accessed 15 Jan. 2019.
Scola, Nancy. "A Picture of You, in Federal Data." *Politico*, 11 Oct. 2017, www.politico.com/agenda/story/2017/10/11/federal-data-individual-portrait-000540?lo=ap_d1. Accessed 15 Jan. 2019.
Skyrim. Bethesda Softworks, 2011.
Star Wars: The Old Republic. BioWare Austin, Electronic Arts, 2011.
Susskind, Richard, and Daniel Susskind. "Technology Will Replace Many Doctors, Lawyers, and Other Professionals." *Harvard Business Review*, 11 Oct. 2016, hbr.org/2016/10/robots-will-replace-doctors-lawyers-and-other-professionals. Accessed 15 Jan. 2019.
"Tanking Guide Battle for Azeroth." *Icy Veins*, 23 July 2016, www.icy-veins.com/wow/tanking-guide. Accessed 15 Jan. 2019.
Wexler, Rebecca. "When a Computer Program Keeps You in Jail." *The New York Times*, 13 June 2017, www.nytimes.com/2017/06/13/opinion/how-computers-are-harming-criminal-justice.html. Accessed 15 Jan. 2019.
World of Warcraft. Blizzard Entertainment, 2004.

Damien B. Schlarb
Narrative Glitches: Action Adventure Games and Metaleptic Convergence

When Neo, the protagonist of the 1999 film *The Matrix*, sees a black cat passing by a doorway twice within a matter of seconds, he chalks off the experience as an episode of déjà vu. His companions explain that, in the virtual world of the matrix, experiencing déjà vu usually means that the matrix, the elaborate procedurally generated virtual-reality computer simulation of the late 1990s (of all things), is adjusting its code to apprehend them. The matrix entraps humans in order to syphon off their body heat and with it power a race of sentient machines that have overtaken the earth. What Neo first dismisses as cognitive dissonance is actually a computational error. This "cat glitch" has a semiotic double valence: it illustrates the perpetual calculations, which are normally imperceptible to those enthralled by it, that are necessary to generate the world of the matrix, and it also signifies an anomaly in the code. In this latter sense, the glitch draws attention to the matrix's basic machine character. Its hardware, which exists in the form of ominous, seemingly endless fields of server towers in the wasteland of the real world, ultimately limits both its virtual world and its capacity for dominating the humans it enslaves. The image of the cat, then, represents the banality of this limitation by invoking the whimsy of superstition (black cats signify bad luck for those whose paths they cross), while the glitch —an error in the code or a sign that a processor's data buffers are overstrained—signifies the material limit against which the matrix's computation constantly struggles. Like any late-1990s computer operating system, the matrix can glitch out, lag, crawl, freeze, or even crash. Given this Achilles' heel, we may therefore have reason to hope that Neo and his comrades can overcome it and save humanity.

From a narratological standpoint, the scene foreshadows the machines' downfall by illustrating the status of the matrix as a medium. Machine actions become visible, momentarily puncturing the protagonist's cognitive frame of reference. As Neo's immersion in the simulated world of the matrix gets interrupted, he is reminded of the fact that all his experiences in the world are mediated. This particular kind of metalepsis, or frame-breaking, reveals to the characters the machinic actions that are necessary to maintain the illusion of a coherent reality. The cat glitch, then, represents a suture in this otherwise seamlessly mediated, immersive world, a moment in which Neo and his friends may confront the matrix as a medium.

https://doi.org/10.1515/9783110659405-013

Media studies theorists Jay Bolter and Richard Grusin define moments in which media alert users to their presence, for example through obtrusive computer operating software interfaces, as instances of hypermediacy (33). What is characteristic of this phenomenon is that it disabuses the operator of the illusion of immediacy and seamlessness that all media strive to create. Such moments can even be epiphanic because they allow us to perceive both the content and the medium simultaneously. Like Neo, we may pause, look back through the looking glass, and marvel at the fabric of the strange wonderland we have stepped into. What makes this scene worth contemplating is that it puts meta-reflection about media convergence in the service of narrative. Hypermediacy becomes part of the story.

Narrative-driven action adventure video games have long employed similar metaleptic techniques to draw player attention whilst striving to increase immersion. Yet the characteristic configuration of video games as what Andrew Galloway terms diegetic and non-diegetic player and machine actions add several semiotic, narrative, and political layers to the phenomenon (11, 16–28). For example, in the action adventure, science fiction game *Metal Gear Solid* (1998), the terrorist Psycho Mantis, a character with telekinetic and telepathic abilities, threatens first the avatar, Snake, and then the player directly with reading their minds. Depending on the player's dialog choices, Psycho Mantis turns players' TV screens black, activates the controller's vibration features, and reads the contents of whichever memory card is inserted into the gaming console. Afterwards, the game continues along its narrative track, and yet the character has momentarily transcended the narrative and ludic confines of the game, thereby creating a moment of heightened sense of the narrative, the medium, and the external material situatedness (console, game pad, TV set, etc.), or what Galloway calls a "moment of unplay" (35), of the game.

In this article, I attend to moments of metalepsis in which simulated machinic failure becomes part of narrative. Video game scholars have theorized purposeful disruptions in terms of players' expectational horizons and even as aesthetic objects in their own right, yet little attention has been paid to the manner in which they become diegetically and semiotically productive.[1] Using the examples *X-Men* (1993), *Batman: Arkham Asylum* (2009), and *Pony Island* (2016), I consider instances in which games reflect their own mediatedness, both in the sense

---

[1] Besides Galloway, see also Bojahr, who I discuss below. On the side of the player, narrative glitches operational in ludic storytelling are similar to what Jesper Juul describes as the paradox of failure, i.e., the fact that we hold games that allow us to fail in higher regard than those who do not (cf. 36). On the aesthetic afterlife of glitches, see John Sharp's discussion of visual artworks based on video game bugs (cf. 24).

of being media that facilitate digital gameplay and in the extended sense that they mediate between the materiality of machinic, diegetic, and player actions. This mediation has itself several vectors of meaning, which I trace out below. I argue that these moments, in which different strains of mediation, materiality, and storytelling come together, mark instances of what I will call metaleptic convergence, which characterizes video games as a medium. When games point to their own extradiegetic situatedness, they underscore their status as media and their material dimensions: a game is the sum of algorithmic calculations required to keep it running, and it may, for example, be embedded on a blu-ray disc spinning in a drive that gathers information via laser read-outs. Materiality and computation become represented momentarily as intersecting in the game's diegesis to advance the stories it tells. In this article, I consider how these interstices between the material and the cultural become significant in narrative.

Galloway's cybernetics-based model of gamic action serves as a referential framework for addressing video games as objects of analysis here; however, I will still strategically refer to them as aesthetic objects at certain points of my analysis. Galloway distinguishes between diegetic machine acts, i.e., the machine calculations which create the game world (cf. 11–12); nondiegetic operator acts, configuration, pausing, enacting the algorithm; diegetic operator acts, commands entered via the interface that drive gameplay and in our case narrative; and nondiegetic machine acts, signs of the machine enacting the game rules, such as granting players power-ups for collecting certain items or killing an avatar for walking off a cliff. These actions are performed "over the contestation of the operator" (28) and carry in themselves signs of material culture, for instance in the response time of the system to certain gamic actions (cf. 33). My theoretic approach here is constructivist in the sense that I identify the layers of meaning that become mobilized in the instances I focus on here. Player activity both mobilizes and is impacted by the diegetic and extradiegetic events in question, and Galloway's model allows me to ponder the formal and political implications of this dialectic.

Theory: Remediation, Convergence, Singularity

Conceptually capturing the phenomena I outlined above requires a theoretical model of media analysis that can apprehend such moments in video games as symbolic (re-)alignments that have narrative valence. What I call metaleptic convergence is made up of building blocks from the fields of media studies, literary studies, and narratology. Drawing on these three discourses, I think about these events as instances of semiotic and media convergence.

Henry Jenkins's model of media convergence usefully allows us to consider within the same referential and analytical framework both material and cultural objects (cf. 282). Convergence, in the instances I outline below, occurs because something shifts simultaneously in the perceptions of players and characters alike. In these moments, the machine dimension of the game, which exists latently all along during gameplay, moves into view and becomes part of the game's narrative. And while the game continues to run normally, its previously opaque machine dimension erupts on the scene and interrupts play and immersion. The game's characteristic procedural generation becomes momentarily inhibited. Like Neo staring down the black cat, players stand confronted with both the gaming system's machine actions—now unveiled as non-diegetic machine actions—that enable player actions in the first place, and their own diegetic actions that drive the game and its narrative. And yet all of this remains part of the simulation of the game. In the next moment, however, this interruption furthers immersion as it becomes framed as metalepsis.

From a media studies point of view, the instances I discuss here are noteworthy because they mark, as Bolter and Grusin acknowledge, moments in which hypermediacy assumes "a playful or subversive attitude, both acknowledging and undercutting the desire for immediacy" (34). They proceed to remind us that both hypermedia and transparent media strive to achieve what they call "the real" in the viewer's experience, i.e., "that which would evoke an immediate (and therefore authentic) emotional response" (53). When games employ glitches as ludo-narrative devices, they give players pause, because they simultaneously feel stumped while also being in on the joke. Players may stop, smile, and continue on playing, even more enthused than before. Bolter and Grusin's notion of playfulness on the side of the medium marks such moments as instances in which players' media literacy, latent technophilia, situational awareness, and preconceptions about the gamic situation become the subjects of both mockery and pleasure.

The appeal, or rather the authenticity of these experiences emerges from the overall conceptual ambiguity of such moments, in which players become involved more closely with the game. At the same time, these instances see players cease their play for a moment, only to start up again on a higher level. Galloway notes how nondiegetic machine acts may "create a generative *agitation* or ambiguity" (34), elevating gameplay to a higher order activity, which he conceptualizes as "*écriture*, the supplement, the new" (38).[2] Philosopher Daniel Martin

---

[2] Galloway adopts the term from Jacques Derrida's poststructuralist manifesto "Structure, Sign, and Play in the Discourse of the Human Sciences" (1970).

Feige, in a recent attempt at defining video games from the vantage point of aesthetics, even implies that such ambiguous playfulness constitutes the defining characteristic of video games. As objects of "determined indeterminacy" ["bestimmte Unbestimmtheit"] (107), Feige argues, games open up spaces of (cognitive, phenomenological, intellectual) possibility that are not accessible via other media.

While I will not speculate here on the creative potential—let alone the conceivable psychological implications—these moments hold for players, I do want to use the phenomenon of narrative glitches to expound on the term *écriture* as Galloway uses it. I use the term here as designating a generative dynamic that exceeds mere passive consumption of or immersion in a medium. Specifically, I am thinking about narrative glitches as convergence events, brief time periods in which something important and different happens that is characteristic for the form of the video game as a remediating medium. Literary scholar Derek Attridge has argued in a similar vein for what he calls the singularity of literature, and his concept may help specify what the aforementioned theorists have called, playfulness, ambiguity, or *écriture*. Attridge proposes that singularity constitutes "the demand that this specific collocation of words, allusions, and cultural references makes on me [the reader] in the event of my reading, here and now, as a member of the culture to whom these codes are familiar" (95). While he describes texts, Attridge's proposition lends itself to being adapted for analyzing video games. I propose that narrative glitches push players towards such higher-order play. Video games, I argue, make the same kind of computational demand, and the manner in which they exert that toll becomes visible in moments of ludo-narrative and machinic convergence. By simulating the breakdown of the machine, gameplay is being defamiliarized and players confront, even if it is only for an instance, their own diegetic action as *gamic* action, in the kinetic sense of putting commands into a machine. In other words, the activity of gaming as an interaction of machinic and player actions gets signified to them as material interaction, all while remaining immersed in the game. The experience therefore remains mediated while moving to a higher order of signification.

In what follows, I analyze three objects from different eras of console homegaming. In each instance, I begin by providing a brief overview of the game's aesthetic sensibilities and gameplay loops. I explicate and analyze moments of metaleptic convergence, in which gameplay gets disrupted in order to further the narrative and players are forced to confront the materiality, cybernetics, and machinic actions that generate the digital artefacts they interface with. In doing so, they enter momentarily into a higher level of play, in which gameplay and narrative absorb and reflect all these dimensions of external situatedness. I distinguish these moments by the material actions and consequences the game suggests to players. The activities of resetting the game, the fear of losing one's data and progress, and even deliberately deleting the game are all moved within the representational compass of a game's narrative through metalepsis. Attridge notes regarding literature that singularity constitutes the synchronic experience of movement through the medium, a movement which in turn generates "depth and density" (97–98). I propose that the same double movement of deepening and condensation occurs in these metaleptic moments in gaming.

Resetting the Game

X-Men appeared late in the Sega Genesis's console life cycle. A third-person, hack-and-slash side scroller, it belonged to the era of so-called licensed action games, i.e., games based on preexisting entertainment franchises such as movies or, in this case, a popular Marvel Comics series. Players assume one of four X-Men characters, mutants with extraordinary physical abilities, and traverse several linear levels as they avoid obstacles and combat disposable minions as well as super villains from the franchise as boss characters, whom they encounter at the end of each level. In terms of graphics, story, and gameplay, the game is typical for its genre and its time, although commercial reviewers considered it extremely difficult, due in part to poor level design and difficulty spikes. However, the game does experiment with interface- and sequence conventions, for instance by foregoing a title screen with menu options and dropping players directly into a first prelude level after they turn on the console.

In level five of the game, players confront Mojo, an obese, humanoid alien who resembles *Star Wars*' Jabba the Hutt. Mojo has no spine but prosthetic robot spider legs, cable appendages for hair, and a maniacal personality. He controls Mojo World, a planet hardwired with cameras and outfitted as an elaborate gladiator pit from where he broadcasts crash-TV-style combat-sports spectacles and deathmatches between those he abducts and enslaves. With a setting straight out of Paul Michael Glaser's 1982 movie *The Running Man*, the character Mojo is a fun-house mirror image of a 1980s entertainment executive, a parody of corporate greed, the declining quality of US-American entertainment under mass culture, and dehumanizing business practices. The original character thus already contains a certain metaleptic and political dimension.

Once players reach Mojo's lair and defeat him, they are prompted by various in-game monitors to "reset the computer" in order to stop a virus that threatens to destroy Mojo's stronghold in an explosion. Players can search the room high and low for any means to reset the network of wires and monitors displayed in the game's level, while a timer on the side of the screen ticks down mercilessly, but to no avail. The solution to the puzzle is to gently press the reset button on the gaming console. Doing so will cause the screen to fade to black and eventually fill up with green binary code. Players are then automatically transported to the next level. The game's regular interface gets momentarily extended to the hardware of the console; the input sequence is never used before or after this point, and there is no other indication of what players must do beyond the text on the screen. Worse yet, the operation is not without risk: holding down the reset button too long may cause the console to reset in earnest, which results in players losing their progress.

Media convergence here has a cognitive basis: players must revise their understanding of the boundaries between the interface of the gamepad and the console in order to solve the puzzle and progress to the next stage. This moment of hypermediation reverberates out both in the direction of narrative—players cannot proceed unless they stop Mojo's virus bomb—and to the game's material basis in the cartridge inserted in the console. Players must recognize the game's extra-diegetic situatedness and adjust their actions accordingly. Having battled their way through a literally nightmarish media landscape, they are prompted to confront the game as medium and reimport that knowledge into the game. Put differently, progress in the game depends on making that cognitive adjustment.

The prompt to reboot the system opens up a tenuous probabilistic space: players too immersed in the game may fail to recognize the extended valance of the word "reset" displayed on their screens and consequently may not progress further. They may even turn off the game in frustration as they fail to solve the puzzle, thus actually—one may say tragically—performing the proximate action to the one required, since apart from the reset button, the Genesis console only has a power button on its face plate. What is more, the interval between pressing and releasing the console's reset button determines which "system" gets rebooted—the virtual system of Mojo's computer or the console's operating system that runs the game's software. As the two systems converge semiotically, progress and failure are brought in precarious proximity.

Metaleptic convergence, in this instance, does not open a creative space of jouissance, as Galloway suggests in his example, but rather constitutes a radical and unexpected elimination criterium: players either recognize the game's overlapping narrative, semiotic, and material valences—and do so within a time limit—or they cannot proceed further. One may chalk this off to bad game design, but the fact that the story of the level revolves around a maniacal media mogul, who rules over a planet whose primary function is to provide a mediascape, suggest that this is indeed a moment of metagaming that frames the kind of singular alignment I have theorized above. Of course, not all games utilize ludo-narrative machinic convergence in quite so harsh a manner. Rather, the phenomenon occurs on a spectrum of narrative integration that runs from jarring to rather seamless.

The Fear of Breaking the Game and the System

Batman: Arkham Asylum by Rocksteady Studios (2009) was widely credited by commercial reviewers with reinvigorating the single-player action adventure genre at the time. The game's central conflict revolves around the DC Comics character Batman and unfolds on the grounds of Arkham Asylum, the mental institution for the criminally insane that houses the pointy-eared superhero's rogues gallery. The asylum has been taken over by the Joker, and Batman must restore order by combating henchmen and traversing the narrow halls and corridors of the facility whilst collecting clues and riddles to solve the mystery surrounding the purpose of the Joker's siege.

Arkham Asylum uses the New England Gothic architecture of the claustrophobic mental institution to construct its narrative setting. Its visual and acoustic cultural subtext includes steampunk, Gothic fiction (e. g. H.P. Lovecraft), and 1980s' horror and action movies. The game reimagines familiar characters from the D.C. Comics/Warner Bros. intellectual property in terms of this specific admixture of cultural references.

The gameplay combines hand-to-hand and stealth-based, "predatory" combat, exploration, and puzzle solving. However, the game's appeal arguably lies in its asymmetrical combat: Batman's wide array of gadgets and tactics enable players to take on hordes of armed enemies. Wielding an arsenal of "wonderful toys"—as Jack Nicholson calls them in the 1983 Batman film, which the game also references at times—Batman's "superpower," as it were, is being prepared, and the gameplay grants players this particular version of a power-fantasy. Combat requires players to assess various parameters such as the terrain, crowd size, as well as enemy attack- and defense capabilities and patterns. Recognizing these patterns and matching them to Batman's arsenal and physical combat skills, combined with the dexterity required to execute offensive and defensive maneuvers, constitutes the challenge here. Stealth combat revolves around Batman sneaking unseen through secluded areas (e. g., hallways, boiler rooms, rooftops) whilst eliminating enemies one by one.

In a key sequence, Batman faces off with one of his arch nemeses, the Scarecrow, who infects him with a fear-inducing aerosol toxin that causes hallucinations based on deep-seated, personal fears. After the first dose of gas, Batman will cough while leaving a room, a slight gesture that one may miss while playing. Minutes later, the hallway will gradually morph into the alley in which young Bruce Wayne's parents were murdered in front of him, setting him on a path to vigilantism. The game thus uses visual storytelling to explore the personal trauma of Batman's alter ego Bruce Wayne, while blurring the distinction between him and the asylum inmates. This scenario unfolds episodically across three separate encounters with the Scarecrow. Visual and aural clues indicate to the player when a sequence is hallucinatory (the hissing sound of the gas being ventilated into the room, Batman's coughing, the orange hue of his eyes, the cockroaches that begin crowding the hallways). One example is the illusion of the death of Commissioner Gordon, Batman's surrogate father figure.

However, the final encounter breaks with player expectations: following the aforementioned whizzing sound of gas in the background and Batman's slight coughing, an off-base announcement over the asylum's PDA system ("did anyone catch the game last night?") signals that something is amiss. Suddenly, the game freezes and the screen begins to fill with graphical artefacts and code fragments. Next, the game seems to restart with its title sequence, only to reveal this to be another Scarecrow-induced fear hallucination.

The ludo-narrative gambit here consists in the game momentarily dissolving the magic circle and letting the story of Batman's struggle with the toxin bleed into the system of the player. The game temporarily aligns players' contextual with Batman's diegetic perspective. The threat of losing hardware functionality becomes the objective correlative of the effects of Scarecrow's fear gas. As Batman loses his grip on reality, players experience the sensation of losing control over their avatar as well as a latent fear that their hardware has been corrupted. Similar to *X-Men*, the game aligns players' outside-world stakes with its diegetic stakes, creating a moment of higher-order play. However, this instance of the phenomenon, I would argue, is more elaborate and better integrated into the game's visual language and overall story. While the game console continues to function normally, this instance of non-play, within the diegetic logic of the game, dramatizes a central trope in Batman's mythos: his fear that he may be the same as the villains he fights.

The disruption, finally, has phenomenological implications for players. The simulated audio-visual glitches draw attention to the algorithmic actions necessary for running the game, specifically, for enabling diegetic and non-diegetic operator actions. During regular play, both sets of actions exist as discrete spheres for players. However, during this moment of convergence, machine and operator actions become symbolized on a diegetic level through the audio-visual misaligned code artefacts, which in turn mark an instance of hypermediation.

Media studies scholar Philipp Bojahr, who draws on Niklas Luhmann's systems model, sees such disruptions and juxtapositions as elucidating the intersections of the discrete systems of player and game. What Bojahr calls "amicable disruptions," of which he deems the episode in *Arkham Asylum* an example (164–65), occurs when the game purposefully behaves "in ways contrary to the player's gameplay-related horizon of expectations" (163, my translation). Game-design scholar Doug Church argues similarly that the appeal of videogames for players lies with their ability to create "perceivable consequences" (qtd. in Fernández-Vara 12).

The consistent correlation of system rules and player expectations creates what narratologists and media studies scholars like Janet Murray (cf. 98–99) and Marie-Laure Ryan (cf. 12) have termed immersive flow, i. e., players being swept up in the intersecting actions of interface manipulation, narrative, play, and what Fernandez-Vara (cf. 58) calls context (hardware is running etc.). Britta Neitzel further distinguishes flow and immersion from player involvement, i. e., the "playful equilibrium of proximity and distance" (["das spielerische Gleichgewicht von Nähe und Distanz"] that is generated via the concerted operations of multiple techniques and on multiple layers technical and symbolic levels (83, my translation). Contrary to Galloway, these approaches usually do not consider non-player acts as part of their respective systems. What all these concepts share is the idea that players need to be somehow entrapped by or tangled up in the game's semiotic structures.

However, in *Arkham Asylum*, the opposite seems true: interrupting flow arguably gets players more invested (if not immersed) in the story.[3] Once they realize that the game did not crash and that the video they see is a parody of the game's opening cut-scene, they will arguably resituate themselves in diegetic action. Meanwhile, *X-Men* makes the same gamble but with higher stakes, as it preconditions progress in the game on recognizing metaleptic convergence. And while the idea of immersion through disruption may seem paradoxical at first, it is consistent with media studies' conceptions of the mutually reinforcing tendencies of hypermediation and immersion.

There emerges yet another, political dimension of metaleptic convergence here, when we read this moment in *Asylum* as a commentary on the state of late capitalism and the investment of millennial Western professionals in personal entertainment technology. Galloway notes that "[a]cts of configuration," like menu settings or inventory arrangements in RPGs, "express processes in culture that are large, unknown, dangerous, and painful [...]. [A]cts of configuration are

---

3 Again, cf Juul, 36.

a rendering of [late capitalist] life" (16). In *The Plague of Fantasies*, Slavoj Žižek identifies a naïve tendency in users to "trust the phenomena" of the interface, a tendency that for him characterizes our traversal of cyberspace (cf. 130–32). For Žižek, interfaces generate the "illusion of continuity": "the user becomes 'accustomed to opaque technology'—the digital machinery behind the screen retreats into total impenetrability, even invisibility" (131).

Arkham Asylum arguably simulates a disruption of play in which what Žižek calls "imbecilic contingency" (129) bursts through this veil of naiveté to momentarily negate the false "sense of interiority that ideological space curvature promises" (130). Because this disruption is only simulated, however, it can be rendered harmless and even become part of this naïve flow of gameplay. Once players see the Scarecrow's inverted bat-symbol on the moon standing high above the skyline of Gotham City, the fear of a possible system corruption and accidental resetting of the game recedes and may even turn to a heightened sense of immersion and investment in the story.

As with *X-Men*, the gambit here is to threaten players with complete data loss. The emotional stakes are even higher in the sense that players are made to briefly suffer the fear of having their systems permanently damaged, whereas *X-Men* merely teases players about possibly losing game data if they incorrectly manipulate the console interface. *Arkham Asylum* integrates more effectively instances of metalepsis with its story as it introduces visual and aural cues associated with the Scarecrow scenario earlier on in the game. Like in any good whodunit, players must become detectives and mentally retrace their steps and recognize that the signs for solving the puzzle were indeed there all along. The previous two examples use metalepsis in select instances to meditate on the medium of video games, i.e., to create metagaming. I have argued from the beginning that the semiotic efficacy of these instances lies in their temporal and spatial limitedness. That being said, it is of course possible to extend such moments and even make them the premise of an entire game, as in the following example.

Deleting the Game to Win the Game

The early 2010s marked the rise of the so-called independent or 'indie' games. Usually produced by a single person or a two-person team, these games often feature retro graphics and gameplay principles (for instance, 8-bit side scrollers). The commercial success of these games continues to be considerable, given that they can be produced relatively cheaply and distributed digitally and independently. Games such as *Braid* (2009) or *Super Meat Boy* (2010) rank among the most prominent examples of such success stories. One subgroup in this genre is the metagame, which reflects on the medium of the video game. While most of the instances I discuss in this article can be considered meta-sequences or -episodes in otherwise linear, narrative games, metagames like *Undertale* (2015) and *The Stanley Parable* (2016) engage directly with the trappings of interface and ludic storytelling through their respective gameplay loop and narrative styles.[4]

In *Pony Island*, players confront a haunted penny-arcade cabinet, which prompts them to "insert" their souls, rather than quarters, to play. Gameplay alternates between a simple side-scrolling jump-and-run, in which they guide an 8-bit animated unicorn across an increasingly menacing obstacle course, and puzzle sections in which players must 'hack' the cabinet's core programming and eventually retrieve their soul by shifting around symbols and enter text commands. These two loops are interspersed with DOS-based text-messenger chats with Satan himself, who taunts players about the impossible odds of beating the game. The game's screen remains framed at all times by the visual representation of an old transistor screen, which adds a layer of signification to play as the game evokes the material impression that the various game elements all 'take place' on one arcade screen. While remaining stationary in space, the arcade cabinet challenges players by offering games of various genres (puzzle, jump-and-run) as well as dialog options. Meanwhile, the interface follows the point-and-click principle of the home PC adventure games from the early 1990s, like *The Secret of Monkey Island* (1990), in which players must solve visual puzzles and choose between various dialog options.

The game references specialized sub-sections of online gamer culture. When trying to start a new game from the main menu, players find menu items disappearing, changing color, or falling to the bottom of the screen like material objects. Players must "fix" the menu by manipulating the base code of the cabinet in the form of moving symbols around to matching, pre-marked positions. Once the right sequence is established, players take on another obstacle-course section with their pony, while Satan quickly thwarts their efforts by deploying unavoidable obstacles causing instant death. Puzzle sections invoke the activity of modifying ("modding") games and trading copies of unfinished games that has been common among online communities since the late 1980s.

Modders, players with programming skills, will break into a game's code and fix errors ("bugs") or make aesthetic modifications, for instance, by changing character appearances. They might also port older games to newer operating systems. Yet, in this case, manipulating the game's corrupted code constitutes one

---

[4] The documentary *Indie Game: The Movie* (2012) traces out this process.

of the two gameplay loops rather than guerilla hacking. Compared to the previous two examples, the chain of signification reaches much further than the immediate material, non-diegetic situatedness of the game. By allowing players to become hackers without the necessary coding skills, *Pony Island* symbolically bridges the skill gap that differentiates the two communities. Players may simulate a more intense practice of 'play'—modding—that encompasses even a game's baseline code, thus defamiliarizing the kind of surface play represented by the pony obstacle course sections.

Evoking modding culture in this manner elevates metalepsis from an incidental occurrence to a design principle. In contrast to *X-Men* and *Arkham Asylum*, frame-breaking here functions not as a story-telling device but becomes the whole point of the game. Players are constantly confronting the fact that they are playing a video game whilst fiddling with its core code. The whimsical secondary gameplay loop, the pony obstacle course, meanwhile gets stripped of its gameplay efficacy. Players may control the avatar on the screen by entering simple commands, but the stages cannot be completed because the code has been corrupted. This part of the game, the actual game in terms of *Pony Island*'s diegesis, becomes stripped of its ludic efficacy while being super-charged with symbolic value. The obstacle course sections exist as referential tokens, signifying, on the one hand, the game's broken state and, on the other hand, the difference between various gaming practices and gamer types: casual players who enjoy games like *Angry Birds*, which feature simple, straightforward control schemes, dedicated players who sink hours into sprawling open-world games with elaborate graphics and complex inventory-management systems, and obsessive players who go to even greater lengths and utilize the very code of a game. It also signifies the simple fact that gameplay is not possible while the game's code remains corrupted. Once players have patched the arcade cabinet's program, they may confront Satan with their pony and shoot laser beams at him in the final level of the game.

Meanwhile, the coding puzzle sections, while simulating the higher-order skill set of programming and constituting the actual primary gameplay loop, are semiotically sparse. Players are simply called upon to match symbols, and like the platforming sections, the puzzle sections merely signify the truism that a game's code must be operational in order for even simple gameplay to take place. This is where the two game play loops intersect: each gameplay section points to the other, thereby creating a spiral of signification.

Like *X-Men* and *Arkham*, *Pony Island* also has a noteworthy instance of metaleptic convergence: the game's signification spiral ends once Satan is defeated and players can retrieve their souls. After the end credits have rolled, a ghost, who had helped players with clues via the game's built-in text-chat feature, appears and asks to be freed. Like the player's avatar was trapped in the arcade cabinet, the ghost claims to be trapped in the game's code on the player's computer. Only when the *Pony Island* file is deleted from the player's hard drive can the ghost be set free. Through the diegetic entity of the ghost, the game prompts players to eradicate its code, i.e., to perform an action diametrically opposed to the principles of the game they just completed. If players delete the game, metalepsis turns to entropy as frame-breaking turns to object-breaking, the erasure of the game's code. Deletion ends the game's signifying spiral while in itself signifying the ultimate end of the object fetish that is modding. The game only ever truly ends when there is no more code and obsessive players can cease "playing" the game in all senses of the term. As with our other two examples, completing the game requires players to take actions in the material world, in this case, uninstalling the game they thought they had just completed and thus erasing their progress.

Conclusion

The ghost in *Pony Island* delivers the same message to players as the black cat in *The Matrix* gives to Neo: get out of the game. Feige notes that the whole "gag" about gaming (he uses this term specifically) is that players really do not play the game so much as they play through themselves while completing a game (cf. 173), and in many respects, the action adventure games that I have considered here all point players outside their own semiotic framework. Yet they do so in order to propel their respective narratives and to enhance immersion. My interest has been in shedding light on this counterintuitive push-and-pull dynamic, which I have called metaleptic convergence in an effort to capture conceptually the way in which their ludo-narrative, semiotic, and material valences align. I have characterized these alignments by their short duration and semiotic density, or what Attridge calls deepening and densifying. In literature, this unfurling conceptual space prompts readers to interlace the text with their knowledge of the cultural world from which it comes. In the realm of video games, *écriture*, in Galloway's sense of "generative agitation," correlates with Attridge's notion of "demand" made by texts to their readers. It designates the higher order of play that players enter once they answer the game's demand for such deeper engagement. Narrative glitches thus are nodal points at which this ever-deepening and densifying, agitative and demanding interstice becomes visible. The games I have discussed here afford players particular responses to these demands, by which all dimensions of gamic activity converge as they become represented in play.

More work has to be done on the conceptual implications of the symbolic spaces that these convergences open up in video games. For instance, if gameplay really constitutes *écriture* in the poststructuralist sense, narrative glitches may help us think about the generative violence, or *trace*, at the center of such 'writing.' They may even enable us to identify and conceptualize a revolutionary potential in video games.[5] The overarching project here is of course to sharpen our image of video games as media object that mean in certain ways. My attempt here was informed by the poststructuralist notion that the characteristic properties of structures emerge at their fault lines, or in moments when they collapse. Action adventure games utilize this notion and operationalize it as narrative, in the process creating litters of black cats for us to pause and contemplate.

Works Cited

Attridge, Derek. *The Singularity of Literature.* 2nd ed., Routledge, 2017.
Batman: Arkham Asylum. Rocksteady Studios, 2009.
Bolter, J. David, and Richard Grusin. *Remediation: Understanding New Media.* MIT Press, 1999.
Bojahr, Philipp. "Störungen Des Computerspiels." Gamescoop, pp. 147–78.
Cixous, Hélèn. "The Laugh of the Medusa." *The Critical Tradition: Classic Texts and Contemporary Trends*, edited by David H. Richter, 3rd ed., Bedford, 2007, pp. 1643–55.
Feige, Daniel Martin. *Computerspiele: Eine Ästhetik.* Suhrkamp, 2015.
Fernández-Vara, Clara. *Introduction to Game Analysis.* Routledge, 2014.
Galloway, Alexander R. *Gaming: Essays on Algorithmic Culture.* U of Minnesota P, 2006.
Gamescoop, editor. *Theorien Des Computerspiels*, Junius, 2012.
Juul, Jesper. *The Art of Failure.* MIT UP, 2013.
Pajot, Lisanne, and James Swirsky. *Indie Game: The Movie.* 2012.
Mullins, Daniel. *Pony Island.* Daniel Mullins Games, 2016.
Murray, Janet H. *Hamlet on the Holodeck: The Future of Narrative in Cyberspace.* MIT Press, 1998.
Neitzel, Britta. "Involvierungsstrategien des Computerspiels." Gamescoop, pp. 75–103.
Ryan, Marie-Laure, editor. *Narrative Across Media: The Languages of Storytelling.* U of Nebraska P, 2004.
Sharp, John. *Works of Game: On the Aesthetics of Games and Art.* MIT UP, 2015.
X-Men. Sega, 1993.
Žižek, Slavoj. *The Plague of Fantasies.* Verso, 2009.

---

5 I am thinking of Hélène Cixous's use of the term "*écriture féminine*" (1644) as emancipatory practice in "The Laugh of the Medusa" (1975) as a potential blueprint for framing this discourse.

Sabrina Mittermeier
Time Travelling to the American Revolution — Why Immersive Media Need American Studies

Using a case study of the depiction of the American Revolution in the video game *Assassins Creed 3* (2012), as well as Disney's treatment of the era in their Magic Kingdom and Epcot theme parks, this paper has two simple arguments to make: first, that video games and theme parks are similar forms of media and that these similarities warrant more attention from scholars, and second, that American studies is a discipline uniquely suited to address this need. While there is a clear overlap in theory between the academic study of video games and theme parks (particularly concerning ideas of immersion or authenticity), nobody so far seems to have bothered to draw direct comparisons. This is a missed opportunity, I argue, since this would likely lead to fruitful collaborations between the small but burgeoning field of theme park studies and the gradually more established field of video game studies. Elsewhere, I have defined the theme park as "a participatory medium that relies on strategies of theming to entertain an audience within a transnational consumer culture" (Mittermeier, *Middle Class* 6). This definition could easily also be applied to digital games. Games are even more participatory in nature than theme parks, and their transnationality is integral to their success, particularly that of the mass-marketed triple-A titles. At the same time, 'theming' is not a term that immediately seems to lend itself well to describe how games tell their stories, but if we expand on its meaning, the similarities become quite apparent. Imagineer (the term Disney uses for their theme park designers) Joe Rohde has called the practice of theming "narrative placemaking," or "the building of ideas into physical objects." While digital games do not let us grasp physical objects, they still let us enter three-dimensional worlds, and thus Rohde's assessment of such "narrative space" as "theatrical space" equally applies here: "Guests make choices as to how to travel through the space or where to look (...) [so,] linear storytelling doesn't read. If the space is designed to allow free, self-directed flow, then the designer cannot know what linear sequence each person may follow." Not all digital games allow for the same freedom, but particularly those with a first-person point of view do, and as virtual or augmented reality experiences become more and more feasible in digital gaming, this strategy should gain even more relevance for game designers. Most importantly, both good theme park and game design involve their respective audience, "they are given roles within the narrative" (Rohde),

https://doi.org/10.1515/9783110659405-014

whether the gameplay or theme park design is more active or passive—hence the discussed participatory nature of both media. When narrative placemaking is successful, the audience suspends their disbelief and thus becomes immersed. Media scholar Erkki Huhtamo has argued that immersion implies "a transition, a 'passage' from one realm to another, from the immediate physical reality of tangible objects and direct sensory data to *somewhere else*" (159, original emphasis). Both a well-designed theme park and a game can 'suck' you into their story and make you feel like you are a part of it, like you are actually in another place or time.

This immersion of theme parks and video games, however, has been seen less as a potential but rather as a threat when the stories being told this way are grounded in historical fact, and since this is such a rich and controversial topic, I want to use video games and theme parks with a historical setting as an example here to explore their similarities. Immersive media give us the possibility of "time travel," as archaeologist Cornelius Holtorf has called it, the opportunity to "experience the presence of another period" (31). Yet such an experience is never straightforward, and it is highly contested within the larger context of a discussion on history and its representation. One of the most notable moments in this ongoing debate occurred in the early 1990s, when the first Culture Wars were waged in the US. Disney had famously tried to open a historical theme park called Disney's America near Manassas Battlefield Park (a Civil War historic site) in Virginia in 1993 and had to cancel the project not even a year later. They had sparked a massive discussion in the media and among professional historians that opposed the project across political divides. Their criticism thus did not just aim at the fear of a disneyfied, whitewashed history from more liberal pundits, as conservatives meanwhile suspected Disney would try to present a history they deemed as too "politically correct"—a weaponized term even then (Mittermeier, "Windows" 134). While the project fell victim to a larger conflict that also included controversies over an exhibit of the Enola Gay, the bomber that dropped the atomic bomb on Hiroshima at the National Air & Space Museum, and a project to revise the National History Standards for school education, it also opened a discussion about the role of popular culture in teaching history to the public (Mittermeier, "Windows" 135). Historical film has been a staple genre ever since the invention of the medium, and while occasional discussions have been had about the authenticity of its depiction, academic interest, particularly from historians themselves, was pioneered by Robert Rosenstone only in the late 1980s and early 1990s. Besides his and other scholars' convincing arguments that historians and other disciplines should equally take interest, there seems to be the persistent idea in some academic circles that the study of film (or other pop-cultural media) should be the sole work of literary disciplines. Yet while historical film unarguably plays an important role in the public's engagement with and understanding of history, digital games and theme parks' immersive nature have raised additional concern as they expand the framework of said debate.

Bob Weis, an Imagineer who had been with the Disney company in 1993 and who today is the president of Walt Disney Imagineering (WDI), had promised that Disney's America would show its visitors "the Civil War with all its racial conflict," and Michael Eisner, then-CEO of the Walt Disney Company, even went so far as to suggest it would convey "what it was like to be a slave or (…) to escape through the underground railroad" (qtd. in Lukas, "A Politics" 276). While such tone-deaf remarks make the outrage from historians somewhat understandable, they also point toward the unique characteristics of the medium that distinguish it from the less participatory media of film or literature. Peter Rummell, then chairman of WDI, eventually submitted to a statement to an OAH (Organization of American Historians) Newsletter on the subject. He explained that Imagineering had intended to use the multiple tools of narrative placemaking and apply them to historical periods in order to "help visitors imagine what it must have been like at certain moments in our nation's history" (Rummell 10). Similar claims are also made almost verbatim by many video game designers that try to bring historical events to life, even to this day. The most prominent example is the *Assassins Creed* franchise by Ubisoft that released its first installment in 2007, and which ties together several radically different historical periods and locations using a meta-narrative that lets the series' protagonist re-live his ancestors' memories via a device called the "Animus." Most of the gameplay takes place in the past, then, and so the protagonist engages in literal, actual time travel, while the player does so only figuratively. This, however, seems to authenticate the player's experience of the past, and is a narrative device that theme parks use frequently; Disneyland famously greets every guest entering with the sign "here you leave today, and enter the world of yesterday, tomorrow and fantasy." To illustrate how such 'time travel' works within those games (and compare and contrast it with theme parks' treatment of the past), I will focus on the third installment in the series, *Assassins Creed 3* (2012), which is set during the American Revolutionary Era.

The developers apparently chose the theme because it fit with their overarching plotline of Templars vs. Assassins, "free will vs. (…) oppression," as lead writer Cory May puts it ("IGN Presents"). Creative designer Alex Hutchinson adds that it was an "unexpected place to set a game, that it was somewhere a game hadn't been set before" ("IGN Presents"). It is true that the American Revolution is a historical period that is still rarely depicted in popular culture, especially in comparison to the other era instrumental for American civil religion, the

American Civil War (cf. Hochgeschwender 432). Not until the success of the musical *Hamilton* (2015) had it found much representation across such divergent media as film, literature or theater. The makers of *Assassins Creed III* offer an unusual entry into the period by giving the protagonist a Native American background. They claim a certain amount of authenticity by hiring language coaches and an actor of Mohawk descent ("Episode One"), a claim which would deserve more critical scrutiny in its underlying assumptions about culture and race than the focus of this essay allows for. Besides the unconventional protagonist, though, the depiction of the past follows familiar strategies of narrative placemaking. Ubisoft produced an official making-of called "Inside Assassins Creed III" as promotional material that is still readily available on their official YouTube channel, in which the game's creative team discuss several aspects of its design. Besides the designers, however, the series of videos also feature other 'experts,' such as reenactors, a member of the Sons of the American Revolution, and a Navy SEAL. All of these add an air of authenticity to the designers' claims of making it possible for the players to be "exploring that time," allegedly even details that "you don't really hear about in the history books" (Hutchinson in "Episode One"). Yet the main draw is clearly the iconography that is familiar to American audience: in order to 'bring the past to life,' the game offers detailed recreations of the cities of Boston and New York, using historical maps as source material ("Episode Four"), as well as those of battle weapons and uniforms, for which reenactors and historians were consulted ("Episode Two"). Such rather cosmetic uses of the past are a staple of pop-cultural historical depictions—one only needs to consider films like *The Patriot* (2000), also set during the Revolution, that essentially dresses up an action-revenge movie in colonial garb, with hardly any historical merit. Holtorf has described this practice as "pastness," the "contemporary quality or condition of being past" (35). In addition to such stylized uses of the past, the player in *Assassins Creed III* gets to be in the proverbial room where it happens, "whether it's the Boston Tea Party or the Boston Massacre, we have these big historic events we can situate our game around" (Hutchinson in "Episode Four"). As the protagonist Connor, the player gets to "assassinate key historical figures, at major battles, at major events during the Revolution" (Hutchinson, "Episode One"). This opens up the potential for telling an alternate history (technically, the mere insertion of a fictional character suffices to do that), which is explored in the DLC "The Tyranny of King Washington," yet the main game still is firmly grounded in a patriotic, 'accurate' depiction of the Revolutionary era. The well-known 'heroic figures' of the American Revolution, as the game's designers have called them ("Episode Three"), are glorified, and the player gets to become one of them. In the promotional making-of, Gary Bohannon, a member of the Sons of the American Revolution, exclaims:

"If George Washington would have had Connor on his team, he wouldn't have needed many other people!" ("Episode One"). The marketing department for the game also released a live-action trailer entitled "Rise" that shows several civilians 'rising up' for the Revolution, and it similarly aligns Connor, and in turn the player, with them. The draw of the game, then, is the promise of time-traveling to the era of the American Revolution and to experience colonial America first-hand: exploring cities, fighting battles on land and sea, and meeting people like George Washington and Benjamin Franklin. As studies of immersion in different media have shown, the key to its success is prior knowledge, and an interest in the story is vital for anyone to be immersed in a narrative (cf. Hofer and Wirth 167). It would be interesting to find out how this setting and particularly its visual iconography resonated with international audiences who are likely less familiar with it than Americans. The game sold well outside the US, but much of this can likely be attributed to the overall success of the very popular franchise. Yet what remains equally important as audience reception is the motivation of its creators, who clearly relied on recognition value to bring this era to life in the game, while at the same time framing this practice in terms of historical accuracy. Yet, and this seems to be the crux of this argument, if they had made an actually historically accurate game, what would it even look like? The result would likely be something that would not be a 'good' game, at least not one that tells a narratively coherent story, and it could even lead to a loss of immersion because it would potentially not conform to prevalent ideas of what the American Revolution should look like; it would simply not tick all the boxes of audience expectation.

Theme parks use exactly the same strategies as digital games to let their visitors 'travel in time.' This becomes abundantly clear when looking at themed spaces that depict the same time and place: colonial America, and specifically the events of the American Revolution. The Liberty Square area in Disney's Magic Kingdom theme park, as well as the American Adventure pavilion in Epcot, both part of Walt Disney World in Orlando, Florida, are prominent examples. Liberty Square opened with the rest of the Magic Kingdom in 1971, as a direct reaction to the upcoming bicentennial celebrations in the US at the time (cf. Wright 66). It features detailed recreations of the Liberty Bell, colonial-style architecture, echoing Independence Hall in Philadelphia or the Virginia House of Burgesses, and nods to Paul Revere's ride. Its sole attraction besides a shop and two restaurants is the Hall of Presidents, a show that tells a much compressed history of the American presidency, featuring audio-animatronic versions of all 45 men. The park's employees, or in Disney-speak "cast members," are dressed in colonial garb, adding to the immersion. As with every Disney theme park setting, it follows the four strategies of what Alan Bryman has called

"Disneyization": the use of theming, hybrid consumption, merchandising, performative labor, and control and surveillance.

The American Adventure pavilion in Epcot similarly tells American history through a patriotic lens. Housed in a massive colonial architecture building, its main attraction, another American history-themed show, features audio-animatronics of Benjamin Franklin and Mark Twain. The food served at the pavilion includes such all-American standards such as funnel cake (a dish actually brought into the country by the Pennsylvania Dutch), and a Five and Drum corps contributes to musical entertainment. Both Liberty Square and the American Adventure pavilion, then, rely on similarly familiar key figures and events, as well as cosmetic, stylized uses of the past, "pastness," in architecture and design to immerse their visitors—to make 'time travel' possible. Laurie Meamber, a marketing scholar, has compared the American Adventure pavilion to other famous historic tourist sites in the US, including Colonial Williamsburg and Mount Vernon. She has found that these attractions equally rely on patriotic, disneyfied storytelling, and that they also increasingly have turned to the tools of Disneyization in conveying their narratives: "As Disney has always utilized technology to immerse the visitor into the site, historical sites are also embracing immersion as a way to make history come alive" (Meamber 140). It seems, then, that the concerns that had brought the Disney's America project to a halt are no longer preventing other attractions from using these tools—and they have never stopped digital games from doing so. Yet, digital games have also received much more vocal backlash from both academics and the media (if not on the scale of the Disney's America controversy) when they have engaged with more harrowing periods of the past, such as Nazi Germany. As neither film nor literature are still the target of such large-scale discussions, especially those that prominently feature historians or politicians, it seems to be their inherent participatory or immersive nature that fuels these debates more than anything. Scott Lukas, one of the most prolific writers on theme parks, has explained this by the "more active role" ("Politics" 278) that visitors take in contrast to the more passive role that spectators of a movie or readers of a book (usually) fill, adding "that the technology of theming itself is often the inciter of controversy" ("Politics" 276). He further argues this is a question of "genre" or "form of the themed space" that dictates the "the type of topics that may be considered" ("Pushing" 53). And yet, immersive media conveying historical periods are hugely successful, and from what we can tell, their popularity will likely not wane anytime soon—the newest installment of the *Assassins Creed* series, *Assassins Creed: Origins*, even features a "Discovery Mode" that lets the player freely explore Ancient Egypt beyond the conventional gameplay, an experience that has been compared to a museum (Tamayo). So what do we make of these immersive media and their popularity as academics in general, and as cultural historians in particular?

The central issue is that of authenticity, of whether such media can ever really offer us more than "pastness," or worse, disneyfied, whitewashed versions of history. Is it really possible for digital games or theme parks to be true to history, give us an "accurate reflection" (Lukas, "Keeping" 90) of it, and thus be 'authentic'? And how do these immersive media challenge and change our notion of what such authenticity means? Could they possibly even make historians question what is authentic and what is not, given that even historians have a similar penchant for telling and teaching history focused on key events and figures— maybe a more personalized, immersive approach could have an impact on this practice? And yet, just because *Assassins Creed III* recreates colonial Boston and New York to a certain extent or because it delves into the brutal details of battle, or even when it lets us have a conversation with Benjamin Franklin, it still does not tell us much about the personal concerns of people that supported or opposed the American Revolution. It does not tell us about politics, the intricacies of war, the reality of lived lives, their suffering and hardship. And yet, prematurely dismissing the potential of immersive media in letting us 'time travel' also seems like a missed educational opportunity, and like a failure to engage with potential new and different forms of how we conceive of historical authenticity. I firmly agree with Holtorf that while we should be diligent to not trivialize the past, we might have a "particular human duty to travel to unpleasant destinations as we may in that way take important lessons and indeed emotions back to present reality" (39). Immersive, participatory media potentially do offer us this chance, if done right. American historians James Oliver Horton and Eric Foner, who had agreed to advise for Disney's America before it was cancelled, seem to have understood these possibilities. Horton even saw it as a democratic effort, arguing that "'we need to educate our people and we need to do that in a variety of places. We can't count on the schools or the universities or even formal mainstream traditional museums to do the education (...) alone'" (qtd. in Zenzen 180). Academics can play an important role in this. Even while most of us will never be able to consult on a historical film, video game, or theme park (not that such consultation would automatically result in a more authentic product), we can write about them, and most importantly, we can teach about them. We can use them to instill and cultivate an interest in history both in our students and beyond the ivy-ranked walls of academia. And we can and must help them interpret these media from a variety of perspectives—we can teach them media literacy.

This is where American studies comes in. The interdisciplinary nature of the field is what makes it so useful for a critical analysis of immersive media, be it theme parks or digital games. It gives us tools from cultural studies, cultural history, literary studies, media studies, gender and race studies, and many other fields, and all of them are necessary to understand the multifaceted nature of digital games. While academic writing usually calls for putting focus on any one of these lenses, the training in this diverse field still equips its practitioners exceptionally well to decode these media from multiple angles. While the narratology vs. ludology debate within video games studies has become stale anyhow, an American studies approach easily does away with it, and it also moves analysis away from being too formalist or intrinsic to the text. American studies done right also always encompasses a cultural historic outlook that calls for consideration of context—not just that of historical decades depicted as in the case studies discussed here, but also, and even more importantly, the context of cultural production. Its toolbox is uniquely suited to understand digital games and other immersive media as the multi-faceted products they are. It is thus more than logical that the discipline embrace them, as it has done with other aspects of popular culture before.

Works Cited

"Assassins Creed 3 – Rise Trailer." *YouTube*, uploaded by Playstation Australia, 4 July 2012, www.youtube.com/watch?v=ySLSt_QLmoQ.
Bryman, Alan. *The Disneyization of Society*. Sage Publications, 2004.
Hochgeschwender, Michael. *Die Amerikanische Revolution. Geburt einer Nation 1763–1815*. C.H.Beck, 2016.
Hofer, Matthias, and Werner Wirth. "Präsenzerleben—Eine medienpsychologische Modellierung." *Montage A/V*, vol. 17, no. 2, 2008, pp. 159–75.
Holtorf, Cornelius. "On the Possibility of Time Travel." *Lund Archaeological Review*, vol. 15, 2009, pp. 31–41.
Huhtamo, Erkki. "Encapsulated Bodies in Motion. Simulators and the Quest for Total Immersion." *Critical Issues in Electronic Media*, edited by Simon Penny, State U of New York P, 1995, pp. 159–86.
"IGN Presents: Making Assassin's Creed 3 – Origins (Part 1)." *YouTube*, uploaded by IGN, 19 Sept. 2012, www.youtube.com/watch?v=zoEqI97-HaU.
"Inside Assassins Creed III: Episode One." *YouTube*, uploaded by Ubisoft, 23 Aug. 2012, www.youtube.com/watch?v=aELBUumQFNw.
"Inside Assassins Creed III: Episode Two." *YouTube*, uploaded by Ubisoft, 30 Aug. 2012, www.youtube.com/watch?v=vep2BzeleyA.
"Inside Assassins Creed III: Episode Three." *YouTube*, uploaded by Ubisoft, 13 Sept. 2012, www.youtube.com/watch?v=o5JKCs-rJw&t=308s.
"Inside Assassins Creed III: Episode Four." *YouTube*, uploaded by Ubisoft, 19 Sept. 2012, www.youtube.com/watch?v=O_0RVLc9hi4.

Lukas, Scott A. "A Politics of Reverence and Irreverence: Social Discourse on Theming Controversies." *The Themed Space: Locating Culture, Nation, and Self,* edited by Scott A. Lukas, Lexington Books, 2007, pp. 271–94.

Lukas, Scott A. "Controversial Topics: Pushing The Limits in Themed and Immersive Spaces." *Attractions Management,* no.4, 2015, pp. 50–54.

Lukas, Scott A. "Keeping It Real (on Authenticity)." *Attractions Management,* no.1, 2017, pp. 90–94.

Meamber, Laurie A. "Disney and the Presentation of Colonial America." *Consumption Markets & Culture,* vol. 14, no.2, 2011, pp. 125–144.

Mittermeier, Sabrina. *Middle Class Kingdoms—A Cultural History of Disneyland and Its Variations, 1955–2016.* 2017. LMU Munich, Doctoral Dissertation. (publication with Intellect Books forthcoming)

Mittermeier, Sabrina. "'Windows to the Past': Disney's America, the Culture Wars, and the Question of Edutainment." *Polish Journal for American Studies,* vol.10, 2016, pp. 127–46.

Rohde, Joe. "From Myth to Mountain: Insights Into Virtual Placemaking." *ACM SIGGRAPH Computer Graphics,* vol. 47, no.3, 2007, DOI: 10.1145/1281324.1281325. Accessed 15 Jan. 2019.

Rosenstone, Robert A. *Visions of the Past. The Challenge of Film to Our Idea of History.* Harvard University Press, 1995.

Rummell, Peter. "A House Divided: Historians Confront Disney's America." *OAH Newsletter,* vol. 22, no.3, 1994, p. 10.

Tamayo, Paul. "Discovery Mode Turns Assassins Creed: Origins Into a Museum." *Kotaku,* 20 Feb. 2018, kotaku.com/discovery-mode-turns-assassins-creed-origins-into-a-mu-1823166019. Accessed 15 Jan. 2019.

Wright, Alex. *The Imagineering Field Guide to the Magic Kingdom at Walt Disney World.* 2nd edition. Disney Editions, 2009.

Zenzen, Joan M. *Battling for Manassas: The Fifty-Year Preservation Struggle at Manassas National Battlefield Park.* Pennsylvania University Press, 1998.

Manuel Franz and Henning Jansen
A Shining City and the Sodom Below: Historical Guilt and Personal Agency in *BioShock Infinite*

"You...you were there...at Wounded Knee...I can see it in your face" (Shotgunnova, "GS 09: Hall of Heroes"). As Elizabeth confronts Booker DeWitt with these words, the main character of *BioShock Infinite*[1] is confronted with his past—a past directly linked to one of the darkest chapters of U.S. history. Video games, such as *BioShock Infinite*, play an integral part in the perception of history in everyday life and in recent years, have increasingly become integrated in commemorative and historical culture (cf. Heinze 26–30). By analyzing the depiction of history-related 'content' in video games, historiographical research may help to understand the impact of this medium on the societal perception of history itself.

Elizabeth's words concisely illustrate the three aspects of commemorative culture this essay addresses: first, the depiction and use of history in relation to historical guilt ("Wounded Knee"), second, the personal agency associated with such guilt ("you were there"), and third, the actions of and effects on players ("in your face"). After introducing *BioShock Infinite*'s historical setting, the essay examines both the narrative and the ludic components of the game. We argue that its depiction of history addresses individual responsibility and guilt as a driving force of commemorative culture; furthermore, we demonstrate the game's attempt to evoke such guilt/responsibility as well as its eventual failure to do so.

BioShock Infinite is set in an alternate version of the year 1912. Booker DeWitt, the game's anti-hero, is a former soldier and Pinkerton agent struggling with alcoholism and gambling debts. A nihilistic cynic ever since he left the U.S. Army, he is making a living by selling his talent for violence to the highest bidder. The game's plot begins when DeWitt is offered a rather unusual job in order to "wipe away the debt": he is to rescue Elizabeth, a young woman held captive in the city of Columbia.

---

[1] *BioShock Infinite* was developed by Irrational Games and published by 2K in March 2013 for Windows, Xbox 360, and PlayStation 3. Two sequel DCLs (*Burial at Sea, Episode One + Two*) were published in November 2013 and March 2014. This essay focuses exclusively on the main game.

https://doi.org/10.1515/9783110659405-015

Columbia soon turns out to be a steampunk metropolis floating above the clouds. A brainchild of the self-proclaimed prophet Zachary Hale Comstock, the technologically advanced city was initially built for the 1893 World's Fair as a showcase for American exceptionalism and was later dispatched around the world. During the 1901 Boxer Rebellion, however, Comstock—without orders from Washington—commanded Columbia's forces to destroy Beijing, thus revealing that his city was, in fact, heavily armed. When the U.S. government disavowed Comstock's renegade actions, Columbia seceded from the United States and vanished above the clouds, claiming to build a better society apart from the "Sodom Below."

When players first arrive in the city, they get the impression of a shining paradise, given Columbia's beautiful architectural appearance combining Roman and colonial American influences. Like all newcomers, DeWitt is being baptized at the city gate, symbolically washing off the impurity he is leaving behind upon entering this "New Eden." Not far into the game, however, the city's true character becomes more and more apparent. Turning out to be a totalitarian dictatorship, Columbian society is built on religious fundamentalism, hyper-nationalism, and white supremacy.

Just moments after DeWitt's arrival, the city's devotion to an odd religious fundamentalism mixing Old Testament leitmotifs with American nationalism is introduced. In fact, Columbians worship America's Founding Fathers as saints, as players witness in a scene where believers pray to statues of George Washington, Benjamin Franklin, and Thomas Jefferson. While deeply reveling in patriotic symbolism, the city has only adapted from the United States what seemed fit to their xenophobic ideology. In their view, their former homeland abandoned its divine purpose not only by turning away from religion but from racial purity as well. In the city's historical narrative, Abraham Lincoln is demonized for having ended slavery, while his assassin, John Wilkes Booth, is portrayed as a martyr. Columbia's social hierarchy rests upon the notion of white supremacy. Jim-Crow-like laws ensure that only the city's Anglo-Saxon population holds positions of political and economic power. Blacks, Catholic Irish, and other ethnic minorities constitute a racial underclass, deprived of rights and only tolerated as a useful pool of cheap labor. Propaganda posters, excessively present in the whole city, warn against the "foreign horde" and fuel a paranoid spirit. Consequently, Columbia is a highly militarized police-state. There is, however, opposition against Comstock's regime. The resistance movement Vox Populi, spearheaded by its black leader Daisy Fitzroy, has rallied the oppressed in order the fight the system. When a violent civil war erupts on the streets of Columbia, DeWitt gets in the crossfire between Comstock's and Fitzroy's forces.

On their quest to rescue Elizabeth, players gradually explore the floating city and decipher its secrets along the way. What begins as a classic damsel-in-distress plot embedded in an unconventional scenario gradually transforms into a more elaborate storyline, especially as it not only reveals the intertwined past of its main characters but also involves traveling between parallel worlds. Referring to quantum physics, the game postulates the existence of an infinite number of universes, each of them based on different decisions made by its inhabitants—hence the title *BioShock Infinite*.

Given Columbia's state of technology as well as a number of other steampunk and supernatural elements in the game world, *BioShock Infinite*'s year 1912 is obviously not our universe's historical year of 1912.[2] However, the values on which Columbian society is based are all too familiar to players from our reality. Supposedly dedicated to American exceptionalism, the city in the clouds is actually a mirror image of the darkest facets of U.S. society in the early twentieth century—and after. Thus, the scenario's hyperbolic character may encourage players to ponder the moral ambivalence of real American history, while the game's alternate world provides a projection surface to reflect on the dilemma of historical guilt (cf. McCarter).

The phrase 'historical guilt' has been a controversial concept in debates on the politics of memory. The notion that members of an "imagined (...) community" (Anderson 6) are personally accountable for the wrongdoings committed in the name of that community is not without flaws. After all, it defies modern standards of individualism and self-responsibility. At the same time, the very nature of the imagined community is such that it is imagined across time. How can an appropriate culture of remembrance be developed as liberal societies struggle to come to terms with the darker chapters of their past? In recent decades, the term 'historical responsibility' has emerged in the public discourse on collective memory. Unlike the notion of historical guilt, the phrase 'historical responsibility' does not indicate that members of a community who did not themselves partake in historical wrongs ought to feel guilty on a personal level. Rather, it en-

---

2 Our historical year of 1912 has also been a rather tumultuous one in American political history, seeing the heyday of the progressive reform movement, a major split in the Republican Party and the ascendancy of Democrat Woodrow Wilson to the presidency. Both a progressive and a war president, Wilson "would come to be one of the best remembered and most argued over of all presidents" (Cooper 599).

courages individuals to face the darker chapters of their collective history, to take their lessons from it, and to not repeat the mistakes of the past.[3]

While the rather abstract idea of historical responsibility dominates the academic debate on commemorative culture, *BioShock Infinite* attempts a more direct approach to this politically sensitive issue. The game does not limit itself to a setting in which the antagonists—namely Comstock and his followers—represent historical wrongdoings that most players would probably identify as reprehensible.[4] As the plot progresses and players learn more about the cruelties that Columbia has committed in its dedication to American exceptionalism, the game merges the themes of historical and individual guilt in a remarkable way. It turns out that DeWitt, the game's protagonist through whose eyes players perceive the world of *BioShock Infinite*, is personally entangled in America's sinister past.

Fittingly, this revelation takes place in Columbia's museum, a whole building complex devoted to commemorative culture. The so-called "Hall of Heroes" is home to several displays dedicated to historical events that have shaped Columbian society. Comstock, however, has made sure that the museum serves as an elaborate propaganda instrument that revises and reinterprets history to extol the city and its leader. For example, the exhibition on Columbia's 1901 raid on Beijing is portrayed as a heroic fight against the Chinese, who are racially stereotyped as devious creatures and bloodthirsty aggressors. The Boxer Rebellion, an actual historic event, is not only partly fictionalized in *BioShock Infinite* but also ideologically revised within the game's narrative itself. This approach is particularly important in the second case of such fictional revisionism: the Wounded Knee Massacre.

The actual Wounded Knee Massacre occurred on December 29, 1890, on the Pine Ridge Indian Reservation in the state of South Dakota. The 7th U.S. Cavalry Regiment confronted the indigenous Lakota tribe and demanded they hand over their weapons. When one of the Lakota refused to give up his gun and a shot went off, the soldiers opened fire. After the guns fell silent, roughly 200 Lakota were dead, more than half of them women and children. Today, the Wounded Knee Massacre is widely seen as the last in a long series of atrocities committed during America's so-called Indian Wars. A hundred years later, the United States

---

[3] Given Germany's decade-long struggle to come to terms with its Nazi past, there is a multitude of literature on commemorative culture published in German. For an overview, see Cornelißen 548–63.

[4] Settings in which players fight antagonists representing historical 'villains' are a common feature in video games. Counter-factional historical scenarios have also been explored in a number of popular games such as the *Wolfenstein* series or *Command & Conquer: Red Alert*.

Congress issued a resolution formally expressing its deep regret for the massacre.[5]

In the lore of *BioShock Infinite*, the Wounded Knee Massacre happened as well. Both DeWitt and Comstock took an active part in it and earned a reputation for their cruelty. In its aftermath, DeWitt was haunted by guilt and nearly broke over it, while Comstock embraced his deeds and became the fanatic founder of Columbia. In the "Hall of Heroes," however, Comstock presents his twisted version of the historical incident. Portraying the massacre as a heroic act of self-defense, the "Battle of Wounded Knee" exhibit displays cut-out caricatures of violent Lakota murdering American soldiers. A mechanical display shows two Indians holding a white woman hostage while aiming a tomahawk at her; another display shows a native holding the woman's scalp while she is lying on the ground. The exhibit ends in a tribal field with a statue of Comstock, "the hero of Wounded Knee," standing triumphant over a horde of aggressive Indians. In the background, an image of George Washington—idolized with toga and sword—looks favorably upon the great victory over America's savage foes.

When players first enter the "Hall of Heroes" in the early mid-game, they are already familiar with Columbia's predominant nationalism. Thus, the misrepresentation of history comes as no surprise. From the beginning, players are invited to look behind the scenes and identify the Wounded Knee exhibition as cheaply ideological. Hyperbolically stereotyping the Indians as aggressive savages while celebrating Comstock's heroic chivalry is easily recognizable as propaganda. To avoid misunderstandings, additional comments by DeWitt make players aware of the true nature of the historic events.

BioShock Infinite makes it almost impossible to miss the game's central point regarding commemorative culture. In a less than subtle way, the "Hall of Heroes" ensures that players are able to see through Comstock's propaganda and grasp the significance of his reinterpretation of history. It becomes clear that Columbia is dedicated to a conception of U.S. history that not only denies the atrocities Americans have committed in the past but embraces them and praises the nation for their perpetration. In this narrative, "America has never (...) done anything wrong" (Psiropoulos) and can never do anything wrong. Consequently, it dignifies even the darkest chapters of its past.

The hyperbolic depiction of a perverted American exceptionalism in the "Hall of Heroes" aims at causing players to ponder the dilemma of commemorative culture: how does a society cope with the wrongdoings committed in its name? Does the process of coming to terms with the past lead to a sense of

---

5 For a detailed account on the Wounded Knee Massacre and its aftermath, see Grua.

guilt or a sense of responsibility? And how does it affect the individual? Remarkably, *BioShock Infinite* not only reflects on the rather abstract level of society's historical narratives that are so obviously epitomized by the game's setting, but it also addresses the individual level. After all, Booker DeWitt, the game's only playable character, was, much like Comstock, personally involved in the atrocities committed at Wounded Knee. During the course of the storyline, the entangled themes of personal and historical guilt are further explored and lead to a remarkable plot twist.

After the confrontation with the supposed end boss Comstock, Elizabeth, who has accompanied players through the game after rescuing her, takes DeWitt through various dimensions to finally reveal his true identity to him. During the final sequence, he realizes that his cryptic mission to rescue Elizabeth—"Bring us the girl and wipe away the debt" (Shotgunnova, "WK 02: Welcome Centre") —is actually a glimpse of lost memory referring to a contract between Comstock and DeWitt himself. Roughly twenty years ago, DeWitt sold his own daughter to pay for his gambling debts. Perfidiously, the main character not only inherits this personal guilt from his own past but even has to relive/replay these crucial events to continue on his quest. After the revelation that his lost daughter and Elizabeth are the same person, DeWitt is convinced that only destruction can end this infinite loop of guilt. Thus, he decides to "smother the son of a bitch in his crib" (Shotgunnova, "GS 20: Ending"). Elizabeth then, after reassuring herself that DeWitt really wants to do this, opens a portal to the birth of Zachary Hale Comstock. Surprisingly, they end up at the baptism DeWitt was considering after the cruelties he committed at Wounded Knee. In his universe, Booker refused to be baptized because he did not believe that a splash of water could wash away his sins (Bosman 111). Yet Elizabeth reveals that, in a different reality, DeWitt actually took the baptism and was reborn as Comstock. Remarkably, either decision—being baptized or refusing it—could not redeem him from his guilt. As Booker DeWitt, he got addicted to alcohol, ran into debt, and sold his own daughter. As Zachary Hale Comstock, he became a fanatic tyrant whose crimes even exceeded those committed at Wounded Knee. He not only established a murderous regime but locked up his 'own' daughter, planning to use her supernatural powers for his designs.

In the combined person of DeWitt and Comstock, the themes of personal and collective guilt merge with one another, and thus reveal *BioShock Infinite's* implicit narrative perspective on history. Reflecting on the long existing historiographical debate over agency within history, the game assumes that history is shaped by (fallible) individual decisions. In the world of *BioShock Infinite*, every individual decision opens a new dimension, in which characters pursue their own path and (hi)story. The narrative level of the game thus claims that historical guilt first and foremost arises from individuals and not collectives or structures.

Yet is this the guilt of the player as well, or is it just that of the avatar? Players do incur guilt in their own ways during the game, namely through their interaction with the game world and their actions mirrored by their surroundings: first—given the genre-conventions of a first-person shooter—by killing innumerous adversaries, and second, by supporting the paramilitary underground group Vox Populi. At first glance, Fitzroy's organization, which has opposed Columbia's charismatic leader[6] and his fanatic followers for years, appears to fight for a good cause. The resistance movement, however, unmasks itself by its extremely violent actions as morally corrupt—for example as Daisy Fitzroy, in her quest for revenge, does not shy away from killing an innocent child.[7]

The intrinsic and extrinsic genre conventions force players to shoot their way through the conflict-oriented storyline, but these game mechanics are not problematized as, for example, in *Spec Ops: The Line* (published a year before *BioShock Infinite* by 2K). Here, players are increasingly unsettled by the tasks they have to fulfill. Faced with options for action which all lead to destruction and violence, players as well as the game's protagonist distance themselves from the methods of war. Subversively, the game lures players to incur guilt (Smethurst 211). In a remarkable sequence the Spec Ops force is confronted by revolting civilians. The task is to rescue a fellow soldier who is about to be hung by a mob. After several hours of gameplay dictating to solve conflicts by shooting, players know only one way to rescue their comrade. They do not even know that there are other options to resolve the situation because the interface abandons players by giving no help and just stating the mission goal. In a perfidious way, the game mirrors the chain of command in the military. The interface permanently instructs and commands players to shoot, so that they rely on this assistance without thinking about and reflecting on their own strategies. Therefore, players shoot and kill civilians although they could just fire in the air to scare them off. Moral dilemmas like this shape *Spec Ops: The Line* and subvert the conventions of its own genre, but this is not how *BioShock Infinite* works.

---

[6] Weber characterizes three possible ways of legitimizing sovereignty: traditional, rational, and charismatic. The focus on charismatic leadership, in the persona of Zachary Hale Comstock, underlines the game's view on agency within history because the other, structure-based legitimizations of sovereignty are subverted and overthrown by the individual charisma of Comstock. For the characteristics of charismatic leadership see Maurer 45.

[7] The question of guilt requires agency, which is rarely given in *BioShock Infinite* directly. Other options to play the game are discussed later.

Players encounter the gory violence of *BioShock Infinite* for the first time roughly fifteen minutes into the game. In the early stages, they are able to explore the beauty of Columbia. The horror that hides within the darker layers of this picturesque city only comes to light when players witness a bizarre raffle where an interracial couple is exposed, shamed, and will be symbolically if not actually stoned. In this horrific sequence, players are for the first time confronted with the grim side of the dystopian setting of the game. At first glance, the game allows them to decide whether they throw the baseball at the announcer or at the couple.[8] In contrast *to Spec Ops: The Line*, a choice of action (throwing at the couple/throwing at the announcer) is given, but the decision is not of any consequence: in both instances, players are hindered from completing the action. On a narrative level, the decision only influences whether they will be able to see the couple alive later in the game or not.

While raising the hand to throw, DeWitt is identified as the False Prophet, although players have no clue what it means yet, and during this brief cutscene the first homicide of the game is committed. Players watch as DeWitt crushes the head of a police officer using the mechanic grappling hook of another policeman. Then DeWitt grabs this hook, and only at this point are players able to interact with the game world again. Nevertheless, the path is predefined: without offering alternative problem-solving strategies, the game has already 'corrupted' players to eliminate their adversaries. The game takes the guilt out of the first killing from players by making them passive observers, but it continues to do so by justifying the deaths that will follow as a result of their direct action. After all, the goal is to rescue a girl—a noble, chivalric task—and from now on DeWitt is simply forced to use his skills and tools in an act of self-defense. Contrary to *Spec Ops: The Line*, violent actions are never reflected. It is possible to kill every NPC[9] without any punishment—the only risk is increased attention from the police, which DeWitt wants to kill anyway.

Yet are there any other ways to play the game? The answer is a limited yes, there are some ways—even though the game does not support these explicitly. While the main game does not offer any stealth mode (in contrast to its DLC *Burial at Sea: Episode Two*), it is possible to complete *BioShock Infinite* without inflicting any direct damage. To be fair, the phrase "direct damage" covers an ex-

---

8 The baseball, a symbol of American everyday culture, functions as an allegory for the game design and narrative strategies, in which American culture works as a toolbox for the game's plot and its mechanics. Furthermore, it implies that stoning/public lynching is as emblematic as baseball is for American culture.

9 Children cannot be killed or harmed; they do not have any life counter and are even more spatial environment than adult NPCs.

ception because some areas cannot be traversed before every adversary is killed. Andrew Walt, then editor of haywiremag.com, has tried to "break *BioShock Infinite*" following this maxim of avoiding direct damage. Direct damage, he defines, consists of "attacks squarely targeted at enemies with all firearms and damage dealing vigors[10] as well as melee maneuvers." Ex negativo, Walt characterizes indirect damage as "use of the Possession vigor on enemy units, vigor traps, tear manipulation and passive abilities from certain pieces of gear." Here, the act of killing is in fact only outsourced, and the reduction of responsibility is at least questionable, but it does constitute an attempt to subvert the game and its mechanics within the game's rules and designs. Another rather ludic or community-driven attempt to avoid killing is 'speedrunning'[11] through *BioShock Infinite*. One way to speedrun is to use glitches within the level design to dodge whole areas (for example the raffle scene). While focusing on beating the game in the shortest time possible and subsequently earning the respect of the speedrunning community, the story and the game mechanics (e.g. killing) recede into the background. Therefore, non-killing is rather a by-product and happens accidentally, not intendedly. However, so-called 'pacifist runs'—intended non-killing runs without exploiting glitches—do not exist for *BioShock Infinite*. This might be the case because they are deemed not interesting enough or appear to be simply impossible because of the game's level design (e.g. gate openers). In sum, other options and ways to play the game exist, but are nothing more than marginal phenomena.

In the "Hall of Heroes", the game introduces another deeply unsettling justification to kill situated in the game's plot. Players inadvertently fulfil the last wishes of a group of adversaries by granting them a soldier's death. Cornelius Slate, a former general at Wounded Knee and the Boxer Revolt, and his fellow veterans have fortified themselves in the museum. Slate sends his soldiers against players—not to hinder their progress within the story but to exploit DeWitt's way of handling things. Slate and his companions have simply lost their purpose, and by fighting against the protagonist, and dying in the process, this void is filled again. By killing the soldiers, players give them their identity back. Not only is the act of killing justified but also it is enhanced and glorified.

After making his way through the "Hall of Heroes," players find a wounded Cornelius Slate on the floor, barely leaning against a pillar. The general begs

---

10 *BioShock Infinite*'s equivalent to *BioShock*'s plasmids, which are liquids to gain greater powers and special abilities.
11 "Speedrunning is the act of playing a video game with the intent of completing it as fast as possible, for the purposes of entertainment and / or competition" (https://www.speedrun.com/about).

DeWitt to kill him and thereby free him from his loss of identity. This time, the game leaves the decision up to players, and they can kill or spare him. Thus, grave questions are forced upon them: is not killing Slate really sparing him? Is granting him a—from his perspective—noble death not rather an act of mercy? Is killing him not freeing players from the guilt of the things Comstock will do to Slate? This time, the decision really matters, as players will face the consequences on a narrative level. If they spare him, Slate will be captured and players will see him later on in the story as a tortured man in a catatonic state. Thus, *BioShock Infinite* indicates there are worse things than death and implicitly blames players for not killing the general before. DeWitt then gets another chance to kill Slate, just to end his suffering. If players chose this option and kill Slate, however, they have to deal with the disgust and horror in Elizabeth's face.

Sources such as this 'subreddit' about 'Decisions in *BioShock Infinite*' supports the thesis of a more abstract emotional punishment of moral questionable decisions, even though it has no impact on a narrative or ludic level:

> However—and this is the point of my argument—these decisions *do* matter. Not to the story, no, as I've clearly established above, but to me as a player. On my first playthrough, I chose to give Elizabeth the bird pin and ended up getting my hand stabbed at the ticket booth. For the rest of the game, whenever Booker used his hands or I looked at Elizabeth, I was reminded of that choice. It was cemented in me, and affected the game far more than most decisions do in other games.
>
> The game gives you response to your choices in a way that feels natural; you're only changing small things, so it's only small things that are changed in this short time-frame, but you are constantly reminded of those changes. In the back of your head, you still know that you shot Slate in front of Elizabeth, or the ticket-man. The decisions might not matter as much to the direction the story is taking, but they do wonders with the player's feelings. (AManHasSpoken)

Elizabeth's detailed facial expressions and her likeability evoke empathy and the players' desire to be liked by her in turn. Due to this deep narrative bond that is carefully constructed by the game in various sequences, her reactions and feeling should influence the way players perceive the game. Her shocked face during and after the death of Slate mirrors the consequences of the brutal deed. However, it is not her first contact with violence. She first witnesses the player killing people within the "Battleship Bay" sequence. After rescuing Elizabeth and falling into an artificial beach setting, citizens of Columbia tasked with catching the fugitives trap them both. The game leaves the player no chance to solve this situation other than to embrace conflict, to use violence, and to kill the pursuers. Overwhelmed by the brutality of the events, Elizabeth temporarily flees from Booker. Within a scripted scene, she confronts him with his acts.

> Elizabeth: You killed those people. I can't believe you did that...they're all dead... You killed those people!
> Booker: Elizabeth, I—
> Elizabeth: You're a monster!
> Booker: What did you think was gonna happen? Hmmm?
> Elizabeth: What?
> Booker: Do you understand the expense people went through to keep you locked up in that tower? You think people like that are just gonna let you walk away? You are an investment... and you will not be safe until you are far away from here.
> Elizabeth: What do...what do they want from me?
> Booker: I don't know. (Shotgunnova, "GS 07: Battleship Bay")

This initial tension, the dehumanization by killing, and the discussion of personal guilt are quickly wiped away by DeWitt's economic explanation, and players are thus shielded, much like Elizabeth, from having to question the ethics of his actions.[12]

The indication of a debate on guilt, which is then quickly avoided, is striking in the game, and especially the gameplay goes against the grain of this narrative implication. On the one hand, Elizabeth confronts players with their guilt; on the other hand she is a reliable scavenger for ammunition throughout the game. She helps DeWitt to survive by offering supplies, thus enabling him to kill further. *BioShock Infinite's* treatment of violence consequently fails due to ludonarrative dissonance.[13] On a narrative level, violence and killing is reflected and questioned; on a gameplay level, it is even celebrated or at least accepted as a genre-specific necessity. The procedural rhetoric[14] of the game subverts and diminishes the story-based discussion over guilt. In terms of gameplay, killing—besides the marginal alternatives introduced above—is unavoidable; it is the core mechanic and what the gameplay is all about. Even within its genre as a first-person shooter, the focus on a body count is significant, while e.g. a stealth mode is not implemented in the game. On top of that, players are even rewarded for killing more. In fact, there are additional achievements waiting to be unlocked for clearing an area of all adversaries.

Yet the setting of *BioShock Infinite* and its entanglements with America's historical guilt is not only interesting but also thought-provoking. Furthermore, its

---

12 On a side note, this sounds like the cynical extradiegetic explanation for the whole violence of the game: it is an investment, and it sells well.
13 Clint Hocking introduced this term 2007 while analyzing *BioShock*. He stated that the player can always act selfishly while the game celebrates selflessness.
14 Ian Bogost uses the terminology of rhetoric to describe the meaning and ideology of play options within a video games (cf. 2).

integration of personal agency within the game's (hi)story opens a wide field of potential. It could have stimulated a level of reflection on these historical events that far exceeds the level in which players' own actions are reflected upon, but it fails in this regard. *BioShock Infinite* does not evoke a sense of (historical) guilt because it sabotages itself within the gameplay. It may only rather represent such a feeling and integrates itself in the commemorative culture as an extraordinary beautiful yet pretentious attempt to exhibit American atrocities to an audience that mostly wants to play. Depending on the character of players—whether they are story- or gameplay-oriented—the guilt-discourse either unfolds or remains meaningless. A sense of historical guilt is either developed and solidified or vanishes like the sound of a fired bullet.

Works Cited

AManHasSpoken. "Decisions that Matter." *Reddit*, www.reddit.com/r/Bioshock/comments/1dzmt8/spoilers_infinite_decisions_that_matter. Accessed 15 Jan. 2019.

Anderson, Benedict. *Imagined Communities: Reflections on the Origin and Spread of Nationalism*. Rev. Ed., Verso, 1991.

Bogost, Ian. *Persuasive Games. The Expressive Power of Videogames*. MIT Press, 2007.

Bosman, Frank. "Accept your Baptism, and Die! Redemption, Death and Baptism in BioShock Infinite." *Gameviroments*, vol 6, 2017, pp. 100–29.

Cooper, John Milton, Jr. *Woodrow Wilson: A Biography*. Random House, 2011.

Cornelißen, Christoph. "Was heißt Erinnerungskultur? Begriff—Methoden—Perspektiven." *Geschichte in Wissenschaft und Unterricht*, vol. 54, 2003, pp. 548–63.

Grua, David W. *Surviving Wounded Knee: The Lakotas and the Politics of Memory*. Oxford UP, 2016.

Heinze, Carl. *Mittelalter Computer Spiele: Zur Darstellung und Modellierung von Geschichte im populären Computerspiel*. transcript, 2012.

Hocking, Clint. "Ludonarrative Dissonance in *BioShock*." *Click Nothing*, 7 Oct. 2007, clicknothing.typepad.com/click_nothing/2007/10/ludonarrative-d.html. Accessed 15 Jan. 2019

Maurer, Andrea. *Herrschaftssoziologie. Eine Einführung*, Campus, 2004.

McCarter, Reid. "Booker DeWitt and the Guilt of a Nation." *Digital Love Child*, 3 Apr. 2013, digitallovechild.com/2013/04/03/booker-dewitt-and-the-guilt-of-a-nation. Accessed 15 Jan. 2019

Psiropoulos, Brian. "In the Sky, Lord, in the Sky: Historical Guilt and *BioShock Infinite*." *Girls Like Giants*, 4 Apr. 2013, girlslikegiants.wordpress.com/2013/04/04/in-the-sky-lord-in-the-sky-historical-guilt-and--bioshock-infinite. Accessed 15 Jan. 2019

Shotgunnova. 4 April 2014, gamefaqs.gamespot.com/pc/605053-bioshock-infinite/faqs/69191 Accessed 15 Jan. 2019

Smethurst, Tobi: "'We Put Our Hands on the Trigger with Him': Guilt and Perpetration in *Spec Ops: The Line*," *Criticism*, vol. 59, no. 2, 2017, pp. 201–21.

Walt, Andrew: "Breaking BioShock." *Haywire Magazine*, 15 July 2013, www.haywiremag.com/features/breaking-bioshock. Accessed 15 Jan. 2019

Jacqueline Blank
The Art of *BioShock Infinite:* Identity, Race, and Manifest Destiny

> For works in which world-building occurs, there may be a wealth of details and events (or mere mentions of them) which do not advance the story but which provide background richness and verisimilitude to the imaginary world. (...) Such additional information can change the audience's experience, understanding, and immersion in a story, giving a deeper significance to characters, events, and details. Audience members and critical approaches that center on narrative, then, may find such excess material to be extraneous, tangential, and unnecessary, while those that consider the story's world will find their experience enhanced.
> Mark J. P. Wolf, *Building Imaginary Worlds: The Theory and History of Subcreation* (2–3)

The idea for this article came from talks with other gamers that made me realize how little attention many players pay to the overall design of the gameworlds they explore. However, especially within the medium of video games, world building—the creation of a believable gameworld—is an important tool for immersion. As Mark Wolf points out in *Building Imaginary Worlds:* "Often when a world is noticed at all, it is only considered as a background for stories set in it, rather than a subject of study itself" (2). In my opinion as well, the overall visual design of a game can be seen as the extension of simple storytelling: think for example of the retrofuturistic design in the *Fallout* series, or of the design of enemies and weapons when they are well-integrated into the setting and story of the game, such as the insects in *Fallout* that have mutated due to radiation, or the Splicers in *BioShock*, who suffer the consequence of Plasmid abuse. Even the placement of simple objects in the gameworld can tell microstories, like the Bibles placed in the smuggler's hideout in *BioShock*'s Neptune's Bounty. This also includes the artwork scattered throughout the gameworld, which will be the focus of this article: my goal here is to identify possible influences on the artwork in *BioShock Infinite* and also show in which ways these artworks are embedded in the game's narrative fabric.

How does narration work within the interactive medium of the video game, and how can narrative information additional to the main story, which is mostly presented though dialogues and cutscenes, be provided? Games must be understood as navigable spaces: while the player travels through this space, he or she will identify and interpret the narrative elements the game provides. Game designers should therefore not be seen as storytellers but rather as "narrative architects," since they do not only devise stories but "design worlds and sculpt places" (Jenkins 121). Thus, games can be interpreted by analyzing the narrative elements the player encounters during gameplay as well as the audiovisual presentation the game provides in general. "Stimulated by the game," as Nitsche says, "the player weaves the connections, creates a narrative context" (43). The player uses the narrative elements presented to him as clustered throughout the game space in order to project meaning onto these objects and events that include them. However, the perception of a game's content is rather individual, given how much or how little interactivity he or she is granted by the game design. Also, artwork can be ignored by the player, depending on his personal preference of how to explore the gameworld. Though it is the player's choice to either disregard or pay attention to his surroundings, game designers have different tools at their disposal to direct and guide the player within the gameworld. This starts with the placement of objects and artwork. A painting placed in the center of a room, for example, will surely catch the player's attention. In addition, whenever the player is unable to move the camera by himself, as is the case in many cutscenes, the playable character's gaze is directed by the game designers and thus the focus of the player is directed as well. Also, sometimes non-playable characters will directly or indirectly comment on objects in the gameworld, providing audio cues to the player on what to look out for. In addition to those methods, there are also elements like objects, posters, and the overall visual design of the game that enhance the general atmosphere of the gameworld in order to create a credible imaginary world, filled with life. If a gameworld feels sterile or empty, it is difficult to achieve an immersive effect on the side of the player. Good game design must therefore focus on the building of such a coherent imaginary world and on ways to guide the player through this world.

The following will give an analysis of some of the artwork presented in *BioShock Infinite* by identifying possible inspirations from American cultural history. I will show how these works of art are connected to the game's plot and how they, as narrative elements, offer added value to the players' experience. I have identified three interrelated topics to classify the artwork of *BioShock Infinite*: identity, manifest destiny, and race. With the secession from the United States, Columbia needed to form a separate, new 'national' identity, and it did so in reference to American beginnings. Comstock created a civil religion that would unify Columbia's residents by connecting the original myth of the exceptional foundation of the United States with his personal myth as God-chosen prophet and founder of the new nation that is Columbia. The Prophet not only created a personal cult surrounding his own person and family but also fostered the deification of the American founding fathers: once Booker awakes after his baptism in a cutscene at the beginning of the game, he finds himself lying in the 'Garden of New Eden.' As he regains consciousness, he looks up at the statues of George

Washington, Thomas Jefferson, and Benjamin Franklin, which are worshiped in the garden.

Fig. 1: Statues in the Garden of New Eden

Each 'deity' carries his respective religious symbol, which signifies his role in the creation of the American nation: Washington holds the Sword as a symbol for justice and power, which can be seen as a reference to his military career. Jefferson is associated with the Scroll representing law and order, pointing to his role in history as the author of the Declaration of Independence. And Franklin's symbol is the Key to knowledge, referring to his reputation as a man of many professions and as a talented inventor. With the inclusion of these mythical founding fathers into his own religious and political system, Comstock clearly hoped to both transfer ideals and virtues associated with these men onto himself and to link Columbia to earlier American history in order to stress the continuation of the American mission, which in Comstock's opinion the US has failed to do since the end of the Civil War. In addition, all attributes assigned to the three Founding Fathers also have their analogy in biblical symbolism and are connected to the Apocalypse: the Sword, wielded by Christ on Judgement Day (Revelation 1:16), the Book of Life stating the names of the Saints (Revelation 5:1–14), and the Key (Matthew 16:19) opening the Pearly Gates (Revelation 21:21).

There are numerous other examples of this deployment and reinterpretation of American symbolism and ideals in Columbia. Next to being called the Prophet, Comstock is also referred to as the Founder, for example. In one of the paintings presenting Columbia's history that are passing by in a parade during the

Raffle and Fair, Comstock is presented as a humble farmer who is visited by the Arch Angel that revealed to him his destiny as leader of the floating city. The scene is reminiscent of typical representations of biblical annunciations by angels in Christian art. In addition, the portrayal clearly refers to Jefferson's accentuation of the American farmer as the archetypical American, as "the appropriate social foundation for a virtuous United States" (Stephanson 15). Jefferson praised farmers as "the chosen people of God" (Jefferson 160).

Fig. 2: The Parade

Some of the artwork in *BioShock Infinite* is also inspired by the paintings of manifest destiny, the ideological justification for the extensive westward migration based on the notion that Americans were destined by divine providence to claim the land. The essence of this ideology is probably best illustrated and summarized by John Gast's famous painting *American Progress* (1872):

The picture shows an allegorical figure, the "Star of Empire," as it moves westward, casting out the dark by its shining example of progress and civilization, symbolized by the book and the telegraph wire she holds. In the dark west, the Native 'savages' flee from her approach; in the bright east, settlers, stagecoaches, and railroads move steadily westward to replace them. The term *manifest destiny* itself was coined by John L. O'Sullivan, who stated in 1845 that

> [the American claim] is by the right of our manifest destiny to overspread and to possess the whole of the continent which Providence has given us for the development of the

Fig. 3: John Gast. *American Progress*. 1872.

great experiment of liberty and federative self government entrusted to us. (...) It is in our future far more than in our past (...) that our True Title is to be found (...). (397–98)

Columbia can be understood as a new West that will continue the American mission and ideals after the US had betrayed them (as Comstock believes), reinvigorating the idea of manifest destiny after the closure of the continental frontier had been announced by Frederick Jackson Turner. Some artworks from *BioShock Infinite* are thus heavily influenced by works representing westwards expansion such as *American Progress*. The game's designers here aesthetically draw on the fact that "American landscapes have been characterized as more didactic, nationalistic, and religious and less purely art for art's sake than Old World pictures" (Aikin 85). This characterization is evident in other famous examples such as Emanuel Leutze's *Westward the Course of Empire Takes Its Way* (1862) and Albert Bierstadt's *The Oregon Trail* (1869).

In both these paintings, the lighting is reversed compared to *American Progress:* the West is glowing as it promises a new beginning. These compositional arrangements stress the idea that "[t]he west is the compass point that still stands metaphorically for national destiny as well as for good prospects, freedom, and personal rebirth" (Aikin 87). Especially one of the artworks in *BioShock Infinite* exhibits features of these expansion paintings, most notably a strong right-to-left compositional movement, which is central to the aesthetics of the

Fig. 4: Emanuel Leutze, Westward the Course of Empire Takes its Way. 1862.

Fig. 5: Albert Bierstadt, Emigrants Crossing the Plains, or The Oregon Trail. 1869.

genre, as Aikin explains: "it is difficult to find any depiction of American westward expansion, or 'progress,' in high art or popular illustration that does not feature strong right-to-left, or 'westward,' movement" (80). This painting of Comstock's 'exodus' to Columbia can be seen twice in the game: at the very beginning when Booker leaves the elevator and enters Columbia for the first time. Players first encounter it as a large glass painting, with light illuminating the scene and shining through the glass from behind. The writing above reads: "And the Prophet shall lead the people to the New Eden." The glass painting undoubtedly offers a memorable first impression of Columbia for the player and already hints at what to expect from this strange city: a utopia defined by religious zealotry.

Fig. 6: The first instance of the painting

The second time we encounter this scene, it is displayed as a painting during the parade at the Raffle and Fair (alongside the portrayal of Comstock as a humble farmer mentioned above). The painting features the same compositional movement as artworks of Manifest Destiny: Comstock points westward to the city in the sky, which is bathed in glistening sunlight, representing a heavenly place that strongly contrasts with the meager and barren earth of the "Sodom Below."[1] Comstock's pose, the surge from right to left, and the beckoning light

---

[1] The term "the Sodom Below" can be encountered numerous times in the game. It refers to everything below the floating city of Columbia. The rest of the world is consequently considered

Fig. 7: The second instance of the painting

in the west all parallel the features of the paintings mentioned above. Columbia is thus constructed as continuing the American need for movement and expansion with its journey to promote American ideals (the city's original purpose at the Chicago World's Fair), as well as the country's exceptionalist position in the world and in history. With these paintings, Comstock stresses Columbia's duty to re-manifest the American identity he saw corrupted in the US.

For Comstock, however, this identity and the American exceptionalist position are solely products of the superiority of the White Anglo-Saxon race. In this respect, Comstock's ideals correspond to the beliefs of Reverend Josiah Strong, expressed in his book *Our Country*, which was first published in 1885, and which is certainly representative of a more widespread racist ideology in nineteenth-century America. As Stephanson explains, the book "introduced a religious version of manifest destiny that was also imperialist at a moment when the old continentalist imagination was beginning to dry up" (79). In his book, Strong claims that the Anglo-Saxon race is the representative of "two great

---

a sinful place, as the biblical reference to Sodom suggests. While the displays of Columbias 'history' at the Raffle and Fair float by, an announcer states: "And so our Prophet led the people away from the Sodom Below—up, up into the city, where he created an even more perfect union." Again, religious terms and references to the foundation of the United States (in this case to the preamble of the Constitution) are combined to emphasize Comstock's ideology.

ideas, which are closely related" (33), civil liberty and "a pure *spiritual* Christianity," which originated among the "Teutonic race" and is synonymous with Protestantism (34). Strong argues that this spiritual Christianity is mostly found among the Anglo-Saxons, "for this is the great missionary race" (35), and he also believes that it has been schooled by God for the "final competition of races" (49). He states that "this race of unequaled energy, with all the majesty of numbers and the might of wealth behind it—the representative, let us hope, of the largest liberty, the purest Christianity, the highest civilization—having developed peculiarly aggressive traits calculated to impress its institutions upon mankind, will spread itself over the earth" (49). The American people, however, play a special role in God's plan, because "[t]here can be no reasonable doubt that North America is to be the great home of the Anglo-Saxon, the principal seat of his power, the center of his life and influence" (40). Unsurprisingly, Strong also believes the Anglo-Saxon race "is destined to dispossess many weaker races, assimilate others, and mold the remainder" (53). Comstock and the Columbian people hold similar views on the inequality of the races. As players soon find out, Columbia is pervaded by segregation as well as racist propaganda. White Anglo-Saxon Columbians isolate the inferior 'other' by marking it in terms of 'lesser' races. The presence of these others in Columbia is explained by Jeremiah Fink in the voxophone "Solution to Your Problems," which can be found between the two cages in which the interracial couple was held prisoner:

> "I told you, Comstock—you sell 'em paradise, and the customers expect cherubs for every chore! No menials in God's kingdom! Well, I've a man in Georgia who'll lease us as many Negro convicts as you can board! Why, you can say they're simple souls, in penance for rising above their station. Whatever eases your conscience, I suppose."

Those deemed inferior had thus been brought to Columbia for their cheap labor so that the founders and the upper classes of this 'great' city would not be forced to perform menial work. As a consequence of racial and social segregation in poor living conditions—many were forced to work in the factories of Fink's industrial empire and lived in the so-called Shantytown visited later in the game—a Civil War breaks out in Columbia between the so-called Vox Populi and the Founders of Columbia.

These views on racial superiority of the Columbian (Anglo-Saxon) people in particular are best represented in-game by the so-called Fraternal Order of the Raven, a Columbian reinterpretation of the Ku Klux Klan. The Order's halls are visited rather early in the game, and this is where players encounter a number of symbolic artworks. A statue of Comstock as he, according to the engraving in the base, "fights the serpent of nations" adorns the Fraternity's courtyard, representing the Prophet as a protector of racial purity and Anglo-Saxon superiority and referring to his role in the Boxer Rebellion (this historical event is also featured at the second display in the Hall of Heroes next to the display of Wounded Knee). In addition, an emblem states the Order's duty: "Protecting Our Race." Once the player enters the Order's halls, he sees a statue of John Wilkes Booth, who is worshiped by the Fraternity for eliminating the "Great Apostate" Abraham Lincoln. Throughout its halls, Lincoln is portrayed as a devilish figure, as Comstock believed America had strayed from its original mission after the Civil War. In comparison, Washington is represented as a Saint. He is portrayed wearing a tunic and adorned by a halo, like apostles or saints in Christian art. Facing west, he commands righteous troops, leading them into battle. His floating figure is bathed in light. In contrast, the background in the painting of Lincoln is covered in black shadows, floating around his body. The troops below him carry torches, resembling an angry mob in contrast to the flag-wielding soldiers in the painting of Washington. The portrait of Lincoln is reminiscent of illustrations of hell, whereas the lighting in the juxtaposed painting evokes scenes from paradise.

Fig. 8 & 9: Lincoln and Washington

In the great hall, a huge painting called "For God and Country" displays Washington, holding the Liberty Bell in one hand and the Ten Commandments in the other. An allegorical Columbia baths Washington in the light of liberty, while stereotypical representatives of different races and nationalities (Irish, Mexican, Native American, Arabic, and Asian) look up at his figure or avert their gaze from the emanating light.

Fig. 10: "For God and Country"

Again, Washington is portrayed as a saintly figure, and the painting reminds one of Christian pictorial traditions and Christian iconography. The painting summarizes Columbia's racist ideology and is probably the best known artwork of the game. Washington, at the center of the painting, is reminiscent of traditional portrayals of Jesus Christ on Judgment Day, only that instead of the Book of Revelations, Washington carries the Ten Commandments. In the right hand, he holds the Liberty Bell as a symbol for American independence, instead of the imperial orb often carried by Christ in Christian art, symbolizing his reign on earth. Behind him, an allegorical personification of Columbia is emanating light, illuminating the scene and especially the figure of Washington. She raises a banner stating "For God and Country." A ring of stars frames Washington, serving as an aureole to indicate his sainthood. The whole arrangement of the figures and emblems in the painting resembles traditional Christian portrayals of the Last Judgment, in which often angels with banners are arranged around Christ, but also portrayals of the Trinity in art, in which instead of Columbia, God stands behind Christ and the holy Spirit (as a dove) is flying above. In the painting of Washington, the dove can be found in the top right corner, representing "Purity." Below that, a garland of corn stands for "Prosperity," the emblems on the left read "Faith," represented by the cross, and "Defense," symbolized by arrows. These symbols also allude to Christ's suffering. Below Washington, the stereotypical portrayal of the minorities resemble similar stereotypical representations in depictions of the Last Judgment, or more precisely the portrayal of the procession of damned souls. To conclude, Washington here is presented Christ-like, in the tradition of Salvator Mundi, as the savior who brings order to the world.

To conclude, the artwork embedded in *BioShock Infinite* is part of the narrative fabric of the game and draws heavily on actual historical artworks from the nineteenth century and their respective cultural context. In the world of *BioShock Infinite*, Columbia was built as an attraction at the Columbian Exposition in Chicago at the end of the century in 1893. The goal was to represent American exceptionalism and to spread American ideals, surpassing previous world fairs by far. It thus makes sense that the game's designers would chose artwork of the nineteenth century that celebrates American exceptionalism, such as the paintings of manifest destiny, as inspiration for their imaginary world. On the one hand, these paintings promised a new beginning in the West—as it was Columbia's mission to offer a new beginning in the sky; on the other hand, the paintings of this time marginalized or excluded all those who supposedly barred the way of progress (think of Native Americans fleeing from the Star of Empire in *American Progress*). In this regard, the historical sources for the art in *BioShock Infinite* also feed into the racist views commented on in the game.

The artwork enriches the game's imaginary world by providing additional information to the player and helps enhance the immersion into said world. However, these types of narrative elements are open to interpretation and can easily be overlooked. It is the player's own choice to notice or disregard them. In my opinion, however, gameworlds should be explored more thoroughly, because these imaginary worlds often reveal more than meets the eye at first glance. In addition, the game designers continuously try to direct our attention to such narrative elements while providing context: though racist propaganda is featured in the game, it does not stand for itself but is part of the world-building that gives meaning to the characters' actions. The playable characters, Booker and Elizabeth, constantly comment on the injustices they encounter. When Elizabeth notices the signs on the segregated bathrooms in in the Arcade of Battleship Bay, for example, she cannot help but note that the whole affair seems "like an unnecessary complication." Her captivity apparently spared her from most of the racist propaganda preached in Columbia, and it is through her and Booker's eyes we as players see this imaginary world.

Theories on world-building, such as that proffered in Wolf's *Building Imaginary Worlds*, provide a new angle for the analysis of video games, as they consider narrative elements such as the artwork as essential components for the creation of the imaginary world in which the action of the game is set. In addition, these narrative elements enrich the gameworld by making the world seem more authentic, as I hope to have shown in my analysis of how Comstock's ideology is mirrored in the artwork placed throughout Columbia.

Works Cited

Aikin, Roger Cushing. "Manifest Destiny: Mapping the Nation." *American Art*, vol.14, no.3, 2000, pp. 78–89. JSTOR, http://www.jstor.org/stable/3109364. Accessed 15 Jan. 2019.

Bierstadt, Albert. *Emigrants Crossing the Plains, or The Oregon Trail*. 1869. The Butler Institute of American Art, Youngstown, OH. butlerart.com/permanent-collection. Accessed 15 Jan. 2019.

BioShock Infinite. Irrational Games. 2K Games, 2013.

Gast, John. *American Progress*. 1873. Museum of the American West, Los Angeles. Library of Congress, www.loc.gov/pictures/resource/ppmsca.09855. Accessed 15 Jan. 2019.

Jefferson, Thomas. *Notes on the State of Virginia*. 1832. Library of Congress, www.loc.gov/resource/lhbcb.04902. Accessed 15 Jan. 2019.

Jenkins, Henry. "Art Form for the Digital Age." *MIT Technology Review*, September/October 2000, www.technologyreview.com/article/400805/art-from-the-digital-age. Accessed 15 Jan. 2019.

Jenkins, Henry. "Game Design as Narrative Architecture." *First Person: New Media as Story, Performance, and Game*, edited by Noah Wardrip-Fruin and Pat Harrigan, MIT Press, 2004, pp. 118–30.

Leutze, Emanuel. *Westward the Course of Empire Takes its Way*. 1862. US Capitol, Washington D.C. Architect of the Capitol, www.aoc.gov/art/other-paintings-and-murals/westward-course-empire-takes-its-way. Accessed 15 Jan. 2019.

Nitsche, Michael. *Video Game Spaces: Image, Play, and Structure in 3D Worlds*. MIT Press, 2008.

Stephanson, Anders. *Manifest Destiny: American Expansionism and the Empire of Right*. Hill and Wang, 2000.

Strong, Josiah. "The United States and the Future of the Anglo-Saxon Race." 1889. *Selections from Our Country*, edited by Micheal George Mulhall. Adam Matthew Digital, 2007, www.empire.amdigital.co.uk/contents/document-detail.aspx?sectionid=72333. Accessed 15 Jan. 2019.

Wolf, Mark J. P. *Building Imaginary Worlds: The Theory and History of Subcreation*. Routledge, 2012.

Veronika Keller
Sounds of Tears: Mozart's *Lacrimosa* in Different Media

Classical music, in its broadest definition, is music written in Europe or European-influenced countries between the middle ages and the twentieth century (Finscher). But more importantly, it is defined by a distinction from folk or popular music, a contrast that is set up by many scholars in terms of classical music being (high) art and popular music being entertainment.[1]

I do not follow this distinction. Most of today's so-called classical music was at one point composed to be entertaining (mostly at court), and there are a numerous examples for pop music being highly conceptualized and artistic. In the public opinion, though, this binary still prevails, and maybe the prejudice about classical music being artistic and therefore hard to listen to is the reason why so many people just say they do not like, hear or know classical music. This disinterest toward classical music is, when it comes to live performances, especially true for younger adults, as a survey by the National Endowment for the Arts (NEA) from 2012 shows: of all US adults attending a classical concert in the past twelve months of the survey, only 9.7 % were between 18 and 24 (NEA 12). The ratio is even lower (7.7 %) when it comes to watching a classical music performance via TV/radio or the internet (NEA 30), so the high prices of tickets for many classical concerts cannot be the only explanation for this disinterest of an age group which at an average has a low income. Of course going to a concert is not the only way to listen to classical music nowadays, and studies show that there is not really an age gap when it comes to just listening to classical music, especially thanks to Youtube and Spotify, but classical music as a whole is, along with Heavy Metal or Singer/Songwriter, one of the less preferred music genres (Audience Net 36).

Despite this relative unpopularity in the US, classical pieces are often used in movies, TV series, and video games. And their function is not only to mirror the common association between classical music and a sophistication by using it in scenes set in a fancy restaurant, the house of a rich person, or using it for the stereotypical mafia godfather listening to Italian arias. More often, classical music is used to evoke emotions in a more general way, and it

---

[1] See for example Johnson, Julian. *Who Needs Classical Music? Cultural Choice and Musical Value.* Oxford, 2002.

thus becomes a part of the narrative itself, as I will show by using the example of Mozart's *Lacrimosa* (part of *Requiem*, KV 626) in this paper.

As William Gibbons wrote in his book *Unlimited Replays. Video Games and Classical Music*, "(...) over significant periods of time, and through a variety of methods, music accumulates multiple layers of meaning" (2). On a strictly individual level, these meanings can be quite different from person to person, depending on situations one connects with a specific piece of music. But there are also more general layers of meaning where a certain understanding of a musical piece is shared by a bigger group and therefore can be used for communication and narrative purposes.

Especially in the nineteenth century, musical scholars and the public went so far as calling music a universal language, which meant that the emotions and stories behind a piece can supposedly be understood by everybody across language and cultural barriers (cf. Gienow-Hecht 2). This position is no longer accepted today, as scholars now recognize that the meaning behind a musical piece has to be learned like any other code. Although it may be argued that European-American-influenced music is so widespread and dominant across the world that many people grow up listening to and therefore learn to understand certain meanings behind the music early on. In many cases, this happens subconsciously by hearing certain musical patterns and connecting them to certain emotions and events.[2] For example, many listeners will understand or at least feel the implication of sadness behind a piece like Chopin's *Marche Funèbre* (op. 35) or connect Mendelssohn's *Wedding March* from his *A Midsummer Night's Dream* (op. 61; MWV M 13) to said happy occasion—even if they may not know the titles or composers of these works.

In this paper, I argue that this subconscious learning process works on three different levels: through the music itself and its original narrative, through different media, and within a single medium.[3] To illustrate this I chose Mozart's *Requiem*, and even more specific its *Lacrimosa*. This piece is embedded in a liturgical background and therefore the original narrative and emotions conveyed through music are quite easily decoded. It is also used quite dominantly in several movies, TV series, and video games, making it a major example of the usage of a musical piece across different media. And finally, it has a prominent role in

---

[2] Recent studies also suggest that people can always differentiate between the purpose a music piece has, and by doing so can distinguish between for example a lullaby and a dance song (see Mehr, Manvis, et al. p. 356–368).

[3] I will ignore the level of connecting music to personal experience, because these connections can be quite different and even conflicting with the broader understanding of a musical piece, as for example even the 'happiest' song can be connected to a sad situation.

the game *BioShock Infinite*, where its own layer of meaning is established inside the game and is even connected to the gameplay itself, so that it becomes a part of the most important difference between games and other media: interactivity.

Liturgical and Musical Background

The *Lacrimosa* is deeply rooted in Western/Christian music traditions, which Mozart also had in mind and considered when composing it. It is part of the *Requiem*, a mass for the dead in Roman Catholic Church. Its parts are, as Mozart composed it, Introitus, Kyrie, Sequentia (*Lacrimosa* is the last piece of this part, while the also famous *Dies Irae* is the beginning), Offertorium, Sanctus, Benedictus, Agnus Dei, and Communio. The Sequentia is, generally speaking, a chant or a hymn sung after the Allelujah and before the Offertory, where bread and wine are placed on the altar. There are different Sequentiae, for example for Easter or Pentecost (cf. Reichert, Kneif). The lyrics for the *Lacrimosa* in the Requiem were written in the thirteenth century; they are as follows, with an English translation:

> Lacrimosa dies illa
> Qua resurget ex favilla
> Judicandus homo reus:
>
> Huic ergo parce Deus
> Pie Jesu Domine
> Dona eis requiem
> Amen
>
> That day of tears and mourning,
> From the dust of earth returning
> Man for judgement must prepare him,
>
> Lord, have mercy on him.
> Gentle Lord Jesus,
> grant them eternal rest.
> Amen.

If you know the liturgical background of this mass of the dead and its lyrics, you already connect the overall theme of death with the piece, and more precisely the actual grieving process with the titular tears plus the major theme of waiting for judgment after death.

Beyond that, there are also some compositional tools which you could understand and therefore relate to the emotion of grieving, if you grew up with the Western musical traditions: It is set in d minor, and minor in general is said to have a darker, maybe even sadder tone. The piece also begins with a motif that is very common in Baroque, Classical and Romantic music, the so-called "sigh motif". This musical figure consists of a slurred note pair of accent and relaxation, usually in a semitone step, which thereby tries to imitate a human sigh. Thanks to this onomatopoeic character the figure possibly could be recognized, at least subconsciously, even by people who never heard of a sigh motif (cf. Kilian 81).

Movie Narratives: *Amadeus*

Understanding these compositional tools like the sigh motif and therefore understanding the meaning behind musical pieces was part of the education of the middle and upper class in the nineteenth century. Therefore, the embedded codes were understood by many people, and references could be used in a different variety of settings and narratives. This also means that classical music in the nineteenth and early twentieth century was used in every entertainment sector, not only concerts or the opera, but also as part of vaudeville shows or for scoring 'silent movies.' With the rise of the 'talkies' in the late 1920s and early 1930s, classical music became therefore part of their soundtracks, too.

There is not much scholarly research about the usage of specific classical pieces throughout different movies up until now, and the Internet Movie Database's collection of soundtracks is huge but certainly not complete. The data currently available indicate that parts of Mozart's *Requiem* were not used much in movie soundtracks from the 1930s through the 1950s; there are movies with Mozart's music from that time, but they mostly use *Eine kleine Nachtmusik* (KV 525) or an aria. Beginning with the 1960s, there are some lesser-known movies using the *Requiem*, like the Spanish-Mexican *Viridiana* (1961), which includes parts of the *Requiem*, though not the *Lacrimosa*. Therefore, it seems that the starting point of this piece's greater public awareness has to be Miloš Forman's *Amadeus* (1984). In this movie, the writing of the *Requiem* itself is part of the plot, though not in a very historically accurate way (for example, there is no evidence of Salieri really being the instigator of Mozart's demise, and the way Mozart always composes in a frenzy and without thinking much about it had nothing to do with his actual working process). Because of these inaccuracies, many scholars still hate the movie, and Maurice Zam, former director of the LA Conservatory of Music, even declared: "*Amadeus* is dangerous to your musical health. It may prevent you from appreciating Mozart's music, and pervert and poison your capacity for intelligent listening to all kinds of music" (qtd. in Kupferberg 240). Nevertheless, the movie made nearly 52 million dollars in the US and won eight Academy

Awards, and it was for many moviegoers a new gateway to Mozart's music (cf. Kupferberg 227). And thanks to a very clear connection between the story, the representation of emotions on screen, and specific music pieces, it was also a way to understand certain layers of this music.

The movie leans quite heavily on Mozart's music within its soundtrack, most prominently *Il Nozze di Figaro* (KV 492), *The Magic Flute* (KV 620), and *Requiem*, whose composing processes and, in the case of the two operas, premieres are also part of the plot. This means that most of Mozart's music in the movie can be called diegetic, being either actually performed within a scene or as an auditive manifestation of Mozart's composing process.

This is also true for the *Requiem*, whose composing process is the main plot of the last third of the movie, beginning with the commissioning of the piece by a black-masked man. The composing process of this mass for the dead from then on accompanies Mozart's failing health and is set in a stark contrast to him composing the more cheerful 'Singspiel' *The Magic Flute*.

In her book about *Amadeus*, Cornelia Szabó-Knotik put together a table of the different uses of Mozart's music, focusing on their diegetic and non-diegetic character (cf. 34–35).[4] Here one can see that, in contrast to the predominantly diegetic use of the other musical pieces in the movie, parts of the *Requiem* are used non-diegetically, beginning with the first chords of the piece when Mozart got the commission. From that scene on, some parts of the *Requiem* therefore become a way for the director to communicate with the audience by foreshadowing and underlining the emotions represented on screen.[5]

Mozart's whole dying process, underscored by parts of the *Requiem*, culminates and ends with his death and funeral, both accompanied by the *Lacrimosa*. These scenes undeniably invoke emotions like grieving and despair (through the acting, the setting, and the story itself) in the audience, which are enhanced by the music itself because of the already stated liturgical and musical reasons. At

---

4 However, she does not use the two terms but speaks about "O-Ton" (literally, 'original sound') when it comes to diegetic music and "Hintergrund" (background) for non-diegetic music. Her "Originalvertonung" (original setting) on the other hand can be part of both categories: the *Dies irae* and *Confutatis* are in a way diegetic as they are the auditive manifestations of the composing seen on screen, whereas *Rex tremendae* is non-diegetic and underscores Mozart's realization that his wife left him.

5 There is no consent among scholars about the different meaning of music if it is diegetic or non-diegetic. Moris B. Holbrook summarized the most common opinion: "(...) diegetic music serves primarily to reinforce the realistic depiction of the *mise-en-scène* (...)," while in contrast "(...) non-diegetic music contributes to a film's dramatic development by fleshing out a character, developing a theme, signaling an impendent event, or otherwise drawing on associations and identifications that add depth to the meaning of the motion picture" (48).

the same time for the viewers the sad meaning of these scenes is now connected to this musical piece and probably can be invoked the next time they hear it. Therefore a layer for understanding the music is added even for people without the liturgical or musical background.

After *Amadeus*, other movies like *The Offering* (1997) or *Kiss Kiss Bang Bang* (2001) used the *Lacrimosa* in similar manners, and thanks to a spoof of Forman's movie in *The Simpsons* episode 15.11 "Magical History Tour" from 2004, this connection between Mozart's death and the *Lacrimosa* was repeated for a younger generation: when Bart/Mozart dies, you hear the first notes from the *Lacrimosa*. Finally, especially since the 2010s, Mozart's *Lacrimosa* was also widely used in TV-series, most prominently in episode 1.4 of *The Crown* when it is foreshadowing the death and despair the city of London will have to face because of the 'Great Fog of London.'

A Layer of Its Own: *BioShock Infinite*

Both purposes mentioned for *Amadeus* and *The Crown*—the foreshadowing of tragedy and the accompanying of a path to death, are also major functions for the *Requiem's* use in *BioShock Infinite*, though here in the end the *Lacrimosa* also gets its own meaning in the game.

BioShock Infinite (2013) is known for its creative use of pre-composed music as a way to comment on the story and foreshadowing future events.[6] This is especially true for the *Requiem*, heard for the first time in Lady Comstock's Memorial Hall. At this point in the game the main protagonist Booker DeWitt, after arriving at the (seemingly) utopian floating city of Columbia, freed a young girl named Elizabeth, and now they are trying to leave the city. Their escape takes them to the mausoleum and memorial exhibition of Lady Annabel Comstock, the martyrized wife of Columbia's leader and self-proclaimed prophet, Zackary Comstock, and, as we learn later on, Elizabeth's mother. The memorial is divided into four different rooms, each dedicated to one part of Annabel's life story and each musically accompanied by a part from Mozart's *Requiem*:

---

[6] For a detailed analysis of the used modern pop-songs and classical pieces see Gibbons, Chapter 3. Here he analyzes the pop songs in *BioShock* and their anachronistic nature in the game's world for "(...) reinforcing and destabilizing the player's sense of time and place" (43), as well as the use of the music of Richard Wagner, a known anti-Semite, in the scene where a mixed-raced couple is almost stoned by a crowd (44).

Location	Movement of Requiem
"The Memorial of Our Lady"	Lacrimosa
"The Transport of the Child"	Agnus Dei (opening only)
"The Murder of Our Lady"	Rex tremendae
"The Vengeance of the Prophet"	Confutatis

In his analysis, Gibbons concentrates mostly on the *Requiem* "as a sonic manifestation of the larger issues of quantum mechanics and uncertainty" (44), as well as the liturgical meaning of the different parts in connection to the story about Lady Comstock (45–47). His analysis of the *Lacrimosa* is quite short, though, and especially since this part of the *Requiem* becomes quite important later on, some additional thoughts are necessary.

As Booker enters the first room of the Memorial Hall, the *Lacrimosa* immediately begins to play. The sound of the music itself at this moment is a little scratchy, as if coming from an old record player, therefore making it a diegetic part of the soundscape inside the world of the game. This is a new take on the non-diegetic use of these musical pieces in the other media discussed before: the music should not only speak to the player but also to the public of Columbia. For them this hall, which includes not only the music but also large oil paintings of Lady Comstock as well as a fountain with a weeping angel, visualizing the titular 'lacrimosa' (lat. for weeping, tearful), should be a place for mourning.

This meaning as a fixture in the world itself becomes even clearer when you think about the question of anachronism represented in the game via music: in *BioShock Infinite* you can hear quite a lot of modern pop-songs like "God only Knows" by the Beach Boys (1966) or "Girls Just Wanna Have Fun" by Cyndi Lauper (1983). They are played in 1910s' versions, in these two cases sung by a Barbershop Quartet and played by a calliope, respectively. These songs therefore "(...) both reinforc[e] and destabiliz[e] the player's sense of time and place" (Gibbons 43). When it comes to the *Requiem*, however, there is no question of anachronism anymore. It was composed in 1791 and can easily be part of a world set in 1912. This means that Mozart's music, and every emotional and narrative function it has, is a natural part of the world that the player does not have to question after hearing the music for the first time.

Even the liturgical meaning behind the *Requiem* seems quite fitting for the memorial hall: there are many Christian themes scattered in the game up to this point (cf. Gibbons 44–47), and when the player visits the other three rooms, it becomes very clear that Lady Comstock's life and death are interwoven with a Christian narrative that strongly parallels the story of the Holy Family, again making the *Requiem* an obvious and quite fitting part of the world. But players at this point in the game already know that all this religious behavior is only a façade, so the whole arrangement must strike them as cynical and ideological rather than genuine. This is proven later on in the narrative by the fact that Lady Comstock was not, as the official story goes, killed by an anarchist, and she was not a martyr of the utopian ideas of Columbia. Instead, her husband had her assassinated because she threatened to reveal the truth about his manipulative and ruthless nature to the public.

This revelation, which subverts both the Christian and utopian aspects of her story, is foreshadowed in the use of an abridged version of the *Lacrimosa* in this scene: if the player knows the original music piece he realizes quite early on that a big part, namely the two lines about the resurrection of the dead and their judgment, was left out. This omits the original Christian meaning behind death from this piece, and it is another indication that this 'Christianity' is only a façade. This also means that even the seemingly fitting *Lacrimosa* in this world is, literally, broken.

The mentioned omission of the parts about the resurrection will seem even more poignant in retrospect, because when we hear the *Lacrimosa* again later in the game Lady Comstock is actually resurrected as a violent ghost, which would make the omission a more complex ironic foreshadowing that is important in what it does *not* announce.[7] This second usage of the *Lacrimosa* in the game happens when Booker and Elizabeth arrive at the tomb of Lady Comstock. There the *Lacrimosa* is played through loudspeakers in an eternal loop, as a reference to the memorial hall and Lady Comstock herself. At this point, the *Lacrimosa* has been inscribed with a new layer of meaning inside the world of *BioShock* as a Leitmotif, a piece of music connected with Lady Comstock. This is expanded even further when the music becomes part of the gameplay: after Lady Comstock is 'resurrected,' meaning the dead one from this dimension is merged with a living one from another, she becomes a screaming siren who sometimes sings the first part of the *Lacrimosa*. Its sound is twisted and electronically manipulated, but on some occasions still recognizable. The player has to shoot this siren and can use this specific music to find her location in the chaos and through other loud noises at the cemetery after her 'resurrection.' Thus, in the end the *Lacrimosa* becomes a kind of fighting marker and therefore gets a totally new layer of meaning for every player of *BioShock Infinite*.

---

[7] Gibbons offers a similar interpretation of the second room and its *Agnus Dei:* the scene shows Elizabeth as a baby and her relocation to the secluded tower in which she lived most of her life until Booker freed her. The *Agnus Dei* comments therefore on her role as the titular Lamb of God and therefore messiah, a role of Elizabeth in Columbia's society we can find throughout the game (Gibbons 46–47).

Conclusion

Up to this point the *Lacrimosa* had a quite stringent narrative meaning of mourning and grieving in all the media I discussed, be it its original liturgical or musical connotation or its use in movies, TV series and *BioShock*. This use of already known musical pieces can enhance the narrative, either by foreshadowing or deepening the shown emotions, if the viewer is familiar with its meaning. This mainly happens via repetition in different media. In the case of the *Lacrimosa*, its original meaning of mourning is present in every given example, and therefore this particular reading is strengthened in the collective mind, even if the individual doesn't necessarily remember every scene in which it is used in detail.

Yet the very last example of the *Lacrimosa* as a battle cry shows that precomposed music can obtain new layers of meaning within a given medium, though in this case it probably will not change the perception of the music piece for the majority of people. Yet precisely this has happened in some cases, and a new layer of meaning became more dominant in popular culture than the original one: two examples of this phenomenon are Richard Strauss's 'Introduction' in *Also sprach Zarathustra* (op. 30), now generally evoking associations with outer space because of Stanley Kubrick's *2001: A Space Odyssey* (1968), and Richard Wagner's *Ride of the Valkyries* (from *Die Walküre*, WWV 86B), which after *Apocalypse Now* (1979) is associated with helicopter attacks. In their very first installments, both pieces had a narrative meaning you could trace back to its original intention, but afterwards the connection between the movie images and the music became much stronger than that between the original narrative and the music. However, if we want to determine a turning point for this change of meaning we need more analysis of just one music piece through all media, including video games. Especially video games with their interactive character could have a great potential for such changes, because the player not only listens to music but also has to react with it to advance in the game world. But they also play an important role in repeating the established interpretation of certain music pieces, and therefore their role in acquiring musical literacy is now as important as that of movies and TV series.

Works Cited

Audience Net. *Music Consumption: The Overall Landscape*. London, 2017.
BioShock Infinite. Irrational Games, 2K Games, for Microsoft Windows, 2013.

Finscher, Ludwig. "Klassik". *MGG Online*, edited by Laurenz Lütteken, Bärenreiter-Verlag, Verlag J. B. Metzler, RILM, 2016, www.mgg-online.com/mgg/stable/12219. Accessed 15 Jan. 2019.

Forman, Miloš, director. *Amadeus*. Orion Pictures, 1984.

Gibbons, William. *Unlimited Replays: Video Games and Classical Music*. Oxford UP, 2018.

Gienow-Hecht, Jessica C. E. *Sound Diplomacy: Music and Emotions in Transatlantic Relations, 1850–1920*. U of Chicago P, 2009.

Holbrook, Morris B. "The Ambi-Diegesis of 'My Funny Valentine.'" *Pop Fiction: The Song in Cinema*, edited by Steve Lannin and Matthew Caley, Intellect Books, 2005.

Johnson, Julian. *Who Needs Classical Music? Cultural Choice and Musical Value*. Oxford UP, 2002.

Kilian, Gerald. *Norm und Subjektivität im Spätstil Mozarts: zur Analyse, Didaktik und Methodik der späten Werke Mozarts*. Die Blaue Eule, 2002.

Kupferberg, Herbert. *Amadeus: A Mozart Mosaic*. McGraw-Hill, 1986.

Mehr, Samuel A., Manvis Singh, et al. "Form and Function in Human Song." *Current Biology* vol. 28, no.3, 2018, pp. 356–68.

National Endowment for the Arts. *A Decade of Arts Engagement: Findings from the Survey of Public Participation in the Arts, 2002–2012* [NEA research report # 59]. Washington DC, 2015.

Reichert, Ursula, and Tibor Kneif. "Requiem." *MGG Online*, edited by Laurenz Lütteken, Bärenreiter-Verlag, Verlag J. B. Metzler, RILM, 2016, www.mgg-online.com/mgg/stable/11933. Accessed 15 Jan. 2019.

Szabó-Knotik, Cornelia. *Amadeus: Milos Formans Film als musikhistorisches Phänomen*. Akademische Druck- u. Verlagsanstalt, 1999.

Nathalie Aghoro
Unspoken Adventures: On Sound, Story, and Nonverbal Gameplay in *Journey* and *Inside*

> "Sound is the invisible layer of the world that shows its relationships, actions, and dynamics." (Salomé Voegelin, *Sonic Possible Worlds* 2)

> "[T]he meanings of play—of video gameplay in particular—are ultimately connected to social and material realities [...]." (Steven Jones, *The Meaning of Video Games* 15–6)

Listening and playing are two interactive abilities that allow individuals to build and actively tap into networks of relationships that constitute their world. In video games, sound design and gameplay promote the cohesion of the gaming experience as they enlist a player's sensory and explorative participation in the game world. Listening *to* the game and playing *with* the rules of the game means to connect with a virtual environment—a connection informed by social, political, economic, or cultural premises.

The 2012 video game *Journey*, developed by the game studio thatgamecompany, and Playdead's *Inside* from 2016 are two story-driven games that combine the relational characteristics of sound and play while completely foregoing spoken or written narration. Instead of vocal renditions or texts, they use other means such as nonverbal sound to convey their stories and, ultimately, to elicit an interpretive response to the gameplay experience. In both games, sound simultaneously involves the players and encourages them to create their own personal stories while playing.

The main stories of *Inside* and *Journey* are embedded in game environments geared toward an immersive and interactive experience that oscillates between the solitary exploration of the world and the cooperative involvement in social connections. Set in an uninhabited desert, *Journey* combines a single-player mode with optional opportunities for cooperation and experimentation in its gameplay. *Inside's* dystopian adventure lets its lone and silent protagonist grapple with institutional power structures that govern every form of interaction with non-player characters in its Foucauldian carceral society.

The absence of verbal explanations or distractions in both games channels the player's attention to the sonic effects of their actions within the game from the beginning and allows for a contemplative engagement with the aural and visual aesthetics of the game environment. They start without preamble with a solitary avatar in a natural setting that is reflected in the acoustic design of the footsteps once the player takes up the controller and starts to move. We can hear the

https://doi.org/10.1515/9783110659405-018

rustling of leaves as a feedback to our actions in the forest of *Inside* and the sand grinding under the avatar's feet in *Journey*'s desert.[1] This first auditory contact when one starts playing the game announces that paying attention to sonic cues is an integral component of the gameplay. It paves the way for the upcoming acoustic definition of the social and environmental structures governing the game world and the aural involvement in non-player character interactions as well as player relations.

Even though the outlook of these two games is almost antithetical, their shared emphasis on the sonic contributions to storytelling and nonverbal gameplay calls for a comparative analysis. When considered together, they raise the question of what makes sound (and this includes the absence of sound within a sonic environment) such an efficient tool for shaping the relations between players, non-player characters, and the virtual game environment. Critical listening provides a framework for the cultural contextualization of video game sound as a formative influence when it comes to the imagination of social dynamics, and it highlights the significance of sound for the interconnectedness between the practice of gaming and the "social and material realities" Jones mentions (16).

In the following, I will argue that the usage of nonverbal sounds in *Journey* and *Inside* generates individual storytelling experiences that invite players to evaluate or rethink social dynamics and world-subject relations. Their approaches on the "invisible layer" of sound—to come back to Voegelin's analogy—directly implicate the player in the sonic and visual events on screen through the close connection of sound to the tactile input and feedback loop between hand and controller. Since the progression in these games is based on the sequential exploration of a story in which the avatar is the protagonist, the gaming experience inevitably also becomes a storytelling experience. Accordingly, the acoustic definition of player actions and social relations not only functions as a major gameplay feature but also affects how the story evolves in the process. In the following, critical listening shall generate insights into the connections between nonverbal gameplay, virtual storytelling, and sound. The ensuing focus on in-game acoustics will delineate the impact of sound design on narrative agency and social practice as well as the participatory dynamics fueled by sonic play in *Journey* and *Inside*.

---

[1] Video material and gameplay sequences for both games can be found on the publisher's website: https://www.degruyter.com/view/product/529432.

Playing Games with Absent Sounds and Fictional Detours

In *Inside* and *Journey*, sound is the determining element for the tension between gameplay and storytelling. The combination of an explicit attention to sound and the evident absence of sounds is a main driving force for engaging the player. It opens up a space for play in the stories that the games unfold and complements the spectacle of the visual aesthetics they display with the interactive potential of listening. As Karen Collins writes in *Playing with Sound*, "[l]istening affects the ways in which the player experiences the game and, in some cases, affects the player's ability to play the game" (5). These two games, however, go a step further than this general notion because they offer players the option to influence the course of the game through the practice of listening and the play with sound reproduction.

When sounds are elements of the game structure and of 'free' play at the same time, the presence or absence of particular sounds can promote alternatives to the predetermination of a story-driven gameplay and may sometimes even lead to its subversion. The double function of sound in both *Journey* and *Inside* engenders a possibility space that Graham Jensen defines as the result of the tension between the rules of the game and the freedom of play in "Making Sense of Play in Video Games: Ludus, Paidia, and Possibility Spaces:"

> In the same way that the Russian thinker Mikhail Bakhtin describes "centripetal" (or "organizing") and "centrifugal" (or "disrupting") forces working constantly against each other in language and culture (...), the forces that characterize *paidia* and *ludus* are in constant tension in video games. The result of this tension is what Will Wright (...) calls a "possibility space," a site of constant but productive, generative conflict between order and chaos, between rules and uninhibited play. (69)

Along these lines, gameplay resides at the interstices between the rules of a game and the player's drive to explore possible courses of action and test the game's boundaries in the process. The rules provide orientation and structure. They ensure the clear determination of the overall outcome of a game and its riddles, challenges, or tasks. By preventing the game from being arbitrary, they facilitate its playability. Play makes gamer agency possible and is characterized by the process of trying different approaches and altering an unsuccessful procedure when stopped by the code. In other words, play calls for experimentation and imagination as it motivates players to choose from a variety of options or even create their own solutions. The possibility space of a game depends on the balance between these two features and the visual, aural, and tactile features of a game function as calibration tools for the balancing of a game. Hence, simultaneously embedding sound in the game structure and playing with acoustics taps into the "transformative and generative power of play, which is derived precisely from the point at which *paidia* and *ludus* necessarily intersect" (Jensen 71). Sound facilitates the recognition of boundaries and required actions. Its temporal characteristics make sonic stimulus particularly useful as a structural element in video games, e.g. for timing tactile input or signaling hidden locations, key positions or action-oriented feedback. Moreover, the multimodality of sound in video games[2] promotes playful experimentation with the game environment: play resides in the selection of what sounds a player chooses to listen to or, if it is a playable feature, in the triggering of sounds within the game as well as in the process of finding out which sounds do what.

From the perspective of critical listening, two types of sonic play are at work in *Inside* and *Journey*. The first one is marked by the absence of language and the presence of other sounds as part of the structured, story-driven progression. In the following, this form of play will be defined as a play of signification. The second type is a sonic play with variation that consists of acoustic choices made by the listening player—choices that may range from possible gameplay actions to free play.

The play of signification in *Journey* and *Inside* is the result of the fictional indeterminacy that arises from the absence of a narrative voice, scripted dialogues or explanatory text passages. Chris Baldick situates the literary notion of indeterminacy within the fields of reader-response theory and deconstruction. It signifies "any element of a text that requires the reader to decide on its meaning" and represents "a principle of uncertainty invoked to deny the existence of any final or determinate meaning that could bring to an end the play of meanings between the elements of a text." Expanding the notion of indeterminacy beyond the scope of literary textuality to other media—as the present study does with a specific focus on video games—does not mean to read games as texts. This move rather arises out of the understanding that the play of signification included in fictional indeterminacy does not necessarily need to be a textual practice and is not confined to processes of interpretation alone.

Gaming ties practices of participation to the experience of epistemic uncertainty. In story-driven video games in particular, the notion of fictional indeterminacy acquires a distinctively interactive and multimodal meaning. Not only

---

[2] Collins highlights that "[s]ound in interactive media such as games is multimodal—that is it involves the interaction of more than one sensory modality and usually contains three (vision, audition, and haptics—action, image, and sound)" (22).

does it depend on the process of interpretation caused by on-screen events seen or heard, it is also affected by tactile feedback signals, multimodal input-response loops linked to player actions, and the general amount of in-game agency granted to the player. Therefore, fictional indeterminacy in video games is closely related to the player's attitude toward uncertain situations that they bring to the game. How uncertainty is actively handled while playing determines the manner in which players get involved with possible pathways through the video game. Moreover, the personal ways of playing the video game defines which parts of the game a player will be able to access and which ones will remain undisclosed.

The joint critical consideration of gameplay and fictional indeterminacy provides insights into the features and functions of a game's possibility space in relation to participatory practices. Based on Wolfgang Iser's literary anthropology, Philipp Schweighauser advocates an interdisciplinary approach to "the cultural work of fiction in a variety of media without leveling the distinctions between different cultural practices" (118). He argues that game studies and literary theory can mutually enrich each other by widening the scope for a more encompassing understanding of fiction. For Schweighauser, a media-independent understanding of fiction is particularly suitable to explore the "participatory nature" (118) of video games and, at the same time, to re-examine the cultural significance of fiction within a broader media ecology. To this end, he reads Iser's definition of fiction in *The Fictive and the Imaginary: Charting Literary Anthropology* as follows:

> Iser points out that 'fiction' is a much more active process than its equation with mimesis or representation suggests. Fiction does not imitate the world: it shapes, forms, fashions or invents a new, fictional world with objects and people in it that do not exist in empirical reality. Fiction, then, is not a mirroring of the world we already know. Instead it is a staging and invention of a new world, which emerges out of an interplay between the projections of the text and the reader's imagination. (125)

The emphasis on the active and generative process of fictional invention is the point of departure for the consideration of fictionality in video games in Schweighauser's work. He suggests that from a comparative perspective the active conceptualization of fiction "makes us think again about Eskelinen's (...) claim that 'the dominant user function in literature, theatre and film is interpretative, but in games it is the configurative one'" (125). In the present context of story-driven video games, the notion of fictional indeterminacy encompasses the configurative function of play. In contrast to literature, where the process of fashioning a story world happens within the reader's mind, video games render the inventive emergence of a fictional world visible, audible, and palpable through the participatory process of the gameplay. What the story means, what kind of story it will be, and how the play of signification unfolds depends to a large extent on the actions of the player.

Listening to story-driven video games thus reveals the significance of sound for the participatory projection of fictional worlds. More precisely with regard to the sound design of *Inside* and *Journey*, it becomes apparent that the nonverbal acoustic and visual cues resonating with musical soundscapes and other forms of environmental storytelling in combination with fictional indeterminacy encourage the players to both undergo and bring to life narratives about human connection. Together, the sound-related actions of the player and the predefined soundscape of the games help navigate their fictional indeterminacies while fundamentally affecting the invention of the fictional world that takes place during the gameplay.

At first glance, the almost rudimentary main plot line appears to be strictly predetermined in both games. Its unfolding is inextricably linked to their underlying story-driven structure. In *Journey*, players perform a "pilgrimage" toward the ray of light at the top of a mountain. The goal to be reached in the game is announced within the first 30 seconds of gameplay. The visual announcement prompts the player to perform a predetermined forward movement that Tom van Nuenen links to "a well-established narrative pattern [that] inflects the main story: Joseph Campbell's 'monomyth' or hero's journey" (468–69). Van Nuenen argues that this forward movement is designed to trigger an affective response which is why he qualifies the game principle as "procedural (e)motion" (466). For him, the emotional experience linked to this "unidirectional" (473) "spatial teleology" is "a cathartic experience, producing awe (…) by following the structure of Campbell's concept" (468–69). Along these lines, the cloaked avatar follows the ray of light until it reaches the top and finally returns as a changed character.

In *Inside*, the puzzle-platformer's side-scrolling principle invariably leads players from left to right in order to reach the end of the game where the story's resolution seems to await. However, the protagonist, a boy with a red sweater, is thrown into a dystopian world in which every social interaction is determined by a surveillance apparatus without any contextualization for the player. The constant forward movement does not reveal who the boy is, where he is going, and why he is being chased by people with firearms, searchlights, and dogs. The single gameplay focus lies on survival in a threatening and opaque system. The lack of a frame story for the events happening on screen creates a heightened sense of uncertainty and anxiety that clashes with the linearity of the gameplay. With reference to Playdead's game *Limbo*, the predecessor of *Inside*, Graham Pedlingham connects the indeterminacy that is a primary trait of the gaming experience to a post-9/11 aesthetic of uncertainty: an aesthetic that seeks to convey an anxiety around the potential precariousness of structures and systems; a sense of vulnerability and disorientation at both a personal and social level; a self-reflective engagement with the iconography of 9/11 and its mediatisation; a permeability of boundaries that are implicitly or explicitly linked with the safety of, as Butler terms it, 'First Worldism'. (157)

In *Inside* the vulnerability of the protagonist becomes palpable through his silent isolation within a controlled environment of scientific experimentation and rigorous supervision. The perception of order as precarious that permeates Western discourses in the early twenty-first century finds its translation in *Inside* into a story world where control dominates. The game reduces the individual to the role of test subject and penalizes any test failed by the avatar.

The absence of dialogue in an adverse environment is consistent with a story about control and subjection to institutional power. It calls for lateral thinking and obliges players to pay particular attention to their surroundings when searching for clues with a strong emphasis on game sound cues for player actions. In a talk at the Game Developers Conference 2016, *Inside*'s sound designer and audio director Martin Stig Andersen calls the platformer "A Game That Listens," thus highlighting the audio-driven gameplay where, as he says, sound "decides when the character should walk" to survive a level (Andersen 00:26:21).[3] *Inside* systematically connects threats to sonic cues and integrates sound into the process of puzzle solving. Dangers announce themselves acoustically, such as the watchdogs that hunt the avatar down at several instances in the game. Their barking can be heard before they appear on the screen, and when the player sees them it is already too late to react. The game thus emphasizes the importance of attentive listening for a successful completion of the puzzles; whenever sound cues are ignored, death becomes unavoidable.

In *Journey*, the absence of language in combination with a strong focus on environmental sound is also justified by the main story that could be categorized as ecofiction. As van Nuenen observes, the adventure is "[m]odeled after [a] (...) threefold structure of rites of passage, [which] (...) involves a fixed narrative pattern of separation, initiation, and return" (469), and the separation in this case is the separation from a historical past. The soundtrack forms an intertextual bridge to a literary past: "*Journey*'s soundtrack (the first gaming soundtrack to be nominated for a Grammy) uses music to help trace the overarching narrative; composer Austin Wintory based the soundtrack on a musical motif, ending in an

---

3 Playdead clearly prioritizes the integrity of *Inside* as a work of art in which sound and visual design are inseparable, even when it comes to press releases and reviews. They grant permission to share footage of the game provided that visuals and sound are presented together.

aria at the game's end, the lyrics referring to hero's journeys, such as *The Aeneid*, *Beowulf*, and *The Iliad*" (van Nuenen 469). The music thus constructs a historical lineage for the game by linking *Journey* to a canonical set of lyrical journeys. In such a depopulated world where sand keeps spreading over the architectural remains of an ancient culture, the use of language seems lost while nature survives.

Nevertheless, the player-protagonist can emit chiming sounds when pushing a controller button. They can use this aural signal to trigger the projection of glyphs and pictorial representations of historical records. The sonic activation of these narrative initiations referencing events that took place at the explored sites is also the key to the next level, i.e. another geographical section of the game. The acoustic command is an example of the "spatial sonic embodiment" that Collins considers as a particularity of interactive sound (57). It is always linked to the avatar's movement pattern. Whenever one pushes the button, the figure emits a tone and performs a small jump at the same time. Collins calls this combination "kinesonic congruence." As she argues, "players have a sonic reaction that matches the action that the body is making, thus embedding personal expressiveness into the game through the character" (57). Through the combination of movement and sound that activates the nonverbal story mode, the avatar becomes a resonance body, vibrating with the artifacts and, as a consequence, reconstructing visuals that call for narrative interpretation. The player initiating this process actively takes part in the teleological unfolding of the game by extension.

Overall, sound negotiates the tension between the linearity of the main story mode and the fictional indeterminacy resulting from the absence of linguistic support in both games. Acoustic features fundamentally shape the gaming experience. Consequently, players have articulated their involvement in the storytelling process online by developing and discussing theories about the meaning of a certain ending as well as sharing their experiences with videos featuring a particularly memorable run. This kind of involvement suggests that the gaming experience is considered personal and unique despite the necessary predetermination of the main storyline. *Journey* and *Inside* particularly encourage this perception through the conversion of the sonic gameplay features established in the story into a second type of play with sound that requires, in Zimmerman's sense of the word 'interactive,' the players' "explicit participation" (160)—a play on variation that includes the recourse to their personal imaginary repertoire.

Narrative Agency and the Social Dynamics of Sonic Play

The sonic play with variation in *Journey* and *Inside* derives from the respective set of acoustic signals that each game establishes as part of the general rules. Therefore, these signals are already known to the player as tools they can utilize to influence the virtual environment. These sonic game elements fulfill the function of furthering the plot as much as they facilitate improvisation in a departure from the linear main pathway. As a consequence, play depends on the degree to which freedom of choice is embedded within the game and provides possibilities for the repurposing of built-in acoustic options according to the player's experiences and imagination, even more so because these sounds are nonverbal and as such not predetermined by any language.

Narrative and agency are inextricably interconnected in story-driven video games because the tension between a fixed outcome and free play needs to be balanced. The notion of narrative agency, as proposed by D. Fox Harrell and Jichen Zhu in their article "Agency Play: Dimensions of Agency for Interactive Narrative Design," factors this tension in. As they argue, "narrative agency is contextually situated, distributed between the player and system, and mediated through user interpretation of system behavior and system affordances for user actions" (44). They recognize two dimensions with an impact on agency in narrative interactive media: the socio-cultural contexts that inform both user and system and the aesthetic experience included in gaming. With reference to Laura Ahearn's anthropological studies, they define agency as "the *socio-culturally mediated* capacity to act," a definition they translate to digital media as follows:

> In digital environments, a user's power to take meaningful actions is mediated through the structure provided by the computational system as well as the socially situated interpretation of actions rendered by the user. A system's capacity to afford certain actions, impose certain constraints, and reward certain behaviors clearly has great effect on user's agency. (47)

Since the system needs to interpret player actions in order to select and match responses that do not randomly jeopardize immersion, the encoded socio-cultural conjectures significantly shape its structure. Moreover, narrative agency includes the reining in of user agency because the latter "also provides an aesthetic experience and needs to be appropriate to its narrative context. A user's capacity to act and make distinction does not necessarily entail narrative consistency" (47). In order for the overarching game development to remain consistent and reach its overarching goals, it requires the specification of a limited framework for free play or the implementation of rewards that encourage the player to return to the main story eventually.

These aspects of digital interactivity are conditioned by agency play, according to Harrell and Zhu: "The interplay and interdependence between the two seemingly oppositional concepts of user agency and system agency provides us a starting point to systematically describe a set of possibilities for deploying agency in interactive narrative media. We call this set of new possibilities *agency play*" (45). The regulation of agency dynamics "focuses on leveraging the relationship between the user and system in order to create a story world that is meaningful and engaging for users to participate in" (48). Along these lines, the balancing of user and system agency is a challenging play with social constraints that *Inside* negotiates through sound while *Journey* partially fosters free play with sound cues but also highlights ideological signposts and orchestrates multimodal impulses within the game environment to pace the progression to the top. In this way, the agency play of both games listens to and plays with sound.

Sonic play is social play because sound positions the subject in relation to others and to their surroundings and both games use this relational quality for their play with variation. Through sound, they negotiate the social norms and socialized behaviors written into the game. From the point of view that gaming consists of "enter[ing] a space *between* two worlds," as Schweighauser suggests by defining "the gaming experience (...) [as] *doubly real*" (125), the negotiation of social dynamics exceeds the game environment because sonic play as a participatory practice has a double connection to the social both on screen and in the experiential world. In the case of fictional indeterminacy, learned sociocultural discourses lend themselves to informing both the system rules and player actions. As Jensen writes, "the possibility space is a site of constant negotiation between implicit and explicit rules that are introduced both by the game and by the player" (76). Consequently, the sonic play with variation becomes the acoustic engagement with a game's possibility space in which a cultural, social, and personal behavioral repository paves the way to improvisation and experimentation with in-game sounds and social practices.

Journey encourages the active usage of the acoustic command and provides gamers with creative possibilities to play with. For instance, producing the chiming sounds makes it possible to connect with the stylized flora and fauna of the virtual world, with which one can but does not necessarily need to interact. If one chooses to engage with characters resembling birds, dragons, flowers, or seaweed, one develops and embellishes the main gameplay with subplots. These side stories revolve around ideas of cooperation between nonhumans and humans in an ecologically challenging environment possibly affected by climate change, and they vary according to the player's actions and individual creative drive.

The choice to cooperate is rewarded with benefits that facilitate the journey such as riding on animals for a faster progression in the level and recharging one's floating power when calling out to the non-player characters or moving close to them. This reward system also functions within the embedded online multiplayer mode that is limited to sharing the virtual space with one random person at a time. The appearance of another unnamed player in the game is announced by a beam of light that points roughly into the direction of the other. Moreover, one can announce one's presence acoustically by emitting the chiming sonic cue. The engagement with the other player is a free choice, and their presence can be ignored just as they may progress without acknowledging you. When the distance between the two players is too great for some time, the other disappears from the individual game space and one is alone again. In her work called *How Games Move Us: Emotion by Design*, Katherine Isbister notes that the player interaction is designed "intentional[ly] (...) [to promote] collaborative exploration and discovery" (118). *Journey* counts on the players' joy of discovery when they are confronted with another after a certain amount of solitary time in the awe-inspiring environment. The sound pattern turns into an unspoken communication when players find each other and play with it to experiment with their newfound connection. Since the sounds are connected to movement, the first encounter often looks like a dance.

The impossibility of verbal communication in this context can be understood as a hard-coded guarantee that no one can openly antagonize someone else and that the game's social dynamics stay based on the premise of cooperation. In combination with the possibility for sonic composition by the players, the lack of language therefore exemplifies the efficient version of a "manipulation rule" (Jensen 73) encrypted into the sound design of the game. Jensen argues that

> [m]anipulation rules (...) are heavily influenced by sociocultural values and thus can develop gradually into goal rules as the "infinite possibilities of *paidia* become mediated by the pragmatics of interaction" (Bateman 2005). This transition is especially likely to occur if the possibilities afforded by a particular set of manipulation rules help a player to work toward a specific goal, whether that goal is defined within the context of the game or without, as in the case of culturally reinforced goals. (74)

In *Journey*, linguistic restriction becomes a shared commonality for the time of the social interaction with another real player's avatar in the game while the play with sonic cues shapes the quality of the anonymous encounter.[4] The underlying rules of nonverbal gameplay and basic sonic expression configurate a possibility space for communication that privileges a cooperative principle for social behavior because of the reward system connected to the sonic command when players establish a close proximity between their avatars. Thus, cooperation has the potential to become a goal in itself for the players, even though it is not indispensable for completing the game.

The simple acoustic command in combination with the provided opportunities to interact with other gamers (and non-player characters) equips the player with extensive narrative agency and generates a wide range of possibilities to vary and to shape the story one experiences during a playthrough. It can be a tale of solitary adventure and survival in extreme climate settings, but also one of fleeting acquaintances, cooperation, moral support, or mentorship when one player chooses to stay and help another to find all the secrets in order to unlock the ultimate trophy. With solitary progression being an integral part of the main story line, the sonic free play becomes a play with variations on the precariousness and serendipity of an encounter with life across a range of moods and tones—melancholy and exaltation being just two examples.

The game explicitly references the double reality that Schweighauser recognizes as a constitutive feature of video games by revoking the anonymity of the players after the end of the game. The end credits reveal the identity of all players met—even if one chose to ignore another spawned avatar—and as a consequence explicitly acknowledge their potential role as companion in the development of the story. By naming them, the game developers highlight that the virtual connection of screen is also a simultaneous real-life connection. When Jones discusses the meanings of play, he argues that "[p]laying usually involves remaining simultaneously aware of both the gameworld and of the real world, of yourself and of other players as performing at the boundary of the two" (15–16). He references online game wikis, walkthroughs, and strategy guides as examples of gaming-related zones of intersection. From a contemporary perspective, one could add let's play videos or the online gameplay in games such as *Journey* to this line of thought. In this sense, the end credits are a reminder of the duality experienced during the practice of gaming. More specifically, the listed names suggest that through the random encounter with strangers within the possibility space of the game, "players engage with socio-cultural values that are

---

[4] The emphasis on single encounters in *Journey* is intriguing. The game only matches two simultaneous players at once, never more. This reinforces the drive toward a dialogic communication between vocalizing and listening resonance bodies.

inscribed in the game but that also exist in 'real life'" (Jensen 76). The time spent while interacting in *Journey* is also time players spend socializing with strangers, possibly from around the world and with differing social backgrounds. The random and anonymous meeting within a virtual environment conditions the social dynamics of in-game interactions as much as it is conditioned by the alignment on cooperation built into the rules of the game. Ultimately, the transfer of the connection to the actual world or other virtual environments literally becomes a possibility through the network features of the console.

Journey's free play with sonic expression contrasts *Inside*'s focus on "active listening," to use Collins' terminology (2). The differing strategies of the sonic gameplay determine the contrasting social dynamics of both games. In *Inside*, it is the environment that sounds and that the silent protagonist is exposed to in dismal ways. The sonic environment or soundscape of *Inside* can be described as what sound studies scholar Brandon LaBelle calls an acoustic territory. In his monograph *Acoustic Territories: Sound Culture and Everyday Life*, he argues that "[a]coustic space (...) brings forward a process of acoustic territorialization, in which the disintegration and reconfiguration of space (...) becomes a political process" (147). Labelle refers to the potential of sound to make the negotiation of power in social space aurally perceivable, and I think that this capacity is used in *Inside* to position the avatar as frail and impotent in light of the power structures at play. When confronted with shock waves that violently disrupt the fabric of a gigantic mechanism at the center of an industrial site, the player moves the avatar from shelter to shelter. In order to get to safety, a distinct sound loop that accompanies each disruption and is determined by a strict time pattern needs to be decoded through active listening. In order to survive, the protective shield as well as the avatar's movement must be timed according to the rhythm of the shock waves every step of the way.

The mercilessness of the waves teaches players to obey the system, to fully abide by the rules in their gameplay. In social settings, blind obedience is rewarded as well (at least in the earlier parts of the game). Another scene in the game in which the protagonist becomes part of a group of test subjects can be considered a turning point in the matter. At first the game enforces conformity to the mainstream, depicted as mindless test subjects, through the necessary alignment of the player actions with their movements. Following the masses guarantees success—a dystopian perspective on social dynamics that is acoustically enhanced by muffled footsteps and the throbbing of heartbeats. Then the barking of dogs present in the room sends mixed messages. As mentioned earlier, the dogs' sounding is connected to the action of running to the next frame early on in the game, and the player who remembers the cue in a situation that technically demands compliance and penalizes autonomous movement needs to decide quickly which one of the diverging signals to follow. However, this is a choice under false pretenses since there is only one way to survive the level, namely, to break the pattern of controlled alignment, to show initiative, and run. The in-game subversion of established rules thus proves that *Inside* pits the agency of the player against the mechanisms of a totalitarian system that enforces social isolation.

With agency play in *Inside* privileging system agency over user agency in the majority of cases, the narrative agency of the player only becomes evident in the long run—most notably at the end of the game or when played for a second time. The imbalance during the game reflects the inescapable constraints imposed by a power that absorbs any opportunity for agency—a power that Harrell and Zhu relate to "[a]n extreme reading of Foucault" in which "omnipresent impersonal discourses so thoroughly pervade society that no room is left for anything that might be regarded as agency, oppositional or otherwise" (47). *Inside*'s long-term agency scope is designed for the detection of a second, secret ending that is only revealed if the player recognizes a hidden side quest early on in the game and successfully manages to interpret the respective clues by listening closely. Harrell and Zhu consider agency scope as a regulatory parameter for the balancing of narrative agency:

> The concept of agency scope describes the impact and narrative focus of user and system actions, ranging from immediate and local impact, such as spatial navigation ability, to less immediately apparent but more global results, such as shaping the narrative structure itself. Either side of the agency scope spectrum can be used effectively to convey meanings in addition to the actual narrative. (49)

The actual interpretive choice that endows the player with narrative agency is ultimately postponed to the regular end of the game with an open end that is almost anticlimactic in its lack of dramatic resolution. *Inside* comes to a halt abruptly after urging the player on from the beginning—particularly through the acoustic buildup of suspense and urgency—and suddenly withdraws gameplay control by inhibiting the response to any kind of tactile input. The game literally expels players and relegates them to the experiential world for making sense of the story they have just experienced. The second, secret ending (for which the player needs to memorize a particular musical sequence that is played back at several instances during the playthrough) suggests that an escape from mind control is only an option for the player crossing the threshold between virtuality and actuality and not for the avatar left behind in the fictional environment of the game. Hence, the finite nature of the playthrough becomes an existential question because both endings repeal the linear determination of the story line by denying an in-game resolution. In contrast to *Journey*, where the final credits refer to the actuality of social relations established during the playthrough, *Inside* emphasizes the fictionality and temporary character of the bond between player and avatar and problematizes their social dynamics with respect to the presumably inevitable obliqueness of power relations.

Conclusion: The Values of Resonant Video Games

Inside and *Journey* both convey intricate value systems through nonverbal gameplay, fictional indeterminacy, and sound. The rules that govern their digital environments inscribe the particular worldviews of each game into its soundscape, allowing the listening player to discover the dynamics and scope of their agency within their story-driven worlds through sonic resonance. Sound adds a meaningful sensory plane to cultural conceptions of the subject and social community and the role of critical listening is to uncover the discourses it initiates. The focus on sound in *Inside* and *Journey* thus not only serves as a means to make room for individual player participation in their respective possibility spaces. It can also be read as a multimodal device for the integration of meta-commentaries on the socio-cultural work of video games into the practice of gaming, such as the exploration of social dynamics in the virtual as well as in the actual world, the reflection on ideological premises that define a specific game structure and their connections to player actions and interactions, and their significance for the formation of social subjects.

Works Cited

Andersen, Martin Stig. "A Game that Listens." *YouTube*, 22 July 2016, www.youtube.com/watch?v=Dnd74MQMQ-E.

Baldick, Chris. "Indeterminacy." *The Oxford Dictionary of Literary Terms*, Oxford UP, 2015. *Oxford Reference*, www.oxfordreference.com. Accessed 15 Jan. 2019.

Collins, Karen. *Playing with Sound: A Theory of Interacting with Sound and Music in Video Games*. MIT Press, 2013.

Harrell, D. Fox, and Jichen Zhu. "Agency Play: Dimensions of Agency for Interactive Narrative Design." *Proceedings of AAAI 2009 Spring Symposium on Intelligent Narrative Technologies II*, 2009, pp. 44–52.

Inside. Playdead, 2016.

Isbister, Katherine. *How Games Move Us: Emotion by Design*. MIT Press, 2017.

Jensen, Graham H. "Making Sense of Play in Video Games: Ludus, Paidia, and Possibility Spaces." *Eludamos. Journal for Computer Game Culture*, vol. 7, no. 1, 2013, pp. 69–80.

Jones, Steven E. *The Meaning of Video Games: Gaming and Textual Strategies*. Routledge, 2008.

Journey. thatgamecompany, 2012.
LaBelle, Brandon. *Acoustic Territories: Sound Culture and Everyday Life.* Continuum, 2010.
Limbo. Playdead, 2010/2011.
Pedlingham, Graeme. "Precarious Playing: Post-9/11 Aesthetics of Uncertainty in PlayDead's *Limbo* (2010)." *Gothic Studies*, vol. 17, no. 2, 2015, pp. 151–70.
Schweighauser, Philipp. "Doubly Real: Game Studies and Literary Anthropology; or, Why We Play Games." *Eludamos. Journal for Computer Game Culture*, vol. 3, no. 2, 2009, pp. 115–32.
Van Nuenen, Tom. "Procedural (E)Motion: Journey as Emerging Pilgrimage." *Journal of Popular Culture*, vol. 49, no. 3, 2016, pp. 466–91.
Voegelin, Salomé. *Sonic Possible Worlds: Hearing the Continuum of Sound.* Bloomsbury, 2014.
Zimmerman, Eric. "Narrative, Interactivity, Play, and Games." *First Person: New Media as Story, Performance, and Game*, edited by Noah Wardrip-Fruin and Pat Harrigan, MIT Press, 2006, pp. 154–64.

Contributors

Jon Adams teaches in the North American Studies Department at Freiburg University. He has used video games in various classes: to discuss features of narrative, and to present visual descriptions of dystopian and postapocalyptic worlds. Currently he is preparing a work on video games and the algorithmic medium.

Nathalie Aghoro is an assistant professor of North American Literary and Cultural Studies at the Catholic University of Eichstätt-Ingolstadt with an interest in auditory culture, postmodern and contemporary literature, and media theory. Her book *Sounding the Novel: Voice in Twenty-First Century American Fiction* (Universitätsverlag Winter, 2018) examines the sonic mediality of voice in the works of Richard Powers, Karen Tei Yamashita, Jennifer Egan, and Jonathan Safran Foer. She is the co-editor of the 2017 JCDE special issue on *Theatre and Mobility* (with Kerstin Schmidt), and her publications include essays on postmodern novels, contemporary literature, and Afrofuturism in music. Her most anticipated game not (yet?) in the making is a reboot of the Brave Fencer Musashi.

Alexandra Bacalu is an assistant lecturer at the English Department of the University of Bucharest, where she teaches eighteenth-century literature. Her main research interests include early modern and Enlightenment intellectual history with a focus on the history of psychology. Her Ph.D. thesis, which addresses the emergence of Stoic disciplining exercises for the imagination in early eighteenth-century poetics, is to be defended in 2019. Unless she's playing co-op, she always chooses the lowest difficulty so she can follow the story.

Jacqueline Blank is a Ph.D. candidate at LMU Munich, where she is part of the Class of Culture and History. She is working on a project on cultural history and ideology as inspiration for video games in general, and on the world-building of the *BioShock* and *Fallout* series in particular. She loves to play fast-paced multiplayer first-person shooters such as *Rainbow Six: Siege*, but takes her time to explore every corner of the game world in single-player games and RPGs such as *Fallout*.

David Callahan is Associate Professor of English at the University of Aveiro, Portugal. His work has mostly dealt with postcolonial issues, in journals such as *Interventions*, *Postcolonial Studies*, *Critique*, *English Studies in Africa* or *Studies in Australasian Cinema*. He has also published on subjects as varied as DNA and Surveillance in CSI, James Fenimore Cooper's Androgynous Heroes, and Ethical Issues Surrounding the Use of Images From Donated Cadavers in the Anatomical Sciences. His most recent publication is the article "The Poetry of Li-Young Lee and Timothy Bewes's Event of Postcolonial Shame," in *Arizona Quarterly* (2018). To his own shame, he has to play every game on easy.

Sebastian Domsch teaches Anglophone literatures at the University of Greifswald. He holds a Ph.D. from Bamberg University, and a Habilitation from LMU Munich. His major fields of interest besides video games are contemporary literature and culture, graphic novels, the history and theory of literary criticism, Romantic literature, and 18th-century literature. He is the author of a book in the series on "Future Narratives" on video games and narrative (*Storyplay-*

ing: Agency and Narrative in Video Games, 2013) as well as books on Robert Coover, Cormac McCarthy, and the emergence of literary criticism in eighteenth-century Britain. He is the editor of a collection on American twenty-first-century fiction, and of the *Kritisches Lexikon zur fremdsprachigen Gegenwartsliteratur*. Since teaching, administration, and kids have largely consigned him to the ninth circle of gaming hell, a.k.a. idle games, he is desperately trying to come up with a way to turn them into an academic research subject.

Manuel Franz is a doctoral candidate in American History at Heidelberg University, Germany. His dissertation, *Preparedness, Paranoia, Patriotism: U.S. Defense Societies and the Quest for Americanism, 1914–1920*, explores the American preparedness movement in World War I. As a gamer, he hates nothing more than border gore in *Europa Universalis IV*.

Michael Fuchs is a fixed-term assistant professor in American Studies at the University of Graz in Austria. He has co-edited six essay collections, most recently *Intermedia Games– Games Inter Media: Video Games and Intermediality* (Bloomsbury, 2019), and has authored and co-authored about 50 published and forthcoming journal articles and book chapters on video games, American television, horror cinema, science fiction franchises, comics, and contemporary American literature. Apart from being the managing editor of *JAAAS: The Journal of the Austrian Association for American Studies* and working on a handful of monographs and co-edited volumes, Michael is involved in too many video games-related shenanigans with fellow contributor Steve Rabitsch. They are developing an introduction to American culture through the lens of video games and, with some outside assistance, are in the early stages of co-editing books on digital games and cities and digital games and nature, respectively. Currently, Michael spends too much time thinking about (rather than actually playing) video games—being an academic working on popular culture is hard. For additional information on Michael's past and ongoing research, see www.michael-fuchs.info.

Henning Jansen is a graduate student in Global History at Heidelberg University, Germany. He is interested in interdisciplinary approaches to video games and video game culture. In his leisure time, he makes a good Arthas Menethil and would have chosen similarly in Stratholme.

Veronika Keller studied musicology and German literature in Leipzig and Halle, Germany. In 2017 she finished her dissertation at LMU Munich called *"Here I am in my Mecca". Die US-amerikanische Musikschülermigration nach Deutschland, 1843–1918* (Olms-Verlag, forthcoming) about the migration of music students from the USA to Germany. Now she is an independent researcher and lecturer at LMU. Her fields of study include transatlantic cultural connections, music and emotions, reception history, and music in pop culture (video games, series, and movies); she has published essays on the pop song in Korean TV series and about the musical comedy series *Galavant*. She loves strategy games and learned everything about trebuchets from *Age of Empires*.

Martin Lüthe is currently an assistant professor at the John F. Kennedy Institute for North American Studies at Freie Universität Berlin. Lüthe published the monographs *"We Missed a Lot of Church, So the Music Is Our Confessional": Rap and Religion* (Lit Verlag, 2008) and *Color-Line and Crossing-Over: Motown and Performances of Blackness in 1960s American Culture* (WVT, 2011). He is working on his Habilitation *Wire Writings: Media Change in the Cul-*

ture of the Progressive Era. He keeps buying the new *PES* ever year and tells himself that it's somehow better than the one before.

Patricia Maier graduated from LMU Munich with an M.A. in American History, Culture and Society, and she is currently working on her doctoral thesis on video games in the context of US-American culture. While video games have changed immensely since she first started playing them, she somehow still finds herself playing *Tomb Raider*.

Dietmar Meinel is currently working as a postdoc in American Studies at the University of Duisburg-Essen. He has published in English and German, and his articles have appeared in the *European Journal of American Culture* and *NECSUS: European Journal of Media Studies*. His monograph *Pixar's America: The Reanimation of American Myths and Symbols* (2016) has been published by Palgrave MacMillan. Together with Elena Furlanetto he also edited *A Poetics of Neurosis: Narratives of Normalcy and Disorder in Cultural and Literary Texts* (2018). His research interests include popular culture, visual culture, nineteenth-century America, and literary and cultural theory. Even as the fire may fade, he still loves everything *Dark Souls*.

Sabrina Mittermeier (University of Augsburg) completed her dissertation titled "Middle Class Kingdoms – A Cultural History of Disneyland and Its Variations, 1955 – 2016" in the field of American Cultural History at LMU Munich in 2018; it is slated to be published as a monograph with Intellect Books in 2020. She is also the co-editor of *The Routledge Companion to Star Trek* (tbd), a forthcoming essay collection on *Star Trek: Discovery* (Liverpool UP 2020), as well as the volume *Here You Leave Today – Time and Temporality in Theme Parks* (Wehrhahn 2017) and has further published on various topics of American popular culture. She is also currently working on a postdoc project on LGBT Public History in the US and West Germany. If she ever actually finds time to play a video game, it is probably yet another round of *Age of Empires*.

Andrei Nae is an assistant lecturer at the University of Bucharest where he teaches American literature and practical courses in English. He defended his Ph.D. thesis "Immersion and Narrativity in the Survival Horror Genre" in 2017 and is currently working on a research monograph based on it. Some of his more recent publications include "Mission Objective: Carry the White Man's Burden to Outer Space—The Gamification of Colonization in *Dead Space*" published in *Ekphrasis* 20.2 (2018) and "Miranda Fights Back: Appropriating Shakespeare's *The Tempest* in Rockstar's Stealth Survival Horror *Manhunt 2* (2008)" included in the anthology *Shakespeare 400 in Romania. Papers Commemorating the 400th Anniversary of William Shakespeare's Death*. Although he holds a Ph.D. on immersion, he cannot stand wearing the Playstation VR headset for more than 30 minutes.

Michael Phillips is a tenured senior lecturer in the English Department at the University of Graz in Austria. He has co-edited *ConFiguring America: Iconic Figures, Visuality, and the American Identity* (Intellect, 2013) and authored and co-authored essays on sports and/as American culture, the cult stardom of Bruce Campbell, the television show *Hannibal* (NBC, 2013 – 2015), and Joseph Conrad's *Heart of Darkness* (1899). Mike tries not to touch video games, as they distract too easily from more important matters, such as family and real life.

Sascha Pöhlmann is Professor of North American Literature and Culture at the University of Konstanz. He is the author of *Pynchon's Postnational Imagination* (2010), *Future-Founding Poetry: Topographies of Beginnings from Whitman to the Twenty-First Century* (2015), and *Stadt und Straße: Anfangsorte in der amerikanischen Literatur* (2018), and the (co-)editor of essay collections on Thomas Pynchon, Mark Z. Danielewski, foundational places in/of Modernity, electoral cultures, American music, and unpopular culture. He has published essays on contemporary fiction and poetry, queer theory, film, and black metal, and also on "Pynchon's Games" as well as David OReilly's *Everything* and the poetics of scale. Gaming ever since he was introduced to *International Soccer* and *Kickman* on the C64 at the age of four, he now enjoys playing *Pikmin* with his sons Jakob and Gregor.

Stefan "Steve" Rabitsch is a fixed-term assistant professor in American Studies at the University of Graz in Austria. Once a hardcore gamer who repeatedly developed tenosynovitis, he has become a selective gamer with a view of weaving video games into the American Studies classroom. His first monograph, *Star Trek and the British Age of Sail: The Maritime Influence throughout the Series and Films*, came out with McFarland in early 2019, while his co-edited volume *Set Phasers to "Teach!": Star Trek at University* was published by Springer in the summer of 2018. Among others, Michael Fuchs and he are currently co-editing a book on American urban spaces in the fantastic imagination and developing a textbook for using video games as a means to teaching American culture and history.

Damien B. Schlarb received his Ph.D. from Georgia State University. He works as an assistant professor (non-tenure) at Johannes Gutenberg University, Mainz, Germany, where he teaches courses on American literature and culture. He currently works on a book on Herman Melville's mediation of Old Testament wisdom literature. His research interests include the American Renaissance, Early American religion, the history of the Bible, and the history of science and religion. His academic service credentials include layout and editorial work for the *South Atlantic Review*, the journal of the South Atlantic Modern Language Association, and *Amerikastudien / American Studies*, the journal of the German Association for American Studies. His new research project examines how video games challenge established analytical paradigms in cultural studies. He once finished *Rocket Knight Adventures* (Konami, Sega Genesis, 1993) in 46.5 minutes.

Stefan Schubert is an assistant professor at the Institute for American Studies at Leipzig University. In 2018, he received his Ph.D. for a project investigating what he calls 'narrative instability' in contemporary US popular culture (specifically films, video games, and TV). His wider research interests include popular and visual culture, narrativity, textuality, new media, game studies, gender studies, and (post-)postmodernism. He has published on questions of narrative and agency in video games like *BioShock*, *Heavy Rain*, and *The Stanley Parable*, and he is a member of the DFG research network "Narrative Liminality and/in the Formation of American Modernities." The first video game he can remember playing (and liking) was *Zak McKracken*, but since then, his gaming interests have diversified among platforms and genres.

Doug Stark is a Ph.D. student in the English and Comparative Literature Department at the University of North Carolina, Chapel Hill. His research concerns the role of play and other forms of intuitive knowing in digital culture across fiction, film, video games, and mediating infrastructure. He owes his obscure catchphrases to a childhood obsession with the *Time-Splitters* series.

Mark J. P. Wolf is a Professor in the Communication Department at Concordia University Wisconsin. He has a B.A. (1990) in Film Production and an M.A. (1992) and Ph.D. (1995) in Critical Studies from the School of Cinema/Television (now renamed the School of Cinematic Arts) at the University of Southern California. His books include *Abstracting Reality: Art, Communication, and Cognition in the Digital Age* (2000), *The Medium of the Video Game* (2001), *Virtual Morality: Morals, Ethics, and New Media* (2003), *The Video Game Theory Reader* (2003), *The Video Game Explosion: A History from PONG to PlayStation and Beyond* (2007), *The Video Game Theory Reader 2* (2008), *Myst and Riven: The World of the D'ni* (2011), *Before the Crash: Early Video Game History* (2012), the two-volume *Encyclopedia of Video Games: The Culture, Technology, and Art of Gaming* (2012), *Building Imaginary Worlds: The Theory and History of Subcreation* (2012), *The Routledge Companion to Video Game Studies* (2014), *LEGO Studies: Examining the Building Blocks of a Transmedial Phenomenon* (2014), *Video Games Around the World* (2015), the four-volume *Video Games and Gaming Cultures* (2016), *Revisiting Imaginary Worlds: A Subcreation Studies Anthology* (2017), *Video Games FAQ* (2017), *The World of Mister Rogers' Neighborhood* (2017), *The Routledge Companion to Imaginary Worlds* (2017), *The Routledge Companion to Media Technology and Obsolescence* (2018), and two novels for which he is looking for a publisher. He is also founder and coeditor of the Landmark Video Game book series from University of Michigan Press, the founder and editor of the Imaginary Worlds book series from Routledge, and the founder of the Video Game Studies Scholarly Interest Group and the Transmedia Studies Special Interest Group within the Society of Cinema and Media Studies. He has been invited to speak in North America, South America, Europe, Asia, and Second Life; has had work published in journals including *Compar(a)ison*, *Convergence*, *Film Quarterly*, *Games and Culture*, *New Review of Film and Television Studies*, *Projections*, and *The Velvet Light Trap*; is on the advisory boards of Videotopia, the International Arcade Museum Library, and the *International Journal of Gaming and Computer-Mediated Simulations*; and is on several editorial boards including those of *Games and Culture* and *The Journal of E-media Studies*. He lives in Wisconsin with his wife Diane and his sons Michael, Christian, and Francis, who often introduce him to new games.

Index of Names

Aarseth, Espen   2, 5f., 8f., 14, 62, 79, 116, 118, 151
Abbott, Carl   39
Aikin, Roger Cushing   239, 241
Althusser, Louis   182
Amadae, S. M.   153, 161f.
Andersen, Martin Stig   265
Anderson, Benedict   37, 185, 223
Anzaldúa, Gloria   82
Attenborough, David   49
Attridge, Derek   199f., 208

Baerg, Andrew   83f., 99f., 102, 106, 108
Baggio, Roberto   97
Bailyn, Bernard   51
Bataille, Georges   45
Baudrillard, Jean   42, 131
Baumgartner, Robert   69f., 73
Beach Boys   255
Benesch, Klaus   82f.
Bercovitch, Sacvan   37, 40
Berger, James   62
Berlant, Lauren   45
Bogost, Ian   115, 131, 178, 231
Bojahr, Philipp   196, 204
Bolter, Jay David   119, 133, 196, 198
Boorman, John   59
Booth, John Wilkes   222, 244
Bosman, Frank   226
Bouet, Elsa   54
Bourdieu, Pierre   151, 153, 155, 159–161, 169
Brians, Ella   98
Brigham, Ann   65, 67–70, 74, 76
Brown, Wendy   155, 158f., 161f.
Buchenau, Barbara   80
Buell, Lawrence   4

Calleja, Gordon   65, 68, 131
Cassell, Justine   11
Cassirer, Ernst   114
Chang, Alenda Y.   4
Chopin, Frédéric   250

Cixous, Hélène   209
Clare, Adam   53, 185
Cline, Ernest   16, 151–155, 160, 163, 166–168
Collins, Karen   261f., 266, 271
Condis, Megan   151, 154, 167
Consalvo, Mia   12, 153, 163, 166
Cooper, John Milton   223
Cornelißen, Christoph   224
Cresswell, Tim   65–67, 74
Czarniawska, Barbara   115

Danielewski, Mark Z.   11, 15, 114
De Peuter, Greig   12, 54, 99
Deleuze, Gilles   159, 169
Denson, Shane   100f.
Derrida, Jacques   5, 198
Dickey, James   59
DuBravac, Shawn   192
Dyer-Witheford, Nick   12, 54, 99

Elsaesser, Thomas   118
Engelns, Markus   76
Ermi, Lara   133
Eskelinen, Markku   115, 263
Everett, Anna   12

Fassone, Riccardo   44
Feige, Daniel Martin   199, 208
Fernández-Vara, Clara   204
Forman, Miloš   17, 252, 254
Foucault, Michel   158, 162, 182, 272
Franklin, Benjamin   215–217, 222, 237
Frasca, Gonzalo   116
Fraser, Nancy   92
Frazer, James George   174
Frissen, Valerie   120
Frye, Northrop   174
Fuchs, Michael   1, 14, 35f., 123

Gadamer, Hans-Georg   44
Galloway, Alexander R.   196–199, 201, 204, 208

Gonzales, Raquel M. 122
Gee, James Paul 71f., 185
Gibbons, William 250, 254–256
Green, Amy 4, 51, 53
Grua, David W. 225
Grusin, Richard 119, 133, 196, 198
Gunzenhäuser, Randi 3
Gurr, Jens Martin 80

Habermas, Jürgen 182
Han, Byung-Chul 155, 158f., 161f.
Harrell, D. Fox 267f., 272
Harrigan, Pat 5
Heinze, Carl 221
Hobbes, Thomas 182
Hocking, Clint 231
Hudson, Casey 43
Huizinga, Johan 44

Isbister, Katherine 269
Iser, Wolfgang 10, 263

Jackson, Andrew 60
Jameson, Frederic 91, 131
Jefferson, Thomas 222, 237f.
Jenkins, Henry 11, 36, 117, 119, 151, 160, 198, 235
Jensen, Graham 261f., 268f., 271
Jones, Steven 143, 259f., 270
Jung, C.G. 174
Juul, Jesper 6, 44, 65, 75, 116, 137, 177, 196, 204

Kanzler, Katja 124
King, Stephen 31, 45, 50, 214
Kiss, Miklós 119
Kubrick, Stanley 257

LaBelle, Brandon 271
Lauper, Cyndi 255
Lefebvre, Henri 15, 54, 80, 86
Leonard, David J. 98
Lerner, Max 35
Levine, Caroline 118
Leyda, Julia 81–83
Limerick, Patricia 60, 82
Lincoln, Abraham 53–56, 222, 244

Lipset, Seymour Martin 35
Lovecraft, Howard Phillips 202
Lowood, Henry 99

MacCallum-Stewart, Esther 62
Macherey, Pierre 58
Malkowski, Jennifer 12
Manovich, Lev 114f., 117, 187
Mao Zedong 182
Martin, Terence 15, 42, 97
Marx, Karl 158f., 182
Marx, Leo 42, 82
Mather, Cotton 36
Maurer, Andrea 227
Mayar, Mahshid 3
Mäyrä, Frans 5, 133
McCarter, Reid 223
Mendelssohn-Bartholdy, Felix 250
Milburn, Colin 4
Miller, Perry 37, 82
Mittell, Jason 119, 125
Morgan, Kathryn 107f.
Mozart, Wolfgang Amadeus 17, 249–255
Murray, Janet 12, 116, 140, 181, 204

Nagle, Angela 168
Neitzel, Britta 204
Newman, Michael Z. 3
Nitsche, Michael 65, 70, 72f., 75, 86, 89, 236
Norman, Don 175f.
Nünning, Ansgar 116
Nünning, Vera 116

Paine, Thomas 40
Panofsky, Erwin 114
Pedlingham, Graeme 264
Penix-Tadsen, Philip 3, 65, 70, 72
Pöhlmann, Sascha 1, 113, 115, 127
Pötsch, Holger 50
Pound, Ezra 10
Psiropoulos, Brian 225
Punday, Daniel 115
Pynchon, Thomas 10

Radway, Janice 6f.
Revere, Paul 54, 215

Ruberg, Bonnie 12
Russworm, TreaAndrea M. 12, 61
Ryan, Marie-Laure 4, 11, 137, 204

Schott, Gareth 62
Schweighauser, Philipp 9, 263, 268, 270
Sharp, John 196
Shaw, Adrienne 12, 154
Shepard, Alan B. 14, 35–42, 44–46
Sicart, Miguel 65, 70f., 73, 76
Slotkin, Richard 35, 82
Smethurst, Tobi 227
Smith, Henry Nash 2, 6–9, 14, 82, 162
Spielberg, Steven 164
Spring, Dawn 49
Stephanson, Anders 238, 242
Stern, David 97, 143, 147f.
Strauss, Richard 257
Strong, Josiah 242f.
Szabó-Knotik, Cornelia 253

Taylor, Diane 57, 115
Thon, Jan-Noël 11, 119
Trump, Donald 12f., 38
Turner, Frederick Jackson 55, 81f., 239

Van Nuenen, Tom 264
Voegelin, Salomé 259f.

Wagner, Richard 254, 257
Walt, Andrew 10, 213, 215, 229
Wardrip-Fruin, Noah 5
Wark, McKenzie 169
Washington, George 214f., 222, 225, 237, 244–246
Weber, Max 16, 154, 227
Welsh, Oli 51
Wigglesworth, Michael 35, 38
Willemsen, Steven 119
Williams, William Carlos 10, 157, 160
Wills, John 3
Wilson, Woodrow 223
Winthrop, John 36, 39f., 55
Wojcik, Daniel 35, 41
Wolf, Mark J.P. 14, 21, 235, 247
Wolfe, Alan 7

Zam, Maurice 252
Zhu, Jichen 267f., 272
Zimmermann, Eric 266
Žižek, Slavoj 205

Index of Subjects

1980s   1, 23–26, 30, 91, 101, 152, 154–156, 160, 165–168, 175, 200, 202, 206, 212
9/11   35, 45f., 265

AAA video games   132, 137f.
affordances   114, 118, 133, 173–179, 267
agency   16f., 43, 81, 116–120, 122, 124, 126, 157, 173, 179–183, 221, 226f., 232, 260f., 263, 267f., 270, 272f.
Agnus dei   251, 255f.
Alan Wake   15, 113f., 119–122, 125–127
algorithm   185–192, 197
Alone in the Dark   134
Also sprach Zarathustra   257
Amadeus   17, 252–254
ambiguity   62, 198f.
American Civil War   214
American exceptionalism   39, 42, 46, 222–225, 246
American Revolution   16, 49, 52f., 57, 132, 211, 213–215, 217
American Studies   1–17, 77, 81f., 98, 113f., 126f., 211, 217f.
apocalypse   15, 35, 38, 41f., 44, 47, 62, 237
Apocalypse Now   257
arbitrary   71, 82, 101, 191, 261
arcade game   21, 25, 29, 167f.
Asian American   89, 92f.
2001: A Space Odyssey   257
Assassin's Creed   92, 117, 132, 175
authenticity   132, 143, 148, 198, 211f., 214, 217
Avatar   68f., 71f., 76, 84, 103, 106f., 122f., 164, 176, 196f., 203, 207f., 227, 259f., 264–266, 269–273

Babylon 5   37
baptism   226, 236
Bible   38, 45, 235
BioShock   16f., 21, 84, 221, 223–232, 235f., 238f., 246, 251, 254–257

BioWare   35f., 44
Black Tiger   167
Boxer Revolt   229

Call of Duty   117
Candy Crush   162, 169
choices   15, 44, 61f., 65f., 70–73, 76, 84, 116–120, 122, 124, 140, 173, 177, 181f., 196, 211, 230, 262
Christianity   36, 39f., 60, 168, 237f., 243–246, 251, 255f.
City upon a Hill   35
class   11f., 30, 69, 82f., 92, 132, 137, 140, 148, 159f., 182, 211, 243, 252
classical music   17, 249f., 252
Clock Tower III   137f.
closed systems   188
code   3, 11, 23, 57, 65, 71, 76, 98, 142, 148, 155, 167, 169, 175, 180, 187, 195, 199, 201, 203, 206–208, 250, 252, 261
Cold War   35, 39f., 46
Command & Conquer   224
commemorative culture   17, 221, 224f., 232
Commodore 64   99
Commodore Amiga   26, 97, 99
convergence culture   119, 126, 151
cooperation   61f., 259, 268–271
Crown, The   39, 98, 254
cultural capital   16, 153, 159–161
culture industry   1, 12f.
cybernetics   197, 199
cyberpunk   151, 157

Dear Esther   117
deep learning   186
defamiliarization   199, 207
Deliverance   59
DeLorean   167
Detroit: Become Human   117
deus ex machina   40, 44
didactic Fiction   16, 151
diegesis   178, 197, 207
Dies irae   251, 253

digital culture   151, 155, 161
Dino Crisis   134
disability   11
Disney   16, 211–213, 215–217
disruption   68, 196, 203–205, 271
Dragon Age   67, 72
dystopia   11, 49, 62, 79, 81, 85, 87f., 90, 92f., 152, 156, 228, 259, 264, 271

Eine kleine Nachtmusik   252
Elder Scrolls III, The: Morrowind   188
Elder Scrolls V, The: Skyrim   15, 66, 70, 73–76, 191
Electronic Arts (EA)   30, 97
electronic book review   5
environment   4f., 15, 22, 41, 54, 59f., 68, 70, 72, 79–81, 84–88, 90, 92f., 104, 141, 178f., 181, 188, 228, 259f., 262, 265, 267–269, 271–273
environmental criticism   4
environmental storytelling   264
e pluribus unum   38
error   42, 176, 187, 195, 206
ethnicity   11, 36f., 69
Everquest   190f.
exploits   187
exploration   1–3, 10f., 17, 29, 33, 62, 67, 100, 115, 122, 141, 178, 202, 259f., 269, 273

Fallout   52, 67, 188, 191, 235
Fatal Frame   137
Federal Commission on School Safety   13
feminism   12, 92, 161
fetish   106, 208
FIFA   97f., 100, 106
first-person shooter   79, 89, 138, 227, 231
Forbidden Siren   141
Founding Fathers   222, 236f.
fragmentation   91–93, 132, 141f., 144, 147
fundamentalism   222

gamebooks   118
game mechanics   79, 83–85, 132f., 137f., 173, 175, 181, 227, 229
gameplay   9, 16f., 23, 38, 49, 63, 71, 75f., 81, 86f., 101–104, 118, 122, 131f., 134, 136, 138–141, 148, 163, 173–180, 183, 197–200, 202, 204–207, 209, 212f., 216, 227, 231f., 236, 251, 256, 259–266, 268, 270–273
gamescape   86–88, 90
game theory   2, 153, 161
game worlds   31, 67, 69f., 86, 151, 153, 190f.
gamification   153, 155, 164, 169
gaming capital   153f., 162–165, 167, 169f.
Garden of Eden   41f.
Gears of War   134
gender   11f., 36f., 69, 106, 127, 132, 138, 218
generative agitation   198, 208
genre   8, 16, 22, 26, 29, 41, 65, 69, 84, 98, 117, 125, 132–134, 137, 140–144, 146–149, 152, 176, 179, 200, 202, 206, 212, 216, 227, 231, 241, 249
Germany   99, 185, 216, 224
glitch   16, 188, 195f., 198f., 203, 208f., 229
Grand Theft Auto V   12, 30, 32, 117
Great Awakening   35
guilt   16f., 221, 223–228, 230–232

Haunting Ground   137
Heavy Rain   116–119
hierarchy   9, 222
historical responsibility   223f.
hypermediacy   15, 131–134, 136, 141–143, 148f., 196, 198, 201, 203f.

identity   11, 17, 21, 36, 43, 47, 58, 60f., 67–69, 72, 74, 82, 137f., 154f., 157, 163, 180, 192, 226, 229f., 235f., 242, 270
Il Nozze di Figaro   253
imagined community   223
Imagism   10
immediacy   132f., 142, 147–149, 196, 198
immersion   4, 15, 65, 68, 131–136, 138–142, 144, 148f., 195f., 198f., 204f., 208, 211f., 215f., 235, 246, 267
incorporation   65, 68–70, 76
indeterminacy   127, 199, 262–264, 266, 268, 273

individualism   29, 43, 84, 223
Industrial Revolution   55–57
Inside   17, 120 f., 144, 214, 251, 255 f., 259–262, 264–268, 271–273
interactivity   4, 17, 22, 25–27, 30, 32, 80, 83, 86, 116, 118 f., 124–126, 132 f., 138, 181, 187, 235 f., 251, 257, 259, 261 f., 266–268
interdisciplinarity   8
interface   101, 109 f., 168, 196 f., 199–201, 204–206, 227
International Soccer   99 f.
inventory   74, 136, 140, 191, 204, 207
isolationism   46
iteration   17, 49, 61, 116, 124

Japan   21, 23–25, 32, 100, 137
Jeremiad   15, 36, 42
Jim Crow   222
John Madden Football   97
Journey   17, 51 f., 68, 167, 242, 259–262, 264–273
Joust Arcade   167
Joust Atari 2600   167

Kick-Off 99
Kiss Kiss Bang Bang   254
Konami   100, 102–104, 132, 139, 141

Lacrimosa   17, 249–257
Last of Us, The   15, 49–51, 55, 57, 60, 62 f.
leitmotif   222, 256
linear   6 f., 73, 76, 116, 122, 124 f., 200, 206, 211, 264, 266 f., 272
listening   249 f., 252, 259–262, 264 f., 270–273
Literary Anthropology   9, 263
ludic textuality   15, 113 f., 119–121, 123, 126
ludification   120, 126
ludology   4, 115, 218
ludonarrative dissonance   231

machines   21, 38, 97, 175, 185 f., 195
Madden NFL   97
Magic Flute, The   253
Magnalia Christi Americana   36

Manifest Destiny 17, 39, 235 f., 238 f., 241 f., 246
Marche Funèbre   250
masculinity   15, 36, 58, 98, 104, 106, 108, 110, 132, 137 f., 140, 154
Mass Effect   15, 35–46, 71, 76
materiality   98, 118, 144, 147 f., 197, 199
media   2, 4 f., 8, 11–13, 16 f., 21, 24–26, 30, 35, 43, 57, 85, 106, 113 f., 118 f., 121–123, 125–127, 131–133, 139–141, 148, 151, 155, 163, 179, 196–199, 201, 204, 209, 211–218, 249–251, 255, 257, 262 f., 267 f.
mediation   15, 81, 86, 90, 131–133, 148 f., 197
metafiction   147
metagame   201, 205, 206
metalepsis   16, 195 f., 198, 200, 205, 207 f.
metatextuality   121 f., 124–127, 132, 143 f., 147 f.
methodology   4, 14
Midsummer Night's Dream, A   250
Minecraft   118, 176
Mirror's Edge   15, 79–81, 83–93
misrepresentation   225
mobility   15, 65–69, 73–76, 80–83, 85, 90, 92
mod   6, 15 f., 24, 30, 62, 69, 87 f., 90 f., 101 f., 104, 147, 155, 158, 166, 169, 179, 206–208, 216, 228, 231, 259, 266, 269
"Model of Christian Charity, A"   39
morality   65, 71, 75
Mormonism   59 f., 62
Mortal Kombat   11
movement   4, 12, 15, 22, 26 f., 43, 51 f., 58, 60, 66–69, 74–76, 79–83, 85 f., 88–90, 92, 104, 106, 108 f., 119, 131, 134 f., 141, 178, 181, 188, 190, 200, 222 f., 227, 239, 241 f., 255, 264, 266, 269, 271
multimodality   262
music   9, 17, 22, 24, 151 f., 159, 249–257, 265 f.

narrative   4, 9–11, 15 f., 35–38, 40, 42–46, 49–51, 53, 57, 61, 63, 65, 69 f., 81, 84, 88–90, 92 f., 101 f., 113–127,

132–134, 137–139, 141 f., 145–147, 151, 153, 157, 160, 167 f., 173–175, 177–179, 181, 183, 195–204, 206, 208 f., 211–216, 221 f., 224–226, 228, 230 f., 235 f., 246 f., 250, 252, 255–257, 260, 262, 264–268, 270, 272
narrative archetypes   16, 173–175, 178
narrative complexity   126
narrative instability   113
narrative liminality   114 f., 127
narrativization   115, 119 f., 134, 136–141, 147 f.
narratology   4, 8–11, 115, 197, 218
nation   3, 7, 21, 40, 45 f., 50–53, 58–62, 74, 81 f., 106, 213, 225, 236 f., 244
National Basketball Association   97
nationalism   222, 225
native Americans   61, 246
naturalization   84, 131 f., 138 f.
Nehemiahs Americanus   36
neoliberalism   83–85, 90, 92 f., 153–155, 158 f., 161 f., 164, 169
New Criticism   2, 7
New England   51 f., 202
NFL2K   98
Nintendo   23–25, 32, 99 f.
Nintendo World Cup   99
nonlinearity   116–119, 122, 124–127
nostalgia   26 f., 42, 152, 155, 166

objective correlative   203
Offering, The   23, 29, 70, 122, 206, 228, 231, 254
Outlast   137

Pac-Man   24, 79, 167
p-actions   135
paradox   196
Parkour   15, 80 f., 88 f., 92
Pax Americana   38
physics engine   179
place   2–6, 14 f., 21 f., 31, 46, 49, 54, 57–59, 62, 65–67, 69 f., 72–74, 80–83, 85, 88, 92, 97, 104, 107 f., 116, 120, 135, 139, 146, 191, 198, 206 f., 212 f., 215, 217, 224, 235, 241 f., 254 f., 264, 266

Planetside   187
play   7, 9 f., 12, 14–16, 21, 26 f., 44, 58, 65 f., 72 f., 75 f., 85 f., 98, 102, 105 f., 108 f., 113–127, 132 f., 151 f., 154–156, 162–168, 173, 177, 185, 187–191, 198 f., 203–208, 213, 217, 221, 227–229, 231 f., 243, 255, 257, 259–264, 266–272
player   15–17, 26 f., 29, 36–38, 40–45, 49, 52, 54, 61 f., 65–76, 79–81, 83–93, 97, 99, 102, 104–110, 116 f., 119–122, 131–141, 148, 154–157, 160, 162–164, 166–168, 173, 175–181, 183, 185, 187–193, 196–208, 213–216, 221–232, 235 f., 241, 243 f., 246 f., 254–257, 259–273
player versus environment (PvE)   179
player versus player (PvP)   179
playfulness   16, 198 f.
pleasure   83, 91–93, 114, 118–120, 122, 124–127, 141, 169, 185, 198
poetry   10, 49
politics   7, 12, 15, 37, 50, 61, 89, 97, 127, 138, 213, 216 f.
politics of memory   223
Pong   79, 117
popular culture   15, 21, 24, 30, 42, 57, 66, 68, 113 f., 119, 124, 126 f., 160, 212 f., 218, 257
popularity   21, 26, 29, 35, 99, 113, 119 f., 126, 216 f.
postnationalism   7
power   12, 26, 36, 45, 47, 50, 52 f., 55, 58, 61, 66 f., 71, 88, 127, 154, 157, 159, 165, 168, 180–182, 191, 195, 197, 201 f., 222, 226, 229, 237, 243, 259, 262, 265, 267, 269, 271–273
predetermination   42, 261, 266
prepper   60
Pro Evolution Soccer   15, 98, 100, 103 f., 106–109
procedural rhetoric   84, 178, 231
propaganda   182, 222, 224 f., 243, 246 f.

queer   12

race 11f., 17, 22, 25, 37f., 46, 61, 66, 69, 73f., 80, 91, 106, 131f., 195, 214, 218, 235f., 242–245
racism 92, 106, 242f., 245–247
Ready Player One 16, 29, 151–160, 162–169
realism 15, 97f., 100, 102–106, 131–133, 138, 142–144, 147f., 190
Reddit 125, 167f.
redundancy 140f.
remediation 86, 119, 197
remembrance 155, 223
Requiem 250–255
Resident Evil 134f., 137f., 140
resonance 45, 62, 159, 161, 266, 270, 273
revisionism 224
Rex Tremendae 253, 255
road narrative 15, 65, 67f., 70, 76f., 83
Robotron 2084 167
role-playing game 26, 36, 65f., 185, 187–192
romance 12, 142, 144

Sand Creek Massacre 58
science fiction 22, 37, 39f., 49, 62, 190, 196
script 15, 49–51, 58, 60, 62, 80f., 83, 85–87, 89–92
segregation 15, 85, 91, 243, 246
self-referentiality 143
semiotics 8
Sensible Soccer 97, 99f.
sex 10, 59
sexuality 11f., 36, 69
signification 65, 199, 206f., 262, 264
Silent Hill 15, 132, 134, 136–139, 141
Simpsons, The 254
singularity 8, 197, 199f.
Societies of Control 159, 169
sound 9, 17, 38, 79, 86, 105, 180, 203, 231f., 249, 253, 255f., 259–262, 264–271, 273
soundscape 255, 264, 271, 273
soundtrack 252f., 265
space 12f., 15, 22f., 36, 39, 41, 56, 58, 60–62, 65–72, 74, 79–83, 85–93, 98, 105, 108–110, 120, 141, 157, 161, 175, 178f., 191, 199, 201, 205f., 208f., 211f., 215f., 235f., 257, 261, 263, 268–271, 273
space opera 36f.
specificity 191
Spec Ops: The Line 227f.
speedrun 229
steampunk 202, 222f.
storyworld 11, 37, 119, 121, 124, 132–134, 137–140, 151, 154, 173
strategy 102, 105, 109, 132, 140f., 180, 189f., 211, 270
subculture 22, 88, 92, 142, 155f., 159
surveillance 79, 88f., 92, 216, 264
survival horror 15, 131–142, 144f., 148
symbolic form 11, 113–117, 119, 121, 123, 126f., 163
symbolism 9f., 222, 237

tactics 106, 166, 189f., 202
tank controls 134f.
terrorism 16, 173, 180, 182f.
Tetris 99, 117f.
textuality 80, 121, 126, 262
theme parks 16, 211–213, 215–218
third-person shooter 135
time travel 212f., 216f.
totalitarianism 88–92, 222, 272
Trail of Tears 58
transmediality 11, 119
transnationalism 2, 14, 33, 82, 211

unintended consequences 187
United States of America 1–3, 5, 14f., 17, 21–23, 25, 28, 32, 46, 49f., 53–57, 60, 62f., 65f., 69, 81–83, 97, 106, 110, 113, 115, 119, 126f., 132, 156, 186, 200, 212, 215f., 237, 239, 242, 249, 252
urban 15, 54, 56, 59, 79–81, 83, 85–93, 156

video game novel 16, 151f., 168
violence 12f., 60, 82, 110, 154, 159, 180f., 186, 209, 221, 227f., 230f.
Viridiana 252
virtual reality 4, 98, 105, 110, 131, 156
visual culture 2
voyeurism 141

vulnerability   93, 110, 134, 137, 140f., 144, 148, 178, 182, 265

Walking Dead, The   71
Walküre, Die   257
westward expansion   39, 55, 57, 239, 241
white supremacy   222
Wolfenstein   132, 224

world building   235
World of Warcraft   190–192
world-subject relations   17, 260
Wounded Knee   221, 224–226, 229, 244

xenophobia   37, 222

zombies   140

www.ingramcontent.com/pod-product-compliance
Lightning Source LLC
Chambersburg PA
CBHW020325170426
43200CB00006B/276